Problem Solving
with FORTRAN

Problem Solving with FORTRAN

DONALD D. SPENCER

Prentice-Hall, Inc., Englewood Cliffs, New Jersey 07632

Library of Congress Cataloging in Publication Data

SPENCER, DONALD D
   Problem solving with FORTRAN.

    Bibliography: p.
    Includes index.
    1. FORTRAN (Computer program language)   2. Electronic digital computers—Programming.   I. Title.
QA76.73.F25S64   001.6′424   76-26040
ISBN 0-13-720094-3

© 1977 by Prentice-Hall, Inc.
Englewood Cliffs, New Jersey   07632

All rights reserved. No part of this book
may be reproduced in any form or by any means
without permission in writing
from the publisher.

10   9   8   7   6   5   4   3   2

Printed in the United States of America

PRENTICE-HALL INTERNATIONAL, INC., London
PRENTICE-HALL OF AUSTRALIA PTY. LIMITED, Sydney
PRENTICE-HALL OF CANADA, LTD., Toronto
PRENTICE-HALL OF INDIA PRIVATE LIMITED, New Delhi
PRENTICE-HALL OF JAPAN, INC., Tokyo
PRENTICE-HALL OF SOUTHEAST ASIA PTE. LTD., Singapore
WHITEHALL BOOKS LIMITED, Wellington, New Zealand

To Sherrie

Contents

PREFACE xiii

1 PROBLEM-SOLVING PROCESS 2

1.1 Importance of Computers 4
1.2 How to Recognize a Computer 6
1.3 Using a Computer to Solve a Problem 8

2 PROGRAMMING THE COMPUTER 16

2.1 The FORTRAN Program 19
2.2 Characters and Symbols 23
2.3 Constants 25
2.4 Variables 26
2.5 Arithmetic Expressions 28
2.6 Arithmetic Statements 30
2.7 Library Functions 33
2.8 Logical Constants, Variables, Expressions, and Statements 33

Contents

    2.9 Input-Output Statements *37*
  2.10 Control Statements *48*
  2.11 Unconditional GO TO Statement *49*
  2.12 Computed GO TO Statement *49*
  2.13 Arithmetic IF Statement *49*
  2.14 Logical IF Statement *51*
  2.15 The STOP Statement *51*
  2.16 The END Statement *52*
  2.17 Examples of Simple Problems *52*

3 ALGORITHMS 56

  3.1 Problem Analysis *58*
  3.2 Algorithm Development *58*
  3.3 An Algebraic Algorithm *64*
  3.4 The Number Game Algorithm *65*
  3.5 Algorithm for Generating Fibonacci Numbers *65*
  3.6 Algorithm for *The 15 Puzzle* *66*
  3.7 Algorithm for Number Selection *68*
  3.8 The Königsberg Bridge Algorithm *68*

4 FLOWCHARTING 72

  4.1 Why Use Flowcharts? *74*
  4.2 What Is a Flowchart? *74*
  4.3 Flowcharting Symbols *74*
  4.4 Flowcharting Guidelines *78*
  4.5 Flowcharting Template *80*
  4.6 Construction of the Flowchart *80*
  4.7 Making Decisions *84*
  4.8 Looping *89*
  4.9 Controlled Loops *92*
  4.10 Nested Loops *95*
  4.11 Using Connectors *99*
  4.12 Adding Notes to the Flowchart *100*
  4.13 Subroutines *102*

5 FORTRAN PROGRAMS FOR STUDY 104

  5.1 Painting the Gazebo *106*
  5.2 Michael's Dog *108*

Contents

- 5.3 Mary Goes to the Circus *109*
- 5.4 The Manhattan Island Problem *109*
- 5.5 Roots of Equation *114*
- 5.6 The *N*-th Fibonacci Number *114*
- 5.7 The Jolly Green Giant *114*
- 5.8 Rodney's New Calculator *117*
- 5.9 Fireball Williams' Auto Races *119*
- 5.10 Square Root *123*
- 5.11 California Chemical Laboratory *125*
- 5.12 How Much Current? *128*
- 5.13 Gas Station Robbery *132*

6 ADVANCED FORTRAN 134

- 6.1 The DO Statement *136*
- 6.2 The CONTINUE Statement *138*
- 6.3 Arrays and Subscripts *140*
- 6.4 The DIMENSION Statement *142*
- 6.5 Additional Input/Output *146*
- 6.6 Sample Programs *149*
- 6.7 Specification Statements *158*
- 6.8 Subprograms *161*
- 6.9 Program Debugging Techniques *173*
- 6.10 A Summary of FORTRAN *180*
- 6.11 More FORTRAN? *187*

7 TWELVE INTERESTING FORTRAN PROGRAMS 188

- 7.1 Michael's Dog *190*
- 7.2 Manhattan Island Problem *190*
- 7.3 Fireball Williams' Auto Races *190*
- 7.4 Class Assignment *191*
- 7.5 Karl Gauss's Calculation *191*
- 7.6 Permutations *194*
- 7.7 Who Was Right? *197*
- 7.8 The Absent-Minded Chemist *200*
- 7.9 Matrix Multiplication *201*
- 7.10 The 15 Puzzle *204*
- 7.11 Magic Squares *208*
- 7.12 Magic Square Checker *211*

Contents

8   PROBLEMS WITH FLOWCHARTS   218

8.1   Interest Calculation   *220*
8.2   Prime Number Polynomial   *221*
8.3   Checkerboard Interchange   *221*
8.4   Law of Cosines   *223*
8.5   Accounting Computation   *224*
8.6   Product Cost   *225*
8.7   Real Estate Purchase   *225*
8.8   Checker Counting   *226*
8.9   Chi-Square   *230*
8.10   Compound Interest   *230*
8.11   Customer Billing   *231*
8.12   Change Maker   *232*
8.13   Trigonometric Functions   *235*
8.14   Employee Payroll   *236*
8.15   Company Payroll   *238*
8.16   The 50 Puzzle   *239*
8.17   Roman Numeralizer   *239*
8.18   Payroll Deduction   *245*
8.19   Slot Machine Simulator   *246*
8.20   Decimal-to-English Conversion   *249*
8.21   Prime Numbers   *250*
8.22   Billiard Simulation   *254*
8.23   Mouse in a Maze   *257*

9   PROBLEMS FOR COMPUTER SOLUTION   260

9.1   3 by 3 Magic Square   *262*
9.2   Christmas Tree   *262*
9.3   Powers of Two   *262*
9.4   Investment Calculation   *263*
9.5   Satellite Speed   *264*
9.6   Football Franchise   *264*
9.7   Payroll   *265*
9.8   Law of Sines   *265*
9.9   Multiplication Table   *266*
9.10   Birds   *266*
9.11   Fourth Powers   *266*
9.12   Average Distance   *266*
9.13   Volume of a Dam   *267*
9.14   Student Averages   *268*

Contents

9.15 Employment *268*
9.16 Largest Number *268*
9.17 Bouncing Ball *268*
9.18 Polygon *268*
9.19 Cricket Thermometer *269*
9.20 Average Temperature *270*
9.21 Number Search *271*
9.22 Drag and Lift Force *271*
9.23 Magic Square Checker *271*
9.24 Student Enrollment Survey *271*
9.25 Statistical Calculation *272*
9.26 Row Interchange *273*
9.27 Mean, Median, and Mode *273*
9.28 Cube Root *274*
9.29 Guessing Game *274*
9.30 What is the Number? *274*
9.31 Batting Average *274*
9.32 Most Popular Player *275*
9.33 Temperature Simulation *275*
9.34 Lot Purchase *276*
9.35 Gas Mileage *276*
9.36 Sales Chart *277*
9.37 Salary Conversion Table *277*
9.38 Radius of Curvature *277*
9.39 Interest Table *277*
9.40 House Mortgage *278*
9.41 Merchandise Cost *278*
9.42 College Admission Record *279*
9.43 Sales Journal *280*
9.44 Accounts Receivable *280*
9.45 College Exam Scores *281*
9.46 One Pile Pickup *281*
9.47 Big Words *281*
9.48 Date Finder *282*
9.49 Lucky Numbers *283*
9.50 Wheel of Fortune *284*
9.51 Perfect Numbers *285*
9.52 Symmetry Game *285*
9.53 The Swimming Pool *286*
9.54 Calculate the Sum *287*
9.55 Table of Trigonometric Functions *288*
9.56 Maze *288*
9.57 King's Tour of the Chessboard *288*
9.58 Flight Path Computation *290*

APPENDICES

A   KEYPUNCHING A SOURCE DECK   295

B   PROGRAM FLOWCHARTING SYMBOLS   301

C   GLOSSARY   303

BIBLIOGRAPHY   309

INDEX   315

Preface

This book is intended for those people who would like to be able to use computers to solve problems and help in making decisions. Thus, it is written for students and for practitioners.

The book is designed for the beginning course in computer programming, assuming one course in algebra as the minimal mathematical level of the reader. The pedagogical goal throughout is to keep the material as understandable as possible. Many photographs, diagrams, flowcharts, and cartoons are used to illustrate specific concepts, techniques, and equipment. Although the computer field is burdened with highly esoteric terminology, the attempt here is to keep technical terms to a minimum.

The basic programming language of the book is FORTRAN (FORmula TRANslation). However, the logic approach to solving a problem is independent of any particular language. The treatment of the FORTRAN language is brief and to the point. No attempt has been made to state the differences between different dialects and implementations of FORTRAN. These should be studied from the relevant manuals. The FORTRAN language used in this book is a subset of the FORTRAN IV language and is included in all versions of FORTRAN.

The key objectives of the text are twofold. The reader is given the opportunity to learn how to take a problem and solve it on the computer in the following two steps:

- *Problem formulation.* The reader learns how to formulate a problem and how to devise the algorithm and flowchart for solving the problem by computer.
- *Problem solution by computer.* The reader learns how to express the problem-solving process in a computer language and to obtain a meaningful solution on the computer.

The reader will note that the book begins with the immediate introduction of FORTRAN programming. Most educators agree that it is important to begin work with the computer as soon as possible—preferably immediately after the first class meeting. The interest of the student is then usually so strong that he or she is motivated to proceed with additional related topics as quickly as possible. After the reader is introduced to FORTRAN, he or she then explores the areas of algorithm development, flowcharting, advanced FORTRAN, and problem solving.

Perhaps a novel feature of this book is the inclusion of a large number of problems from many diversified areas: mathematics, engineering, business, physics, chemistry, education, statistics, game playing, number theory, accounting, and others. Problems were purposely chosen to illustrate that FORTRAN programming can be used to solve a variety of moderate-size problems. All of the solved problems in this book are accompanied by flowcharts. The 23 problems for reader solution in Chapter 8 also include accompanying flowcharts. Chapter 9 includes 55 problems for reader solution. The reader's learning process will be greatly enhanced if his or her study is supported by doing the many review exercises contained in each chapter, and if careful attention is paid to the examples and solved problems.

Appendix A includes a short discussion of keypunching a source deck, which should be helpful to readers who are unfamiliar with keypunching their own programs. Appendix B contains a description of program flowcharting symbols. A short glossary of terms is included in Appendix C. The book also includes a bibliography. An instructor's manual is available, containing answers to review exercises and teaching suggestions.

I wish to thank the IBM Corp., Burroughs Corp., Federal Aviation Agency, and Sperry Rand Corp, who supplied me the photographs used in the book and David Lynas for his imaginative cartoons. I also wish to thank my wife, Rae, for pounding the keys of the IBM Selectric, and Sue Collings for keypunching and executing the FORTRAN programs on a computer.

I welcome the reader to a world of reward and accomplishment in his or her encounter with this amazing tool—the computer.

DONALD D. SPENCER

Ormond Beach, Florida

Problem Solving
with **FORTRAN**

Chapter 1

It is estimated that over 20 percent of the total output of goods and services in the U.S. is devoted to reports, statistical information, billing, payroll, and other paper work. Computer systems, such as the one shown here, have helped business people to improve these administrative functions. (Courtesy *IBM Corp.*)

Problem-Solving Process

This chapter is designed to give you a general overview of problem solving with computers. We will begin with a discussion of computer applications and what part they play in modern society. The basic components of a computer system are introduced and the relationships between them are briefly discussed.

Computers are capable of performing large numbers of operations at very high speeds with very little human involvement. However, a computer has to be told *exactly what operations to perform and in what order to perform them. These sets of instructions are called* computer programs. *A program is a series of instructions written in a coded form that the computer is able to translate into its own language. In this chapter, the process of preparing programs is discussed in general terms, the specifics being covered in Chapters 2, 3, 4, and 6.*

1.1 IMPORTANCE OF COMPUTERS

In the United States alone, there are several hundred thousand computers solving problems in almost every area of human activity. The computer is reshaping century-old ways of doing things. This machine, man's most remarkable invention, is invading every area of society, opening up vast new possibilities by its extraordinary feats of rapid manipulation. It has made it possible to multiply by millions of times the capa-

bilities of the human mind. In short, the computer is becoming so essential a tool, with so much potential for changing our lives and our world, that most people should know something about it.

Computers have radically altered the world of business. They have affected military strategy, increased human productivity, made many products less expensive, and lowered barriers to knowledge. They have opened new horizons to the fields of science and medicine, improved the efficiency of government, and changed the techniques of education.

Computers can store every variety of information that humans record and almost instantly recall it for use. They can calculate tens of millions of times faster than the brain and can solve in seconds many problems that would take batteries of experts years to complete. If the computer had not been developed, for example, American astronauts would have been unable to land on the moon.

Computers have given science and technology the greatest tool ever developed for turning the forces of nature to human use. The reason is simple. The computer is more than a prodigy of information and analysis. It never forgets what it has acquired. In time, it will even respond to oral commands and report in both written and spoken English.

Figure 1-1 Computer displays, similar to the common TV set, are used by businesses to provide easy access to computer generated information. (*Courtesy* IBM Corporation.)

Chapter 1   Problem-Solving Process

1.2 HOW TO RECOGNIZE A COMPUTER

We can describe a computer* as a machine that accepts information, processes it, and then provides the results as new information. For example, you might give the computer the following information: *add* the numbers *6421* and *328*. The machine uses these three pieces of information to provide the new information, *6749*.

Computers vary considerably in size and complexity; however, they are all similar in many ways. Each computer must be able to *read in* instructions and data, *remember* the problem being solved and the data to use, *perform calculations* (and other manipulations) on the data, *print out* the results, and *control* the entire operation. Thus, for a machine to process data it must contain five logical elements:

1. A means of input.
2. A means of output.

Figure 1-2 Line printer producing printed information at 1200 lines per minute. (*Courtesy* IBM Corporation.)

*Throughout this book the term "computer" is meant to be "digital computer."

Section 1.2   How to Recognize a Computer   7

3. An arithmetic unit.
4. A means of storing data.
5. A control unit.

The five logical elements all work together in solving a problem, and numerical data and instructions constantly are being sent back and forth between them.

A computer system consists of a number of individual components, each having its own function. The system is made of units to send information to the computer (such as the Cathode Ray Tube display device shown in Figure 1-1), the computer itself, auxiliary storage units, and equipment to accept information from the computer (such as the line printer shown in Figure 1-2). Figure 1-3 shows a large computer system with many different pieces of hardware.*

The various parts of the computer are activated with some input material, which may be punched on cards or input via a typewriter. The cards or typed input specify a set of instructions prepared by the person going to use the computer. This set of instructions is called a *program*.

A program presented to a computer is a complete set of instructions that solve

Figure 1-3 A large computer system—IBM System/370 Model 165. (*Courtesy* IBM Corporation.)

Hardware refers to the physical units that make up a computer system, for example, card readers, line printers, magnetic disk file units. The programs that can be used on a computer are called *software*.

a particular problem. The set of instructions is not always unique, for there may be more than one way to solve a given problem. Without a program, a computer is a helpless collection of electronic circuitry. With a proper program, a computer can direct city traffic, play chess, navigate ships, compose music, or guide a satellite into orbit. A computer does not do any thinking and cannot make unplanned decisions. Every step of each problem it handles has to be accounted for by a program.

You should remember that computers are used to implement solutions to problems. Computers do not solve problems; *people* solve problems. The computer carries out the solutions as specified by people.

REVIEW EXERCISES

1.1 List 10 applications of computers.

1.2 How do you think a bank might use a computer system?

1.3 List the five logical parts to a computer system.

1.4 Define *hardware* and *software*.

1.3 USING A COMPUTER TO SOLVE A PROBLEM

Before we begin the discussion of how to develop computer programs, let us look at the steps that are required when one uses a computer as a problem-solving tool. In fact, there is a prescribed pattern for the solving of most problems with a computer. This pattern involves the following steps, which are illustrated in Figure 1-4.

Step 1: Problem Definition

Your first step in the solution is to understand the problem completely. You must be able to determine if it is feasible to solve the problem on a computer. Many problems are simply *not computer problems*.

Problems that are based on single formulas very well may be solved best on electronic hand calculators. Computer problems should involve as much repetition as possible, because repetition is what computers do best. Whatever a computer can be programmed to do, it can do over and over.

A computer problem also should be useful. Computer time is often expensive and should be used wisely. In a school environment, however, any problem that illustrates some point is useful to the extent that it educates. Many of the problems in this book are rather simple and are included for training purposes. Outside the learning area, in the real world, one should attempt to use computer time to solve problems of a useful nature.

Before a problem can be solved on a computer, the following questions must be answered:

- Is the problem properly defined?
- Can the problem be solved with a computer?

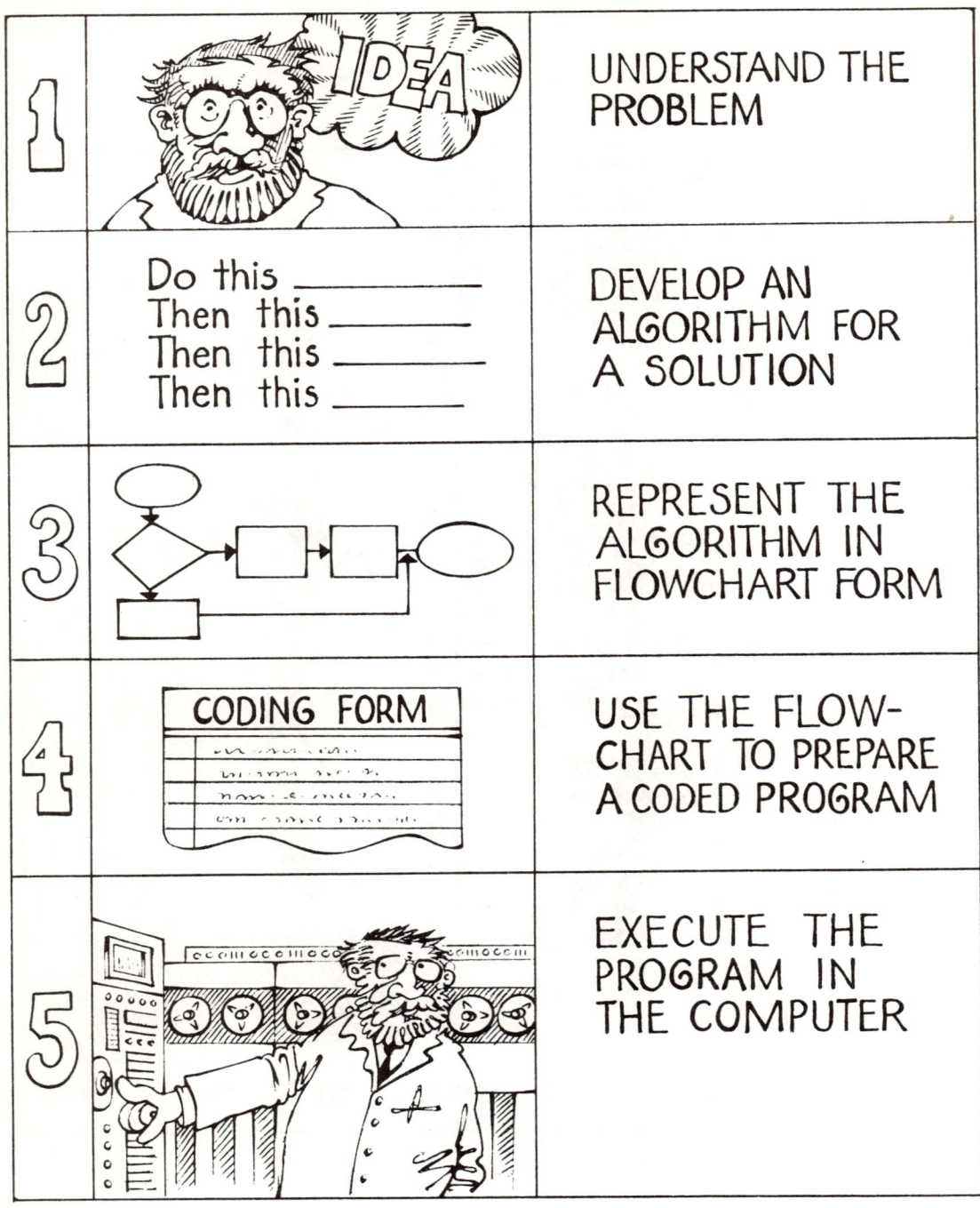

Figure 1-4 Prescribed pattern for the solving of any problem on a computer involves the five steps shown.

Section 1.3   Using a Computer to Solve a Problem

- Will the problem fit the machine that is available?
- What are the inputs to the problem?
- What outputs are expected from the problem?
- Is a computer solution the most cost-effective way of solving the problem?

People often ask such questions as, "Can you play chess with a computer?" "Can you simulate the operations of a jet aircraft with a computer?" "Can you automate a business accounting system on a computer?" "Can you monitor the operation of a plant with a computer?" Of course, all of these things can be accomplished with a computer, but it first may take several months or even years to define the problem adequately. Although it may sound strange to say, we must know *exactly* what the problem is before we attempt to solve it.

A problem need not be described by an exact mathematical equation to be solvable by a computer, but it does need a definite set of rules that the computer can follow. If a problem requires intuition or guessing, or is so hard to define that it cannot be put into precise words, the computer cannot solve it. A great deal of thought must be put into defining the problem exactly and setting it up for the computer in such a way that every possible alternative is taken care of.

Step 2:   Develop a Solution

Once you fully understand the problem, you can proceed to develop a method for its solution. This method of solution is embodied in what we will call an algorithm. An *algorithm* is simply a precise, unambiguous procedure for the solution of the problem. It specifies a sequence of operations that provides the solution in a finite number of steps. Simply stated, an algorithm represents the logic involved in arriving at the solution to a problem. The development of algorithms is discussed in Chapter 3.

Step 3:   Flowcharting

The English language is an unsatisfactory means of representing an algorithm. The language itself is inherently ambiguous, and the logical flow of complex problems is not easily explained in words. A technique widely used in computer problem-solving for representing algorithms is the flowchart (see Figure 1-5). So, once the problem has been defined and an algorithm developed, a flowchart should be drawn to illustrate in symbolic figures the logic of the solution to the problem. Flowcharts are perhaps the best method available for expressing what you want computers to do. They are simple, easy to prepare and use, and eliminate ambiguities.

An example flowchart, which is really too simple to have any practical value, is shown in Figure 1-6. (Chapter 4 will explain how to prepare flowcharts.) Observe that it is composed of several boxes, each representing some particular computer activity as described therein, and directional lines with arrows to designate the logical progression of the solution.

Figure 1-5 Flowcharts are a pictorial description of the procedure used by the computer to solve a problem. (*Courtesy* IBM Corporation.)

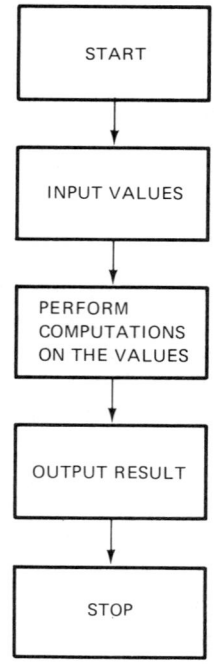

Figure 1-6 A simple flowchart.

12

Section 1.3 *Using a Computer to Solve a Problem* 13

Step 4: Translating a Flowchart into a Program

The flowchart is used as a guideline to the actual coding of the program in a *programming language*. The program, or list of computer instructions, will cause the computer to produce the solution to the problem (see Figure 1-7).

Figure 1-7 Coding instructions for a computer involves writing many error-free (hopefully) statements. (*Courtesy* IBM Corporation.)

An example of what a program would look like when written in an actual programming language is shown in Figure 1-8. This program, written in the FORTRAN programming language, computes the number of bites (assuming that the eater only takes square-inch bites) in a 10-inch diameter pizza. When executed on a computer, the program would result in the following printed message:

THERE ARE 78.5398 SQUARE-INCH BITES IN A 10-INCH PIZZA

An introduction to the FORTRAN language is found in Chapter 2. Chapter 6 contains more advanced topics concerning this language.

Step 5: Communicating with the Computer

After the program has been written, you must input the program and data (if required) into the computer and instruct the machine to execute (perform, run) the program (see Figure 1-9). If the program contains no mistakes, the computer will execute the

FORTRAN CODING FORM

PROBLEM NAME .... DATE ....
STUDENT'S NAME .... CLASS ....

```
C   PIZZA PROGRAM
    D = 10.0
    R = D / 2.0
    A = 3.14159 * R * R
    WRITE(3,10) A
10  FORMAT(10H THERE ARE,F8.4,
   236H SQUARE-INCH BITES IN A 10-INCH PIZZA)
    STOP
    END
```

Figure 1-8.

Figure 1-9 Once the program is coded, it is ready to be submitted to the computer. Shown here is a student entering her program into the computer. In the background is a punched card reader. (*Courtesy IBM Corporation.*)

program and output the desired result. If the program contains mistakes, you must find out why the program failed, make necessary corrections, and try again. This process is called *debugging* the program. You must keep in mind, however, that if the program executes, and answers are printed, there is no guarantee that these numbers are accurate. You must perform some check to see if the results are "correct."

REVIEW EXERCISES

1.5 Discuss the main aspects of the problem situation with which you must be concerned before developing a problem solution.

1.6 List the five steps that are used in the solution of a problem by a computer.

1.7 Explain the reasons for each of the five steps listed in Exercise 1.6.

Chapter 2

Computers are used at Walt Disney World, in Orlando, Florida, for a variety of interesting applications. They control the movements of space vehicles in "Space Mountain." They control the movement—even the fluttering of an eyelash—of every animated figure in the Magic Kingdom. They also control projectors, lights, fire sensors, and many other devices.

Programming the Computer

This chapter is an introduction to computer programming. It is designed to show you how programs are written in the FORTRAN (FORmula TRANslation) programming language. First, we will introduce a few elementary concepts of FORTRAN. Then we will show how these concepts can be used to write programs to solve simple problems. After we discuss algorithm development and flowcharting in Chapters 3 and 4, we will examine additional concepts and techniques of programming in FORTRAN (Chapters 5, 6, 7).

FORTRAN was one of the first high-level programming languages. Developed in 1954, it has undergone several modifications and improvements. FORTRAN II evolved shortly after the original version became available. In 1963, FORTRAN IV came into use. Although these variations of FORTRAN had many common characteristics, they were sufficiently different so that a program written in one version ordinarily could not be processed as if it were another version. A further dilemma was that each computer manufacturer implemented a slightly different form of the language. For example, FORTRAN IV on one computer would not be exactly the same as FORTRAN IV on a different computer. Thus, although programs were written in the same language (theoretically), they could not be processed on different computers without modification.

To overcome this problem of incompatibility, the American National Standards Institute developed ANSI FORTRAN and a subset of this standard called ANSI Basic FORTRAN. Programs written in either of these standard forms of the FORTRAN language should be able to be processed on any computer that implements the standard.

The version of FORTRAN discussed in this text is ANSI FORTRAN. All of the language features are found in most implementations of FORTRAN IV. Thus, all of the programs included in the text may be executed on any computer that has implemented the FORTRAN IV language.

FORTRAN is designed as a mathematically oriented language for the development of scientific computer programs. The language, however, has been used very successfully in developing programs in business, social studies, and fine arts. It has been applied to large and small problems for a wide range of applications.

2.1 THE FORTRAN PROGRAM

A FORTRAN program is a sequence of instructions, or FORTRAN statements, designed to direct the computer to a solution of a given problem. These instructions are punched on standard cards, one FORTRAN statement to a card. The computer user can either punch the cards him- or herself,* or can write the commands on special coding forms, which are submitted to a professional keypunch operator. A typical coding form is shown in Figure 2-1. The computer carries out the commands in the order they are written unless instructed to do otherwise. The 80-column cards on which computer instructions and data are punched are illustrated in Figures 2-2 and 2-3. The complete program written in FORTRAN is called a FORTRAN *source program*. When this program is punched on cards, it is referred to as a *source deck*.

The subsequent discussion applies to both the coding form and the source program card because the format of one line of program coding is identical to the format of one statement punched into one source program card.

Statement numbers. Each line on the form (or card) is divided into 80 columns. Columns 1 through 5 are reserved for the *statement number*. The statement number is used for reference and will be described later in this chapter. It now suffices to say that the statement number consists of 1 to 5 digits. For example, 130 and 4120 are statement numbers.

Statement field. Columns 7 through 72 are reserved for the actual FORTRAN statement. The statement may begin anywhere between columns 7 and 72.

Continuation code. Column 6 is the *continuation* column and is used only when a statement exceeds one line of the coding form. For example, a three-line FORTRAN statement would have a blank in column 6 on the first line and nonzero characters (1, 2, 3, . . . , 9) in column 6 on the next two lines.

Comments. Not all coding on a coding form must represent instructions to the computer. Column 1 is used for *comments*. A comment is made by placing C in column 1 and the comment in columns 2 through 72. The comment statement gives you the capability of adding clarifying information into the program. The comment statement does not become part of the final program that is executed by the computer, so it cannot affect the execution time of the program. It is advisable to use comments freely throughout your programs.

Identification field. Columns 73 through 80 are used for program identification. A typical method of identifying a particular program is to formulate an eight-character name for the program and to record that name on every line of the program. Sometimes the identification field is used to contain a *sequence number*. If, after the program

---

*Appendix A is written for students who are required to do their own keypunching, but who have had no experience in doing so.

Chapter 2 Programming the Computer

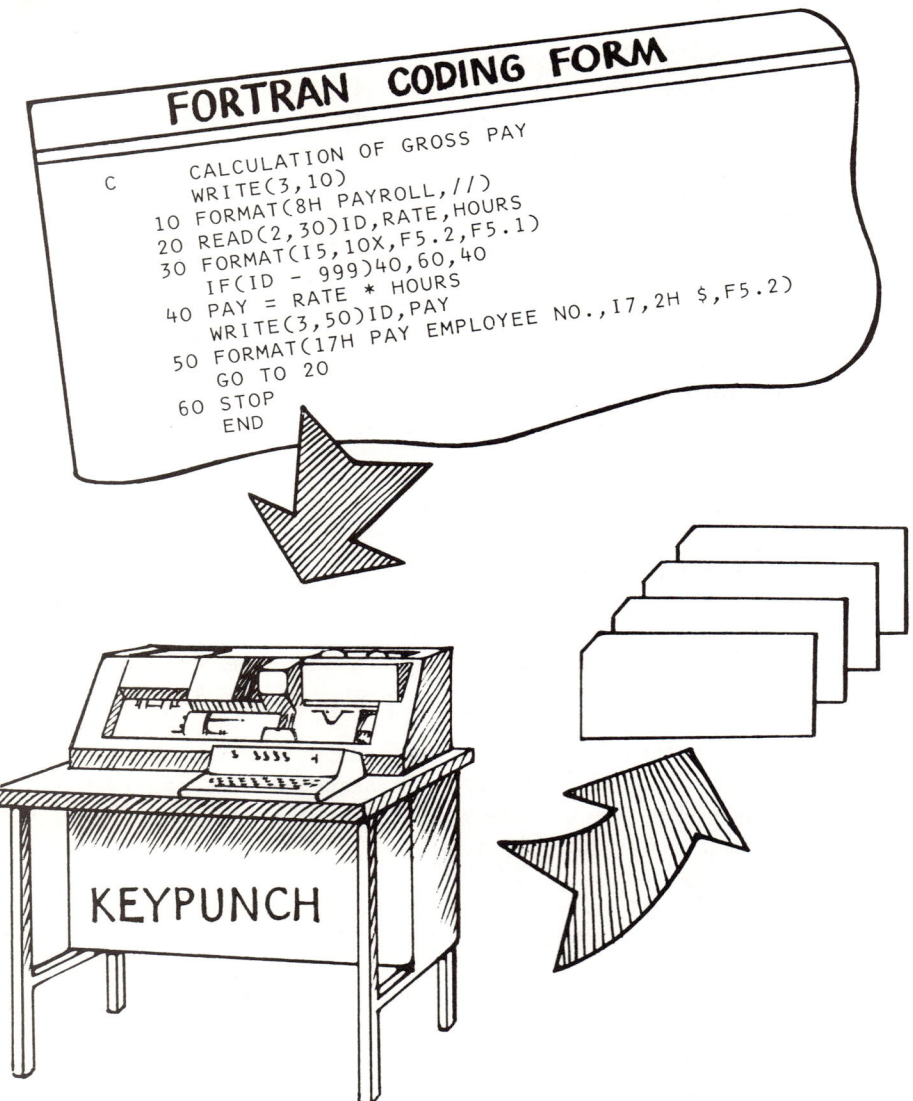

Figure 2-1 A computer user first writes the sequence of FORTRAN statements on a coding form. The statements are then punched on standard cards.

has been keypunched, the program deck is dropped (by accident), the cards can be quickly put into proper sequence again if sequence numbers were recorded in the identification field.

It is extremely easy to make mistakes in writing the program on the coding sheet,

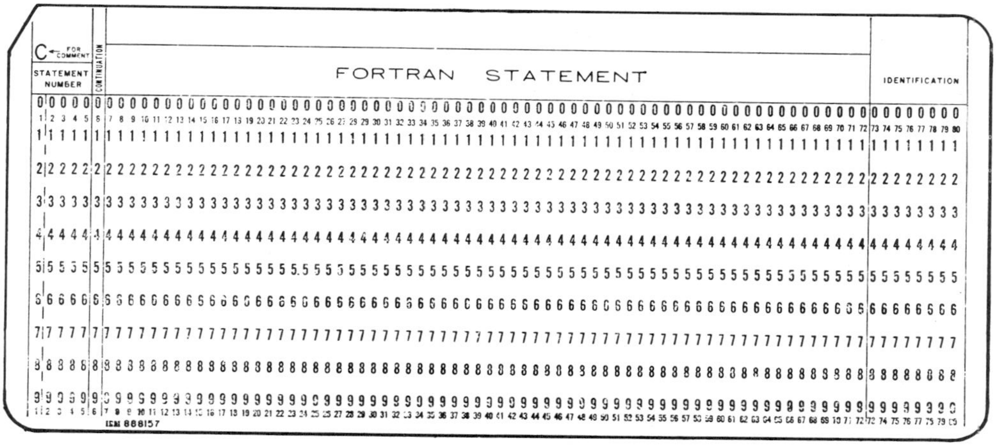

Section 2.1   The FORTRAN Program

Figure 2-2 Punched card used for FORTRAN statements.

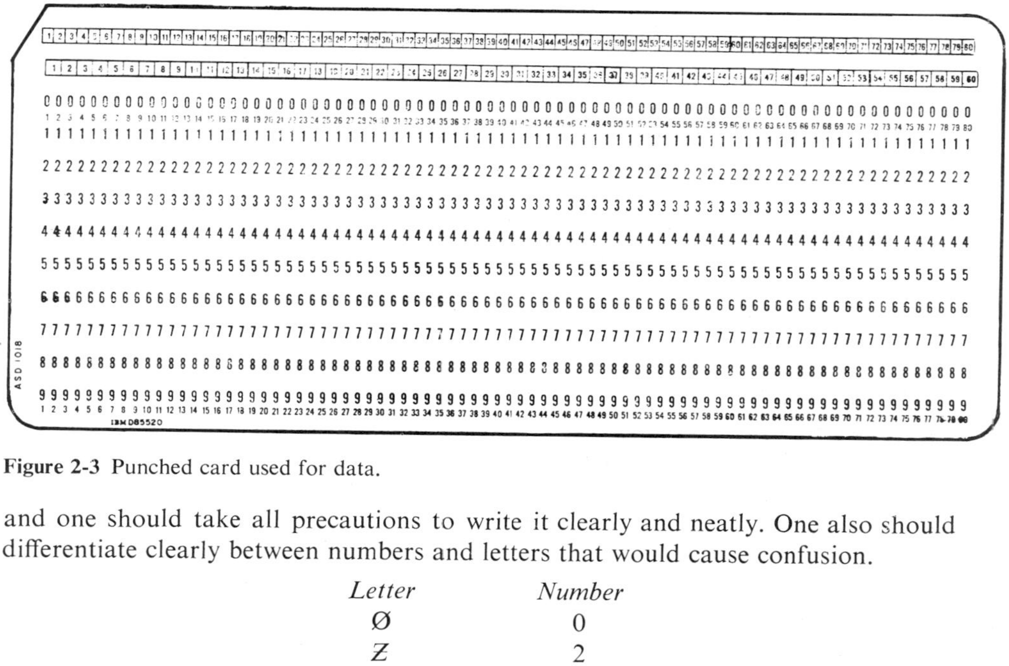

Figure 2-3 Punched card used for data.

and one should take all precautions to write it clearly and neatly. One also should differentiate clearly between numbers and letters that would cause confusion.

Letter	Number
Ø	0
Z	2
I	1
S	5

As an example of the general appearance of a FORTRAN program, consider a program to calculate a value for y given by the equation

$$y = ax^2 + bx + c$$

Chapter 2   Programming the Computer

for a given set of values for *a*, *b*, *c*, and *x*. One solution for this problem is:

```
C          A SAMPLE FORTRAN PROGRAM
     10    READ(2,20)A,B,C,X
     20    FORMAT(4F10.3)
           IF(X.EQ.0)GO TO 40
           Y = A * X ** 2 + B * X + C
           WRITE(3,30)Y,A,B,C,X
     30    FORMAT(4H  Y = ,E17.7,/,3HA =,F10.3,4X,3HB =,F10.3,4X,3HC =,F10.3,4X,3H
    1 2X  =,F10.3)
           GO TO 10
     40    STOP
           END
```

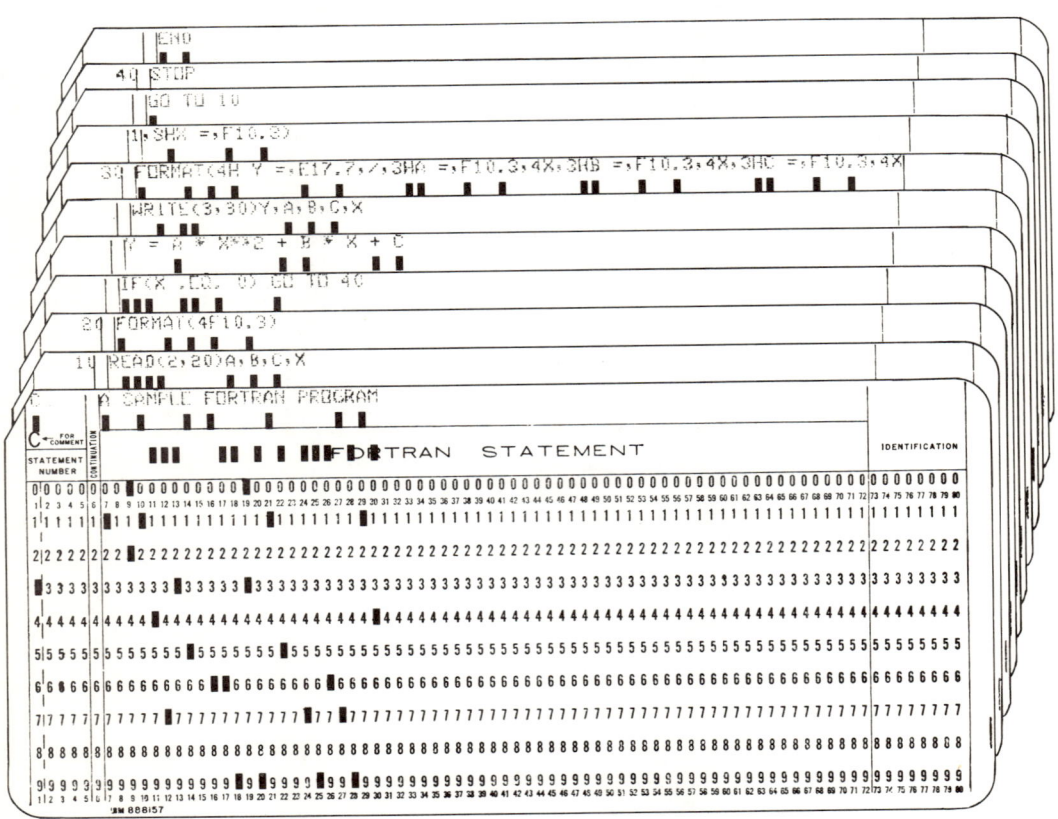

Figure 2-4 Source program deck for sample FORTRAN program.

Section 2.2   Characters and Symbols   23

When this program is punched on cards (see Figure 2-4) and executed on a computer, the following results are printed.

```
Y =    0.1439588E02
A =    14.200    B = 30.300    C = 3.560    X = 0.312
Y =    0.1738750E02
A =    2.510     B = 3.160     C = 7.000    X = 1.500
Y =    0.1500000E01
A =    0.500     B = 0.500     C = 0.500    X = 1.000
```

The outline of the program logic can be diagrammed as in Figure 2-5. The reader should not at this time try to determine how the FORTRAN program works. This example is given only to illustrate a complete FORTRAN program. The reader should, however, try to obtain a feeling for the way a problem is expressed in a language understandable to a computer.

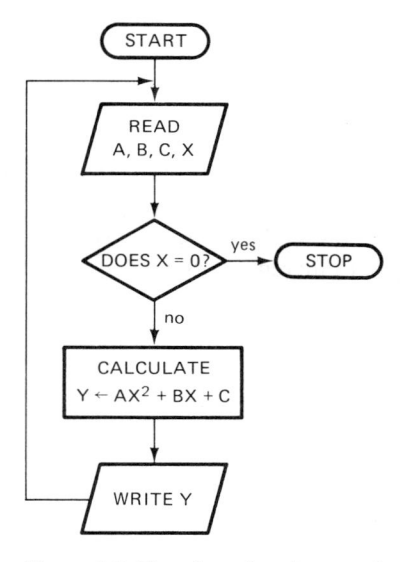

Figure 2-5 Flowchart for the sample FORTRAN program.

2.2 CHARACTERS AND SYMBOLS

A computer program is essentially a coded form of an algorithm for solving a given problem on a computer. In this book the statements of a program are encoded in the alphabet of FORTRAN using established conventions. It is necessary to distinguish between characters of the alphabet and symbols of the language.

A character in FORTRAN is an entity that has a representation internally and externally to the computer. The letter A, for example, is a character and has meaning through the manner in which it is used. Table 2-1 lists the FORTRAN alphabet.

Chapter 2   Programming the Computer

Table 2-1.   Characters of the FORTRAN Alphabet

Alphabetic Characters
   A, B, C, D, . . . , Z

Digits
   0, 1, 2, 3, . . . , 9

Special Characters

Name	Character
Blank	(no visual representation)
Equal sign	=
Plus sign	+
Minus sign	−
Asterisk	*
Comma	,
Decimal point (period)	.
Left parenthesis	(
Right parenthesis	)
Solidus (slash)	/
Currency symbol (dollar sign)	$

A *symbol* in FORTRAN is a series of one or more characters that has been assigned a specific meaning. Typical symbols are the plus sign (+) and the comma, used as a separator. A symbol consisting of more than one character is called a *composite symbol* that is assigned a meaning not inherent in the constituent characters

Table 2-2.   Symbols of the FORTRAN Language

Symbol	Function
+	Addition or prefix +
−	Subtraction or prefix −
*	Multiplication
/	Division
**	Exponentiation
,	Separator
.	Decimal point
=	Assignment symbol
( )	Enclose lists or group expression
.LT.	Less than (<)
.LE.	Less than or equal to ($\leq$)
.EQ.	Equal to (=)
.NE.	Not equal to ($\neq$)
.GE.	Greater than or equal to ($\geq$)
.GT.	Greater than (>)
.AND.	Logical conjunction (AND)
.OR.	Logical disjunction (OR)
.NOT.	Logical negation (NOT)

Section 2.3 Constants

themselves. Typical composite symbols are ** for exponentiation and .LE. for "less than or equal to." The symbols of FORTRAN are listed in Table 2-2 and explained in relevant sections of this chapter.

Spaces (or blank characters) are ignored in FORTRAN (except in Hollerith format) in the statement portion of a line, and they should be used freely to improve readability.

REVIEW EXERCISES

2.1 For what purpose is the keypunch used?

2.2 What is a source program; source deck?

2.3 Indicate the coding form column numbers that correspond to the following fields:
   (a) Statement number
   (b) Comment
   (c) FORTRAN statement
   (d) Continuation column

2.4 Give an example of a comment statement.

2.5 List the characters that may be used in FORTRAN programs.

2.6 Define symbol.

2.3 CONSTANTS

Constants and variables are used in mathematical expressions such as $3x + 12y - 6z$. The constants are 3, 12, and 6, and the variables are x, y, and z. In FORTRAN, constants are numbers such 63 or 12.7, and variables are names such as X, MAP, or PRIME. (Variables are discussed in the following section). Constants are numbers that do not change during computation. The two most used types of FORTRAN constants are *integer constants* (also called *fixed-point constants*) and *real constants* (also called *floating-point constants*). An integer constant is a value that does not have a decimal point or a fractional part. It contains only whole numbers. Real constants always include a decimal point and may or may not have a fractional part. Real constants may also contain an exponent, that is, a number represented by a base, mantissa (significant digits of a number), and a characteristic or exponent. For example, the value 86.3×10^2, where 86.3 is the mantissa, 10 is the base, and 2 is the exponent, would be represented in FORTRAN by the real constant 86.3E2, where 86.3 is the mantissa, 2 is the exponent, and E means *with exponent*. The number is to the base 10.

There are several ways of representing the same value. For example, the values

$$-1.5E3, \quad -15.0E2, \quad -150.0E1$$

are all equivalent to the value -1500.

In a real value, the mantissa may be either positive or negative, and the exponent also may be either positive or negative. This form of constant allows us to express very large or very small numbers.

Table 2-3. Examples of Constants

Integer	Real Constants
1000	0.
301	.162
−6	−36.71
1108	.0012
−360	631.
0	−2.61E+2
76439	36.00E−6
−1	.3641E2

2.4 VARIABLES

A FORTRAN variable may be either a single symbol, such as A, X, or K, or it may be a name consisting of up to six letters and digits only, the first of which must be a letter. Examples are M23, CAT, MAGIC, SUM. A variable represents a quantity that may take on different values during the execution of a program.

There are several types of variables. However, the two most used types are *integer* and *real*. (Other types are discussed in Chapter 6.) An integer variable is one that may be assigned any of the values permitted for an integer constant and is represented by a name starting with one of the letters I, J, K, L, M, or N.* The name of a real variable must begin with a letter other than I, J, K, L, M, or N, and may be assigned any of the values permitted for a real constant.

Table 2-4. Examples of Variables

Integer Variables	Real Variables
MASS	VOLT
I	SUM
JVOLT	WALL
NEW	OLD
K2	A123
MMM	BILL

*This naming convention can be overridden by a FORTRAN statement. The integer and real statements are discussed in Chapter 6.

Section 2.4   Variables

The following FORTRAN program contains only integer constants and variables. The reader should not be concerned about understanding the programs shown below. Understanding will come later when the various statements are described.

```
C         THIS PROGRAM USES ONLY INTEGER CONSTANTS
C         AND INTEGER VARIABLES
C         THIS PROGRAM COMPUTES THE SUM OF THE FIRST
C         TWENTY INTEGERS SQUARED
          ISUM = 0
          K = 0
       10 K = K + 1
          ISUM = ISUM + K * K
          IF(K .LT. 20) GO TO 10
C         PRINT VALUE OF SUM
          WRITE (3,20) ISUM
       20 FORMAT (7H1ISUM =, I10)
          STOP
          END
```

The following program uses only real constants and variables.

```
C         THIS PROGRAM USES ONLY REAL CONSTANTS
C         AND REAL VARIABLES
C         THIS PROGRAM COMPUTES A VALUE FOR P WHERE
C         P EQUALS THE SQUARE ROOT OF SINSQ(A * B * C)
C         +COSSQ(A-C)
          READ(2,10)A,B,C
       10 FORMAT(3F10.5)
          P = SQRT(SIN(A * B * C) ** 2 + COS(A-C) ** 2)
C         PRINT ANSWER TO P
          WRITE(3,20) P
       20 FORMAT(4H1P =,F16.5)
          STOP
          END
```

REVIEW EXERCISES

2.7 Identify all fixed-point constants.
    (a) −62   (b) 41.3   (c) 0   (d) 61.2
    (e) −3.   (f) 167.E04   (g) 32   (h) 0.0
    (i) 0.000E1   (j) 641390   (k) 3.14   (l) −6

2.8 Identify all real constants.
    (a) 13.E6   (b) −3E2   (c) 16   (d) −3.0E.02
    (e) 64.E3   (f) 14329   (g) .00062   (h) 0
    (i) 99.E+2   (j) 0.44E−1   (k) −0.1   (l) 0.0

2.9 Write each of the following numbers as real numbers with the decimal point just preceding the first nonzero digit.
  (a) 62100.3
  (b) 6.00E02
  (c) 4417.632
  (d) 0.00042E−2
  (e) 0.00006E+1
  (f) 63.7

2.10 Express the following numbers as fixed-point constants.
  (a) 36.4
  (b) 0.326
  (c) 14.0E+2
  (d) −36.4E−1

2.11 Identify the illegal fixed-point variables.
  (a) K
  (b) A
  (c) MAX
  (d) N540
  (e) SUM
  (f) 2NUM
  (g) K$10
  (h) NUMBER
  (i) J22R
  (j) NAVY
  (k) L+4
  (l) XM14
  (m) MAGIC
  (n) 1ABC
  (o) 126
  (p) K.12

2.12 Identify the illegal real variables.
  (a) ABC
  (b) IJK
  (c) R63
  (d) 2D
  (e) NUMBER
  (f) CON.2
  (g) KSUM
  (h) ADD
  (i) AVER
  (j) DIVIDE
  (k) ARMY
  (f) IBM
  (m) B6204
  (n) D+10
  (o) AAAAA
  (p) 7+R

2.5 ARITHMETIC EXPRESSIONS

An *arithmetic expression* is a properly formed sequence of variables, special symbols, constants, and functions operated on by arithmetic operators. The five arithmetic operators are shown in Table 2-5.

Table 2-5.

Operator	Operation	FORTRAN Expression
+	Add	A + B
−	Subtract	A − B
*	Multiply	A * B
/	Divide	A / B
**	Exponentiation	A ** B

The order in which expressions are evaluated is governed by the rules of precedence, with all operations of a higher precedence being performed prior to those of a lower precedence. When parentheses are used, the operations contained within parentheses are performed first. Operations of equal precedence are performed from left to right.

The following hierarchy of operations may be used to determine processing order:

First: operation within parentheses.
Second: exponentiation.
Third: multiplication and division
Fourth: addition and subtraction.

Section 2.5   *Arithmetic Expressions*   29

As an example, the expression

$$A*X**2 - B*X + SUM/F$$

would cause the following actions to occur:

1. Calculate X^2.
2. Multiply X^2 by A.
3. Multiply B by X.
4. Divide SUM by F.
5. Subtract the product BX from AX^2.
6. Add SUM/F to the difference of $AX^2 - BX$.

Table 2-6.   Examples of Arithmetic Expressions

FORTRAN Expression	Mathematical Expression
I + 1	$i + 1$
X + 1.0	$x + 1$
A + B * C	$a + b \times c$
A * B + C * D	$a \times b + c \times d$
SQRT(X) − 36.0 + A	$\sqrt{x} - 36 + a$
(A+B)/(C+D)	$(a+b)/(c+d)$
2**(3**4)	2^{3^4}

One can see the value of using parentheses by closely examining the last two examples. Without parentheses, the expression $A + B/C + D$ represents the calculation

$$a + \frac{b}{c} + d$$

instead of

$$\frac{a+b}{c+d}$$

The expression 2**(3**4) will result in a value of 2^{81}. If parentheses had not been used, 2**3**4, the expression would have a resulting value of 8^4, or 4096.

The modes of constants and variables should be the same; that is, one should not mix integer and real quantities in the same expression. An exception to this is a real quantity raised to an integer power.

Table 2-7.   Examples of Mixed-Mode Arithmetic

Mixed Mode	Correct
X + 3	X + 3.0
A + B + 63 − 10.0	A + B + 63.0 − 10.0
K + 3.0	K + 3
N/2 − A/6	N/2 − IA/6

Chapter 2   Programming the Computer

However, there are several implementations of FORTRAN that allow mixed-mode arithmetic.

There are significant differences between calculations involving integers and real numbers. Consider the integer expression N/J. If N is 11 and J is 2, the result of evaluating this expression is 5.5. But since the result must be integer, the fractional part is lost. Thus, the actual answer is 5. Note that the answer is not rounded; it is truncated (chopped off). This rule, together with the rules for the order of executing of operations in an arithmetic expression, yields some peculiar results:

$$1/2 = 0$$
$$1/2 + 1/2 + 1/2 + 1/2 = 0 + 0 + 0 + 0 = 0$$
$$2/3 * 3 = 0 * 3 = 0$$
$$1/4 * 3/4 = 0 * 3/4 = 0/4 = 0$$

REVIEW EXERCISE

2.13 Write FORTRAN expressions for each of the following mathematical phrases:

(a) $\dfrac{a - b}{c + d}$

(b) $(x^2 - y^2)^3$

(c) $\left(\dfrac{a}{b}\right)^{x-1}$

(d) $1 + x^2 + x^3$

(e) $x + \dfrac{y}{2} + Z$

(f) $\dfrac{a + 2}{b + c^3}$

(g) $6 + \dfrac{a}{b}\dfrac{c}{d}$

(h) $(a + b)^5$

(i) $a - \dfrac{b}{x + y}$

(j) $\dfrac{1}{2}\left(x - \dfrac{a}{x}\right)$

(k) $\left(\dfrac{a + b}{c + d}\right)^3 + x^3 + 10$

(l) $k/l + j/n$

2.6 ARITHMETIC STATEMENTS

In algebra a statement is of the form $c^2 = a^2 + b^2$ and represents a mathematical equation. In FORTRAN an arithmetic statement is quite similar to the conventional algebraic equation. It consists of the variable to be computed on the left side of the statement, followed by a "replaced by" symbol and an arithmetic expression on the right side of the statement. The general form of the arithmetic statement is

$$v = e$$

Section 2.6   Arithmetic Statements

where *e* represents the expression to be evaluated, the symbol = means "replaced by," and *v* is the variable that is set to the value of the expression. If the mode of the expression is different from that of the variable on the left of the "replaced by" symbol, it is converted to the mode of the variable.

The statement

$$K = K + 1$$

is an arithmetic statement and is interpreted as follows:

1. The expression $K + 1$ is evaluated by adding 1 to the current value of K.
2. K is then set equal to the value of the expression.

Table 2-8. Examples of Arithmetic Statements

FORTRAN Statement	Mathematical Statement
Y = X + Z	$y = x + 3$
X = SQRT(B**2−40*A*C)	$x = \sqrt{b^2 - 4ac}$
N = A * (A−C)	$n = a(a - c)$
X = (A+B)/C+2.0	$x = (a+b)/c+2$
K = A + 1.0	$k = a + 1$

One must not confuse mixed-mode arithmetic with different modes on opposite sides of the "replaced by" symbol. Mixed mode applies only to the mixing of variable modes of an *expression*. It is very often desirable to perform some computation in one mode (say, real mode) and store the result in an integer variable. For example, in the statement

$$K = 46.3 + 12.2$$

the value of the expression is first determined as 58.5, then truncated (not rounded) to 58, and then assigned to the variable K.

REVIEW EXERCISES

2.14 Each of the following FORTRAN statements has at least one error. Find the error(s) and write the correct statement.

Mathematical Statement	FORTRAN Statement
(a) $a = a + 1$	A = A + 1
(b) $y = \dfrac{a + b}{c + d}$	Y = A + B/C + D
(c) $z = \left(\dfrac{a + b}{c + d}\right)^3$	Z = (A + B)/(C + D)**3
(d) $R = \dfrac{1}{x^2}\left(\dfrac{a}{4}\right)^2$	R = 1/X**2*(A/4)**2

(e) $x = a^{b^c}$ X = A**B**C

(f) $p = \dfrac{3+x}{12y}$ P = (3 + X)/12Y

(g) $y = \dfrac{a}{b} + \dfrac{c}{d}\,r^2$ Y = A/B + C/D*r**2

(h) $a = (x+y)^{1/2}$ A = (X + Y)**1/2

2.15 What would be the value of H after execution of the following sequence of statements?
```
A = 3.0
B = 2.0
C = 5.0
F = A + B
G = F + C − A
H = G*B/20
```

2.16 Compute the value assigned to the left-hand variable by using the arithmetic statements.
   (a) A = 7.0 + 3.0
   (b) I = (3/2) * 2
   (c) N = 2.0 * 3./2.
   (d) L = 2.0 * (3./2.)
   (e) B = (3./2.) * 2.0
   (f) J = 36.4 + 12.2 − 1.0

2.7 LIBRARY FUNCTIONS

The FORTRAN library contains a large number of mathematical functions. These routines are so frequently required that instructions for their evaluation have been programmed previously and are permanently stored where they are always available to the FORTRAN compiler.

A few commonly used functions available in all FORTRAN systems are shown in Table 2-9.

Table 2-9.

Function Name	Mathematical Expression
SQRT(X)	$\sqrt{x}$
SIN(X)	$\sin x$
COS(X)	$\cos x$
TAN(X)	$\tan x$
EXP(X)	e^x
ATAN(X)	arctan x ($\tan^{-1}$)
ABS(X)	$\lvert x \rvert$
FLOAT(K)	Convert k to real
IFIX(X)	Convert x to integer

A library function may be used in an arithmetic expression in the same way that a variable is used. The following three examples of arithmetic statements use library routines:

FORTRAN Statement	Mathematical Statement
Y = SQRT(B**2 − 4.0 * A * C)	$y = \sqrt{b^2 - 4ac}$
Z = ABS(A) + ABS(B)	$z = \lvert a \rvert + \lvert b \rvert$
K = FIX(A) + N + FIX(X)	$k = a + n + x$

2.8 LOGICAL CONSTANTS, VARIABLES, EXPRESSIONS, AND STATEMENTS

Many computer applications involve the handling of nonnumeric data. The logical capabilities of FORTRAN allow one to perform operations that deal with logical relations between pieces of information. The result of such an operation is an indication that the relationship was either *true* or *false*.

A FORTRAN *logical constant* can represent either true or false. It must be either .TRUE. or .FALSE.. A *logical variable* is a variable that has been declared so in a LOGICAL type statement.* A logical variable can take on only the values .TRUE. and .FALSE..

A *logical expression* may consist of a sequence of logical variables, logical constants, or certain arithmetic expressions separated by either logical or relational operators. The solution to a logical expression is a value that is either true or false.

The FORTRAN logical operators are

$$a \text{ .AND. } b \qquad a \text{ .OR. } b \qquad \text{.NOT. } a$$

where *a* and *b* are logical expressions. In the logical expression *a* .AND. *b*, the effect of the operator is to make the total expression *true* only if *a* and *b* are true, but *false* if both *a* and *b* are false or if either *a* or *b* is false.

In the expression *a* .OR. *b*, the effect of the *or* operator is to make the total expression *true* if either *a* or *b* is true or both *a* and *b* are true, but *false* only if *a* and *b* are both false.

The expression .NOT. *a* makes the expression *true* if *a* is false, and *false* if *a* is true.

The logical operators are always preceded and followed by a period.

Table 2-10. Examples of Logical Expressions Using the Logical Operators

Logical Expression	Mathematical Phrase
A .OR. B	$a \lor b$
C .AND. (A .OR. B)	$c \land (a \lor b)$
RED .AND. BLACK	Red $\land$ Black

A logical expression also may be a *relational expression*, that is, an expression involving the FORTRAN relational operators. These relational operators are:

Relational Operator	Definition
.GT.	Greater than ($>$)
.LT.	Less than ($<$)
.EQ.	Equal to ($=$)
.NE.	Not equal to ($\neq$)
.GE.	Greater than or equal to ($\geq$)
.LE.	Less than or equal to ($\leq$)

The relational operators also are preceded and followed by a period.

*This statement is discussed in Chapter 6.

Section 2.8   Logical Constants, Variables, Expressions, and Statements

A relational operator is used to connect two real or two integer arithmetic expressions. Mixed mode arithmetic is not allowed, that is, A .EQ. K would not be allowed, and logical expressions must not be used with these operators. Relational expressions have the value .TRUE. if, and only if, all comparisons in the expression are true. For example, see Table 2-13.

Relational Expression	Solution
1 .GT. 4	.FALSE.
2 .LE. 5	.TRUE.
X .GT. 14.0	Will be .TRUE. or .FALSE. depending upon the value of X.

Table 2-11. Examples of Relational Expressions

Relational Expression	Mathematical Phrase
A .GT. C	$a > c$
K .EQ. NUMBER	$k = $ number
X .LE. 14.0	$x \leq 14$
A .NE. 12.0	$a \neq 12$

FORTRAN also provides means for using relational expressions as parts of a larger logical expression. For example, the logical expression

(X .LE. Y) .OR. W

means that if the real variable X is less than or equal to the real variable Y, or logical variable W is .TRUE., then the expression has a value of .TRUE.. Any other combination would result in the expression having a value of .FALSE..

Table 2-12. Examples of Logical Expressions Using Relational Expressions

Logical Expression	Mathematical Phrase
X .OR. A .NE. 12.0	$x \lor (a \neq 12)$
A .GT. B .OR. C .LT. D	$(a > b) \lor (c < d)$
D .LE. A .AND. K .EQ. 10	$(d \leq a) \land (k = 10)$

Logical and relational expressions are processed from left to right, using the hierarchy of operations to determine the priority. If parentheses are absent and the operators are of equal priority, the operations will be performed from left to right. If the operators are of different priority, the one with the highest priority will be processed first. Quantities within parentheses always will be processed first.

The hierarchy of operations is as follows:

Priority	Operation
First	Quantities within parentheses
Second	Evaluation of functions
Third	Exponentiation (**)
Fourth	Multiplication and division (* and /)
Fifth	Addition and subtraction (+ and −)
Sixth	Relational operators (.GT. .LT. .EQ. .NE. .GE. .LE.)
Seventh	.NOT.
Eighth	.AND.
Ninth	.OR.

A *logical statement* consists of a logical variable name followed by the "replaced by" symbol, followed by a logical expression. The general form is

$$a = L,$$

where *a* is a logical variable that has been declared in a LOGICAL-type statement and L is a logical expression. In the statement

$$Y = A \ .GT. \ B$$

the real variable Y will be set to .TRUE. if the value of A is greater than the value of B, and to .FALSE. if A is equal to or less than the value of B. Both A and B are real variables and Y must have appeared previously in a LOGICAL-type statement.

Table 2-13. Examples of Logical Statements

Logical Statement	Mathematical Statement
A = C .GT. D	$a = c > d$
C = .NOT. A	c is not a
Y = (A .AND. B) .OR. C	$y = (a \wedge b) \wedge c$

REVIEW EXERCISES

2.17 Library functions are used to:
  (a) input information into a computer.
  (b) evaluate common mathematical relationships.
  (c) tell the printer how many printouts there will be.
  (d) keep track of loops in a program.

2.18 Express the following mathematical statements in FORTRAN:
  (a) $y = \sqrt{27} + a$
  (b) $z = |a| + |b| + 10$
  (c) $x = \dfrac{-b + \sqrt{b^2 - 4ac}}{2a}$

Section 2.9   Input-Output Statements

2.19 If A = 4.0, B = 10.0, and C = 2.0, indicate which of the following relations have the value *true* and which *false*.
(a) A .NE. 2.0∗C
(b) B .EQ. A∗∗2 − 3 ∗ C
(c) B .GT. C
(d) C .LE. 0
(e) A ∗ C .GT. B
(f) A ∗ 2.0 .LE. 4.0 ∗ C

2.9 INPUT-OUTPUT STATEMENTS

Input/output statements make it possible to communicate with peripheral devices external to the computer. Such devices are card readers, line printers, magnetic tape units, CRT display devices, paper tape readers, typewriters, paper tape punches, card punches, and magnetic disk units. Input statements enable a program to receive information from external sources; output statements transmit information from computer storage to an external device.

The FORTRAN input/output statements are READ, WRITE, BACKSPACE, REWIND, and ENDFILE. The last three are used with magnetic tape and magnetic disk equipment. Most FORTRAN systems include the previous statements plus PRINT and PUNCH statements.

READ and WRITE statements include a list that defines what information or data are to be processed by the statement. Input lists specify variables to which incoming data are to be assigned. Output lists specify variables or expressions whose values are to be transmitted to an external output device. The elements of a list are specified in the order of their appearance in the list (from left to right). An example of an input/output list would be A, Y, Z, SPEED. If the list contains more than one variable name, the names must be separated by commas. A list must not contain constants. In addition to variable names, the input/output list also may contain the name of an array, an array element name, or an implied DO list. These elements are discussed in Chapter 6.

The READ Statement

The READ statement is of the form

$$\text{READ } (u,f) \text{ L}$$

where u is an integer constant or an integer variable that identifies the input unit,* f is the statement number of the FORMAT statement associated with this READ statement, and L is an input list. The elements of the list are scanned and converted as specified by the FORMAT statement specifications. Thus, the input list actually specifies what quantities are to be transmitted from the input media to the computer.

---

*A u equal to 2 is used for all examples in this book, and it represents a card reader. Number are assigned to input/output devices by the computer manufacturer or user. These numbers must then be used to reference the input or output device.

When you write

$$\text{READ (2,20) A,B,C}$$

the program will read from a punched card the values for the variables A, B, and C. The number 20 identifies the FORMAT statement used: the data on the cards must be in the same order as the variables in the input list.

The WRITE Statement

Whereas the READ statement is used to specify that data be transmitted from punched cards to the computer, the WRITE statement specifies that data be transmitted from the computer to some output media.

The WRITE statement is of the form

$$\text{WRITE } (u,f) \text{ L}$$

where u is an integer constant or an integer variable that identifies the output unit,* f is the statement number of the associated FORMAT statement, and L is an output list. The elements of the list are converted and positioned as specified by the FORMAT statement specifications. This output list actually specifies what quantities are to be transmitted from the computer.

An example of a WRITE statement is

$$\text{WRITE (3,300) A,B,X,SUM}$$

which would direct the computer to output to the printer the values of A, B, X, and SUM according to the specifications of FORMAT statement 300.

It is possible to use the WRITE statement without an output list. A statement such as

$$\text{WRITE (3,20)}$$

would inform the compiler to produce output on the printer using FORMAT statement 20. This FORMAT statement would contain the actual information to be printed.

The FORMAT Statement

FORMAT statements are used in conjunction with input/output statements. Each READ or WRITE statement has a FORMAT statement associated with it. The input/output statement specifies what is to be done, and what variables and unit are to be used. The FORMAT statement describes the form of the data to be read, printed, punched, and so forth. For READ operations, it provides information as to where variable values are located on a card, what form they take (integer or real), and how

---

*A u equal to 3 is used for all examples in this book, and it represents a line printer.

Section 2.9   Input-Output Statements

large they are. For WRITE operations, it specifies where each output value is to be placed on the paper, punched card, and so on, and in what form it should be printed.

The general form of the FORMAT statement is

$$n\text{FORMAT } (S_1, S_2, S_3, \ldots, S_m)$$

where *n* is a statement number and each S represents a separate format field descriptor or separator. The FORMAT statement is not executable; therefore, it may be placed anywhere in the program.

FORMAT Field Descriptors

There are nine field descriptors in FORTRAN. Only the five most used are discussed in this book. They are the I, F, E, X, and H descriptors.

$$\boxed{r\,I\,w}$$

This descriptor is called the *integer descriptor*, and it indicates that the value is to be treated as an integer having a length specified by *w*. The field width *w* includes the sign as well as the integer number. The value *r* represents a repeat count and indicates the number of times to repeat the field descriptor. For example, I7 is used to mean that the program will transmit no more than seven digits for that variable. Every value does not have to be seven digits long. If the number of digits of a value is less than the field width, then the digits are *right-justified*. If a field specification of I7 was used with an actual value of 67, then the value would appear on a card and on a printout, as shown in Figure 2-6, where the b's represent blanks.

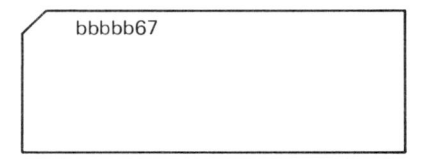

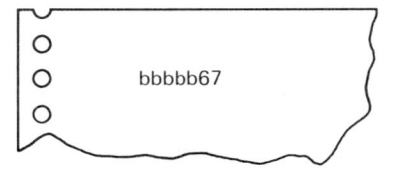

bbbbb67

bbbbb67

Figure 2-6.

The statements

READ (2,20) I,J,K,L,M,N
20   FORMAT (6I4)

specify that the program is to read values for I, J, K, L, M, and N, using the specification of I4 for each. The FORMAT statement could have been written as

20   FORMAT (I4, I4, I4, I4, I4, I4)

However, the repeat count allows us to use the same field specification a specified

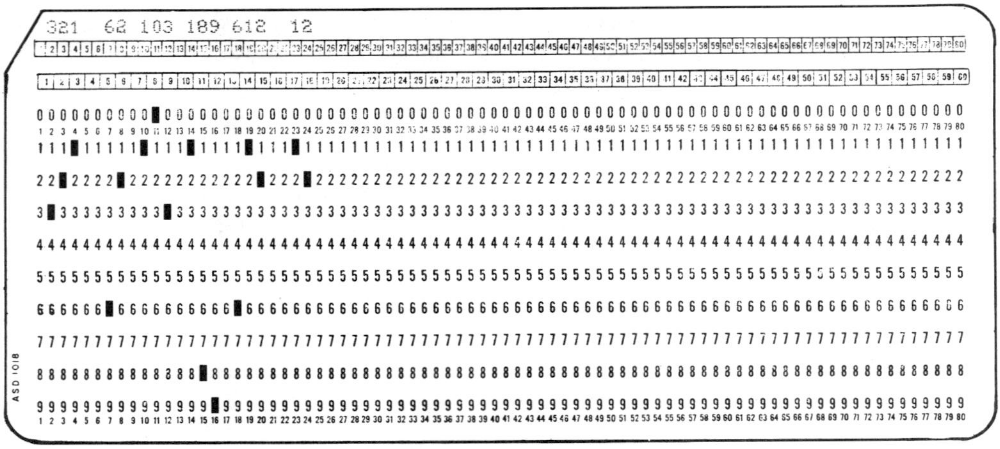

Chapter 2   Programming the Computer   40

Figure 2-7 Data card containing the values 321, 62, 103, 189, 612, and 12.

number of times. This can be used only when the field specifications are identical. If the data values for this READ operation were 321, 62, 103, 189, 612, and 12, they would appear on a data card, as shown in Figure 2-7.

After the READ operation was complete, the variables listed in the input list would contain the following values:

$$I = 321$$
$$J = 62$$
$$K = 103$$
$$L = 189$$
$$M = 612$$
$$N = 12$$

If the field width of the descriptor is less than the number of significant digits in a stored value, the leftmost digits will be lost. For example, if the value 632401 were printed using the field descriptor I4, it would appear as 2401.

$$rFw.d$$

This *floating-point descriptor* indicates that the value is to be treated as a floating-point value: w specifies the width of the field, d specifies the number of decimal places to the right of the decimal point, and r is a repeat count. When the F descriptor is used to describe an output value, the field width w must allow for a decimal point, and a leading sign, if minus.

The specification F8.3 would indicate that an eight-digit floating-point number with three decimal places could be transmitted (seven-digit if the specification is used

Section 2.9   Input-Output Statements

with a **WRITE** statement, and six-digit, if the value is less 3640216 were punched on a card and the statements

```
      READ (2,100)A
100   FORMAT (F8.3)
```

were executed, the variable A would have the value 3240.2 that the decimal point does not have to be punched on the card, because a decimal point is specified in the F descriptor. However, if a decimal point is punched on the card, it will override a FORMAT decimal point specification.

Assume that you write the statements

```
      WRITE (3,20)A,B,C,D,E
20    FORMAT (F3.0,3F6.1,F10.4).
```

and in memory the variables A, B, C, D, and E have the following values:

```
A =      36.1
B =     406.1
C =     532.016
D =   44631.0
E =    -345.6782
```

When the output statement is executed, the printout will contain the following values:

36.	b406.1	b532.0	4631.0	b-345.6780
A	B	C	D	E

$$rE w.d$$

The exponential specification is used to specify floating-point numbers with exponents: r is a repeat count, d is an integer constant representing the number of digits to the right of the decimal point, and w is the width of the field.

When using the E specification for output, one must remember to make the field width w large enough to take care of the mantissa sign, the exponent sign, E, the exponent, the decimal point, and zero. For example, if we had a value in the computer such as -56.1234, and we wanted to print it using the specification E13.6, the printout would appear as follows:

$$-0.561234E\ 02$$

This example points out that a number on output will have the form

$$\pm 0.XXX\cdots XXXE\pm ee$$

where the X's are significant digits of the number, and ee is the exponent.

As in the F specification, the use of the decimal point on input is optional; however, if it appears on a card, it will override the FORMAT specification. There are several valid ways of representing the exponent value of input numbers. The general form of the exponent is $E \pm ee$, and all the following forms are valid ways of representing the exponent *minus* 4: $E - 04$, $E - 4$, and -4. *Plus* 4 can be represented as $E + 04$, $E + 4$, $+4$, E04, E 04, and $E + 4$. Note that the exponent value must be right-justified, that is, Eb4 = E4 and $E - 4b = E - 40$.

$$\boxed{wX}$$

The X specification is a method that FORTRAN provides for skipping spaces. The value w is the number of card columns to be skipped on input or the number of blank spaces to insert on output. For example, assume that IA, IB, and IC have the following values in the computer:

IA = 3641
IB = 6232
IC = 7627

The execution of the following output statement

```
       WRITE (3,36)IA,IB,IC
36     FORMAT (3I4)
```

would look like this:

364162327627

There are two ways of producing spacing in the printout. One is to use a larger field with the I specification and other is to specify blanks with the X specification. The FORMAT statement

```
36     FORMAT (I4,3X,I4,3X,I4)
```

would result in a printout that is slightly more readable:

3641bbb6232bbb7627

Proper use of the X specification can result in a better looking printer output. Consider the following example.

The data card illustrated in Figure 2-8, when used with the statements

```
       READ (2,200) I,SPEED,KK
200    FORMAT (I6,2X,F5.1,6X,I3)
```

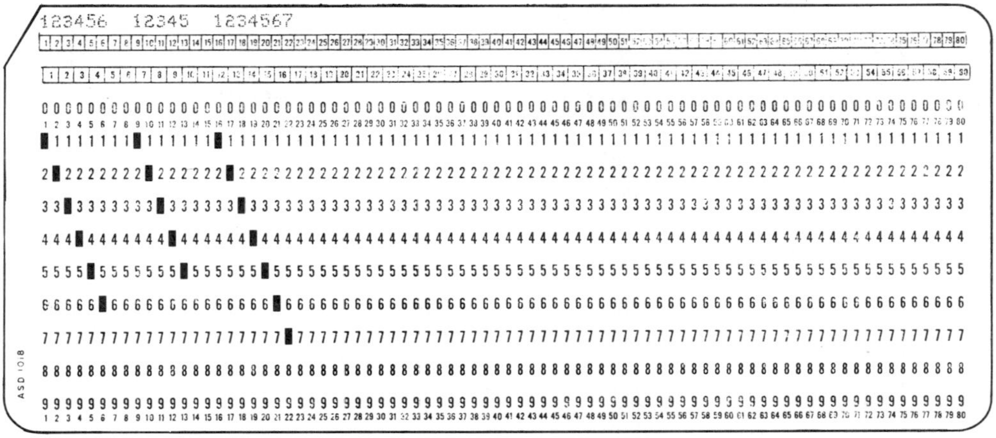

Section 2.9   Input-Output Statements   43

Figure 2-8 Data card containing the values 123456, 12345, and 1234567.

would result in the following assignments in the computer memory:

$$I = 123456$$
$$SPEED = 1234.5$$
$$KK = 567$$

```
wH
```

The Hollerith or H specification provides a method for transmitting nonnumeric information into or out of the computer. The w specifies that the number of characters immediately following the H is transmitted in accordance with the specifications position in the FORMAT statement. Any character, *including blanks*, may be used with this specification. When using the H specification, it is not required to put anything in the input/output list of the associated READ or WRITE statement.

Suppose you wanted to print a heading such as

DENSITY OF AIR AT VARIOUS ALTITUDES

The statements

```
      WRITE (3,18)
 18   FORMAT (1H1,16X,35HDENSITY OF AIR AT VARIOUS ALTITUDES)
```

would accomplish this task.

The 1H1 was used to start a new page, 16X was used to print 16 blank columns to the left of the heading, and 35HDEN...DES was used to print the heading.

The 35 was obtained by adding the 30 characters of the message and the 5 blank spaces between words.

The first column of a printed page is reserved for controlling the print carriage. This is why the 1H1 was used in the last example. The control characters are:

    1: skip to start of new page
    0: double space
   + : suppress spacing
Blank: single spacing

Let's print another message. This time let's also let the FORMAT statement contain an integer value to be printed.

    GROUND SPEED IS n MILES PER HOUR

GROUND SPEED IS and MILES PER HOUR are printed using the H specification, and n is the value of the integer variable KGS and is printed using the specification I4. Assume that KGS had a value of 364 in the computer memory; then the statements

    WRITE (3,222)KGS
 222 FORMAT (16H1GROUND SPEED IS,I4,1X,14HMILES PER HOUR)

would cause the following printout to be generated:

    GROUND SPEED IS 364 MILES PER HOUR

The first H specification started the printout at the top of a new printer page and caused the printout of GROUND SPEED IS, and the second H specification caused the printer to print MILES PER HOUR. Note that it was not necessary to include a print carriage control character in the second H specification. The X specification was used to introduce a blank after the printed value of the variable KGS.

When the H specification is used for input, w characters of input data replace the w characters in the FORMAT statement. For example, if HORSEPOWER was punched on a card in columns 1 through 10, and the statements

    READ (2,20)
 20 FORMAT (10Hbbbbbbbbbb)

were executed, HORSEPOWER would be placed in the computer storage location that previously contained the 10 blank characters of FORMAT statement 20.

Many FORTRAN systems include a simpler way of handling literal data. For example, the statement

    FORMAT ('THE CUBE OF THE DISTANCE IS')

would cause the message

    THE CUBE OF THE DISTANCE IS

to be printed. This type of FORMAT statement accomplishes what an H specifica-

Section 2.9   *Input-Output Statements*   45

tion FORMAT statement would, yet it is much easier to use because one does not have to count the number of characters and spaces between the apostrophes.

> / and ,

FORTRAN has two field separators—the *slash* and the *comma*. The comma is used to separate *field descriptors*. Whenever a slash (/) appears in a FORMAT statement, it means either a *new card* or a *new line of print*. When used with a READ statement, the slash means to read a new card. When used with the WRITE statement, the slash means to start a new line of print.

For example, the statements

```
      WRITE (3,100) A,B,C
100   FORMAT (F6.1,/,F6.1,/,F6.1)
```

would result in A being printed on one line, B on the next line, and C on the third line.

Figure 2-9 illustrates three data cards. Each card contains a data value punched in columns 6 through 10. The statements

```
       READ (2,1000) I,J,K
1000   FORMAT (5X,I5,/,5X,I5,/,5X,I5)
```

or the statements

```
       READ (2,1000) I,J,K
1000   FORMAT (I10,/,I10,/,I10)
```

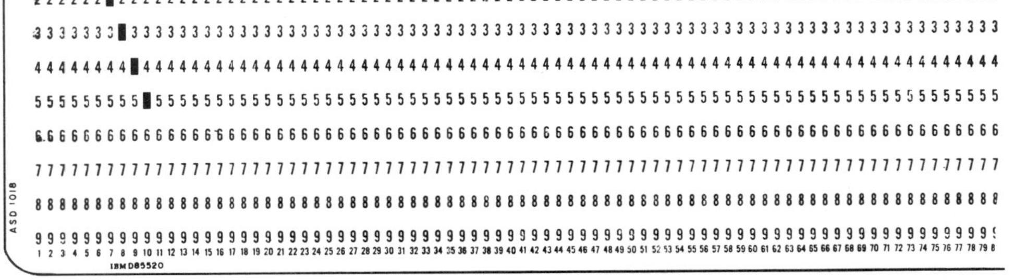

Figure 2-9 Data card containing the values 12345, 67897, and 43210.

or the statements

$$\text{READ (2,1000) I,J,K}$$
$$1000 \quad \text{FORMAT (I10/I10/I10)}$$

or the statements

$$\text{READ (2,1000) I,J,K}$$
$$1000 \quad \text{FORMAT (I10)}$$

or the statements

$$\text{READ (2,1000) I,J,K}$$
$$1000 \quad \text{FORMAT (I10,/,5X,I5,/,I10)}$$

would cause the three cards to be read and the data values contained on the cards to be assigned to I, J, and K in computer memory.

If you wanted to print the values of A, B, and C on one line, skip three lines, then print a line containing the values of D, E, and F, the statements

$$\text{WRITE (3,44) A,B,C,D,E,F}$$
$$44 \quad \text{FORMAT (1H1,3F5.0,////,3F5.0)}$$

would create this printout.

REVIEW EXERCISES

2.20 Indicate the printed value that was directed by the statements

$$\text{WRITE (3,200)} \quad (see\ column\ a)$$
$$200 \quad \text{FORMAT} \quad (see\ column\ b)$$

where *a* and *b* are listed as follows:

	a	b	Value of a in Computer Memory	Printed Value
(a)	A	F4.1	26.3	
(b)	K	I6	237	
(c)	J(3)	I3	1234	
(d)	POWER	F6.0	126.23	
(e)	ACE	F6.2	−74.361	
(f)	AREA	E10.5	12.345	
(g)	MASS	I3	.123	
(h)	N	I4	−27	
(i)	K3	I8	+6321	

2.21 The FORMAT statement
    (a) must be located after a WRITE statement.
    (b) must be located before a READ statement.
    (c) may be located anywhere in a program.

Section 2.9   Input-Output Statements   47

   (d) must be associated with the COMMENT statement.
   (e) must have a statement number.

2.22 The WRITE statement
   (a) is used to write values in computer storage.
   (b) must have a statement number.
   (c) must have an output list.
   (d) is used to output values on the card reader.
   (e) is a method of getting information out of the computer.

2.23 Write a READ and associated FORMAT statement that would cause the values punched on the cards to be assigned in memory as follows:

$$I = 264, \ J = 3486, \ A = 26.1.$$

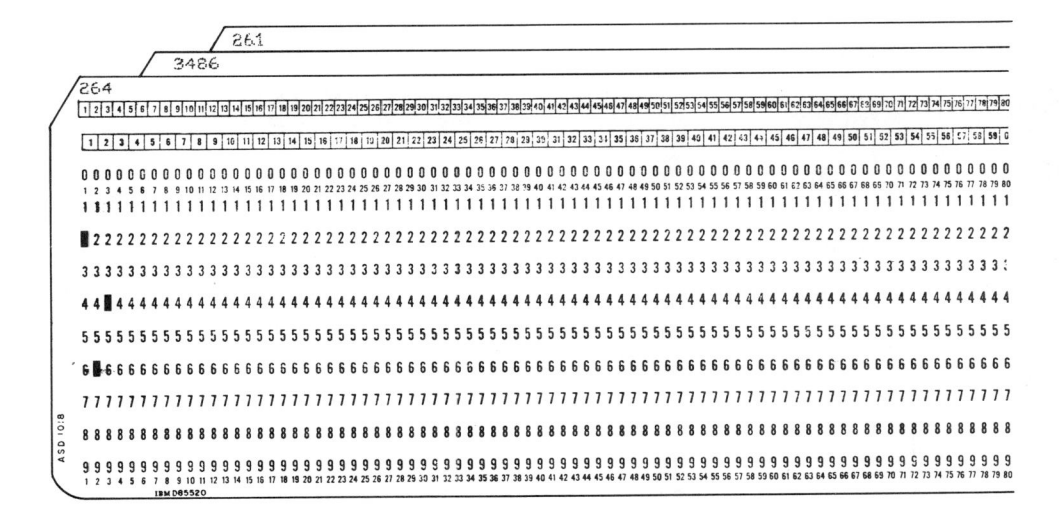

Exercise 2.23

2.24 Indicate the line of print that would be generated by the following statements:

2.25 Indicate the one FORMAT statement that will cause the printer to leave 6 blank spaces.
   (a) 10   FORMAT (6H,I14,F5.1)
   (b) 10   FORMAT (I14,F5.1,6X)
   (c) 10   FORMAT (I14,//,6X,F5.1)
   (d) 10   FORMAT (6XI14,F5.1,6X)
   (e) 10   FORMAT (6X,/,I14,F5.1)

```
          WRITE (3,20)
     20   FORMAT (1H1,6X,14HSUM OF NUMBERS)
```

2.26 What five letters may be used in FORMAT specifications?

2.27 The following card contains values for I, X, and Y.

Chapter 2 Programming the Computer   48

Write READ and FORMAT statements that will read these values into memory so that no significant digits will be lost.

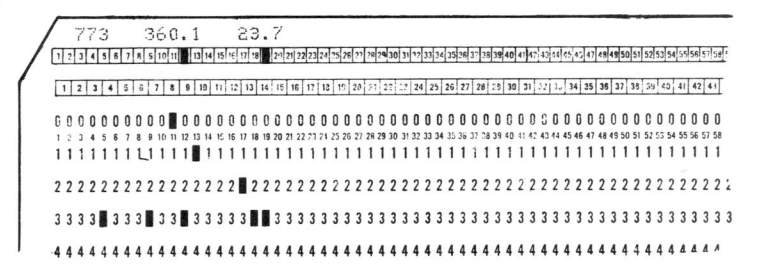

Exercise 2.27

2.28 If the next data card in the card reader is as follows:
(a) What would be read from the card if the statement being executed is

          READ (2,100) M,N1,N2,N3
     100 FORMAT (I2,6X,3I2,10X,F5.2)

(b) What would have been read from the card if the statements had been

          READ (2,100) M,N1,N2,N3,ACE
     100 FORMAT (I2,6X,3I2,5X,F10.2)

Exercise 2.28

2.10 CONTROL STATEMENTS

Each statement in a FORTRAN program is executed in the order of its appearance in the source program, unless this order is modified by a *control statement*. Control statements allow one to transfer program control to any statement in the program. They also allow the testing of various conditions and variables and the repeating of a particular sequence of statements a specified number of times. The control

Section 2.13   Arithmetic IF Statement   49

statements discussed in this section are the unconditional GO TO, computed GO TO, arithmetic IF, and logical IF statements.

2.11 UNCONDITIONAL GO TO STATEMENT

The GO TO statement permits the computer user to transfer program control to another statement in the program *unconditionally*. The form of this statement is

GO TO n

where *n* can be any statement number in the same program.
When you write

GO TO 104

the computer transfers program control to statement number 104. After the statement identified by 104 is executed, control continues with the statements following statement number 104.

2.12 COMPUTED GO TO STATEMENT

The computed GO TO statement permits transfer of control to one of a group of statements, the particular statement being chosen at the time of the computer run. The statement is of the form

$$\text{GO TO } (k_1, k_2, k_3, \ldots, k_n), i$$

where $k_1, k_2, k_3, \ldots, k_n$ are statement labels and *i* is an integer variable. Execution of this statement causes the statement identified by the statement label k_j to be executed next, where *j* is the value of *i* at the time of the execution. The value of *i* must be in the range of 1 to *n*, where *n* denotes the number of statement labels contained between the parentheses. If *i* is not in the range, the results are unpredictable.

When the programmer writes

GO TO (10,20,30,40),K2

the computer transfers program control to statement number 10 if K2 equals 1 at execution time, to 20 if K2 equals 2, to 30 if K2 equals 3, and to 40 if K2 equals 4 at execution time.

2.13 ARITHMETIC IF STATEMENT

The *arithmetic* IF statement has the form

IF (e)a,b,c

where *e* is any arithmetic expression and *a, b, c* are statement numbers in the same program. This statement permits the programmer to alter the order of executing statements, depending upon the results of a computation, the value of a variable, or the sign of a number. The statement works this way: if the value of the expression *e* is *negative*, program control is transferred to *a*; if the value of *e* is *zero*, control is transferred to *b*; and if the value of *e* is *positive*, program control is transferred to *c*. The statement numbers *a*, *b*, and *c* may be the same or all different. For example, when you write

$$\text{IF } (N-6)10,12,36$$

the computer computes a value for the expression $N - 6$, and transfers control to either statement number 10, 12, or 36 depending upon the value of $N - 6$.

If N-6 is negative, control goes to 10.

If N-6 is zero, control goes to 12.

If N-6 is positive, control goes to 36.

The *arithmetic* IF statement is quite versatile and permits you to make most tests. For example, if you want to test to see whether the real variable R is less than, equal to, or greater than 36, you should write

$$\text{IF } (R-36.0) \ 10,20,30$$

Control goes to statement 10 if $R < 36.0$, to statement 20 if $R = 36.0$, and to statement 30 if $R > 36.0$.

For a simple example of the use of an arithmetic IF statement, consider the problem of computing a value for *x*, which is based on the following equations:

$$x = 3y + 36 \quad \text{if} \quad 0 < y \le 11,$$
$$x = y^2 - 10 \quad \text{if} \quad 11 < y \le 33,$$
$$x = y^3 + y^2 - 1 \quad \text{if} \quad 33 < y \le 64,$$
$$x = 0 \text{ for all other values of } y$$

```
      IF(Y)70,70,10
10    IF(Y-11.0)20,20,30
20    X = 3.0 * Y + 36.0
      GO TO 80
30    IF(Y-33.0)40,40,50
40    X = Y * Y - 10.0
      GO TO 80
50    IF(Y-64.0)60,60,70
60    X = Y ** 3 + Y ** 2 - 1.0
      GO TO 80
70    X = 0.0
80    continue
```

The previous segment first determines if the value of Y is either negative or zero and, if so, transfers control to statement 70, where X is set to 0.0. If Y is a positive value, control is transferred to statement 10. This decision was performed by the statement

$$\text{IF } (Y) \ 70,70,10$$

Statement 10 checks to see if the value of Y is less than 11.0 and, if so, computes a value for X using

$$X = 3 * Y + 36.0$$

After this is performed, the statement GO TO 80 transfers program control over the remaining statements.

The IF statement at statement 30 checks to see whether Y is less than or equal to 33.0 and, if so, computes $x = y^2 - 10$, and transfers control to statement 80 via the GO TO statement.

Statement 50 contains another IF statement that performs a similar check. If Y is 64.0 or less, then $x = y^3 + y^2 - 1$ is computed, and GO TO 80 is executed. If the value of Y exceeds 64, statement 70 is executed where X is set to 0.

2.14 LOGICAL IF STATEMENT

The general form of the *logical* IF statement is

$$IF\ (e)\ L$$

where e is a logical expression and L is any executable statement except another logical IF statement or a DO statement.* When this statement is executed, the expression e is evaluated and statement L will be executed if the value of e is .TRUE.. If the value of e is .FALSE., the statement following the logical IF statement is executed. The statement following the logical IF also will be executed if e is .TRUE., and if the statement L does not cause a transfer of control to occur, that is, a statement such as GO TO 360.

If you write the statement

$$IF\ (X\ .AND.\ Y)A = B * C + 36.0$$

and both logical variables X and Y are .TRUE., then compute a value for A using the expression $B * C + 36.0$. If both variables are not .TRUE., the statement is skipped and program control continues with the statement following the logical IF statement.

The statement

$$IF\ (K\ .GT.\ 34)\ GO\ TO\ 300$$

would cause a transfer of program control to statement 300 if, at the time of execution, the value of the real variable K is greater than 34.

2.15 THE STOP STATEMENT

The STOP statement is written to inform the computer to terminate the execution of the program. The form of the STOP statement is:

$$STOP$$

*The DO statement is discussed in Chapter 6.

In an operating system environment, execution of the STOP statement causes an exit to the operating system to *terminate* program execution. This statement provides a convenient method of terminating program control and also provides a smooth transition from one program to the program immediately following. The STOP statement can be located anywhere in a program.

2.16 THE END STATEMENT

In addition to the STOP statement, every FORTRAN program must have an END statement as the last statement in the program. The STOP statement specifies the *logical* end of the program during execution, and the END statement signals the *physical* end of the program for the FORTRAN compiler. During translation of the FORTRAN source program into the basic language of the computer (machine language), the compiler processes each statement in turn until it encounters the END statement. At that point the compiler knows that there are no more source statements, and program compilation is terminated.

REVIEW EXERCISES

2.29 In the arithmetic IF statement IF(?)10,20,30, the value of ? can be:
    (a) $X < Y$ (b) $X > Y$
    (c) $\sqrt{X}$ (d) $X - Y$

2.30 Which one of the following statements will transfer control to statement 22 when R is negative and to statement 32 when R is positive or zero?
    (a) IF (R)32,22,32   (b) IF (R)22,32,32
    (c) IF (R)22,22,32   (d) IF (R)32,32,22

2.31 Write an arithmetic IF statement that will transfer program control to statement 40 whenever X + Y is less than 200.0 and to statement 50 whenever X + Y is greater than or equal to 200.0.

2.32 Write a statement that will transfer control to statement 10 if M is 1, to 20 if M is 2, and so on, up to statements 60 if M is 6.

2.33 What is the purpose of the STOP statement?

2.34 What is the purpose of the END statement?

2.17 EXAMPLES OF SIMPLE PROBLEMS

EXAMPLE 1

An airplane flying at an altitude of 10,000 feet and at 150 miles per hour develops relative wind of 300 miles per hour just above the wing and 80 miles per hour just below the wing. If the wing area is 160 ft², how large is the force perpendicular to the wing?

Section 2.17   *Examples of Simple Problems*   53

SOLUTION

Assume that the density at 10,000 ft is $p = 0.001756$ slug/ft³. The formula

$$F = A \times \frac{1}{2}p(v_1^2 - v_2^2)$$

may be used to compute the resulting force, F in pounds. The factor 44/30 should be used to transform miles per hour to feet per second.

```
C          FORCE PROGRAM
           A = 160.0
           P = .001756
           V1 = 300.0
           V2 = 80.0
           F = A * .5 * P * ((V1 * 44.0/30.0)**2-(V2*44.0/30.0)**2)
           WRITE (3,10) F
     10    FORMAT (8H FORCE =, F 10.2)
           STOP
           END
```

EXAMPLE 2

Given that the three sides of a triangle are $A = 321$, $B = 614$, and $C = 201$, find the area of the triangle.

SOLUTION

The area may be computed from the formula

$$\text{Area} = \sqrt{S(S - A)(S - B)(S - C)}$$

where

$$S = (A + B + C)/2.$$

```
C          TRIANGLE AREA PROGRAM
           A = 321.0
           B = 614.0
           C = 201.0
           S = (A + B + C) / 2.0
           AREA = SQRT(S*(S-A)*(S-B)*(S-C))
           WRITE (3,10) AREA
     10    FORMAT (7H AREA =, F 6.2)
           STOP
           END
```

EXAMPLE 3

The following rates are used to determine Eli Marley's electric bill for the month of June.

Ormond	14 KWH or less	$3.20
Beach	Next 51 KWH	$0.15 per KWH
Electric	Excess over 65 KWH	$0.097 per KWH
Co. Rates		

Write a program to compute Marley's bill, knowing that he used 130 KWH during June.

```
C         ELECTRIC BILL PROGRAM
          AKWH = 130
          CHARGE = 3.20
          IF(AKWH .LE. 14.0) GO TO 20
          IF(AKWH .GT. 65.0) GO TO 10
          CHARGE = CHARGE + .15 * (AKWH - 14.0)
          GO TO 20
       10 CHARGE = CHARGE + 7.65 + .097 * (AKWH - 65.0)
       20 STOP
          END
```

EXAMPLE 4

Write a program to compute and print the sum of the first 100 integers.

```
C         INTEGER SUM PROGRAM
          I = 0
          KSUM = 0
       10 I = I + 1
          KSUM = KSUM + I
          IF(I .LT. 100) GO TO 10
          WRITE (3,20) KSUM
       20 FORMAT (I5)
          STOP
          END
```

EXAMPLE 5

This program computes the average of 15 numbers (for example, examination grades) stored on cards, and prints out the average.

```
C         AVERAGE OF 15 NUMBERS
          SUM = 0.0
          I = 1
       10 READ(2,40)X
          SUM = SUM + X
          I = I + 1
       20 IF(I .LE. 15) GO TO 10
       30 AVER = SUM/15.0
          WRITE (3,40) AVER
       40 FORMAT (F6.2)
          STOP
          END
```

In lines 10 through 20, the values of X are read into the computer and the sum is

REVIEW EXERCISES

2.35 Write a program to compute the value of CAT that will depend upon one of the following relationships:
(a) $CAT = (A+B)(C+D)$ if $X > 0$
(b) $CAT = \dfrac{A + B}{C + D}$ if $X = 0$
(c) $CAT = A + B - C + D$ if $X < 0$
Use the statement $X = 22.0$ to establish a value for X.

2.36 Write a program to calculate 10! (10 factorial) and print the result.

$$10! = 1 \times 2 \times 3 \times 4 \times \ldots \times 10$$

2.37 Write a program that will determine the grade for steel under the following requirements: steel is considered grade 1 if T1 exceeds .95 and if T2 exceeds .75; grade 2 if T1 exceeds .95 but T2 does not exceed .75; and grade 3 if T1 does not exceed .95.

2.38 The formula

$$y = 41.298 \sqrt[3]{1 + x^2 + x^{1/3}}$$

is to be evaluated for

$$x = 1.01, 1.02, 1.03, \ldots, 3.00$$

Each *x,y* pair is to be printed on a line, with headings at the top of the columns. Write a FORTRAN program for this problem.

2.39 A girl drops her purse from the top of the Sears Tower (1454 feet high). Code a FORTRAN program for determining the impact velocity at the street level. Use the formula

$$v = \sqrt{2gh}$$

where *h* is the height of the Sears Tower and $g = 32$ ft/sec² is the earth's gravitational constant.

2.40 A Chinese merchant visiting Boston wants to set his hotel room thermostat for 28° Celsius, but the thermostat is marked off in a Fahrenheit scale. Write a FORTRAN program to make the conversion. *Hint:* use the formula $C = 5/9(F - 32°)$.

Conclusion

In this chapter you were introduced to programming problems in FORTRAN. You have learned the vocabulary and those elements of the grammar of this language that will enable you to solve simple problems. More advanced techniques and problems are discussed in Chapters 6 and 7. However, first you should become familiar with writing and executing simple FORTRAN programs on a computer, and learn how to set up problems for computer solution. Setting up problems will be examined in the next two chapters, where you will be introduced to algorithm development and flowcharting techniques.

Chapter 3

Air traffic controllers use computerized radar systems to supervise air traffic at all major airports. The computer system tracks, identifies, and displays all aircraft at all times. (Courtesy *Federal Aviation Agency*.)

Algorithms

In this chapter we consider a few simple examples of step-by-step procedures for solving problems. The first example is a familiar one. It solves the problem of generating a magic square. This example introduces the general idea of an algorithm, *that is, a list of instructions for solving a problem*. Whenever a computer is used to solve the problem, an algorithm provides the logical steps the computer will follow in the solution.

Then we will consider several examples of algorithms. Most of the examples in this chapter are too simple to be of any use in applications. They are intended only to introduce the topic.

3.1 PROBLEM ANALYSIS

A very important aspect in the process of developing a solution to any problem is the analysis of the problem. *Problem analysis* is the process by which the problem is defined and all of the information needed for problem solution is identified. The importance of properly defining a problem cannot be overemphasized, since any method developed for solving the wrong problem will be unsatisfactory. For example, a trip plan for driving to Las Vegas will not solve the problem if the problem really involves making a trip to Kansas City. There are usually an unlimited number of methods available for solving any given problem. To choose the best method, however, we first must adequately define the problem that needs a solution.

Problem analysis is very subjective in nature. A pat method for analyzing a problem, which always will give all of the information required for the solution, does not exist. The analysis will, however, require that we recognize the problem, identify its inputs and variables, list the outputs desired, formulate a precise problem statement, and determine whether or not a computer is needed to solve the problem.

After a problem has been properly analyzed, we are ready to develop a method for its solution. In the following section we will examine how to develop precise computer approaches to the solution of problems.

3.2 ALGORITHM DEVELOPMENT

How many of us have ever failed to be impressed by a magic square? The magic square shown here is arranged so that the sum of the numbers in any row, column, or diagonal is always 15.

8	1	6
3	5	7
4	9	2

This type of magic square can be generated as follows:

1. Place the number 1 in the center cell of the top row.
2. Assign consecutive numbers in an oblique direction up and to the right. When this procedure carries the number out of the square, write that number in the cell at the opposite end of the column or row.
3. After each group of three numbers has been assigned, move down one box and repeat rule 2.

This set of rules is called an algorithm. Simply stated, an algorithm is a recipe or list of instructions for doing something. More precisely defined, it is a complete, unambiguous procedure for solving a specified problem in a finite number of steps.

"IT'S THE MOST IMPORTANT DISCOVERY OF THE CENTURY... C'MON, LET'S RELAX."

Chapter 3   Algorithms 60

If a computer is used to solve the problem, an algorithm provides the logical steps that the computer will follow in the solution.

The word "algorithm" is derived from the name of a ninth-century Arabian mathematician, al-Khowarizmi. He devised a number of methods for solving certain problems in arithmetic. These methods were presented as a list of specific instructions, and his name has become attached to them. He also wrote the book *al jabr w' al muquabalah* (the reunion and the opposition). The words referred to the two main processes used in solving "equations" problems, *reunion* being presumably the bringing together of terms involving the unknown quantity, and *opposition* the final state, when a "reunited" unknown quantity was faced by some number. The book was translated into Latin, and the Latin title eventually was reduced to our familiar word *algebra*.

A recipe in a cookbook is a good example of an algorithm. The preparation of a certain dish is broken down into many simple instructions or steps that anyone experienced in cooking (and most who are not) can understand. Another example is the procedure used to play the following game. You and your opponent take alternate turns in removing matches from a pile. The minimum number of matches that can be removed from the pile is 2 and the maximum number is 6.* The winner of the game is the one who forces his or her opponent to take the *last* match. For example, consider the following game with an original pile of 76 matches.

- You take 3 and leave 73
- Opponent takes 5 and leaves 68
- You take 3 and leave 65
- Opponent takes 6 and leaves 59
- You take 2 and leave 57
- Opponent takes 6 and leaves 51
- You take 2 and leave 49
- Opponent takes 6 and leaves 43
- You take 2 and leave 41
- Opponent takes 4 and leaves 37
- You take 4 and leave 33
- Opponent takes 6 and leaves 27
- You take 2 and leave 25
- Opponent takes 5 and leaves 20
- You take 3 and leave 17
- Opponent takes 4 and leaves 13
- You take 4 and leave 9

*There are many variations of this game. Any number of matches may be in the original pile, and the number of matches that can be picked up can vary. This game is a special case of Nim.

Section 3.2   *Algorithm Development*   61

- Opponent takes 2 and leaves 7
- You take 6 and leave 1
- Opponent takes 1

The opponent moved last; you win. The strategy of this game is based on modulo arithmetic. If the maximum number of objects a player may remove in a turn is M, then to gain a winning position a player at the end of his or her turn must leave a stack of 1 modulo (M + 1) coins. The set of playing rules that will always insure you a win is called an algorithm.

We solve most decision problems by using algorithms—by breaking down the problem into many unambiguous steps. Problems for computer solution must be broken down into many simple steps or instructions. The algorithms for many problems are rather simple; however, algorithms for complicated scientific problems can be quite complex. The algorithm for determining if 639 is a prime number is simple. One only has to divide 639 by each of the numbers 2, 3, 4, . . . , 637, 638.* If any division results in a zero remainder, the number is not prime; otherwise it is a prime number. The algorithm for simulating the internal operations of a nuclear power plant is complex and involves several thousand steps.

Algorithms are used unknowingly every day—in road maps, rules for adding numbers, directions for performing experiments, instructions for adjusting the carburetor of a car, rules for playing games, instructions for using a tape recorder, directions for opening a combination lock. An algorithm precisely describes the sequential procedure to follow to accomplish a stated task. It is important to note that an algorithm does not give an exact answer to the problem, only *how* the answer can be derived.

An algorithm must have the following four characteristics to be useful. It should be (1) unambiguous, (2) precisely defined, (3) finite, and (4) effective. The following examples illustrate these characteristics.

Consider an algorithm for locating Joe's Pizza Parlor. A *poor* algorithm for this process is:

>   Go north a little ways, then turn left for several blocks.
>
>   Joe's Pizza Parlor is just around the corner of 158th street.

This is an ambiguous, poorly defined procedure. A better, more effective algorithm is:

>   Go north for four blocks, then turn left on 158th street.
>
>   Go down this street until the street crosses Southern Boulevard.
>
>   Turn right; Joe's Pizza Parlor is located at 1236 Southern Boulevard.

This procedure is clearly defined and limited.

*There are much more efficient algorithms for this problem.

Another poor algorithm is:

Take two numbers and multiply them.

This algorithm does not identify the numbers. A better algorithm is:

Take x, multiply by 27, and call it y.

This algorithm can be expressed in mathematical notation as

$$y = 27x$$

Algorithms can be represented in several different ways. One way is to list the steps involved in the process. For example, the algorithm for finding the average of a set of measurements is as follows:

Step 1. Locate the first measurement.
Step 2. Add the second measurement.
Step 3. Is this the last measurement?
Step 4. If so, go to step 7.
Step 5. If not, add another measurement.
Step 6. Repeat Step 3 until all measurements are exhausted.
Step 7. Determine the number of measurements.
Step 8. Divide the sum of the measurements by the answer to Step 7.

If the measurements were 6, 7, -3, and 34, the steps would involve the following operations:

Step 1. 6
Step 2. $6 + 7 = 13$
Step 3. no
Step 4. —
Step 5. $13 + (-3) = 10$
Step 6. $10 + 34 = 44$
Step 7. 4
Step 8. $44 / 4 = 11$

Almost everyone is familiar with the algorithm for placing a station-to-station telephone call. If not, you may find it in any city telephone directory.

(1) Dial "1."
(2) Dial the Area Code, if it is different from your local area code.
(3) Dial the 7-digit telephone number for the place you want.
(4) Give the operator your number, if asked for it.

Another algorithm involves the opening of a particular combination lock. The lock can be opened by carrying out the following sequence of instructions.

COMPUTER ROOM

"FIRST YOU FORGET HOW TO TAKE A SQUARE ROOT. THEN YOU FORGET LOGARITHMS. THEN IT BECOMES DIFFICULT TO DO LONG DIVISION. THEN YOU FORGET THE MULTIPLICATION TABLE..."

Chapter 3   Algorithms

(1) Turn the dial clockwise for three complete revolutions, stopping at 14.
(2) Turn the dial counterclockwise to stop at 27.
(3) Turn the dial clockwise to stop at 7. The lock should open.

Coded, the combination looks like: C14, C14, C14, CC27, C7.
Let us now examine some problems and algorithms.

3.3 AN ALGEBRAIC ALGORITHM

A very simple algorithm involves finding the average of a set of numbers. The algorithm is described as follows:

1. Add the given numbers.
2. Count the given numbers.
3. Divide the answer to (1) by the answer to (2).

For example, let us determine the average age of a family of five. Their ages are 43, 39, 20, 9, and 4. The average is found in three steps.

JUNIOR 4   MOM 39?   DAD 43   BIG BROTHER 20   LITTLE SISTER 9

Section 3.5   *Algorithm for Generating Fibonacci Numbers*   65

1. The sum is $43 + 39 + 20 + 9 + 4 = 115$.
2. The number of people is 5.
3. The average age is $\frac{115}{5}$, or 23.

The algorithm works for all possible sets of numbers.

3.4 THE NUMBER GAME ALGORITHM

Have you ever had someone ask you to think of a number and tell you several things to do with it? Then, without knowing your original number, the person is somehow able to tell you what number you ended up with. For example: "Choose a number. Add 5. Double the result. Subtract 4. Divide by 2. Subtract the number you started with. Your result is 3."

The result is always 3, no matter what the original number was. How does this trick work? Let's look at an algorithm that proves the result is *always* 3.

1. Choose a number. n
2. Add five. $n + 5$
3. Double the result. $2n + 10$
4. Subtract four. $2n + 6$
5. Divide by two. $n + 3$
6. Subtract the number you started with, and the result is three.   3

Now it is easy to see why the original number does not make any difference in the final result.

3.5 ALGORITHM FOR GENERATING FIBONACCI NUMBERS

Leonardo Fibonacci, a wealthy Italian merchant of the thirteenth century, introduced a set of numbers now known as *Fibonacci Numbers*. The first 16 of them are: 1, 1, 2, 3, 5, 8, 13, 21, 34, 55, 89, 144, 233, 377, 610.

Each number of a Fibonacci number sequence is the sum of the two numbers immediately preceding it. That is:

$$1 + 1 = 2$$
$$1 + 2 = 3$$
$$2 + 3 = 5$$
$$3 + 5 = 8$$
$$5 + 8 = 13$$
$$8 + 13 = 21 \ldots$$

Chapter 3   Algorithms   66

The number sequence has practical applications in botany, electrical network theory, and other fields.

The Fibonacci number sequence is formed by the following algorithm:

1. Set A, B, and S equal to 1.
2. Write down A and B.
3. Replace A with B, and B with S.
4. Let $S = A + B$.
5. Write down S in the sequence.
6. Go back to Step 3 and proceed through Step 6 again.

3.6 ALGORITHM FOR THE 15 PUZZLE

The *15 Puzzle* consists of the numbers from 1 to 15 and one blank arranged in a square array. The only rule is this: any one of the numbers to the immediate *right*, *left*, *top*, or *bottom* of the blank space can be moved into the empty space. In the above figure, only 15 or 12 can be moved. The problem posed by the puzzle is: given some other number arrangement as a *goal*—for example, the three following arrangements—can the numbers in the original configuration be so maneuvered as to achieve the goal?

Mathematically it can be shown that there are 16 factorial (20, 922, 789, 888, 000) different number arrangements possible. Exactly half of these (over 10 trillion) number arrangements are impossible ever to achieve. There is an algorithm for determining whether a given goal is possible or not.

1. First consider the individual squares (the positions) as having permanent letter names as shown in the following diagram.

A	B	C	D
E	F	G	H
I	J	K	L
M	N	O	P

2. Consider the number (call it *x*) in position A, of the goal, and count how many numbers smaller than *x* are in positions higher lettered than A.
3. Do this for all the positions, and add up the numbers that were obtained for positions A through P.
4. If the blank square is one of the squares B, D, E, G, J, L, M, or O, add 1 to the sum; if the blank square is in any other lettered position, the sum is left alone.
5. If this final sum is even, the goal is *possible*; if odd, impossible.

Check the algorithm logic by determining that the arrangements X and Y on page can be achieved. Likewise, the arrangement Z cannot be achieved.

Arrangement x   Arrangement y   Arrangement z

Figure 3-1.

3.7 ALGORITHM FOR NUMBER SELECTION

There are often several different algorithms for solving the same problem in a variety of ways. Some people are very clever at finding algorithms that give an answer quickly. Others tend to use familiar approaches, which may require longer time. For example, let us develop an algorithm for finding the largest number in the following list of numbers:

26, 114, 9, 82, 61, 155, 4, 19, 3, 183

We first scan the list and eliminate all one-digit numbers, leaving

26, 114, 82, 61, 155, 19, 183

Next we eliminate all two-digit numbers, leaving

114, 155, 183

Next we eliminate all three-digit numbers. But there is nothing left! Then we back up one step and examine the three-digit numbers, as the answer is among those numbers. Let us compare the first to the second—155 is larger than 114, so we throw out 114. This leaves

155, 183

Comparing these two and throwing out 155 leaves us the final answer of

183

Another way of solving the same problem would have been just to compare the first two numbers and throw out the smaller. Then we continue this process until only the answer is left. For example, in the original set of numbers

26, 114, 9, 82, 61, 155, 4, 19, 3, 183

we would compare 26 to 114 and throw away 26; then 114 to 9 and throw away 9; then 114 to 82 and throw away 82; and so forth until we compared 155 to 183, which would determine the final answer.

One must remember that a number selection algorithm must work for any problem of this type. For example, the algorithm must work for 26, 148, 0, 61, 182, as well as 14, −68, 142, −1, 18.

3.8 THE KÖNIGSBERG BRIDGE ALGORITHM

Most of the algorithms shown in this chapter are for number problems. Algorithms also are useful for solving problems that are not easily put into mathematical terms. Consider the problem of Königsberg Bridges. The map in Figure 3-2a shows the Prussian city of Königsberg and the river loop that divides it into four areas (marked A, B, C, and D). Connecting the areas are seven bridges. The heavy dotted line indicates all the possible routes between A, B, C, and D using the bridges. It has been a tradition among the townspeople that the seven bridges could not all be crossed in

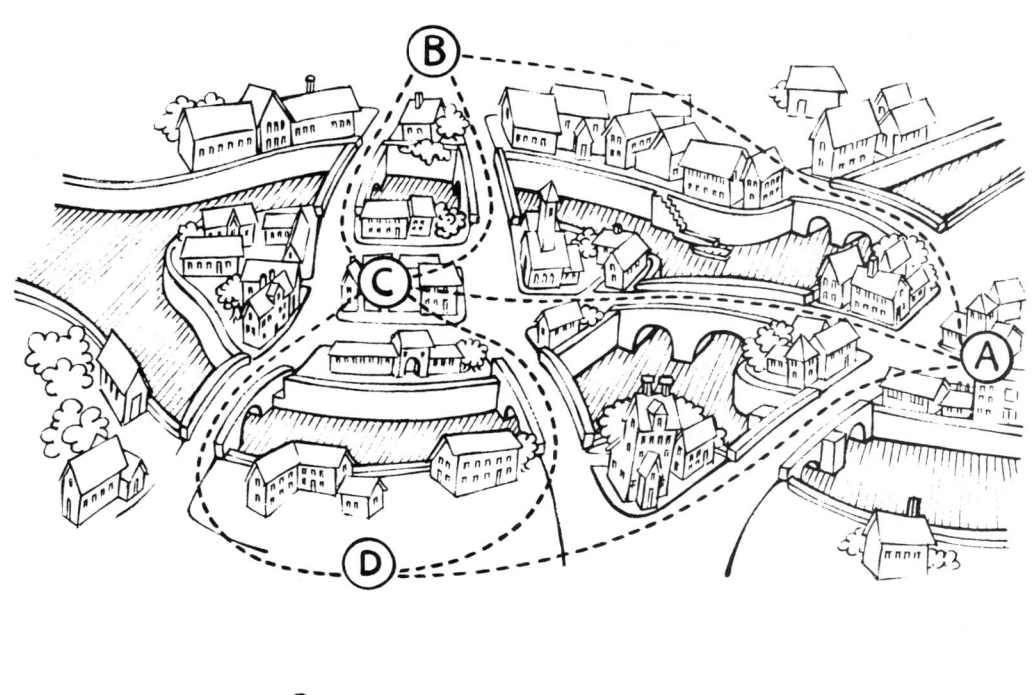

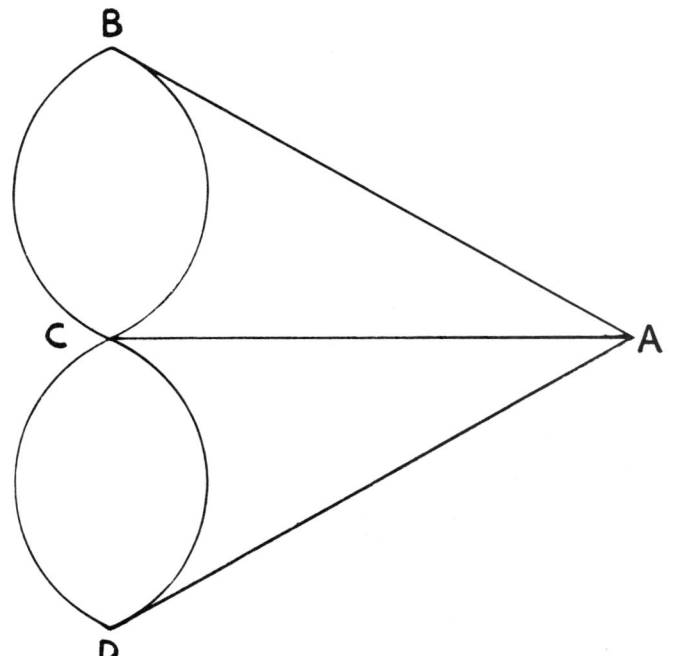

Figure 3-2 The bridges of Königsberg.

a continuous walk without recrossing the route at some point, but no one knew the explanation. When Leonhard Euler, a Swiss mathematician, heard of the Königsberg bridges, he realized an important principle was involved, and he proceeded to design an algorithm that demonstrated why such a walk was impossible.

To understand the solution, consider the diagram in Figure 3-2b. The lettered points and the lines of this diagram correspond to those marked on the map. Each line in Figure 3-2b represents a bridge. Each point, called a *vertex*, represents a land region. The diagram has four vertices and seven lines. Suppose we can travel over each bridge once and only once. If the total route starts from A, we might go first to B. We would enter B on one line and leave on another line. Thus, each time we pass through a vertex, there must be exactly two lines connected to that vertex.

After the total path is drawn, we can say: every vertex has an even number of lines connected to it. The only possible exceptions are the vertex from which we start and the vertex at which we end. Thus, a closed path covering all bridges is possible only if:

1. Every vertex has an even number of lines (then we start and end at the same point), or
2. Exactly two vertices have an odd number of lines (then we start at one of these and end at the other).

Figure 3-2b reveals that the vertices have the following number of lines: A—3, B—3, C—5, and D—3. All four numbers are odd. Hence there is no hope of walking over all seven Königsberg bridges without retracing any path.

REVIEW EXERCISES

3.1 Write an algorithm for determining the average height of the Smith family. Their respective heights are shown in the accompanying figure.

Exercise 3.1

Section 3.8   The Königsberg Bridge Algorithm   71

3.2 The girl at the checkout counter in a supermarket has to make change. Write an algorithm that would describe the process whenever a customer gave her a $5 bill for goods costing $3.66.

3.3 Develop an algorithm for getting a date for Friday night.

Chapter 4

Centralized hospital computer can receive and send information on patients, drugs, room availability, and clinic appointments from terminals, as shown above, located throughout the hospital. System provides complete patient records almost instantly. (Courtesy *Burroughs Corp.*).

Flowcharting

As stated in Chapter 1, an important step in the development of a computer program is the drawing of a flowchart. This chapter is devoted to flowcharting techniques.

The flowchart is used as a guide in writing programs in FORTRAN or any other programming language.

4.1 WHY USE FLOWCHARTS?

In Chapter 3 we described algorithms in the English language and mathematical notation. There are several drawbacks to this method:

- The algorithm is usually not concise.
- The English language is inherently ambiguous.
- This manner of expression does not reveal the logical flow of the algorithm.

A *flowchart* is another way of describing and expressing algorithms. The magic square algorithm, the Königsberg bridge solution, or any of the other algorithms discussed in Chapter 3 could be represented by a flowchart. So could a cookbook recipe for making chocolate cake or a procedure for making a telephone call.

Many algorithms are difficult to express in words. Consider trying to describe a problem solution in natural language—say, something simple like changing a flat tire on a car. Is it the front tire or rear tire that needs changing? Once determined, get the spare tire out of the trunk. Remove hub cap from wheel, loosen lugs, place jack on car bumper, jack up the car, and so on. One can easily see that natural language is serial in nature and produces a rather long description of what is to be done. The same procedure is shown in flowchart form in Figure 4-1. One can readily see the flow of what work is to be performed. Branches are easily indicated in a flowchart (in Figure 4-1, reference the boxes that contain "Is the spare tire flat" and "Is it the front tire").

4.2 WHAT IS A FLOWCHART?

A flowchart is another "language" for describing and expressing algorithms. The word language is used to indicate a means of expressing information for communication. A flowchart is a graphic representation of the solution of a problem. A flowchart uses, in addition to words, geometric symbols to express different types of operations. It is simply a pictorial description of the algorithm, showing the pertinent operations, points of decision, and the sequence in which they should take place to solve the problem correctly.

A flowchart is perhaps the best method available for expressing what computers can do—or what you want them to do. They are simple, easy to prepare, easy to use, and free of ambiguities.

4.3 FLOWCHARTING SYMBOLS

The first computer flowchart ever drawn used only two symbols—a rectangle and a small circle for connecting widely separated parts of the chart. Today's working flowcharts are quite similar; however, most people use more than two symbols. The flowchart shown in Figure 4-1 uses three different symbols.

Section 4.3   *Flowcharting Symbols*

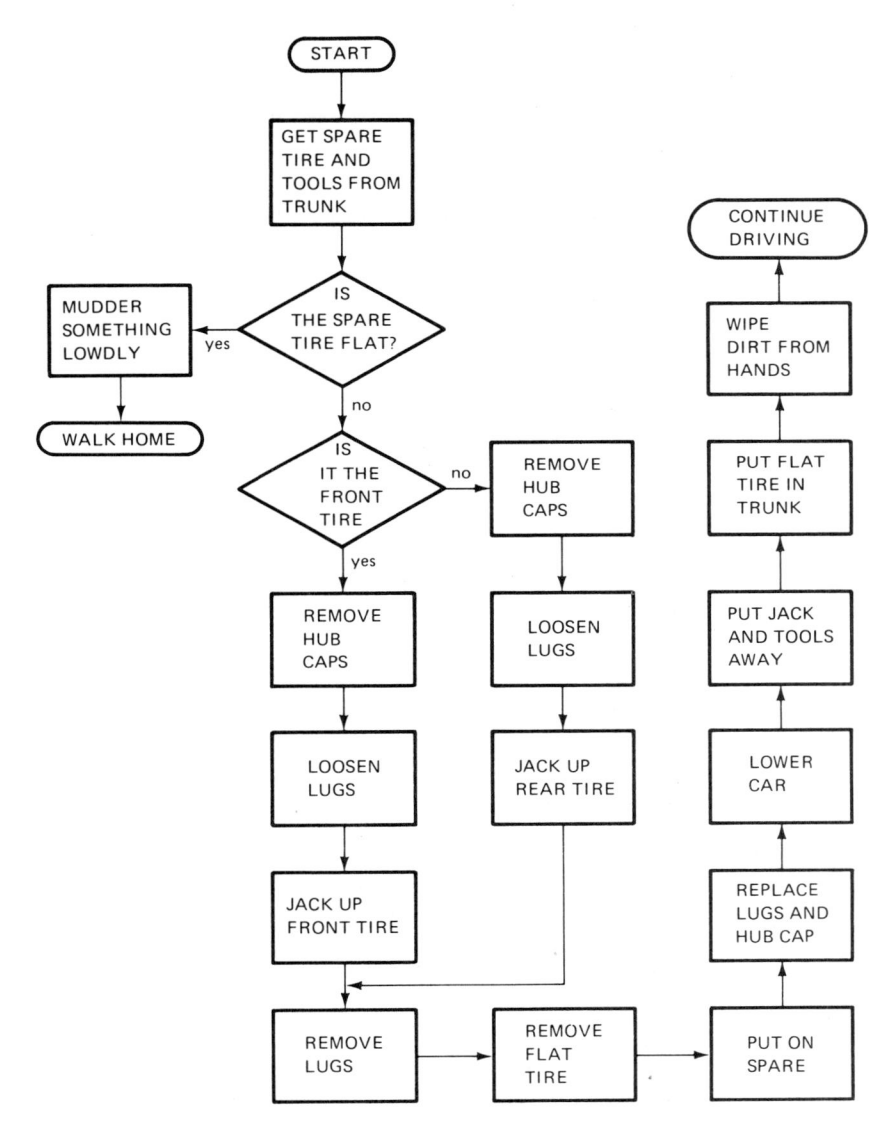

Figure 4-1 Changing a flat tire.

Rather than a set of different symbols for every flowchart, there is a standard set—ANSI Standard Flowchart Symbols for Information Processing. These standard symbols were established by the American National Standards Institute. The complete set of symbols is fairly large; however, we will use only the symbols shown in Figure 4-2. This set will allow us to prepare flowcharts for a wide selection of problems.

Chapter 4   *Flowcharting*   76

Process Symbol. A group of instructions which process information. Often one algorithm step. Used to represent calculations, processing or any function not described by a more specific symbol.

Decision Symbol. The decision function, used where a branch to alternate paths is possible, based on a decision.

Terminal Symbol. Used to represent the beginning or end of a procedure.

Input/Output Symbol. A function of either an input or output device.

Annotation Symbol. Contains descriptive comments or clarifying notes about the procedure.

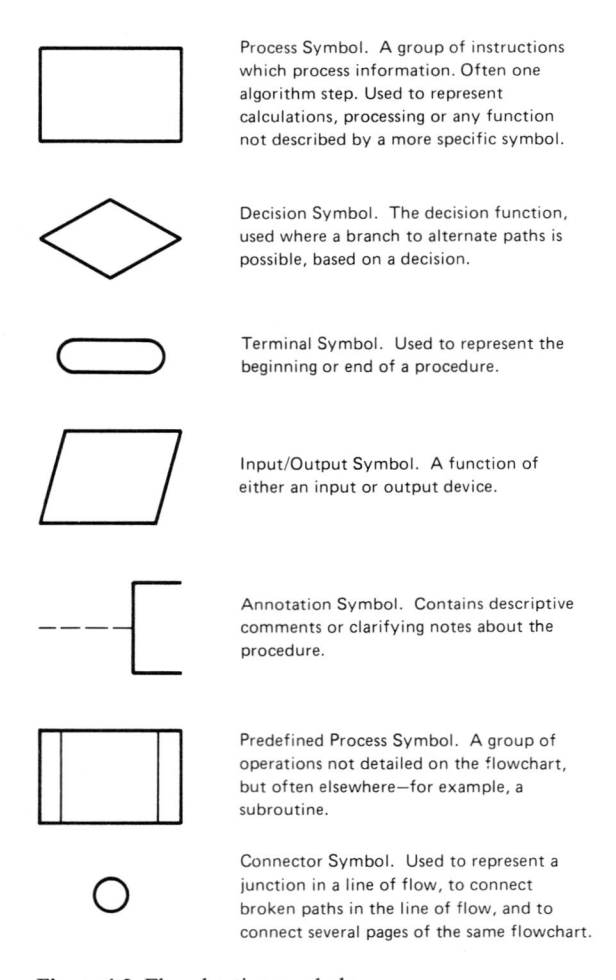

Predefined Process Symbol. A group of operations not detailed on the flowchart, but often elsewhere—for example, a subroutine.

Connector Symbol. Used to represent a junction in a line of flow, to connect broken paths in the line of flow, and to connect several pages of the same flowchart.

Figure 4-2 Flowcharting symbols.

The terminal symbol is used to indicate the beginning or ending of an algorithm.

(START)   (STOP)

The parallelogram symbol indicates either the need of information by the algorithm (input) or the availability of information in the form of an answer (output).

/ READ A /   / PRINT X /

This symbol is used to show what goes into or comes out of a procedure or program.

Section 4.3   Flowcharting Symbols

A rectangle indicates processing, such as a computation. The information written in this symbol may be an English statement, an algebraic statement, or some kind of meaningful shorthand. "Calculate $R = A/B$," "Move A to B," and "Compute $X \leftarrow X + 1$," are examples of processing and would be represented in flowchart notation as follows:

$$\boxed{\text{CALCULATE } R = \frac{A}{B}} \qquad \boxed{\text{MOVE A TO B}} \qquad \boxed{X \leftarrow X + 1}$$

The last example uses the symbol $\leftarrow$, which is often used when making variable assignments. Other ways of representing this same computation follow.

$$\boxed{\text{COMPUTE } X = X + 1} \text{ or } \boxed{\text{INCREASE } X \text{ BY } 1} \text{ or } \boxed{X = X + 1}$$

A diamond symbol is used to indicate that a decision of some sort is to be made. This symbol usually has one entrance and two exits as shown below.

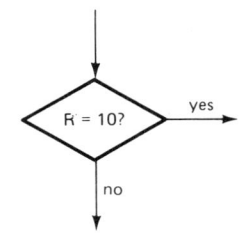

It may, however, have three exits.

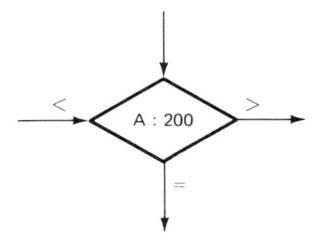

An open-ended rectangle symbol is used to provide descriptive comments or explanatory notes for clarification. For example, the following annotation symbol:

Chapter 4   Flowcharting   78

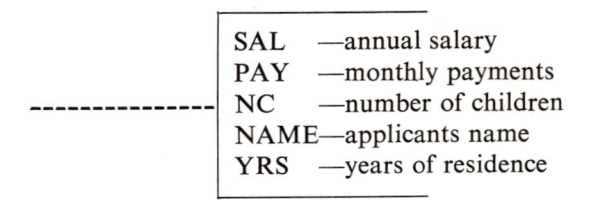

```
                          SAL   —annual salary
                          PAY   —monthly payments
        ----------------  NC    —number of children
                          NAME—applicants name
                          YRS   —years of residence
```

could be used to add a clarifying comment to a flowchart. Note that it is connected to the procedure flow by a dashed line.

Flowcharting symbols are connected by directional flow lines, that is, straight lines with arrows. The normal direction of flow is from left to right and from top to bottom. In certain cases, however, it is not always possible to conform to the normal flow direction. Arrowheads are then included on the flow lines to indicate direction.

Mathematical symbols are also used in flowcharts. Some of the more common ones are:

:	Compare (X: Y)
=	Equal to (X = Y)
$\neq$	Not equal to (X $\neq$ Y)
>	Greater than (X > Y)
<	Less than (X < Y)
$\geq$	Greater than or equal to (X $\geq$ Y)
$\leq$	Less than or equal to (X $\leq$ Y)
Y	Yes
N	No

4.4 FLOWCHARTING GUIDELINES

Although there are many different levels of flowcharts, five general rules should be followed in the preparation of all flowcharts, regardless of the complexity of the problem.

1. Use standard symbols.
2. Develop the flowchart so that it reads from top to bottom and left to right when ever possible. Do not cross flowlines. Use arrowheads to indicate direction.
3. Keep the flowchart clear, readable, and simple. Leave plenty of room between symbols. If a problem solution is large and complex, break it down into several flowcharts.
4. Write simple, descriptive, to-the-point messages in the flowchart symbols.
5. Be legible—print clearly and use a flowcharting template to draw the symbols.

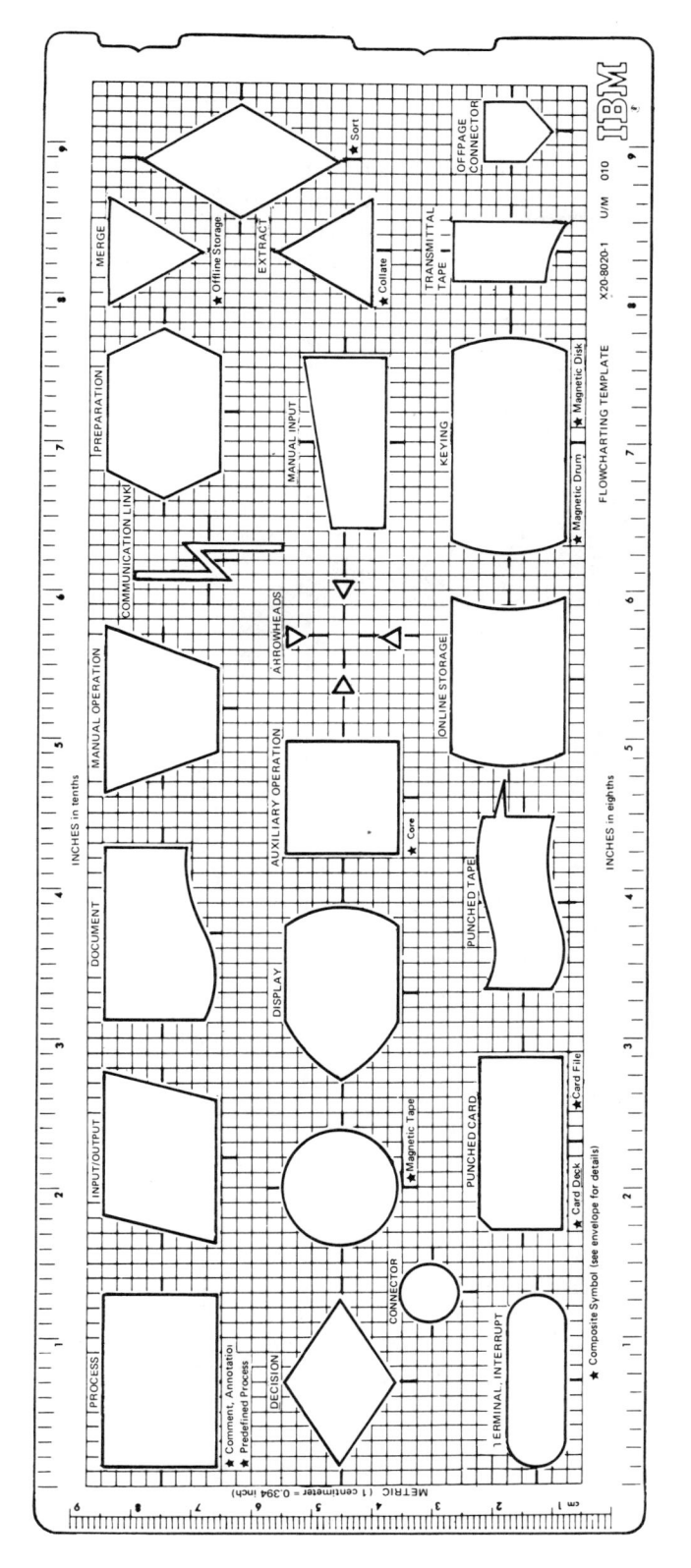

Figure 4-3 Flowcharting template. (*Courtesy* IBM corporation.)

Chapter 4   Flowcharting

4.5 FLOWCHARTING TEMPLATE

A flowcharting *template* (Figure 4-3) is a simple means of drawing the various shaped symbols of a flowchart. Templates are usually available in college bookstores or from various computer manufacturers. A template is a tool that enables anyone, with or without drawing ability, to prepare acceptable, clear, neat flowcharts (see Figure 4-4).

Figure 4-4 Programmer using a template to help her draw a flowchart. (*Courtesy* IBM Corporation.)

REVIEW EXERCISES

4.1 A program flowchart is a pictorial description of the logic to be carried out in the solution to a problem. True or False?

4.2 Why is it necessary to use common symbols when drawing flowcharts?

4.3 List the general rules that should be followed when preparing flowcharts.

4.4 The word STOP can be found in a _____ symbol.

4.5 The symbol $\leq$ is used to represent _____.

4.6 A _____ symbol is used to indicate computer processing.

4.7 What is a template?

4.6 CONSTRUCTION OF THE FLOWCHART

To illustrate the steps in developing a flowchart, let us consider a simple problem: determine the sum of the numbers 63, 12, 88, and 29. We wish to develop a procedure that will add these numbers, two at a time, and output the final result. Look at the flowchart of Figure 4-5.

Section 4.6   Construction of the Flowchart

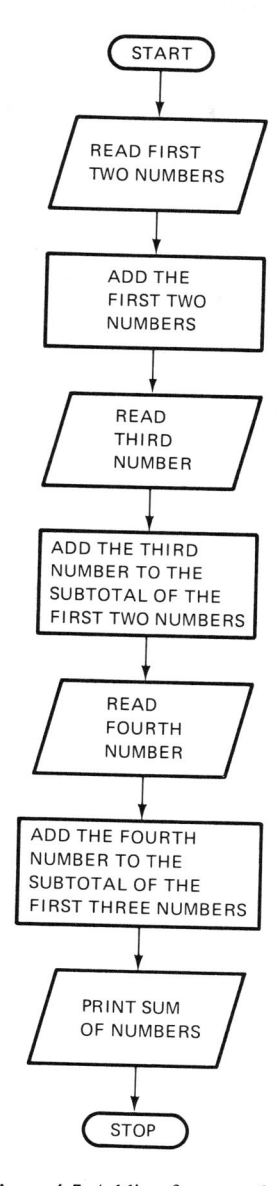

```
                    ┌─────────┐
                    │  START  │
                    └─────────┘
                         │
                         ▼
                  ╱─────────────╲
                 ╱  READ FIRST   ╲
                 ╲  TWO NUMBERS  ╱
                  ╲─────────────╱
                         │
                         ▼
                  ┌─────────────┐
                  │   ADD THE   │
                  │  FIRST TWO  │
                  │   NUMBERS   │
                  └─────────────┘
                         │
                         ▼
                  ╱─────────────╲
                 ╱     READ      ╲
                 ╲     THIRD     ╱
                  ╲   NUMBER    ╱
                   ╲───────────╱
                         │
                         ▼
                  ┌─────────────────────┐
                  │   ADD THE THIRD     │
                  │  NUMBER TO THE      │
                  │  SUBTOTAL OF THE    │
                  │ FIRST TWO NUMBERS   │
                  └─────────────────────┘
                         │
                         ▼
                  ╱─────────────╲
                 ╱     READ      ╲
                 ╲    FOURTH     ╱
                  ╲   NUMBER    ╱
                   ╲───────────╱
                         │
                         ▼
                  ┌─────────────────────┐
                  │   ADD THE FOURTH    │
                  │  NUMBER TO THE      │
                  │  SUBTOTAL OF THE    │
                  │ FIRST THREE NUMBERS │
                  └─────────────────────┘
                         │
                         ▼
                  ╱─────────────╲
                 ╱   PRINT SUM   ╲
                 ╲  OF NUMBERS   ╱
                  ╲─────────────╱
                         │
                         ▼
                    ┌─────────┐
                    │  STOP   │
                    └─────────┘
```

Figure 4-5 Adding four numbers.

First, notice that the symbols at the beginning and end of the procedure are oval-shaped. These symbols indicate a terminal point in an algorithm. That is, they identify a starting or ending point in an algorithm.

The other symbols in the flowchart have shapes of rectangles and parallelograms.

Chapter 4   Flowcharting

The parallelogram-shaped symbol is called an input/output symbol and is used whenever information is to be read into the algorithm or whenever computed results are to be printed or recorded. In this problem, the first input/output symbol is used to input the first two numbers. The next input/output symbol is used to input the third number, and the third input/output symbol is used to input the fourth number. The last input/output symbol is used to output the computed sum.

The remaining symbols are rectangular in shape. They describe processing operations to be performed during the execution of the algorithm. The processing being performed by this procedure is "addition operations."

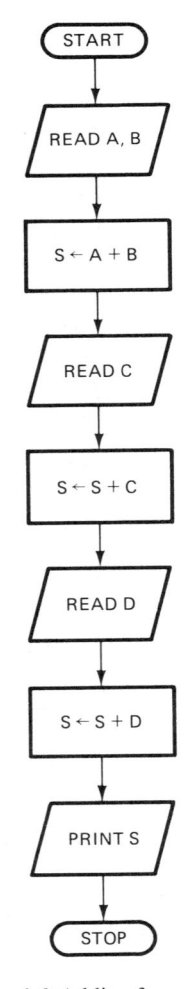

Figure 4-6 Adding four numbers.

Section 4.6 Construction of the Flowchart

The symbols in Figure 4-5 contain messages; however, they could have been written in a variety of other ways. Figure 4-6 illustrates another flowchart that accomplishes the same procedure. This flowchart uses a more concise notation for messages written in the flowchart symbols. In this flowchart, the four numbers are represented by the variables A, B, C, and D. The variable S is used to accumulate the sum.

Sometimes you may want to fill in the flowcharting symbols with words and phrases closely related to the programming language that will be used to implement the procedure. For instance, this flowchart could be written as shown in Figure 4-7. It is almost a one-for-one representation of the program statements of the following FORTRAN program.

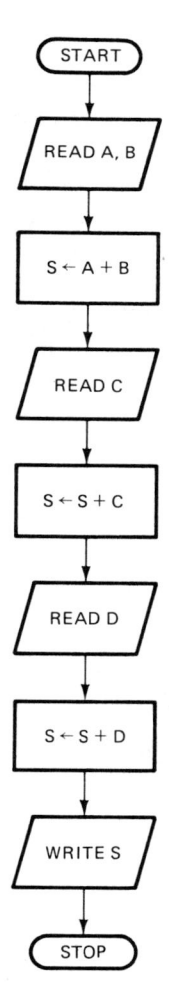

```
       START
         │
       READ A, B
         │
       S ← A + B
         │
       READ C
         │
       S ← S + C
         │
       READ D
         │
       S ← S + D
         │
       WRITE S
         │
       STOP
```

Figure 4-7 Adding four numbers.

Chapter 4   Flowcharting   84

```
        READ(2,10)A,B
  10    FORMAT(2F5.0)
        S = A + B
        READ(2,20)C
  20    FORMAT(F5.0)
        S = S + C
        READ(2,30)D
  30    FORMAT(F5.0)
        S = S + D
        WRITE(3,40)S
  40    FORMAT(3H S=,F5.0)
        STOP
        END
```

"I WAS HOPING FOR A LITTLE MORE DETAIL!"

4.7 MAKING DECISIONS

The diamond-shaped symbol is used when a decision is to be made at some point in a flowchart. There is only one point of entry into the decision symbol. The message of this symbol usually contains a question that can be answered *Yes* or *No*.

Section 4.7   Making Decisions

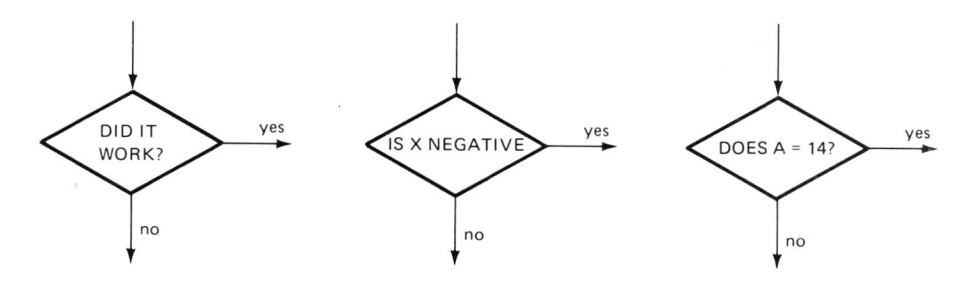

```
    DID IT  ──yes──>        IS X NEGATIVE ──yes──>        DOES A = 14? ──yes──>
    WORK?
      │                          │                              │
      no                         no                             no
      ▼                          ▼                              ▼
```

Questions should be asked in whatever way seems natural. Consider the case where we want to know if a variable is negative.

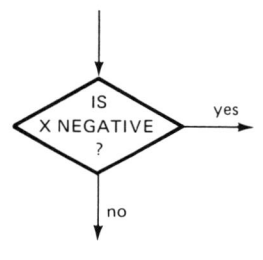

```
        IS
     X NEGATIVE ──yes──>
        ?
        │
        no
        ▼
```

We could also write it as a true-false statement

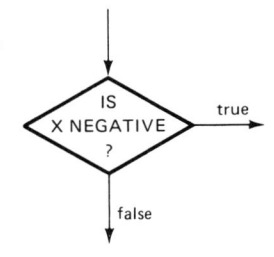

```
        IS
     X NEGATIVE ──true──>
        ?
        │
        false
        ▼
```

or compare X to zero

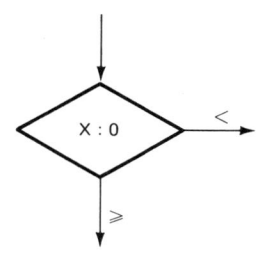

```
       X : 0 ──<──>
         │
         ≥
         ▼
```

Chapter 4   Flowcharting

or simply

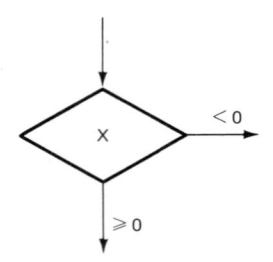

```
        ┌───┐
        │ X │ ──< 0──→
        └─┬─┘
          │ ≥ 0
          ▼
```

It is possible to have three or more exits for a given question. For example, you may desire different exits for X less than 50, X equal to 50, or X greater than 50.

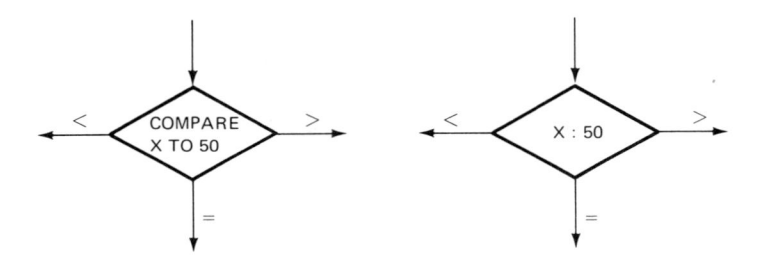

```
    <──┤ COMPARE ├──>          <──┤ X : 50 ├──>
       │ X TO 50 │                 
         │ =                        │ =
         ▼                          ▼
```

Suppose at some point in a procedure you wish X to take on the value of the larger of A and B. The following figure illustrates this task in flowchart form.

Another similar task would be a problem to read the values of A and B and print the greater of these values if $A \neq B$ or print ZERO if $A = B$. Figure 4-9 illustrates a possible flowchart for this procedure. Can you think of other ways to write this procedure? There are frequently are several ways to write correct flowcharts for a problem.

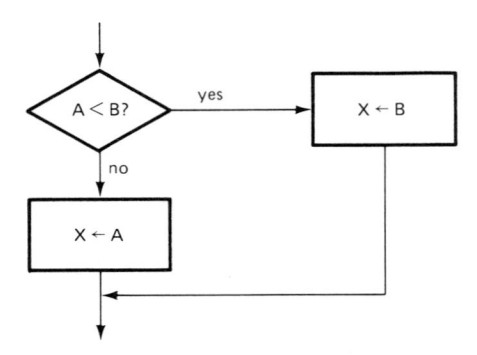

```
         ┌───────┐   yes    ┌───────┐
         │ A < B?├─────────→│ X ← B │
         └───┬───┘          └───┬───┘
             │ no               │
         ┌───▼───┐              │
         │ X ← A │              │
         └───┬───┘              │
             │◄─────────────────┘
             ▼
```

Figure 4-8.

Section 4.7   Making Decisions

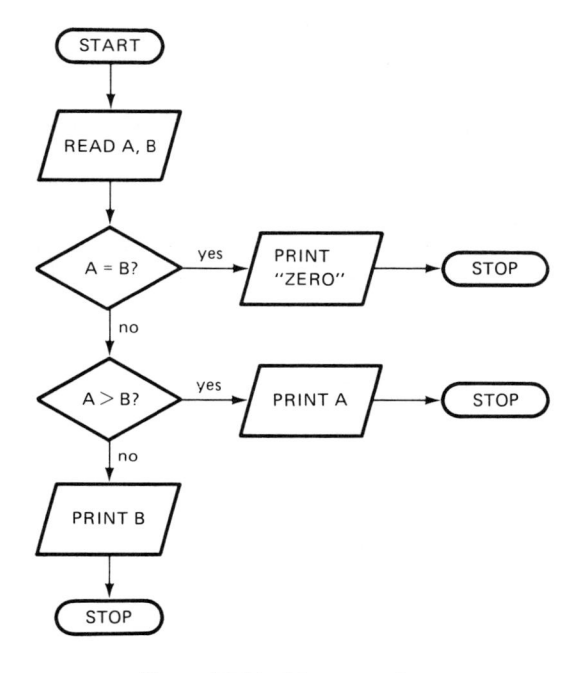

Figure 4-9 Decision example.

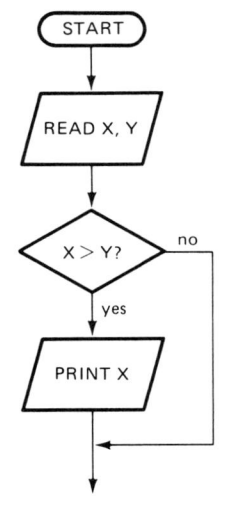

Figure 4-10 Decision example.

Chapter 4   Flowcharting   88

Figure 4-10 illustrates a procedure that inputs values for X and Y, compares these values, and causes X to be printed only if X is larger than Y.

Let us now look at an example where we read a value and, based on it, select one of several courses. In Figure 4-11, the procedure reads a student's name and age. It will select one of three paths to follow, depending on the student's age. Each path causes the student to be assigned to a proper living quarters and the student's name to be added to the building roster. This procedure will read only one student's name and age, perform the classification only once, and terminate. Algorithms of this type are often useful in sorting and classifying type problems.

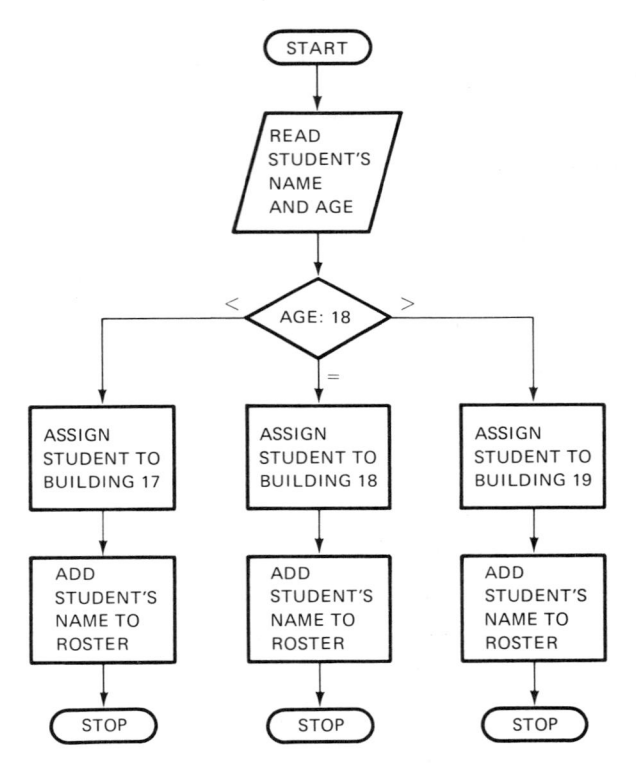

Figure 4-11 Branching—parallel tracks.

REVIEW EXERCISES

4.8 Draw a flowchart for one of the algorithms discussed in Chapter 3.

4.9 Draw a flowchart symbol to decide whether x is 1, 2, or 3.

4.10 Can you think of a way to combine the two decisions $y < x$ and $x < z$ into a single decision symbol?

Section 4.8   *Looping*

4.11   Draw a flowchart to input a number, find the absolute value of the number, and output both the number and the absolute value.

4.12   Draw a flowchart segment that allows Z to take on the value of the larger of X and Y.

4.13   Draw a flowchart to input a number, square and cube the number, and output the number together with its square and cube.

4.14   Draw a flowchart for a problem to read three values and determine if these values can be the sides of a right triangle. Print the word YES if they can and NO otherwise.

4.15   Draw another flowchart that would accomplish the problem illustrated in Figure 4-8.

4.16   Draw a flowchart to read four numbers and determine if any of the numbers are zero. If any of the values are zero, print the word ZERO, otherwise print NO.

4.17   Draw the flowchart of a procedure that will read a value for A, then compute and print out the sum of the 8 numbers, $1, 1 + A, 1 + 2A, 1 + 3A, \ldots, 1 + 7A$.

4.18   Draw the flowchart for a procedure that will input the values of four integers A, B, C, D and output YES or NO depending on whether $A/B = C/D$ or not. If either B or D is zero, the procedure should output UNDEFINED.

4.19   A farmer's pigs will sell for premium rates if their weights are between 350 and 400 pounds. Draw a flowchart and write a FORTRAN program for determining which pigs fall within the desirable weight range.

4.20   A class in ecology has five members who make the following scores on the midterm test: 74, 86, 95, 43, and 65, and the teacher wants to compute the average exam score. Help the teacher out by drawing a flowchart and coding a FORTRAN program for doing the job.

4.21   A second-order polynomial equation has the form

$$y = x^2 + 4x - 3$$

Assuming that $x = 4$, flowchart and write a FORTRAN program to evaluate this equation and print out the resulting value of y.

4.22   Draw a flowchart corresponding with this FORTRAN program segment.

```
         A = 1000.0
10       C = .075 * A
         WRITE(3,20)  C
20       FORMAT(F7.2)
         A = A + 100.0
         GO TO 10
```

4.8   LOOPING

In Section 4.7 we discussed a procedure to add four numbers. If we had to determine the sum of a larger set of numbers, one way to solve this problem would be to extend the flowchart developed for adding four numbers. Figure 4-12, however, illustrates a more compact flowchart for adding any list of numbers. This flowchart uses a *loop*,

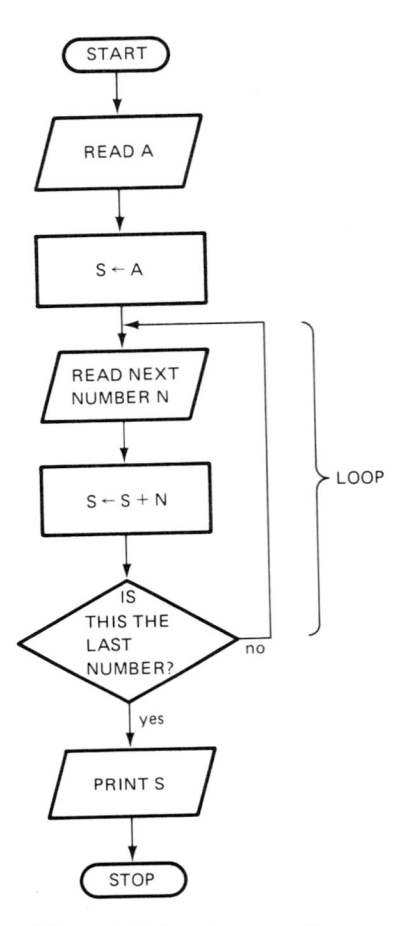

```
                    ┌─────────┐
                    │  START  │
                    └────┬────┘
                         │
                    ╱─────────╲
                   ╱  READ A   ╲
                   ╲_____╱
                         │
                    ┌─────────┐
                    │  S ← A  │
                    └────┬────┘
                         │
                         ▼  ◄──────────┐
                  ╱───────────╲        │
                 ╱ READ NEXT   ╲       │
                 ╲  NUMBER N   ╱       │
                  ╲_____╱        │
                        │              │   LOOP
                  ┌───────────┐        │
                  │ S ← S + N │        │
                  └─────┬─────┘        │
                        │              │
                      ╱   ╲            │
                     ╱ IS  ╲           │
                    ╱THIS  THE╲  no    │
                    ╲  LAST   ╱────────┘
                     ╲NUMBER?╱
                      ╲   ╱
                        │ yes
                  ╱───────────╲
                  ╲  PRINT S  ╱
                   ╲_____╱
                        │
                    ┌─────────┐
                    │  STOP   │
                    └─────────┘
```

Figure 4-12 Looping example.

which involves using a set of one or more steps that are to be done over and over again.

Processing steps within the loop cause a new number to be read and added to the previous subtotal. A check is made to determine if the last number read was indeed the last number in the list. If not, a branch is made back to the beginning of the flowchart, and a new number is read. Whenever the last number is encountered, the sum of the numbers is to be printed.

Have you ever flown in an aircraft and had the pilot say "We are now cruising at 33,000 feet," or "The ceiling is 42,000 feet"? Although this information is certainly helpful, one may still want to know what the altitude is in miles. The conversion can be accomplished by dividing the altitude in feet by 5280, the number of feet in a mile. Figure 4-13 shows a procedure that will produce an altitude conversion table for 0

Section 4.8   Looping   91

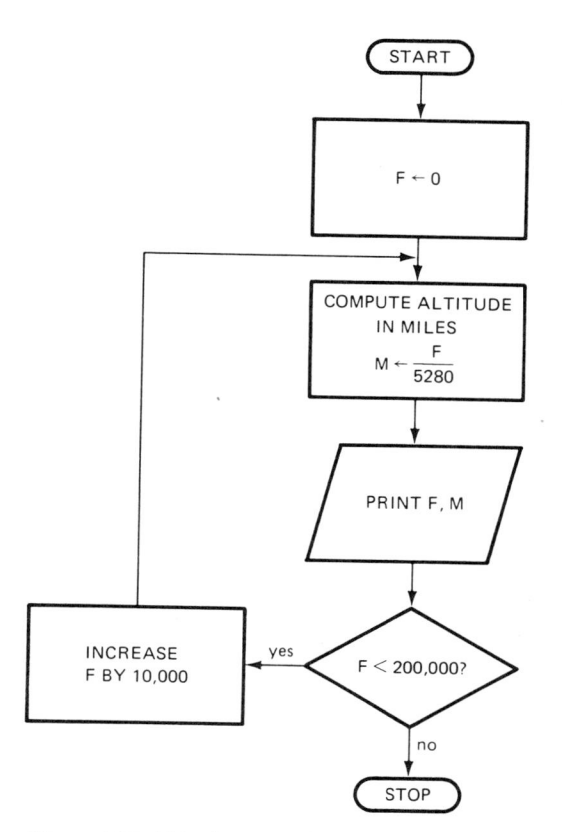

```
                    START
                      │
                      ▼
              ┌───────────────┐
              │    F ← 0      │
              └───────────────┘
                      │
         ┌────────────▼────────────┐
         │  ┌───────────────────┐  │
         │  │ COMPUTE ALTITUDE  │  │
         │  │     IN MILES      │  │
         │  │            F      │  │
         │  │      M ← ────     │  │
         │  │          5280     │  │
         │  └───────────────────┘  │
         │            │            │
         │            ▼            │
         │      ╱ PRINT F, M ╲     │
         │            │            │
         │            ▼            │
  ┌──────────────┐  yes   ╱ F < 200,000? ╲
  │   INCREASE   │◄──────│                │
  │  F BY 10,000 │        ╲              ╱
  └──────────────┘              │
                                │ no
                                ▼
                             ( STOP )
```

Figure 4-13 Altitude conversion.

to 200,000 feet in steps of 10,000 feet. This procedure uses a loop where the variable F (altitude in feet) is increased by 10,000 each time through the loop. For example, F = 0, F = 10,000, F = 20,000, F = 30,000 and so forth, until F = 200,000. The conversion of feet to miles is specified in the process symbol.

Another example of looping is shown in the flowchart procedure to encrypt a message (see Figure 4-14). The first step in the flowchart is to read a message symbol. Next, the procedure determines if the symbol is a letter or number (it could be a space or a punctuation mark, but these are usually ignored in encryption). If the symbol is a letter or number (YES branch of the flowchart), then the procedure causes a key symbol to be read. After obtaining both key and message symbols, the procedure looks up the corresponding cipher letter in the Vigenere Table and causes it to be printed. The procedure then reads the next message symbol and repeats the process. The enciphering steps are skipped if the symbol is not a letter or a number (NO branch from the decision symbol). Before repeating the process, the procedure checks to see if there are more message symbols; if not, it stops (NO branch from the decision

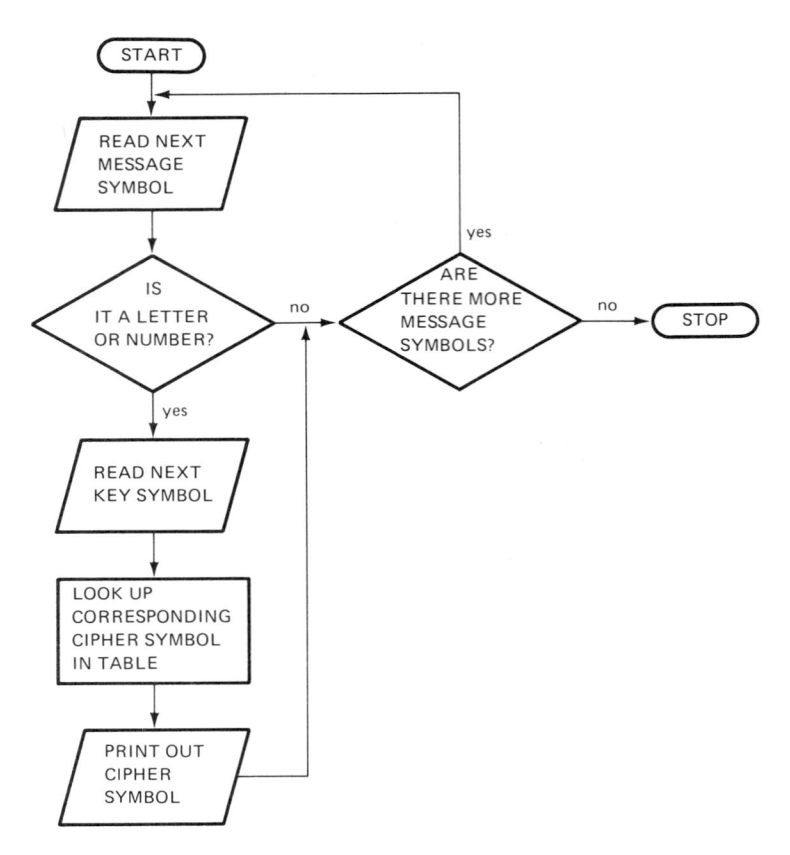

Figure 4-14 Enciphering message procedure.

symbol). Thus, the procedure runs through the loop as many times as there are message symbols. When it finally stops, the ciphered message will have been printed.

A loop is a useful device because several calculations can be performed many times without having to write new instructions for each pass. The procedure will go back to the beginning of the loop and recycle over and over. The weakness of this simple loop is that there is no control over the number of times it is executed.

4.9 CONTROLLED LOOPS

Most programs contain one or more loops. The loop shown in Figure 4-11 is called an *endless* loop. In practice, most loops are terminated when certain conditions are satisfied. For example, one method of limiting the number of times a loop will be executed is with a counter. The procedure would keep track of the number of times a given calculation or operation is performed.

Section 4.9   Controlled Loops

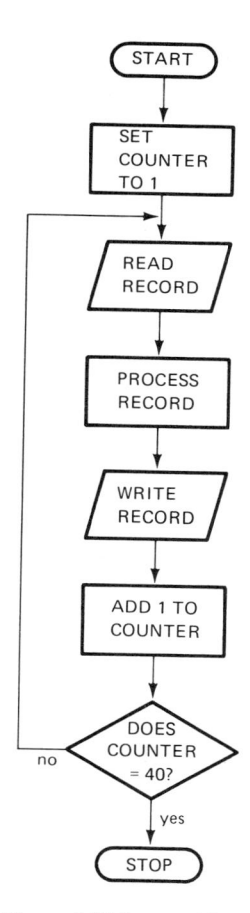

```
                START
                  │
                  ▼
              SET
              COUNTER
              TO 1
                  │
    ┌────────────▶▼
    │         READ
    │         RECORD
    │             │
    │             ▼
    │         PROCESS
    │         RECORD
    │             │
    │             ▼
    │         WRITE
    │         RECORD
    │             │
    │             ▼
    │         ADD 1 TO
    │         COUNTER
    │             │
    │             ▼
    │          DOES
    └──no──    COUNTER
              = 40?
                  │
                 yes
                  ▼
                STOP
```

Figure 4-15 Loop with counter.

A counter is used to perform this function. The example shown in Figure 4-15 illustrates a procedure that will process 40 records and then stop. The counter is initially set to 1. Each time through the loop, the counter is incremented by 1. Then the counter is tested to see if it equals 40. When the counter equals 40, the procedure ends.

Counters may be set up anywhere in a procedure. They can be used to keep track of calculations, count, or limit the number of times something is to be performed. Counters may run in a positive direction (1, 2, 3, 4, 5, 6, . . .) or in a negative direction (100, 99, 98, 97, . . .).

Let us examine the flowchart for another example, one concerning the analysis of English text. Suppose we have the text of a book in punched card form including all the punctuation, space, and paragraph marks. One step in analyzing the author's writing style might be to find the average word length in the book. To do this, a computer would have to count the number of words and the number of letters, then divide to obtain the average. A corresponding flowchart is shown in Figure 4-16. The procedure used here has the form of a loop so that the same instructions are used over and over again to process the string of input symbols. The procedure outputs a single number, the average word length.

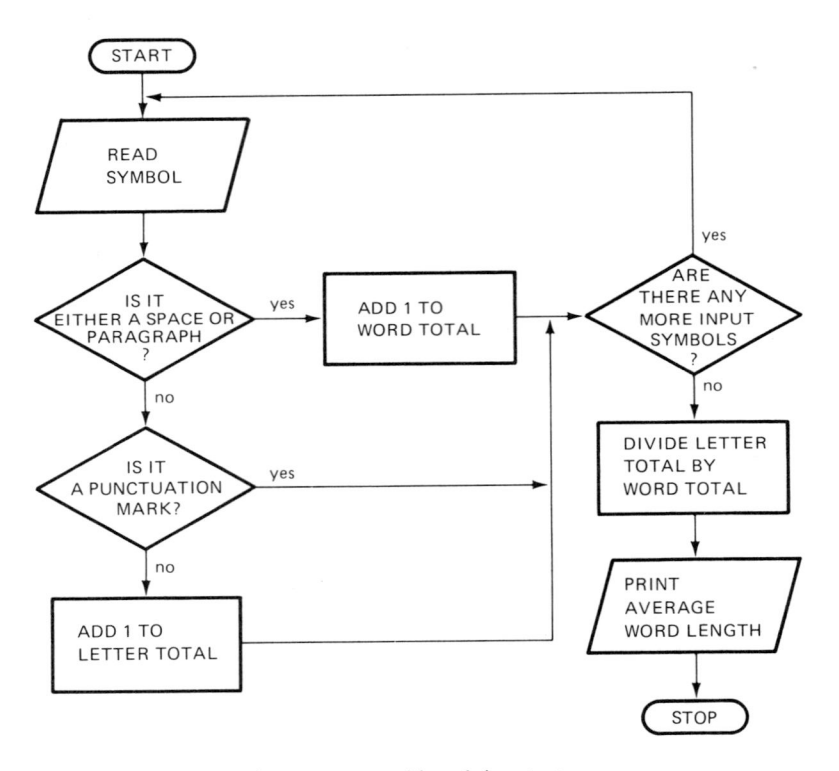

Figure 4-16 Compute the average word length in a text.

Another way of controlling a loop is to use an *end record*, for example, a deck of cards with the last card (trailer card) containing a test value (asterisks, negative value, large number, and so on) punched in it. The last card test may be placed at the beginning or end of the procedure, as shown in Figure 4-17. Let us assume that the last card included a 9999 in a specific card field. The procedure would simply test this field in each card for 9999. When this card is reached, the procedure knows it is the last card in the file.

Section 4.10   Nested Loops

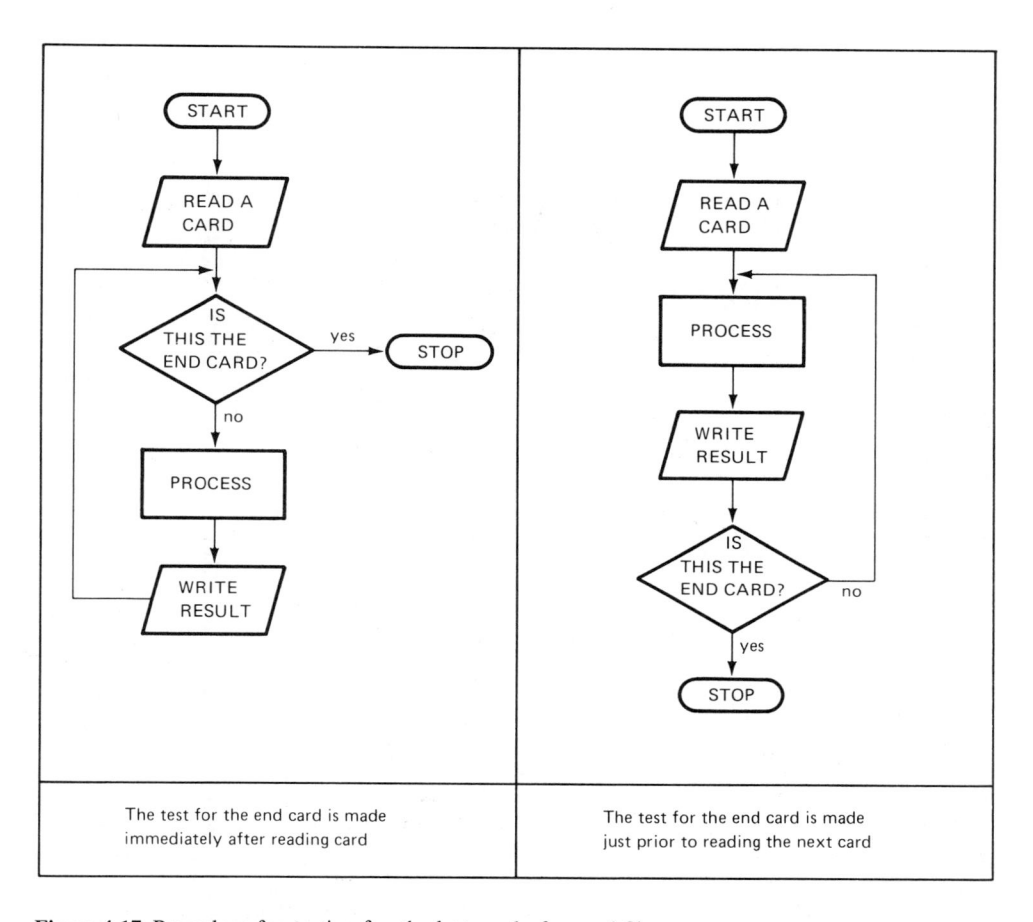

[Flowchart: Figure 4-17 showing two procedures for testing for the last card of a card file. Left side: test made immediately after reading card (START → READ A CARD → IS THIS THE END CARD? → yes: STOP; no: PROCESS → WRITE RESULT → loop back to read). Right side: test made just prior to reading the next card (START → READ A CARD → PROCESS → WRITE RESULT → IS THIS THE END CARD? → no: loop back; yes: STOP).]

Figure 4-17 Procedure for testing for the last card of a card file.

4.10 NESTED LOOPS

Loops may be contained within other loops. Loops of this type are called *nested loops*. Let us examine a nested loop procedure, one to determine the greatest common divisor of two numbers.

If a and b are two integers, any number that divides both a and b is called a *common divisor* of a and b. If a and b have more than one common divisor, one must be greater than the other(s). It is called the *greatest common divisor* (GCD) of a and b. For example, the GCD of 2 and 6 is 2, and the GCD of 24 and 56 is 8. The flowchart of a procedure to compute and print the GCD of two positive integers, a and b, is shown in Figure 4-18.

FLOWCHART
START
X=Y
YES
R=√X
R=|X|
Y= 6
STOP
FLOWCHART
START
YES
X=Y
R=|X|
R=√X
Y=6
EDUCATIONAL
TV
CHANNEL
24
"SO YOU SEE, STUDENTS, FLOWCHARTING CAN BE EASY..."

Section 4.10   Nested Loops

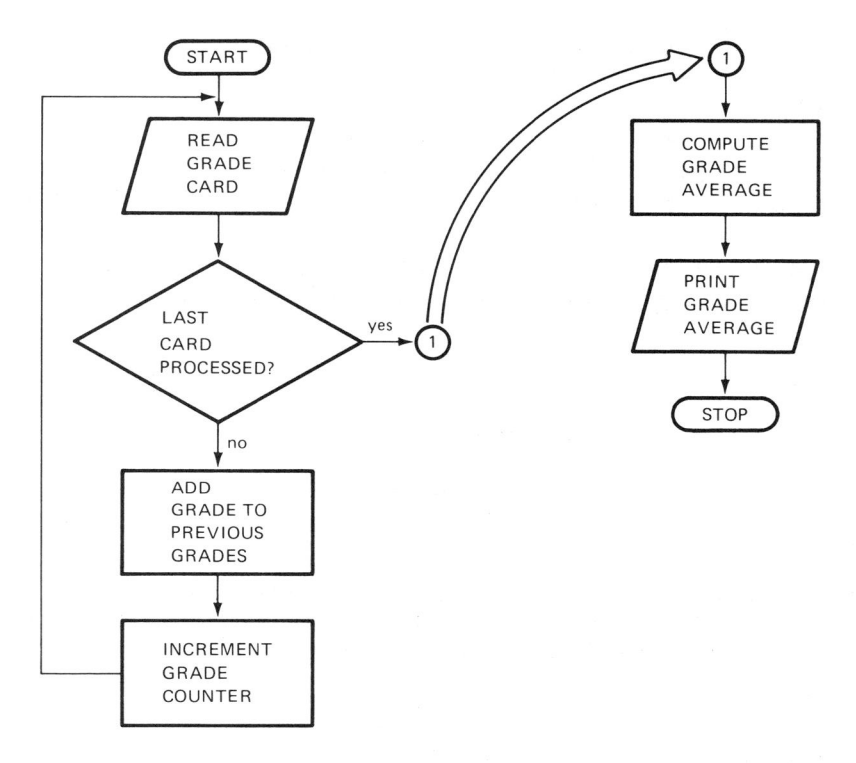

Figure 4-18 Connector symbols often are used in place of a flowline to designate a loop.

This procedure determines whether X divides A and B. If both remainders are zero, then X is a divisor of both A and B. When the procedure finds this condition, it replaces the value of Z with the current value of X. Since X increases by 1 each time through the loop, Z will be the largest such divisor at the termination of the loop. The procedure then specifies that the values of A and B, as well as the GCD of A and B, are to be printed.

You will notice that this procedure contains a *loop within a loop*. When working with loops, you must be careful where you show a returning flow line. If you point it incorrectly, your program will be coded incorrectly.

REVIEW EXERCISES

4.23 How does a single pass computation differ from a simple loop?

4.24 Draw a flowchart that will loop and compute the value of C, represented by

$$C = \sum_{i=1}^{4} a_i b_i = a_1 b_1 + a_2 b_2 + a_3 b_3 + a_4 b_4$$

Chapter 4   Flowcharting   98

4.25 A stack of 50 punched cards contains the final exam grades for a class of 50 history students. Draw a flowchart that will count how many grades there are below 70, and print this number.

4.26 Draw the flowchart to compute the sum of the first 2000 integers.

4.27 You are a clerk in a store, and a woman hands you a $10 bill to pay for a purchase of x dollars. Draw a flowchart that will determine what bills and coins she should receive in change.

4.28 Explain what is meant by the term "nested loops."

4.29 Draw a flowchart corresponding with this FORTRAN program.

```
         A = 1000.0
10       C = .075 * A
         WRITE(3,20)C
20       FORMAT(F7.2)
         A = A + 100.0
         IF(A.LT.3000.0) GO TO 10
         STOP
         END
```

4.30 The computer is to be used to generate a mathematics table. Draw a flowchart and write a FORTRAN program to print the table for N varying from 0 to 100 in increments of 1. The program should print the following table heading:

N   N² $\sqrt{N}$ $\sqrt{10N}$ N³ $\sqrt[3]{N}$

4.31 A salesman has made several sales. He wants to know how many sales were $200 or less, how many were above $200 but not more than $400, and how many were above $400. Draw a flowchart and write a FORTRAN program to supply this information. You may supply the input data.

4.32 Given a list of 25 integers, flowchart and code a FORTRAN program to compute the difference between each number in the list and the average of the numbers.

4.33 The rate of heat conduction Q through a solid material is proportional to the temperature difference and to the area perpendicular to the heat flow and is inversely proportional to the length of the materials. This relation is known as Fourier's law and is expressed as:

$$Q = \frac{KA}{L}(t_1 - t_2)$$

where K = thermal conductivity of the material
A = area of the object
L = length of the object
$t_1 - t_2$ = temperature difference

The thermal conductivity of copper is approximately 226 Btu/[(hr)(ft²)(°F/in.)]. Assuming an ambient temperature of 80°F and heat source of 400°, flowchart and code a FORTRAN program to calculate Q for a 2-inch thick copper block with area specifications:

width 18 to 24 inches, in 1-inch increments
height 18 to 24 inches, in 1-inch increments

Section 4.11 Using Connectors

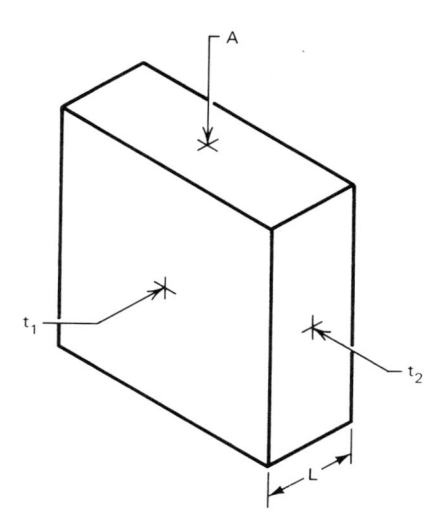

Exercise 4.33

4.34 At the Seminole Chair Factory, the pay for employees is based on a rate per hour plus some bonus amount, depending on the number of chairs produced during the day. Given a deck of cards for 40 employees, compute their wage. For example, at $3.50 per hour base salary and 60 cents bonus for each chair produced over 50, an employee who assembled 76 chairs would earn:

$$(3.50)(8) + (76 - 50)(0.60) = 28.00 + 15.60 = \$43.60$$

Flowchart and write a **FORTRAN** program to compute and print the daily wages of all employees. For each employee, the program should determine the pay earned (base pay plus bonus pay).

Exercise 4.34

4.11 USING CONNECTORS

Look at the flowchart in Figure 4-18. Notice a new symbol? The small circle is called a *connector* symbol, and it is used to tie parts of the flowchart together. It allows you to draw portions of a flowchart on different places of the page or on different sheets of paper. The symbol is especially useful when flowcharts have many branches or run onto many pages.

Chapter 4   Flowcharting   100

There are two types of connectors. An *out-connector* is one that has a line with an arrowhead pointing to the connector circle. An *in-connector* is in line with the flowline or has a line leading from it and pointing to a flowchart symbol or the line connecting two symbols. Out-connectors indicate that flow is to resume in some other portion of the flowchart. An in-connector is a point in the flowchart where flow is to resume. For example, in Figure 4-18 the connector containing the number 1 at the center of the left column of symbols is an out-connector. It indicates that flow is to resume with some in-connector containing the number 1. The in-connector indicates the continuation of a flow sequence that starts somewhere else in the flowchart. In this example, the continuation point is the in-connector at the top of the right column of symbols in the flowchart.

You can enclose any letter, alphabetic character or symbol within connector symbols. The following connector symbols are acceptable:

⟶ Ⓐ   Ⓐ ⟶
⟶ ②   ② ⟶
⟶ ⊛   ⊛ ⟶

4.12 ADDING NOTES TO THE FLOWCHART

You may wish to add clarifying notes or messages to a flowchart such as shown in Figure 4-19. Information is given in these notes about variable assignments, computations being performed and what information is to be printed. The symbol for doing this is called the *annotation symbol*. It is a rectangular-shaped symbol that has one end left open. Annotation symbols may be connected to any symbol, or the line connecting two symbols at a point where the annotation is useful. They are connected to other symbols by *broken lines* instead of solid flowlines.

Use of the annotation symbol is optional. However, it permits you to insert valuable information that cannot be included in other flowcharting symbols. The symbol may contain any type of explanatory material, such as that shown below.

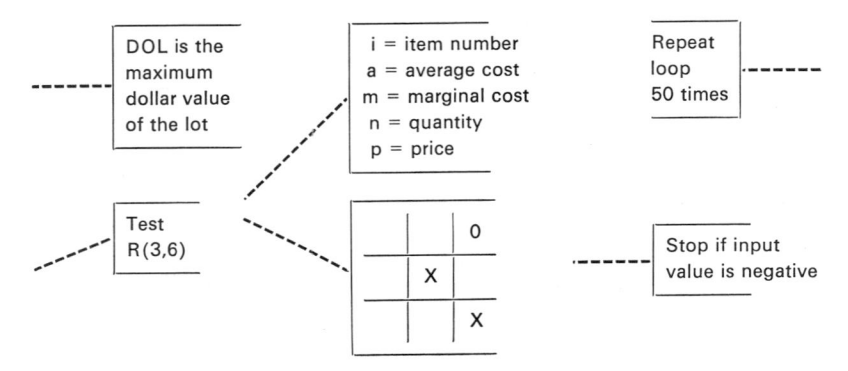

Section 4.12   *Adding Notes to the Flowchart*   101

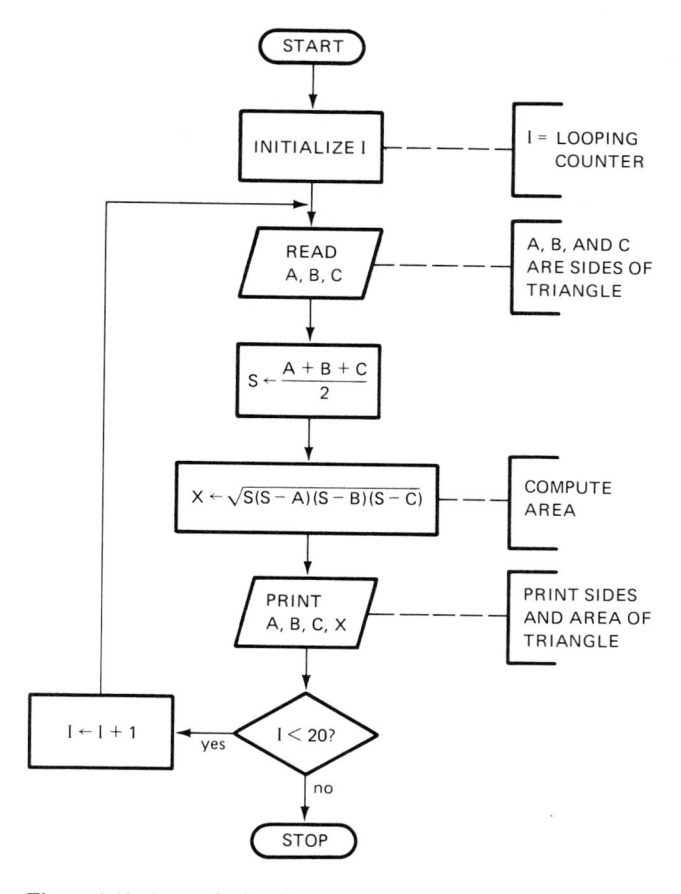

Figure 4-19 Area of triangle procedure (with annotation).

The annotation symbol simply provides a means of relating explanatory information to a particular procedure step.

REVIEW EXERCISES

4.35 Redraw the flowchart shown in Figure 4-12 by using connector symbols.

4.36 Modify the flowchart shown in Figure 4-16. Use connector symbols instead of flowlines to indicate loops.

4.37 The _____ symbol is used to add notes and remarks to a flowchart.

Chapter 4   Flowcharting

4.13 SUBROUTINES

Subroutines* are indicated on flowcharts by using the *predefined process symbol*. For example, a flowchart reference to a square root subroutine might appear as shown in Figure 4-20. The flowcharting symbol contains the name of the subroutine. FORTRAN subroutines are discussed in Chapter 6.

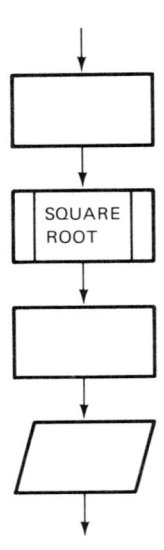

Figure 4-20 Predefined process symbol indicating a reference to a square root subroutine.

REVIEW EXERCISES

4.38 What symbol is used on a flowchart to represent a subroutine?

4.39 Draw a flowchart and write a FORTRAN program to compute a table of values for n varying from −20 to +20. The program should print the following heading:

$$N \quad \sqrt{N} \quad |N|$$

The program should use subroutines (or FORTRAN library functions) to compute the square roots and absolute values of N.

4.40 Draw a flowchart and write a FORTRAN subroutine that determines the second largest number in a list of 20 numbers supplied as data.

4.41 Draw a flowchart and write a FORTRAN program that will do the following:
(a) Read three numbers from one card.
(b) Find the smallest of these numbers.
(c) Print the smallest number (sufficiently identified) and the other two numbers.

*A subroutine is a set of instructions that are used by other programs to direct the computer to execute a specified mathematical or logical operation.

Section 4.13   Subroutines 103

4.42 A depositor banks $10 per month. Interest is 6 percent per year compounded monthly. Draw a flowchart and write a FORTRAN program to compute the amount the depositor has in his or her account after 25 years.

4.43 Given a set of numbers of the form:

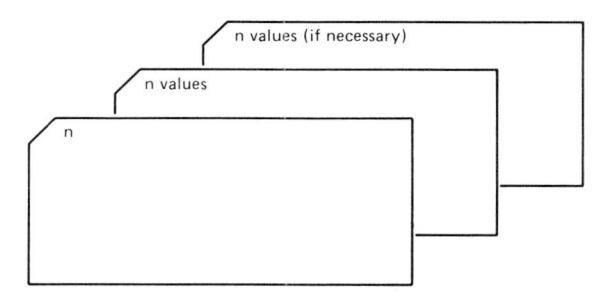

Exercise 4.43

Allow for at least 60 values. Draw a flowchart and write a FORTRAN program that computes and prints the following:
(a) Sum of the numbers in the list.
(b) Smallest number.
(c) Largest number.
(d) Number of numbers equal to 25.
(e) Number of numbers greater than 20 and less than 70.

Chapter 5

Airline passenger seat reservation systems use hundreds of remotely located CRT display terminals, which are connected to a computer system. (Courtesy IBM Corp.)

FORTRAN *Programs for Study*

In Chapter 1 we discussed the necessary steps to solve problems with a computer. In Chapter 2 we learned the fundamentals of the FORTRAN language, allowing you to begin work with the computer as soon as possible. Chapters 3 and 4 were devoted to writing algorithms and drawing flowcharts. Only extensive practice of what you have learned will permit you to utilize effectively your newly learned ways of solving problems by computer. In this chapter you will have the opportunity to consider various types of problems and to carry these problems from formulation through to final solution. Each problem is independent of the other problems in the chapter. Hence you may, if you wish, skip some of the problems if you are not familiar with or interested in them and the techniques used for solution.

You are encouraged to study the problems carefully and then test your problem-solving ability by expanding and/or modifying the problem as well as the associated flowchart and FORTRAN program.

5.1 PAINTING THE GAZEBO

An elderly lady wants to paint the floor of her gazebo without wasting any paint. She knows from experience that it takes one quart of paint to cover 37 square feet of surface area. If the gazebo floor is 10 feet in diameter, how much paint should she buy?

A FORTRAN program for determining the answer is shown in Figure 5-1. The first statement is a comment statement. The second statement, $D = 10.0$, directs the computer to set the diameter of the gazebo equal to 10 feet. The third statement directs it to compute the radius of the gazebo. The fourth statement computes the area of the gazebo's floor from the relationship $AREA = \pi r^2$. Once the floor area has been determined, the computer is directed to divide the AREA by 37 to determine the value of QUART—the number of quarts of paint that will be needed. The last four statements cause the answer to be printed and terminate the program execution.

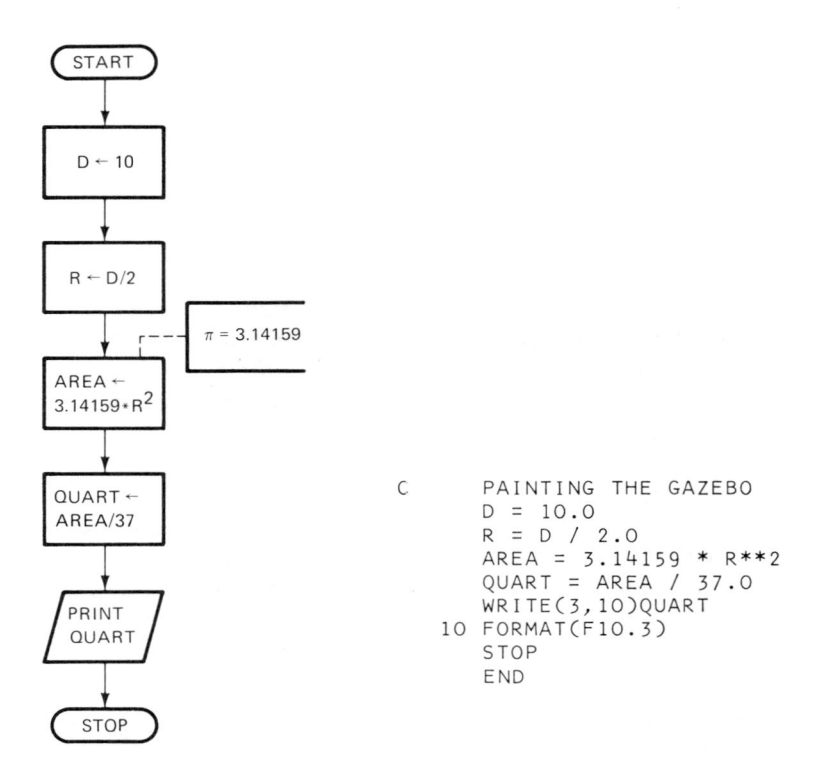

```
C        PAINTING THE GAZEBO
         D = 10.0
         R = D / 2.0
         AREA = 3.14159 * R**2
         QUART = AREA / 37.0
         WRITE(3,10)QUART
      10 FORMAT(F10.3)
         STOP
         END
```

Figure 5-1 *Painting the Gazebo.* An elderly lady used the above program to determine how many quarts of paint she needed to paint her favorite gazebo.

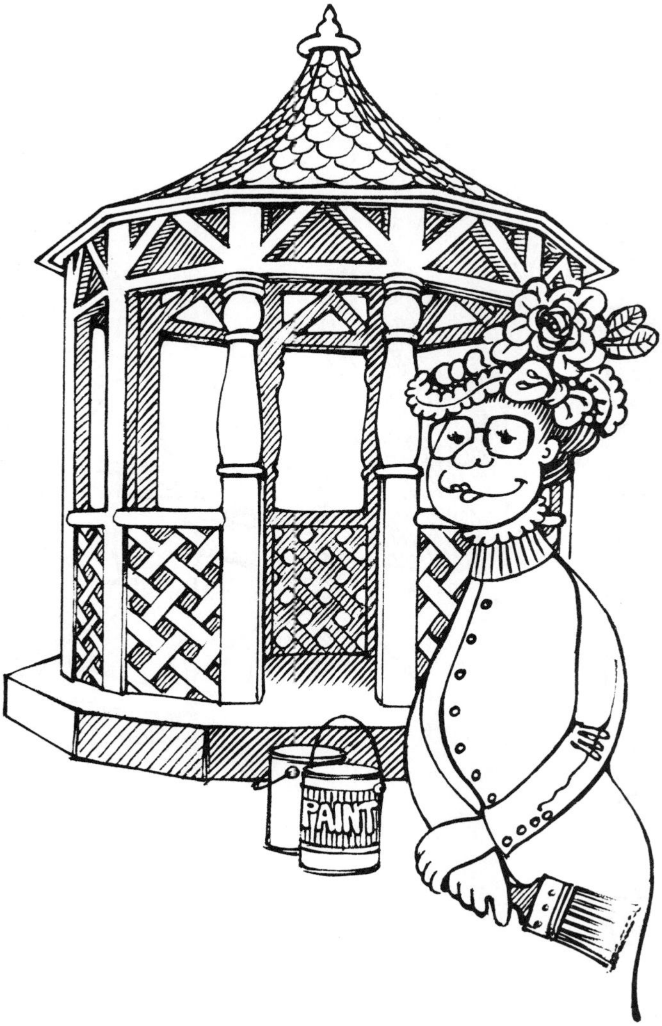
PAINT

5.2 MICHAEL'S DOG

Michael Sicard borrowed $200 from a banker to buy a purebred dog. He pays 12 percent interest on his five-year loan, compounded annually. Figure 5-2 shows the program that Michael used to compute the total amount he paid for the dog.

```
C       MICHAEL'S DOG
        P = 200.0
        N = 0
10      P = P + 0.12 * P
        N = N + 1
        IF(N .LT. 5)GO TO 10
        WRITE(3,20)P
20      FORMAT(4H P =,F14.3)
        STOP
        END
```

Figure 5-2 *Michael's Dog.* Michael Sicard borrowed $200 from a banker to buy a purebred dog. He used the above program to determine the total amount he paid for his dog.

Let us trace through the program to see how the compounding is accomplished. The first statement is a comment statement. In the next two commands, P is set equal to $200 and N is set equal to 0. The first time statement 10 is reached, P equals 200, so P = P + 0.12 * P equals $224. In the next statement N = N + 1, so N equals 1. Thus, *N* is less than 5, and program control loops back to statement 10. At this point, P = $224. Thus the value of P = P + 0.12 * P is 250.88. This procedure is repeated until the looping is terminated (N $\geq$ 5) and the final value of P is printed.

5.3 MARY GOES TO THE CIRCUS

Mary Wolcott's algebra teacher asked the class to determine all Fibonacci numbers* less than 300—a boring assignment if there ever was one! Mary wanted to go to the circus instead; so rather than spending her entire afternoon scribbling out these numbers, she has decided to code the problem for solution on the school's computer. Her program is shown in Figure 5-3.

The first statement is a comment statement. The next two statements direct the computer to set LATST and NEXT equal to 0 and 1, respectively. This is called "initializing the variables." The next statement causes the first two Fibonacci numbers (0 and 1) to be printed. Statement 20 causes the third and subsequent Fibonacci numbers to be computed and assigned to the variable NEWNE. If NEWNE is greater than 300, program execution terminates. Otherwise, the value of NEWNE is printed, the value of NEXT is assigned to LATST, the value of NEWNE is assigned to NEXT, and program control loops back to statement 20 to compute the next Fibonacci number. This looping process will continue until the value of NEWNE exceeds 300.

5.4 THE MANHATTAN ISLAND PROBLEM

In 1626, Peter Minuit purchased Manhattan Island from the Indians for $24 worth of beads and trinkets. If this money had been invested at 6 percent interest and the interest had been compounded annually, what would the investment be worth in 1976?

The program for solving this problem is fairly straightforward and is shown in Figure 5-4. The first statement is a comment statement. The next three statements initialize the variables PRI, K, and RATE. The variable K is a counter used to control the number of program iterations, which, in this problem, is 349 (1976–1627). The interest for a given year is computed as PRI * RATE and the principal at the end of a given year is computed as PRI + PRI * RATE. Statements 10 through 20 constitute a program loop; the principal is recomputed as K decreases from 349 to 0. After the loop is completed (that is, the number of iterations specified by K has been satisfied), the resulting principal (PRI) is printed in statement 30. Statement 50 terminates execution of the program.

---

*Fibonacci numbers were described in Chapter 2. Each number is equal to the sum of the previous two numbers.

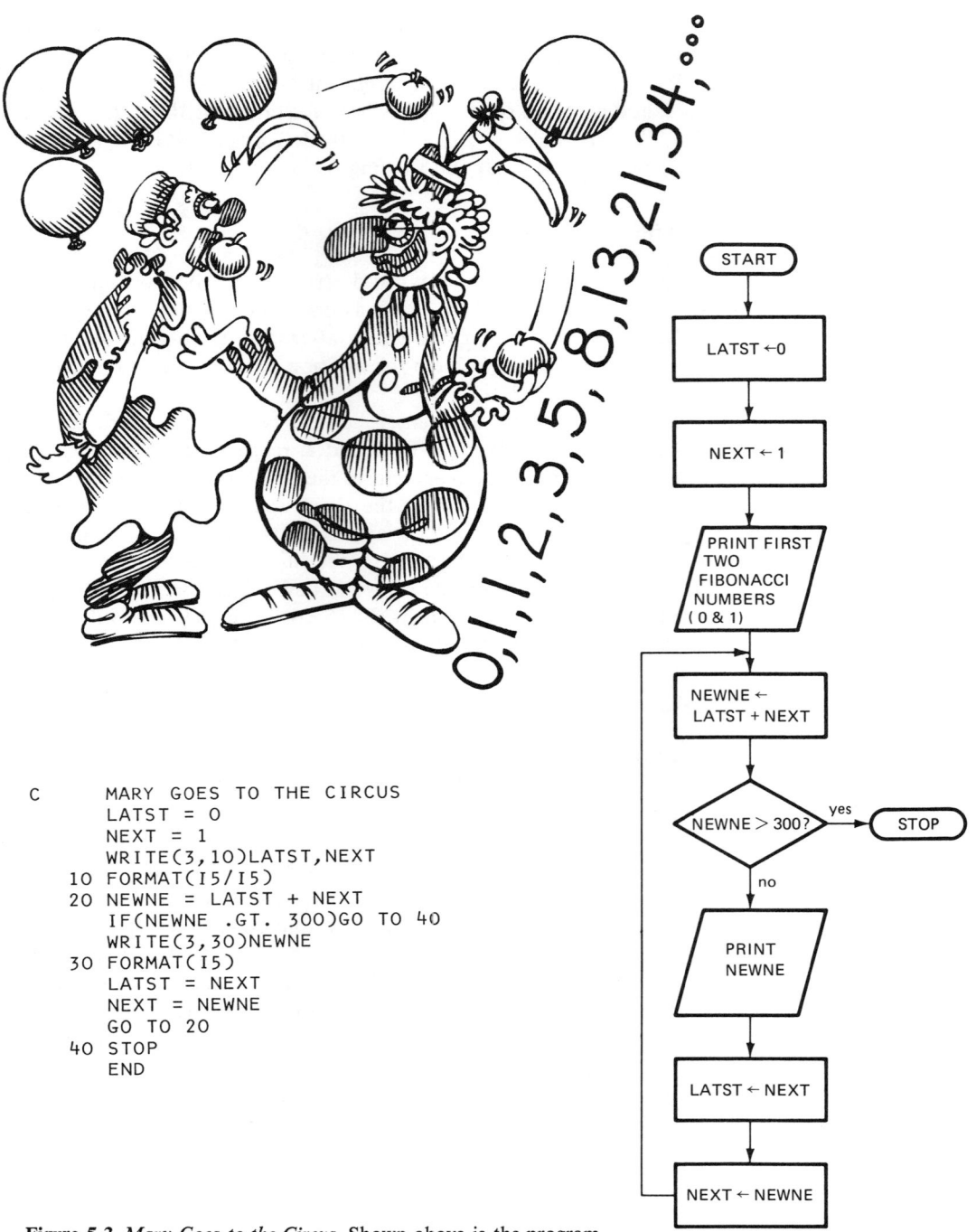

```
C     MARY GOES TO THE CIRCUS
      LATST = 0
      NEXT = 1
      WRITE(3,10)LATST,NEXT
   10 FORMAT(I5/I5)
   20 NEWNE = LATST + NEXT
      IF(NEWNE .GT. 300)GO TO 40
      WRITE(3,30)NEWNE
   30 FORMAT(I5)
      LATST = NEXT
      NEXT = NEWNE
      GO TO 20
   40 STOP
      END
```

Figure 5-3 *Mary Goes to the Circus.* Shown above is the program that Mary wrote to generate all the Fibonacci numbers less than 300.

110

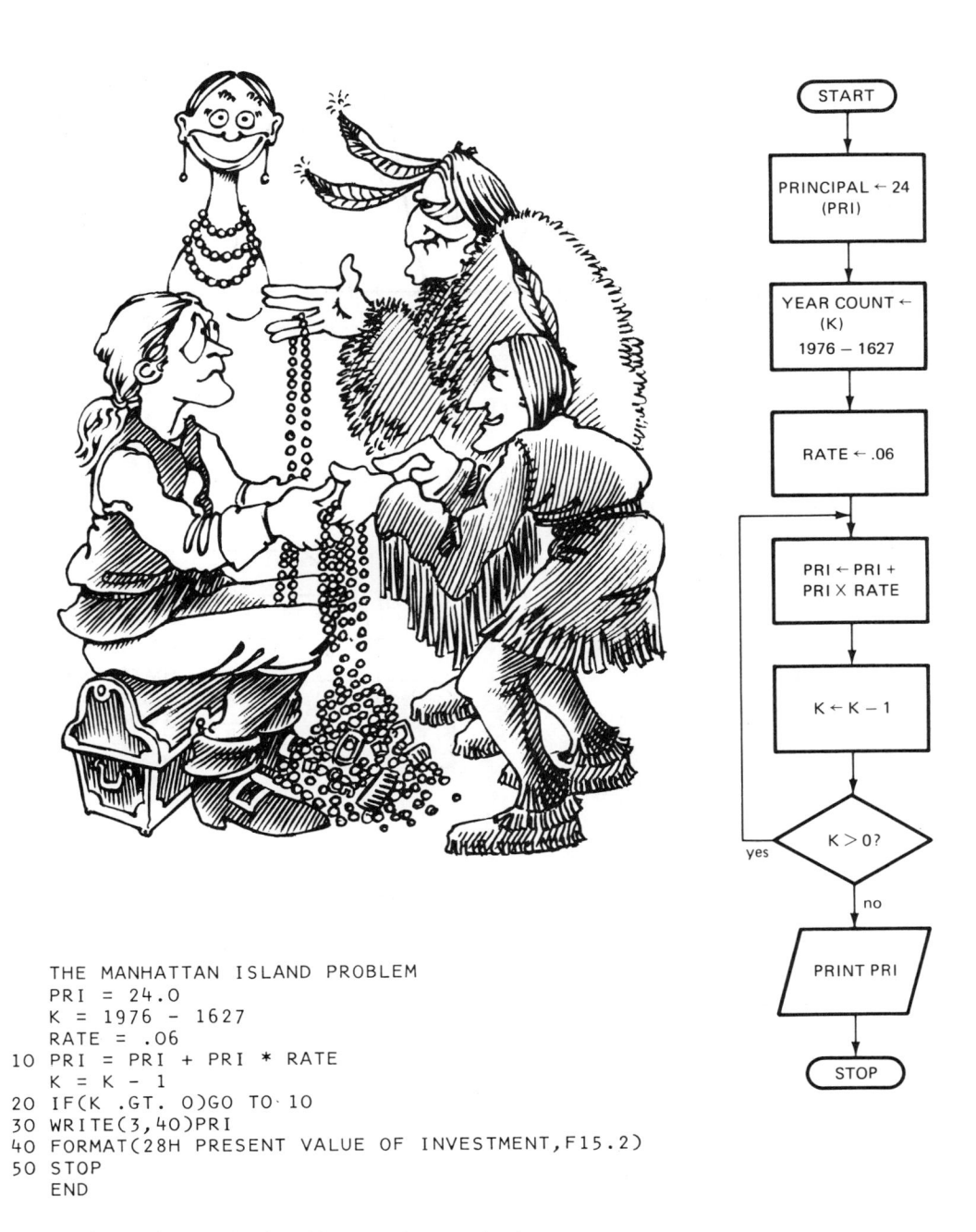

```
C       THE MANHATTAN ISLAND PROBLEM
        PRI = 24.0
        K = 1976 - 1627
        RATE = .06
10      PRI = PRI + PRI * RATE
        K = K - 1
20      IF(K .GT. 0)GO TO 10
30      WRITE(3,40)PRI
40      FORMAT(28H PRESENT VALUE OF INVESTMENT,F15.2)
50      STOP
        END
```

Figure 5-4 *The Manhattan Island Problem.* Manhattan Island was sold by the Indians to the settlers in 1627 for $24 worth of beads and trinkets. This program computes what the investment would be worth today if it had been invested at 6 percent interest, compounded annually.

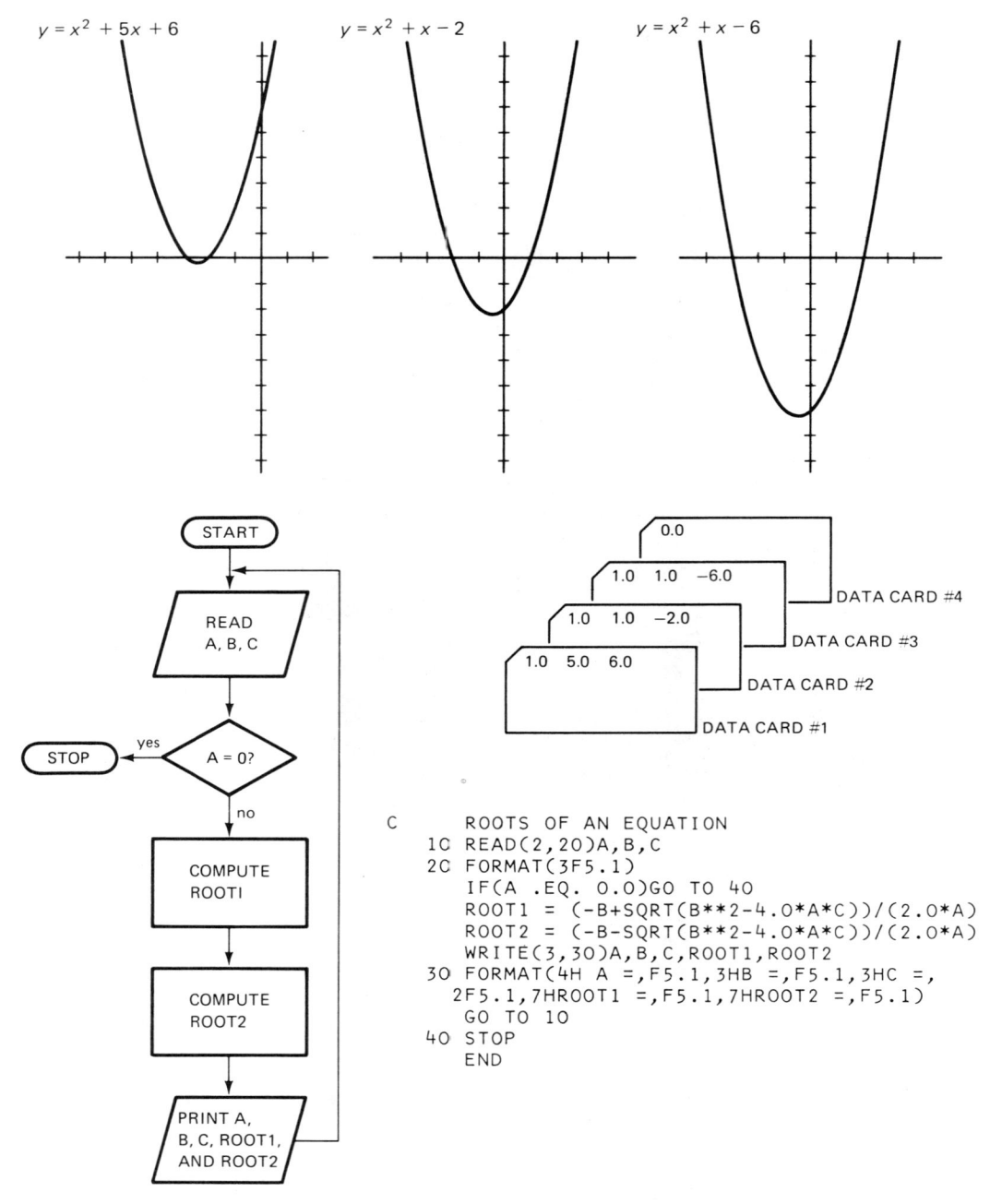

```
C      ROOTS OF AN EQUATION
10     READ(2,20)A,B,C
20     FORMAT(3F5.1)
       IF(A .EQ. 0.0)GO TO 40
       ROOT1 = (-B+SQRT(B**2-4.0*A*C))/(2.0*A)
       ROOT2 = (-B-SQRT(B**2-4.0*A*C))/(2.0*A)
       WRITE(3,30)A,B,C,ROOT1,ROOT2
30     FORMAT(4H A =,F5.1,3HB =,F5.1,3HC =,
      2F5.1,7HROOT1 =,F5.1,7HROOT2 =,F5.1)
       GO TO 10
40     STOP
       END
```

Figure 5-5 *Roots of an Equation.* This program uses the quadratic formula to compute the roots of the equations $x^2 + 5x + 6 = 0$, $x^2 + x - 2 = 0$, and $x^2 + x - 6 = 0$.

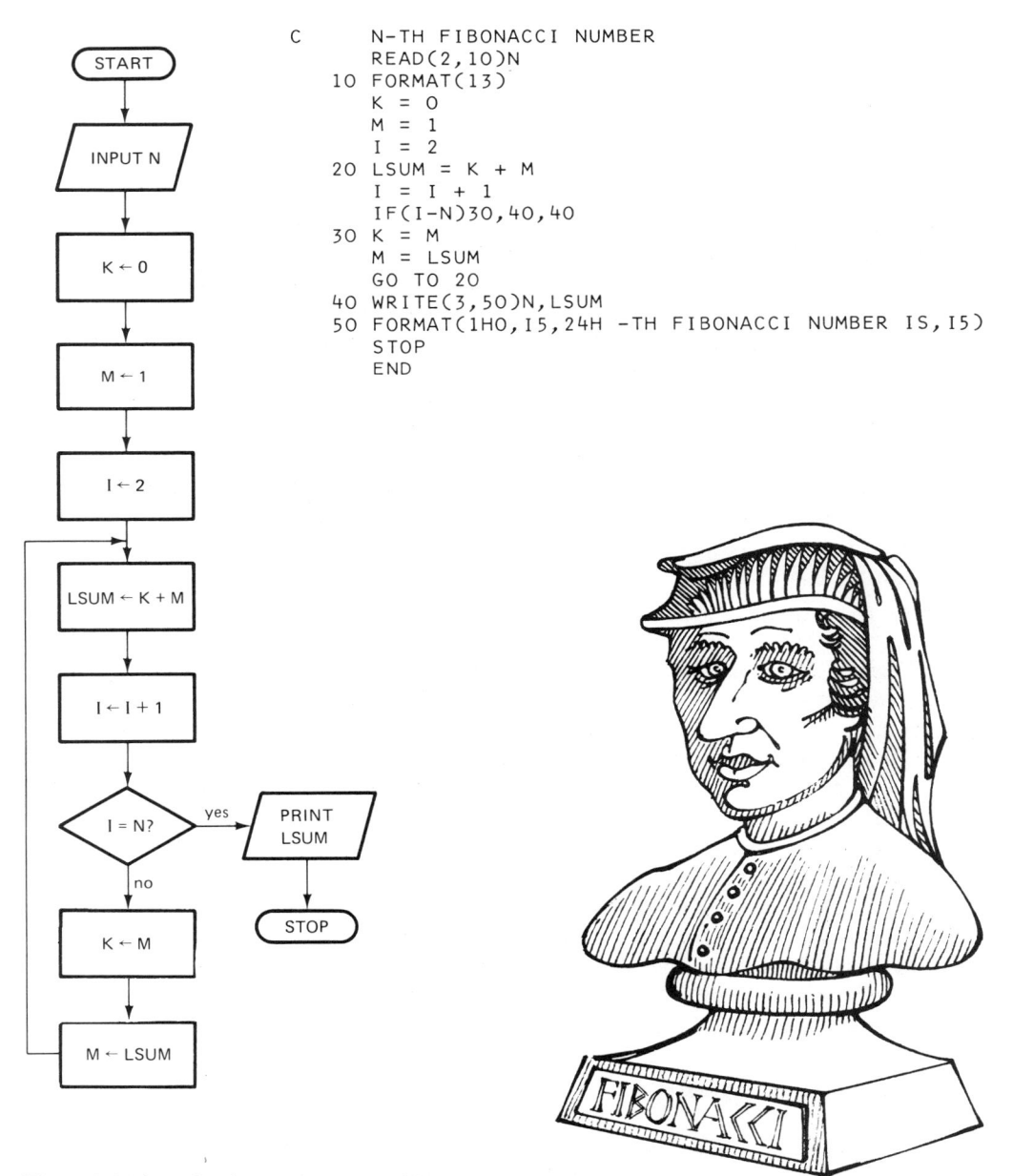

```
C     N-TH FIBONACCI NUMBER
      READ(2,10)N
10    FORMAT(I3)
      K = 0
      M = 1
      I = 2
20    LSUM = K + M
      I = I + 1
      IF(I-N)30,40,40
30    K = M
      M = LSUM
      GO TO 20
40    WRITE(3,50)N,LSUM
50    FORMAT(1H0,I5,24H -TH FIBONACCI NUMBER IS,I5)
      STOP
      END
```

Figure 5-6 *The Nth Fibonacci Number.* This **FORTRAN** program computes the *n*th number in the Fibonacci number sequence, assuming *n* is greater than 2.

Chapter 5   FORTRAN Programs for Study   114

5.5 ROOTS OF AN EQUATION

The roots of a quadratic equation of the form:

$$Ax^2 + Bx + C = 0$$

are given by the quadratic formula:

$$\text{root} = \frac{-B \pm \sqrt{B^2 - 4AC}}{2A}$$

For example, the equation $x^2 + 5x + 6 = 0$ can be factored as $(x + 2)(x + 3) = 0$ and the roots are known as $x = -2$ and $x = -3$. The FORTRAN program given in Figure 5-5 uses the quadratic formula to solve a quadratic equation.

The first statement in the program is a comment statement. Statement 10 reads the values for the coefficients A, B, and C. The fourth statement checks to see if the last data card (A = 0.0) has been read, and, if so, terminates the execution of the program. The fifth and sixth statements use the quadratic formula to compute values for ROOT1 and ROOT2. These statements use the SQRT library function to find the square root. The next statement prints the values for the three coefficients and two roots. The program then loops back to statement 10 to read the next set of coefficients. The example shown includes data cards for the three equations $x^2 + 5x + 6 = 0$, $x^2 + x - 2 = 0$ and $x^2 + x - 6$ and the terminating card.

5.6 THE NTH FIBONACCI NUMBER

We previously considered the algorithm for the Fibonacci number sequence (Chapter 2) and wrote a FORTRAN program (Mary Goes to the Circus) to generate these numbers. Figure 5-6 illustrates a program for generating and printing out the nth Fibonacci number, where it is assumed that n is greater than two.

All the variables in this program are integer variables. After the program reads a value for N, it initializes the values of K, M, and I. Statement 20 computes the sum of K and M, and the following statement advances the counter I by one. The IF statement determines if we have generated the nth number. If (I–N) is negative, the loop is continued by proceeding to statement 30 and completing the assignment of M to K and LSUM to M. The program then returns to statement 20 to generate the next Fibonacci number. The loop is terminated when I = N, and program control is transferred to statement 40 where the value of N and LSUM are printed. After printing these values, the program terminates.

5.7 THE JOLLY GREEN GIANT

The Jolly Green Giant laughed at a stupid network manager and was fired from his job of hulling peas on television. Outraged and discouraged, he has decided to rob a local bank and then take off for Canada. While robbing the bank, he plans to conceal his identity by wearing a mask over his nose and mouth. The giant's tailor estimated that the triangular mask would have the following dimensions:

Section 5.7 The Jolly Green Giant 115

Using the equation

$$\text{AREA} = \frac{1}{2}bh$$

the giant wrote the FORTRAN program shown in Figure 5-7. This program calculated the number of square yards of material that was needed to make the mask as well as the total cost of the mask. The material used for the mask sold for $4 per square yard.

Statements 1, 4, and 8 are comment statements. Statements 2 and 3 initialize B and H. Next the area is computed and printed. Statement 20 computes the cost of the mask by converting the area to square yards and multiplying by $4 per square yard. The next statement prints the cost of the mask. The program then terminates.

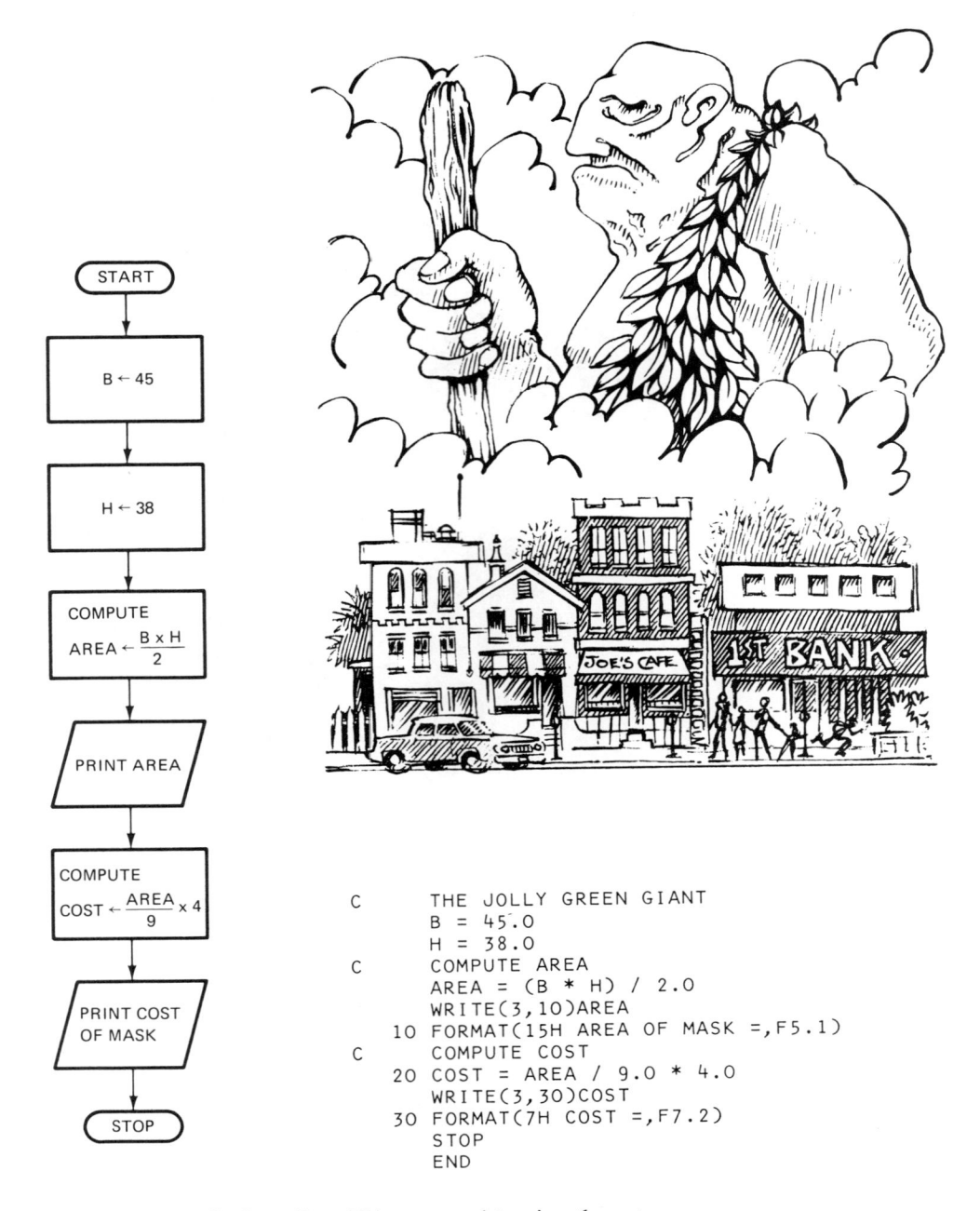

```
C         THE JOLLY GREEN GIANT
          B = 45.0
          H = 38.0
C         COMPUTE AREA
          AREA = (B * H) / 2.0
          WRITE(3,10)AREA
10        FORMAT(15H AREA OF MASK =,F5.1)
C         COMPUTE COST
20        COST = AREA / 9.0 * 4.0
          WRITE(3,30)COST
30        FORMAT(7H COST =,F7.2)
          STOP
          END
```

Figure 5-7 *The Jolly Green Giant.* This program determines the cost and area of the mask that the Jolly Green Giant plans to use in his bank robbery.

116

5.8 RODNEY'S NEW CALCULATOR

Many of the larger problems in the engineering field are now being tackled by computer programs, written by professional programmers, for which the individual engineer need only supply the particular data from the case with which he or she is concerned. However, this example shows how Rodney Butterfinger, a civil engineer in Mountain Top, Kentucky, uses the computer to solve small, tedious calculations. Rodney accomplishes this by writing a short FORTRAN program that simply reads in the data, carries out straightforward calculations, and produces the answers required. An example of a problem that Rodney used the computer to solve is as follows.

Find the height, C, of the neutral axis and the moment of inertia, I, of an H-beam. Pictorially, the beam dimensions appear as follows:

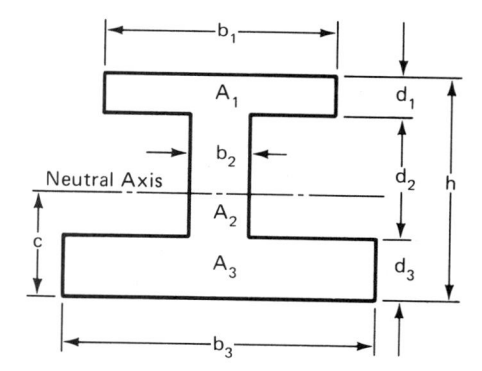

Figure 5-8.

The values of h, d_1, d_3, b_1, b_2, and b_3 are to be given as data, and C and I are calculated from the following formula:

$$I = \frac{b_1 d_1^3}{12} + A_1\left(h - c - \frac{d_1}{2}\right)^2 + \frac{b_2 d_2^3}{12} + A_2\left(d_3 + \frac{d_2}{2} - c\right)^2 + \frac{b_3 d_3^3}{12} + A_3\left(C - \frac{d_3}{2}\right)^2,$$

$$C = \frac{A_1[h - (d_1/2)] + A_2[d_3 + (d_2/2)] + A_3(d_3/2)}{A_1 + A_2 + A_3}$$

where

$$d_2 = h - (d_1 + d_3),$$
$$A_1 = b_1 \times d_1,$$
$$A_2 = b_2 \times d_2,$$
$$A_3 = b_3 \times d_3.$$

Using the previous equations, Rodney wrote the program shown in Figure 5-9.

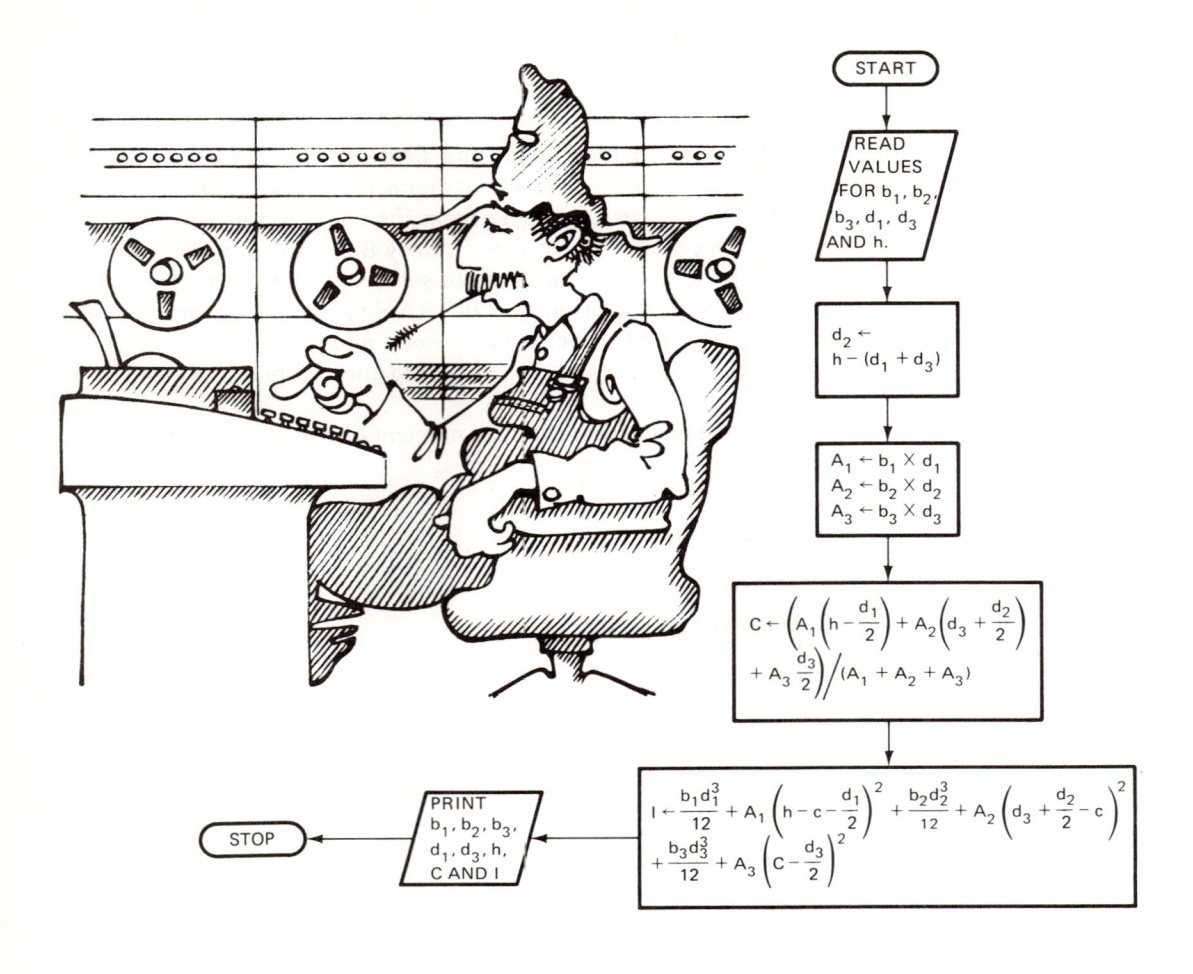

```
C     RODNEY'S NEW CALCULATOR
      REAL I
      READ(2,10)B1,B2,B3,D1,D3,H
   10 FORMAT(6F5.1)
      D2 = H - (D1 + D3)
      A1 = B1 * D1
      A2 = B2 * D2
      A3 = B3 * D3
   20 C = (A1*(H-D1/2.0)+A2*(D3*D2/2.0)+A3*(D3/2.0)) / (A1 + A2 + A3)
   30 I = ((B1*D1)**3)/12.0+A1*(H-C-D1*2.0)**2+((B2+D2)**3)/12.0+A2*(D3+
     1D2/2.0-C)**2+((B3*D3)**3)/12.0+A3*(C-D3/2.0)**2
      WRITE(3,40)B1,B2,B3,D1,D3,H,C,I
   40 FORMAT(5H B1 =,F5.1,5H B2 =,F5.1,5H B3 =,F5.1,5H D1 =,F5.1,
     25H D3 =,F5.1,4H H =,F5.1,/,4H C =,F15.5,4H I =,F25.5)
   50 STOP
      END
```

Figure 5-9 *Rodney's New Calculator.* This program shows how Rodney Butterfinger, a civil engineer in Mountain Top, Kentucky, uses the computer to perform small tedious calculations.

Section 5.9   Fireball Williams' Auto Races

The first statement in the program contains a comment. The next statement reads data values for B1, B2, B3, D1, D3, and H. Statements 4 through 7 compute values for D2, A1, A2, and A3. Statements 20 and 30 perform the tedious calculations for the height, C, of the neutral axis and the moment of inertia, I. The next statement causes the values for B1, B2, B3, D1, D3, H, C, and I to be printed. Program execution stops at Statement 50.

5.9 FIREBALL WILLIAMS' AUTO RACES

Fireball Williams, a race car driver from Atlanta, Georgia, won 17 NASCAR races last year. With the help of his friend, a programmer at one of Atlanta's insurance companies, he was able to write a program to determine the mean speed of those races. The average speeds of his races are as follows:

Daytona Racetrack	—	156 mph
Atlanta Racetrack	—	201 mph
New Orleans Racetrack	—	147 mph
Miami Racetrack	—	176 mph
Houston Racetrack	—	182 mph
Dallas Racetrack	—	196 mph
Barbersville Racetrack	—	190 mph
Tampa Racetrack	—	200 mph
Washington Racetrack	—	153 mph
Louisville Racetrack	—	183 mph
Huntsville Racetrack	—	204 mph
Little Rock Racetrack	—	177 mph
Ashville Racetrack	—	171 mph
Orlando Racetrack	—	159 mph
New York Racetrack	—	169 mph
Boston Racetrack	—	170 mph
Chicago Racetrack	—	168 mph

Fireball used the following equations in his FORTRAN program. The mean (or average), which is a measure of the central tendency of a statistical distribution,

Chapter 5   FORTRAN Programs for Study

is determined by

$$X = \frac{1}{n} \sum_{i=1}^{n} X_i,$$

where X_i for $i = 1, 2, 3, 4, 5, \ldots$, with n representing the value of X at the ith race. The variance, which is a measure of the dispersion or spread of a statistical distribution, is determined by

$$V = \frac{1}{n-1}\left[\Sigma X_i^2 - \frac{(\Sigma X_i)^2}{n}\right],$$

where $X_i = 1, 2, 3, 4, 5, \ldots, n$ represents the value of X at the ith race.

The standard deviation is also a measure of the dispersion of a statistical distribution and is defined as the positive value of the square root of the variance (V).

$$\sigma_x = \sqrt{V} = \sqrt{\frac{1}{n-1}\left[\Sigma X_i^2 - \frac{(\Sigma X_i)^2}{n}\right]}$$

For this problem, Fireball used an n of 17 and the following values of X:

$X_1 = 156$ $X_9 = 153$
$X_2 = 201$ $X_{10} = 183$
$X_3 = 147$ $X_{11} = 204$
$X_4 = 176$ $X_{12} = 177$
$X_5 = 182$ $X_{13} = 171$
$X_6 = 196$ $X_{14} = 159$
$X_7 = 190$ $X_{15} = 169$
$X_8 = 200$ $X_{16} = 170$
                  $X_{17} = 168.$

Fireball's program is shown in Figure 5-10.
The program caused the following message to be printed.

FIREBALL'S CAR SPEEDS
NUMBER OF RACES = 17
STANDARD DEVIATION = 17.4894
VARIANCE = 305.8824
MEAN = 176.5882

```
C       FIREBALL WILLIAMS' AUTO RACES
C       COMPUTES THE MEAN, VARIANCE, AND STANDARD DEVIATION
        SUMX = 0.0
        SUMSQ = 0.0
        AN = 0.0
C       INPUT CONSTANT AND NO. OF X VALUES
        READ(2,10) ZN
   10   FORMAT(F5.0)
C       READ VALUES OF X
   20   READ(2,30) X
   30   FORMAT(F5.0)
        SUMX = SUMX + X
        AN = AN + 1.0
        SUMSQ = SUMSQ + X ** 2
        IF(AN - ZN) 20,40,40
C       COMPUTE MEAN
   40   XBAR = SUMX / AN
C       COMPUTE VARIANCE
        VAR = (SUMSQ - (SUMX**2/ AN)) / (AN - 1.0)
C       COMPUTE STANDARD DEVIATION
        STDEV = SQRT(VAR)
C       PRINT STANDARD DEVIATION, VARIANCE, MEAN
        WRITE(3,50)STDEV,VAR,XBAR
   50   FORMAT(22H FIREBALL'S CAR SPEEDS,/,21H NUMBER OF RACES = 17,/,21H
       2STANDARD DEVIATION =,F16.4,/,11H VARIANCE =,F16.4,/,7H MEAN =,
       3F16.4)
        STOP
        END
```

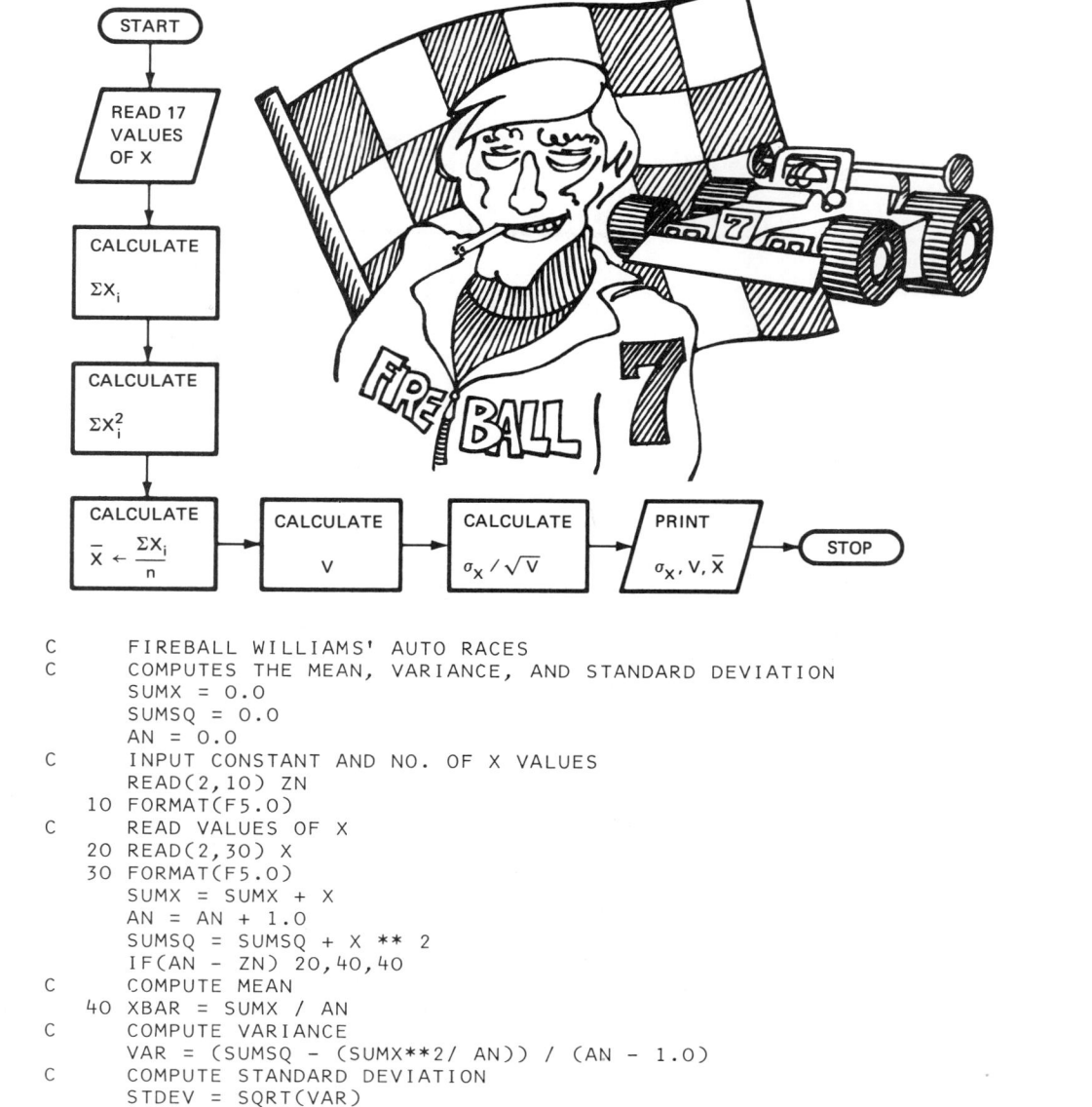

Figure 5-10 *Fireball Williams' Auto Races.* This program computes the mean, variance, and standard deviation of the speed of Fireball's auto races last year.

"IT HURTS WHEN I DO SQUARE ROOTS."

5.10 SQUARE ROOT

The square root of a positive number can be calculated using the Newton-Rapson recursive method:

$$x_i = \frac{1}{2}\left(X_o + \frac{A}{X_o}\right)$$

where A is the number and X_o is the first guess.

This introduces the idea of iteration. To obtain an approximation of A, start with a first guess, X_o, and calculate a value for X_i. Set $X_o = X_i$, and repeat the process. A few steps are:

$$X_1 = \frac{1}{2}\left(X_0 + \frac{A}{X_0}\right)$$

$$X_2 = \frac{1}{2}\left(X_1 + \frac{A}{X_1}\right)$$

$$X_3 = \frac{1}{2}\left(X_2 + \frac{A}{X_2}\right)$$

$$X_4 = \frac{1}{2}\left(X_3 + \frac{A}{X_3}\right)$$

$$\vdots$$

$$X_i = \frac{1}{2}\left(X_{i-1} + \frac{A}{X_{i-1}}\right)$$

Taking the value 4 and computing the $\sqrt{4}$ to three significant digits will make the foregoing procedure clear. The procedure uses a first guess of 1.

$$X_0 = 1.00$$

$$X_1 = \frac{1}{2}\left(1.00 + \frac{4.00}{1.00}\right) = 2.50$$

$$X_2 = \frac{1}{2}\left(2.50 + \frac{4.00}{2.50}\right) = 2.05$$

$$X_3 = \frac{1}{2}\left(2.05 + \frac{4.00}{2.05}\right) = 2.00.$$

There are several ways to determine when to stop the iteration. However, we will stop when the difference between successive estimates are less than some degree of accuracy (EPS).

$$|X_i - X_{i-1}| < \text{EPS}$$

```
C        SQUARE ROOT
C        READ INPUT VALUES (NUMBER, ACCURACY CONSTANT, FIRST GUESS)
         READ(2,10) A,EPS,XN
      10 FORMAT(F5.0,F5.3,F5.0)
      20 XO = XN
C        CALCULATE SQUARE ROOT
         XN = .5 * (XO + A / XO)
C        DETERMINE IF THE COMPUTED ROOT IS TO THE SPECIFIED ACCURACY
         IF(ABS(XN - XO) - EPS) 30,30,20
C        PRINT VALUES OF NUMBER, SQUARE ROOT, AND ACCURACY CONSTANT
      30 WRITE(3,40) A,XN,EPS
      40 FORMAT(9H NUMBER =,F5.0,15H  SQUARE ROOT =,F11.5,7H  EPS =,F5.3)
         STOP
         END
```

Figure 5-11 *Square Root.* This program reads input values for A, EPS, and the first guess; computes and prints the square root.

Section 5.11   *California Chemical Laboratory* 125

Another example where $A = 6561$, $EPS = 0.001$, and $X_o = 60$ is as follows:

$$X_n = \frac{1}{2}\left(60 + \frac{6561}{60}\right) = 84.67500 \qquad |X_n - X_o| = 24.67500$$
(which is greater than 0.001)

$$X_n = \frac{1}{2}\left(84.67500 + \frac{6561}{84.67500}\right) = 81.07975 \qquad |X_n - X_o| = 3.59525$$
(which is greater than 0.001)

$$X_n = \frac{1}{2}\left(81.07975 + \frac{6561}{81.07975}\right) = 81.00004 \qquad |X_n - X_o| = .07971$$
(which is greater than 0.001)

$$X_n = \frac{1}{2}\left(81.00004 + \frac{6561}{81.00004}\right) = 81.00000 \qquad |X_n - X_o| = .00004$$
(which is less than 0.001)

Therefore, the computed square root of 6561 to seven significant digits is 81.00000.

The FORTRAN program in Figure 5-11 computes $\sqrt{A}$ by the Newton-Raphson technique. The program reads input values for A, EPS, and the first guess. After the program computes a value for the square root, it prints the computed root, the original number A, and the accuracy value EPS.

5.11   CALIFORNIA CHEMICAL LABORATORY

Data processing is a term describing computer applications that use a large amount of data but usually only a small amount of computation performed on the data. A few data processing applications are payroll, inventory control, billing, classroom scheduling, credit card accounting, income tax bookkeeping, information retrieval, and similar tasks.

The following problem involves the computation of the weekly wages of every person on the payroll at California Chemical Factory. The FORTRAN program shown in Figure 5-12 reads a data card, computes the employee's weekly wage, and prints the computed value after the employee's identification number. Each data card, shown on page 127, contains the employee's identification number, hours worked, standard weekly pay rate, and overtime rate.

After determining the number of hours that an employee worked, the program computes the wage using either the standard rate or the overtime rate. If the number of hours exceeds 40, the program uses the overtime rate for all hours over 40 and the standard rate for the first 40 hours. If the number of hours was 40 or less, the program multiplies the number of hours by the standard rate. The program prints a list showing each employee's number and total weekly wages.

The last data card to be read by the program is a termination card. It tells the program that there are no more cards to process.

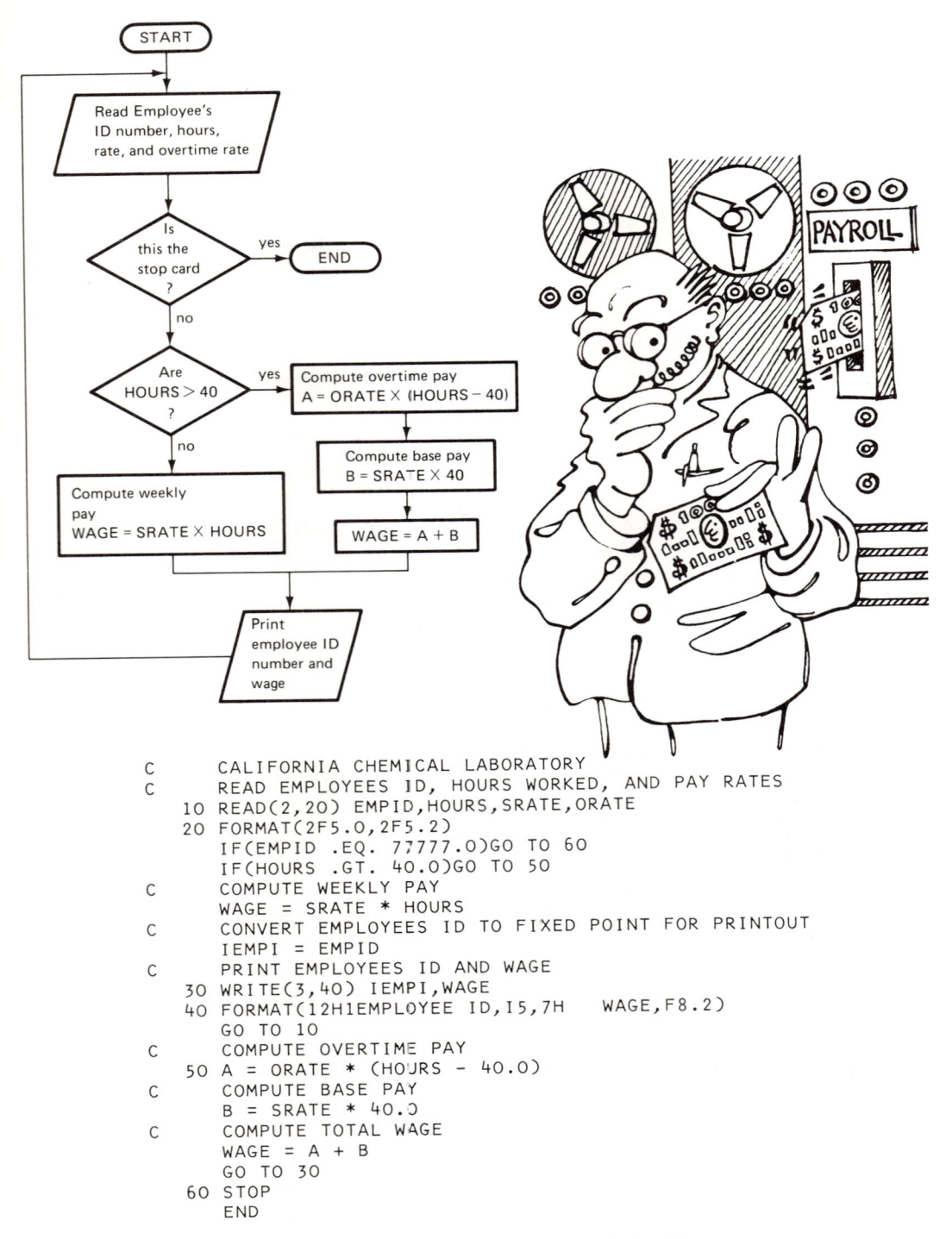

```
C          CALIFORNIA CHEMICAL LABORATORY
C          READ EMPLOYEES ID, HOURS WORKED, AND PAY RATES
        10 READ(2,20) EMPID,HOURS,SRATE,ORATE
        20 FORMAT(2F5.0,2F5.2)
           IF(EMPID .EQ. 77777.0)GO TO 60
           IF(HOURS .GT. 40.0)GO TO 50
C          COMPUTE WEEKLY PAY
           WAGE = SRATE * HOURS
C          CONVERT EMPLOYEES ID TO FIXED POINT FOR PRINTOUT
           IEMPI = EMPID
C          PRINT EMPLOYEES ID AND WAGE
        30 WRITE(3,40) IEMPI,WAGE
        40 FORMAT(12H1EMPLOYEE ID,I5,7H   WAGE,F8.2)
           GO TO 10
C          COMPUTE OVERTIME PAY
        50 A = ORATE * (HOURS - 40.0)
C          COMPUTE BASE PAY
           B = SRATE * 40.0
C          COMPUTE TOTAL WAGE
           WAGE = A + B
           GO TO 30
        60 STOP
           END
```

Figure 5-12 *California Chemical Factory.* This program computes the weekly wages of every employee at a chemical factory in California.

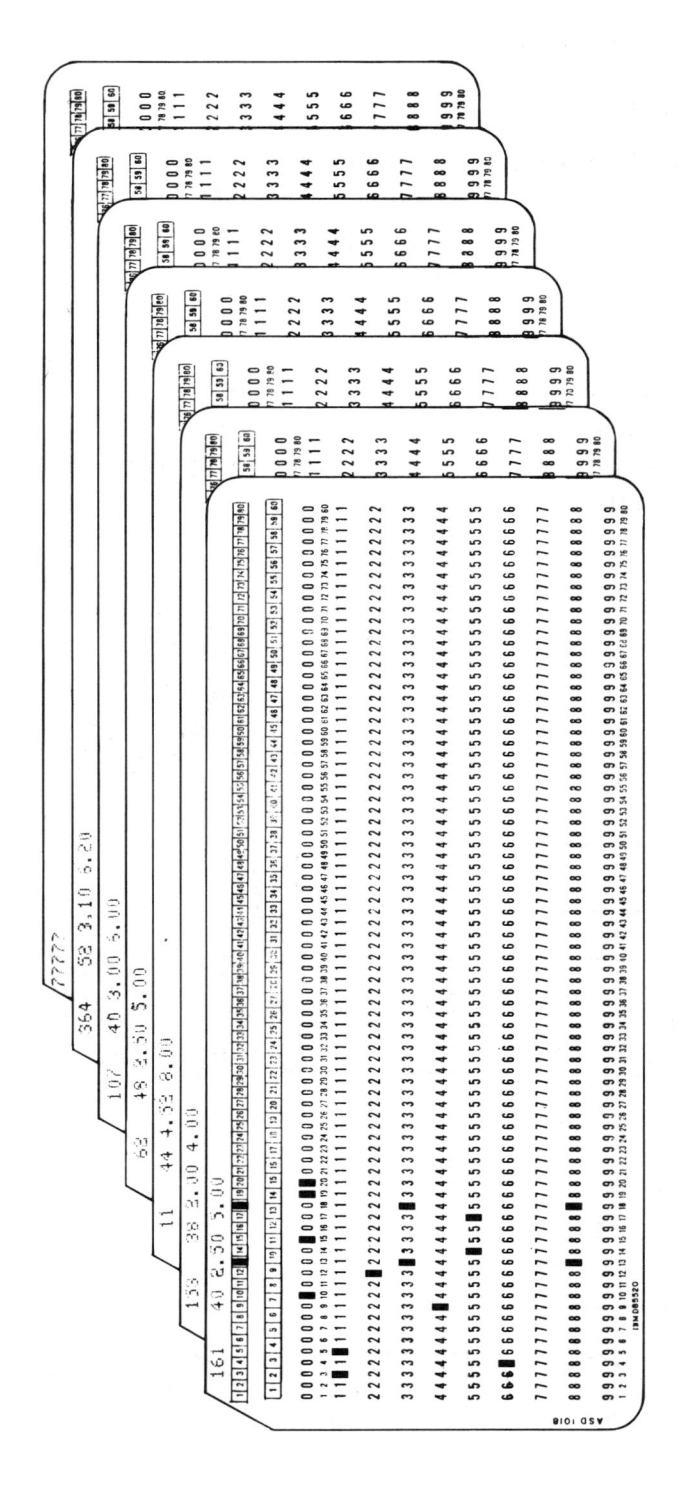

Figure 5-13.

Chapter 5 FORTRAN Programs for Study   128

5.12 HOW MUCH CURRENT?

The equation for determining the current flowing through an alternating circuit is

$$I = \frac{E}{\sqrt{R^2 + \left[2\pi FL - \dfrac{1}{2\pi FC}\right]^2}}$$

where

I = current (amperes) E = voltage (volts)
R = resistance (ohms) L = inductance (henrys)
C = capacitance (farads) F = frequency (cycles per second)
π = 3.1416

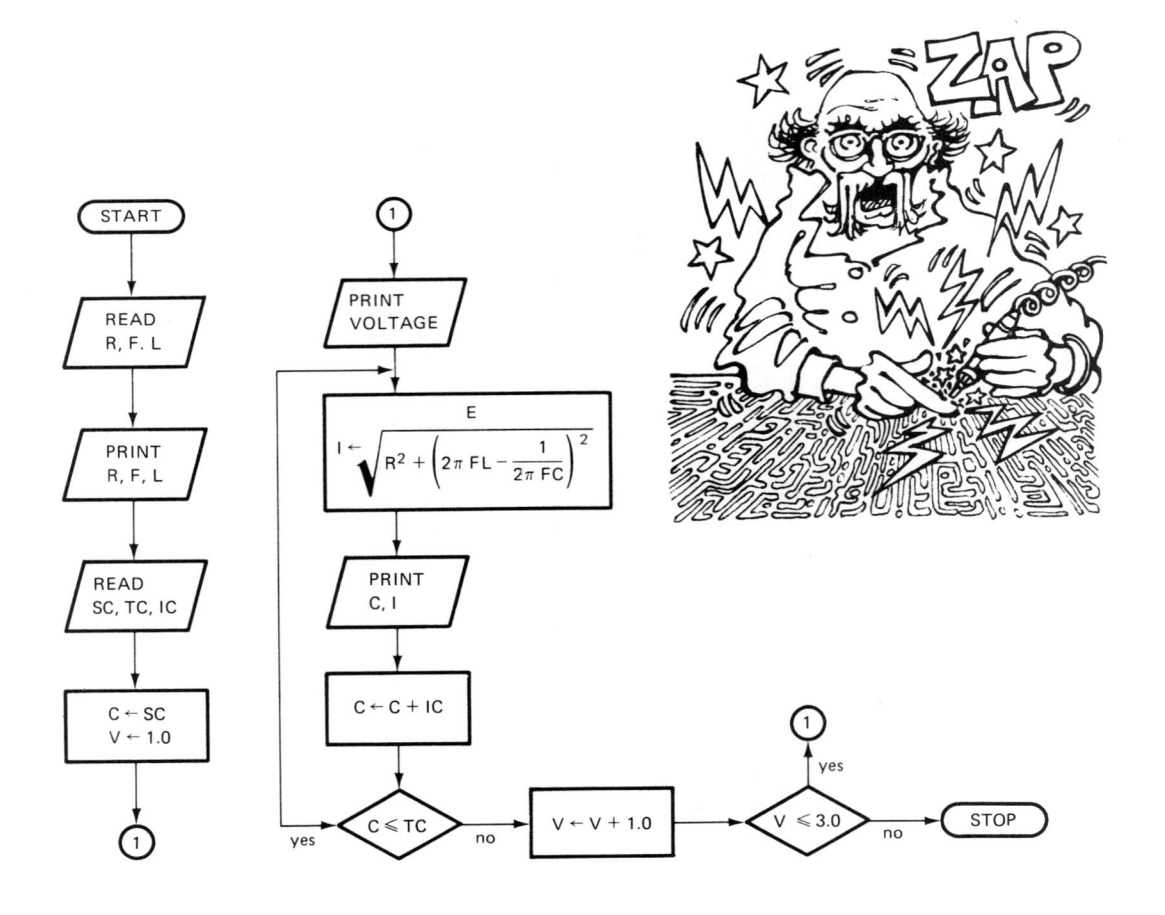

Section 5.12 *How Much Current?*   129

```
C         HOW MUCH CURRENT
C         INPUT VALUES FOR RESISTANCE, FREQUENCY AND INDUCTANCE
          READ(2,20) R,F,L
   20     FORMAT(3F10.4)
C         PRINT VALUES OF RESISTANCE, FREQUENCY AND INDUCTANCE
          WRITE(3,30) R,F,L
   30     FORMAT(3H1R=,F14.4,4H  F=,F14.4,4H  L=,F14.4)
C         INPUT STARTING AND TERMINATING VALUES OF CAPACITANCE AND INCREMENT
          READ(2,40) SC,TC,IC
   40     FORMAT(3F10.6)
C         SET CAPACITANCE TO STARTING VALUE
          C = SC
C         SET VOLTAGE TO STARTING VALUE
          V = 1.0
C         PRINT VALUE OF VOLTAGE
   50     WRITE(3,60) V
   60     FORMAT(3HOV=,F5.0)
C         COMPUTE CURRENT AI
   70     AI = E / SQUT(R**2 +
   70     AI = E / SQRT(R**2 + (6.2832*F*L - 1.0/(6.2832*F*C))**2)
C         PRINT VALUES OF CAPACITANCE AND CURRENT
          WRITE(3,80) C,AI
   80     FORMAT(3HOC=,F7.5,4H  I=,F7.5)
C         INCREASE VALUE OF CAPACITANCE
          C = C + IC
          IF (C .LE. TC) GO TO 70
C         INCREASE VALUE OF VOLTAGE
          V = V + 1.0
C         STOP IF VOLTAGE IS GREATER THAN 3.0
          IF (V .LE. 3.0) GO TO 50
          STOP
          END
```

Figure 5-14 *How Much Current?* This program computes the current for a number of equally spaced values of capacitance for voltages of 1.0, 2.0, and 3.0.

The values of R, F, and L are input to the program via a data card:

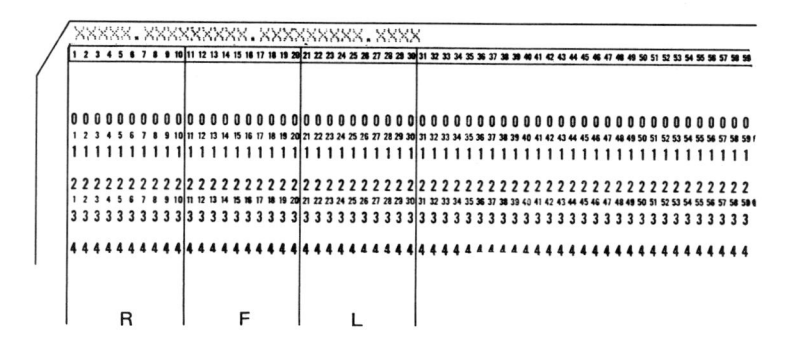

Figure 5-15.

Chapter 5 FORTRAN *Programs for Study* 130

The program shown in Figure 5-14 computes the current for a number of equally spaced values of capacitance for voltages of 1.0, 2.0, and 3.0. The starting and terminating values of capacitance, as well as the increment, are contained on an input card of the format shown below.

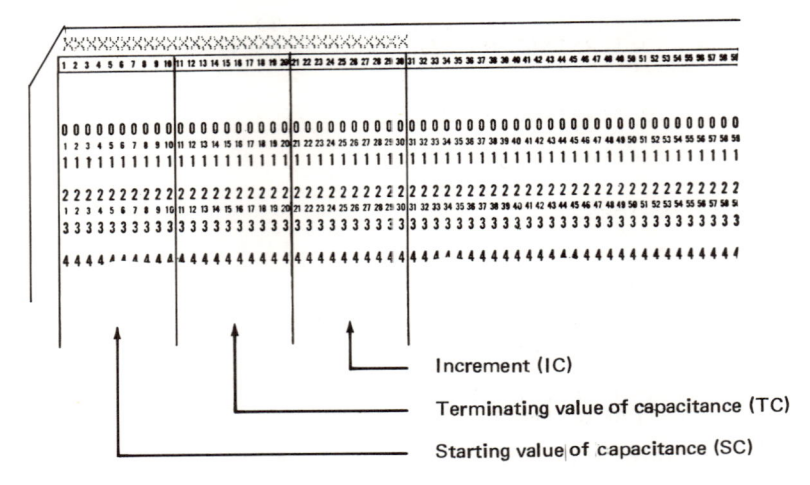

Figure 5-16.

Sample input data cards are shown below with the following values:

R = 100   SC = .0003
F = .006   TC = .001
L = 50   IC = .0001

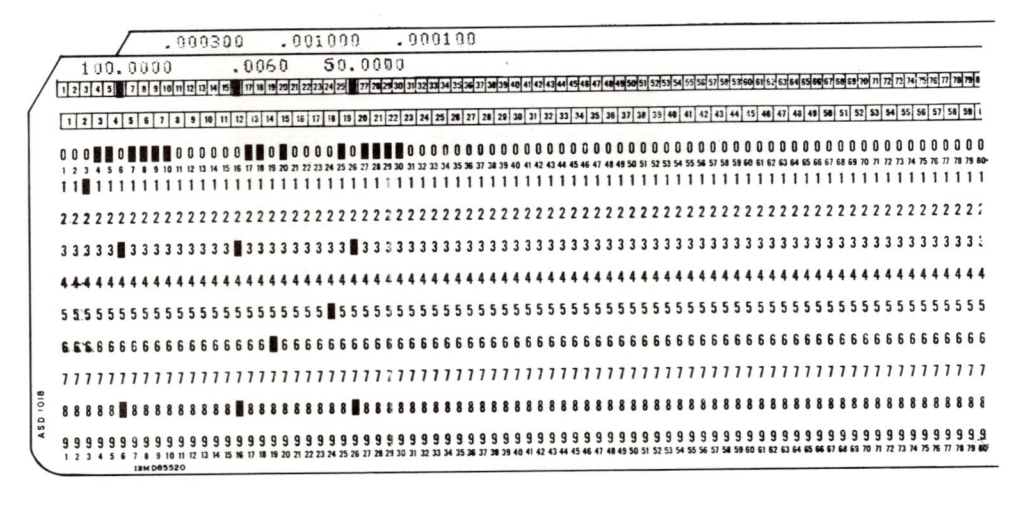

Figure 5-17.

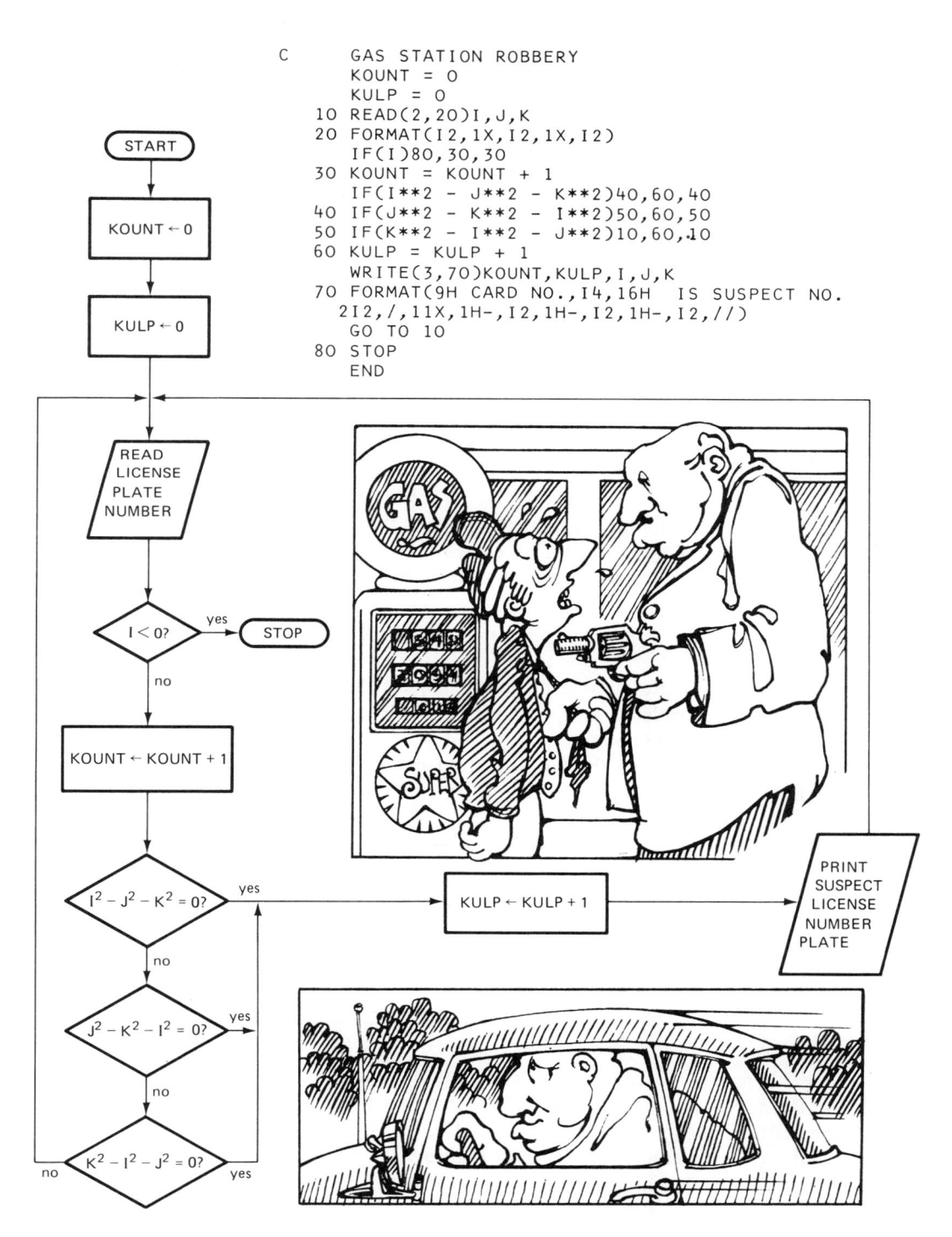

```
C        GAS STATION ROBBERY
         KOUNT = 0
         KULP = 0
   10    READ(2,20)I,J,K
   20    FORMAT(I2,1X,I2,1X,I2)
         IF(I)80,30,30
   30    KOUNT = KOUNT + 1
         IF(I**2 - J**2 - K**2)40,60,40
   40    IF(J**2 - K**2 - I**2)50,60,50
   50    IF(K**2 - I**2 - J**2)10,60,10
   60    KULP = KULP + 1
         WRITE(3,70)KOUNT,KULP,I,J,K
   70    FORMAT(9H CARD NO.,I4,16H  IS SUSPECT NO.
        2I2,/,11X,1H-,I2,1H-,I2,1H-,I2,//)
         GO TO 10
   80    STOP
         END
```

Figure 5-18 *Gas Station Robbery.* This program examines all the license plate numbers of a midwestern state to determine suspects in a robbery and murder case.

5.13 GAS STATION ROBBERY

This problem involves a knowledge of the Pythagorean theorem. Let us first review the elementary trigonometry involved.

The Pythagorean theorem is one of the most basic theorems we have today. It concerns, in particular, so-called right triangles, that is, triangles containing a 90° angle. These right triangles have a unique property:

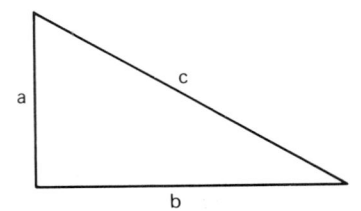

In any triangle containing a right (90°) angle, the square of the hypotenuse is equal to the sum of the squares of the other two sides. (The longest side—the side opposite the right angle—is called the hypotenuse.) Thus, if the triangle *abc* shown contains a right angle, then

$$c^2 = a^2 + b^2$$

There are an infinite number of integer triplets that conform to this pattern. Such a Pythagorean triplet is 3, 4, 5, where $5^2 = 3^2 + 4^2$. Another is 5, 12, 13, where $13^2 = 5^2 + 12^2$, and so on.

Now let us examine the problem. In a midwestern state, the automobile license numbers are of the form:

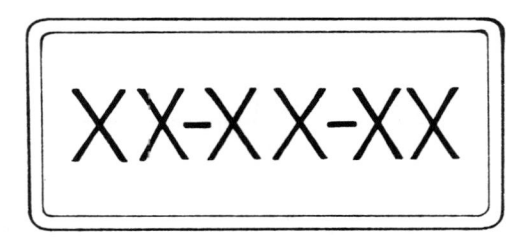

XX-XX-XX

where X can be any digit from 0 to 9.

For every license plate issued there is a punched card containing the number of the plate. The format of the card is (I2, 1X, I2, 1X, I2). A typical batch of such cards would look something like those in Figure 5-19. The exact number of cards is not known, but a special card (called a *trailer card*) with -6 punched in columns 1 and 2 is placed behind the last card.

Section 5.13   Gas Station Robbery

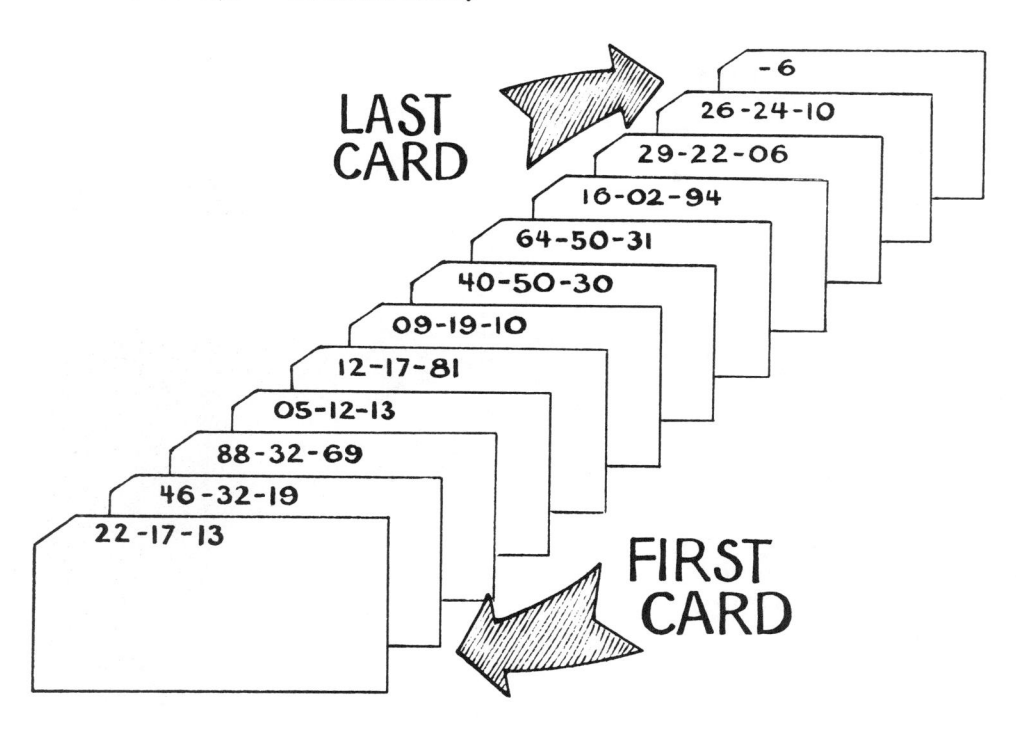

```
-6
26-24-10
29-22-06
16-02-94
64-50-31
40-50-30
09-19-10
12-17-81
05-12-13
88-32-69
46-32-19
22-17-13
```

LAST CARD

FIRST CARD

Figure 5-19.

Subsequent to a robbery of his gas station, the owner, a former mathematics teacher, gave chase while the robbers were making their getaway in a truck. As he approached the truck, the owner was shot just as he managed to catch a glimpse of the license plate. The sheriff soon came on the scene and immediately questioned the gravely wounded owner about the license plate number. His last words were: "... *the sides of a right triangle*."

The sheriff, who has been using computers for years, quickly wrote the FORTRAN program shown in Figure 5-19. This program examines all the license plate numbers in the state and determines what automobiles are possible "suspects."

The program output produced the following license plate numbers:

| 5-12-13 | 40-50-30 | 26-24-10 |

A short while after watching the owners of the automobiles with these license plates, the sheriff caught the men who committed the robbery and murder. The murderers are now spending time in the penitentiary—thanks to a modern-day sheriff.

Chapter 6

A self-service banking machine connected to the bank's computer permits customers to transact their banking business at any hour of the day or night. The above unit can be installed in an exterior bank wall, in the bank's lobby, or in remote locations such as shopping centers or airports. (Courtesy Burroughs Corp.)

Advanced FORTRAN

In Chapter 2 you were introduced to a new language to enable you to communicate with the computer. The essentials of FORTRAN were presented and you were shown how to write complete computer programs. Several complete FORTRAN programs were also discussed in Chapter 5.

This chapter contains additional statements and techniques in FORTRAN programming, and, when applied, they will allow you to solve more sophisticated and challenging problems.

6.1 THE DO STATEMENT

In Chapter 2 we discussed a way of looping by using the IF statement. However, a much more convenient way to implement a program loop is the DO statement. It is one of the most used statements in the FORTRAN language, and it greatly simplifies the writing of loops.

A program loop consists of one or more statements to be executed a number of times, each time altering one or more variables in these statements, so that each pass through the loop is different from the preceding one.

A FORTRAN DO loop looks like this:

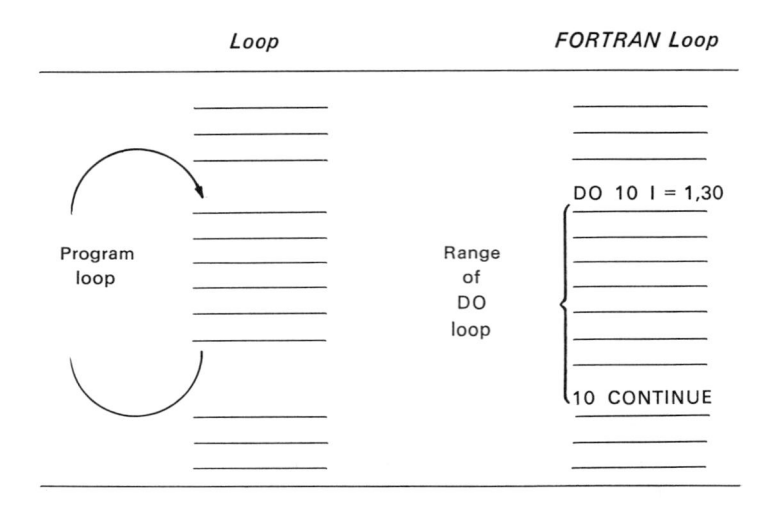

Loop   *FORTRAN Loop*

Program loop   Range of DO loop   DO 10 I = 1,30

10 CONTINUE

The above DO statement instructs the computer to do 30 times all the instructions from the DO statement up to and including the CONTINUE statement. The first pass through the loop I is 1, the second time 2, the third time 3, and so on, until I equals 30 on the last pass.

The general form of the DO statement is

$$DO\ ni = a,b,c$$

where

1. n is the statement number of the last statement in the loop.
2. i is the index that must be an integer variable.
3. a is an integer variable or constant that represents the initial value of the loop variable i (initial parameter).
4. b is an integer variable or constant that represents the limit for the loop variable i (terminal parameter).

5. c is an integer variable or constant that is used to modify the loop variable (incrementation parameter). If $c = 1$, it may be absent.

In the case where $c = 1$, the general form becomes

$$DO \ ni = a,b$$

A few rules that apply to the DO statement are:

1. a, b, and c may not be subscripted variables.*
2. Once the loop has been executed the appropriate number of times, the index is not available for use.
3. The values of a, b, and c must not be changed in the middle of a DO loop. At the time of execution they must be greater than zero.
4. If c is absent, it is understood to be 1.
5. The last statement in the loop cannot be a GO TO (all forms), IF, DO, or STOP.
6. DO loops may be *nested* if all statements in the inner loop are contained in the outer loop. Both the inner and outer loops may end on the same statement.

```
                        ─────DO 20 K = 1,10
         ┌─INNER LOOP─────DO 10 I = 1,6
                        ────10
                        ────20
```

7. Control may be transferred out of a DO loop but not into it.

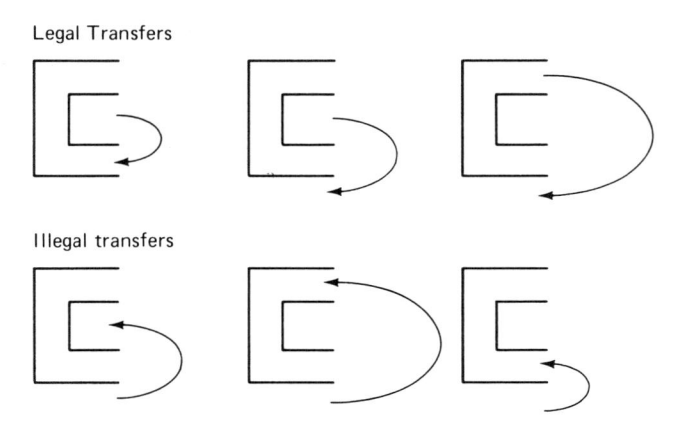

Legal Transfers

Illegal transfers

8. Control can be transferred within a DO loop; however, none of the DO loop parameters can be modified.

*Subscripted variables are discussed later in this chapter, under Arrays and Subscripts.

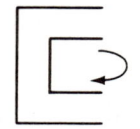

9. The DO loop index variable may be used by any statement in the loop. The DO statement

$$DO\ 70\ K = 1,15,2$$
$$\ldots$$
$$\ldots$$
$$\ldots$$
$$70\ \ldots$$

says "execute the statements immediately following the DO statement up to and including statement number 70." The first time through the loop, K will have a value of 1; the second time, a value of 3; the third time, a value of 5; and so on, until the last time, when K will have a value of 15. The variable K is increased by 2 each time through the loop.

6.2 THE CONTINUE STATEMENT

The CONTINUE statement may be called a null (or do nothing) statement, which can be placed anywhere in the source program without affecting program execution. Its only function is to provide a statement number that serves as a reference point in the program. It can be used, for example, as the last statement in a DO loop to avoid a loop terminating in a GO TO statement, an IF statement, STOP, or another DO statement. Since it does not cause the FORTRAN compiler to generate instructions, it can be used to improve program clarity.

In the following example, the continue statement is used to avoid the DO statement terminating in an IF statement.

```
            _____
            _____
            _____
            DO  30   K = 1, 40
            _____
    20      _____
            _____
            _____
            _____
```

Section 6.2 The Continue Statement

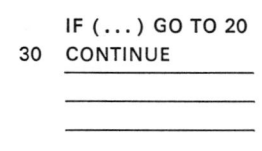

```
        IF ( ... ) GO TO 20
    30  CONTINUE   _____
            _____
            _____
            _____
```

The following example uses the CONTINUE statement to identify a point to which a branch can be made to go around statement 50.

```
        DO 60 K = 1, 4
        IF (X - Y) GO TO 50
        X = Z
        GO TO 60
    50  X = 0
    60  CONTINUE
```

REVIEW EXERCISES

6.1 Is the CONTINUE statement an executable statement?

6.2 The statement DO 30 K = 1,107, −6 contains an error. Identify it.

6.3 What are some of the dangers when incorporating nested DO loops in a program?

6.4 Determine whether the following DO statements are valid or invalid.

DO Statement	Valid or Invalid
(a) DO 60 X = 1,20,2	
(b) DO 16 K = 22	
(c) DO K = 1,30,3	
(d) DO 9999 L = 2,12,1	
(e) DO 9, K = 10,20	
(f) DO 55 J = 1,K+1	
(g) DO VEL I = R,J,K	
(h) DO 77 M = 1,A	
(j) DO 22 I = 1,36,2	

6.5 Write a DO statement that will accomplish what the following IF loop is doing.

```
         K = 0
    10   K = K + 1
            _____
            _____
            _____
            _____
         IF(K .LT. 20)GØ TØ 10
```

Chapter 6 Advanced FORTRAN 140

6.6 Which of the following DO loop nests are valid?

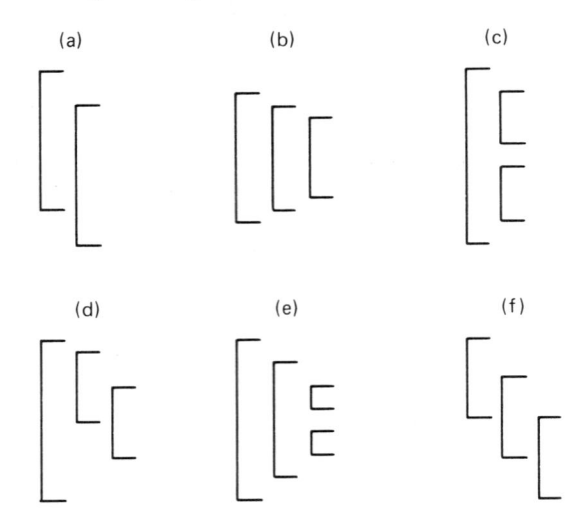

(a)   (b)   (c)

(d)   (e)   (f)

6.7 Write a program to calculate and print out the values of N factorial (N !) given N as an input number. Use a DO loop to accomplish the iteration process.

6.8 Draw a flowchart and write a FORTRAN program that can convert the weights of the college swim team members from pounds to kilograms (*hint:* 1 pound = 0.373 kilograms).

6.3 ARRAYS AND SUBSCRIPTS

Arrays are sequences of values listed in some given order. Using mathematical notation, a value in an array is located by using a *subscript*. For example, in a list of values of SPEED,

$$SPEED_1$$
$$SPEED_2$$
$$SPEED_3$$
$$SPEED_4$$
$$SPEED_5$$

if we wanted the fourth value, we would use $SPEED_4$. The small four is called a subscript and is used to identify a specific element or value within an array.

If the listing is simply sequential, then the array is called a *one-dimension array*, and only one subscript is needed to locate any element within the array.

A *two-dimension array* uses two subscripts separated by commas. This type of array is used when both rows and columns of values are present. For example, the checkerboard shown in Figure 6-1 illustrates the use of subscripts in a two-dimensional

Section 6.3   *Arrays and Subscripts*   141

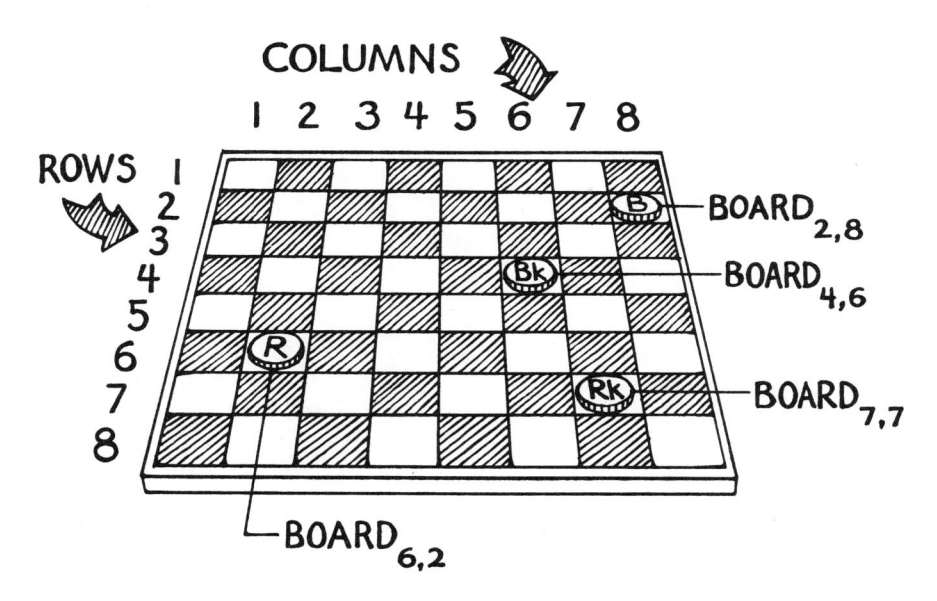

Figure 6-1 A checkerboard containing eight rows and eight columns.

array. The checkerboard contains eight rows and eight columns. Therefore, it is an 8×8 array. The first subscript denotes the row, the second subscript denotes the column. Thus, $BOARD_{2,3}$ would specify the board position or element in the second row and the third column. Checker locations on the board in Figure 6-1 are:

Element	Board Position	Subscripts
Red Checker (R)	Row 6, Column 2	$BOARD_{6,2}$
Black Checker (B)	Row 2, Column 8	$BOARD_{2,8}$
Red King (RK)	Row 7, Column 7	$BOARD_{7,7}$
Black King (BK)	Row 4, Column 6	$BOARD_{4,6}$

In FORTRAN, only certain expressions are allowable for subscripts, and they must be in *integer* mode. The most common ways of expressing subscripts are

X_i where *i* is an integer variable

X_n where *n* is a positive constant integer

$X_{i \pm n}$ where *i* is an integer variable and *n* is an integer constant

Examples of these forms and how they are written in FORTRAN are:

Mathematical Form	*FORTRAN Form*
x_i	X(I)
x_2	X(2)
x_{k-3}	X(K − 3)
x_{j+2}	X(J + 2)

Three other allowable forms of a subscript are:

$$\left.\begin{array}{l} x_{ni} \\ x_{ni+n} \\ x_{ni-n} \end{array}\right\} \text{where } i \text{ is a variable and } n \text{ is a constant}$$

In FORTRAN these forms would appear as

        X(3 * K)   X(3 * K + 6)   and   X(3 * K − 6)

A *subscripted variable* is a FORTRAN variable appended with one or more subscripts. Most FORTRAN systems allow up to three subscripts; however, there are a few systems that allow more. The form of a subscripted variable is VN(S), where VN is any allowable FORTRAN variable name and S is one or more subscripts separated by commas. The subscripts must be unsigned integer values or expressions, and they all must be enclosed within one set of parentheses.

Calculated subscripts must never result in a zero or negative value. For example, in the subscripted variable VEL(K − 6), the value of K must never be 6 or less.

6.4 THE DIMENSION STATEMENT

Every subscripted variable that appears in a FORTRAN program also must be listed in a DIMENSION statement. This statement must precede the first use of the subscripted variable in the program.

The DIMENSION statement is used by the FORTRAN compiler to allocate the proper computer storage for a subscripted variable. The DIMENSION statement has the form

        DIMENSION *v(s)*, *v(s)*, *v(s)*, . . .

where *v* is a subscripted variable name and *s* is one or more integer values that specifies the maximum number of rows, columns, or levels.

A DIMENSION statement to allocate storage for a list of 10 items (named LIST) would appear as

        DIMENSION LIST(10)

The statement

        DIMENSION CHECK(8,8)

reserves storage for an 8 × 8 array named CHECK.

Several subscripted variables may be *dimensioned* in one DIMENSION statement. For example, the statement

        DIMENSION POWER(100), X(20,30), FORCE(3,4,6)

"I'D LIKE TO HELP YOU WITH YOUR COMPUTER HOMEWORK BUT IT'S FORTRAN TO ME."

Chapter 6   Advanced FORTRAN

sets aside computer storage for a 100-element one-dimensional array, a 20×30 two-dimensional array, and a three-dimensional array (named FORCE) that contains a maximum of 3 rows, 4 columns, and 6 levels.

REVIEW EXERCISES

- **6.9** In your own words, define the following terms:
  - (a) DO loop
  - (b) array
  - (c) subscript
  - (d) subscripted variable
- **6.10** Every subscript must be:
  - (a) in real mode
  - (b) in integer mode
  - (c) listed in a comment statement
  - (d) used in a DO loop
- **6.11** What is an array? Can you explain its purpose?
- **6.12** Can a subscript be a literal?
- **6.13** Assume that you are defining two arrays in a DIMENSION statement. Will the maximum value of the subscripts specified for one array influence the maximum value of the other array in any way?
- **6.14** DIMENSION statements are used to:
  - (a) free the computer to begin its computations
  - (b) identify real variables
  - (c) reserve computer storage for arrays
  - (d) evaluate common mathematical operations
- **6.15** Distinguish between an array name, a subscript, the value of the subscript, and the element(s) of the array.
- **6.16** A *magic square* consists of a number of integers arranged in the form of a square, so that the sum of the numbers is the same in every row, in every column, and in each diagonal. Identify the elements of the following magic square array named MAGIC:

16	3	2	13
5	10	11	8
9	6	7	12
4	15	14	1

(a) MAGIC (1, 1) = _____   (e) MAGIC (1, 2) = _____
(b) MAGIC (2, 1) = _____   (f) MAGIC (2, 2) = _____
(c) MAGIC (3, 1) = _____   (g) MAGIC (3, 2) = _____
(d) MAGIC (4, 1) = _____   (h) MAGIC (4, 2) = _____

Section 6.4   The Dimension Statement   145

(i) MAGIC (1, 3) = _____   (m) MAGIC (1, 4) = _____
(j) MAGIC (2, 3) = _____   (n) MAGIC (2, 4) = _____
(k) MAGIC (3, 3) = _____   (o) MAGIC (3, 4) = _____
(l) MAGIC (4, 3) = _____   (p) MAGIC (4, 4) = _____

6.17 Give the following two-dimensional array A:

	Column 1	Column 2	Column 3
Row 1	16	6	13
Row 2	3	9	6
Row 3	14	1	4
Row 4	9	41	11
Row 5	12	2	8

how would the elements of array A be stored in computer memory if the elements were stored in column order?

```
              Memory
             Location
```

(a) n   = _____
(b) n + 1 = _____
(c) n + 2 = _____
(d) n + 3 = _____
(e) n + 4 = _____
(f) n + 5 = _____
(g) n + 6 = _____
(h) n + 7 = _____
(i) n + 8 = _____
(j) n + 9 = _____
(k) n + 10 = _____
(l) n + 11 = _____
(m) n + 12 = _____
(n) n + 13 = _____
(o) n + 14 = _____

6.18 Find the intermediate and final values of R in the following program segment:

```
                                       Array B
                                       B(1) = 2.0
         R = 3.0                       B(2) = 0.0
         DO 20 I = 1,4                 B(3) = 3.0
      20 R = R*2.0+B(I)                B(4) = 4.0
```

(a) R = 3.0
(b) R = _____   for   I = 1
(c) R = _____   for   I = 2
(d) R = _____   for   I = 3
(e) R = _____   for   I = 4

6.19 Find the final value of N in the following program segment:

```
        N = 1
        DO 20 I = 1,2
        DO 20 K = 1,2
     20 N = N + L(I,K)

        N = _____
```

Array L

2	2
3	4

6.5 ADDITIONAL INPUT/OUTPUT

In Chapter 2, the READ and WRITE statement input/output list contained only variable names. Subscripted variable names with indexing also can be used in the input/output list. The general forms of the READ and WRITE statements with subscripted variables names are

$$\text{READ } (u,f) \text{ L}$$
$$\text{WRITE } (u,f) \text{ L}$$

where u is an integer constant or an integer variable that identifies the input or output unit; f is the statement number of the FORMAT statement that is associated with this input/output statement; and L is the list that specifies the arrays names or elements.

The statement

```
        READ (2,20) A(3), B(6), C(2)
     20 FORMAT (3F5.0)
```

would cause three values to be read from the data card and assigned to the third element of array A, the sixth element of array B, and the second element of array C.

The general forms of the READ and WRITE statements with subscripted variables and indexing is

$$\text{READ } (u,f) \ (v(i), i = m_1, m_2, m_3)$$
$$\text{WRITE } (u,f) \ (v(i), i = m_1, m_2, m_3)$$

for one-dimensional arrays or lists and

$$\text{READ } (u,f) \ ((v(i,j), i = m_1, m_2, m_3), j = m_1, m_2, m_3)$$
$$\text{WRITE } (u,f) \ ((v(i,j), i = m_1, m_2, m_3), j = m_1, m_2, m_3)$$

for two-dimensional arrays or matrices.

In the previous formats, u and f are as discussed; v is the name of the subscripted variable; i is a nonsubscripted integer variable; and the m's are either unsigned integer constants or nonsubscripted integer variables representing, respectively, the initial value, the test value, and the increment to be used in the indexing. When m_3 is omitted in the previous format, it is understood to have a value of 1.

Section 6.5 Additional Input/Output

Let us now look at an input statement that will cause an array of data to be brought into the computer:

READ (2,33) (A(K),K = 1,20)

This statement will set up a loop that will read 20 values from one or more cards as directed by the specifications in FORMAT statement 33. These values will be stored in array elements A(1), A(2), A(3), ..., A(20).

A statement that would read the data associated with a two-dimensional array would have the form

READ (2,20) ((A(I,J),I = 1,2),J = 1,3)

This statement would read data into the computer in this order:

A(1,1)
A(2,1)
A(1,2)
A(2,2)
A(1,3)
A(2,3)

If the statement had been written

READ (2,20) ((A(I,J),J = 1,3),I = 1,2)

the data would be transmitted in the following sequence

A(1,1)
A(2,1)
A(3,1)
A(1,2)
A(2,2)
A(3,2)

If the preceding array had been defined in a **DIMENSION** statement, as

DIMENSION A(3,2)

the statement also could be written simply as

READ (2,20) A

and the entire array would be read into memory in *column order*.

An example of a WRITE statement is

WRITE (3,30) ((A(I,J),I = 1,3),J = 1,3)

This statement would cause the nine elements of array A to be printed according to the format specifications of FORMAT statement 30.

Chapter 6   Advanced FORTRAN

Consider the following example. The values for nine integer values in computer memory are

```
MAGIC(1,1) = 8
MAGIC(2,1) = 3
MAGIC(3,1) = 4
MAGIC(1,2) = 1
MAGIC(2,2) = 5
MAGIC(3,2) = 9
MAGIC(1,3) = 6
MAGIC(2,3) = 7
MAGIC(3,3) = 2
```

These values in memory represent the values of a 3 × 3 magic square.* If one wanted to print these values in a square arrangement, the statements

```
      WRITE (3,55) ((MAGIC(I,J),I = 1,3),J = 1,3)
   55 FORMAT (3I5///3I5///3I5)
```

could be used. When the WRITE statement was executed, the first row of the magic square would be printed:

```
    8    1    6
```

Then two lines of blanks and the second row of the square would be printed:

```
    3    5    7
```

Then two more lines of blanks and the third row of the square would be printed:

```
    4    9    2
```

The resulting magic square would appear as follows:

```
    8    1    6
    3    5    7
    4    9    2
```

The same square could be printed by using several other FORMAT statements. The statements

```
   55 FORMAT (3I5//)
```

or

```
   55 FORMAT (3(3I5//))
```

*Magic squares were discussed in Chapter 3.

or

$$55 \quad \text{FORMAT } (//3\text{I}5)$$

would produce the same printout.

REVIEW EXERCISES

6.20 Write WRITE and FORMAT statements that could cause the following printout.

1	15	14	4
12	6	7	9
8	10	11	5
13	3	2	16

6.21 Indicate which one of the following input/output lists is incorrect.
    (a) ((C(I,J),I = 1,7),J = 1.7)
    (b) A,B,C(4),K
    (c) MAGIC,POWER,I
    (d) (A(K),K = 1,8),ACE
    (e) B(3),4,K
    (f) I,J,K,SPEED

6.22 Indicate which one of the following input/output statements is incorrect.
    (a) READ (2,200)A,B
    (b) WRITE (3,30),NUM,BEAM
    (c) WRITE (3,6)(A(K),K = 1,10)
    (d) READ (2,30)(A(I),I = 1,100)
    (e) WRITE (3,61)A(3),K
    (f) READ (2,20)I,J,K

6.6 SAMPLE PROGRAMS

The examples in this section will help to illustrate some uses of arrays and the DO statement.

EXAMPLE 1. SUM OF THE FIRST 150 INTEGERS

The following FORTRAN program computes and prints the sum of the first 150 integers. A flowchart is shown in Figure 6-2.

```
C         NUMBER SUM PROGRAM
          ISUM = 0
          DO 10 I = 1, 150
   10     ISUM = ISUM + 1
          WRITE(3,20) ISUM
   20     FORMAT(6H SUM = , I10)
          STOP
          END
```

Chapter 6   Advanced FORTRAN

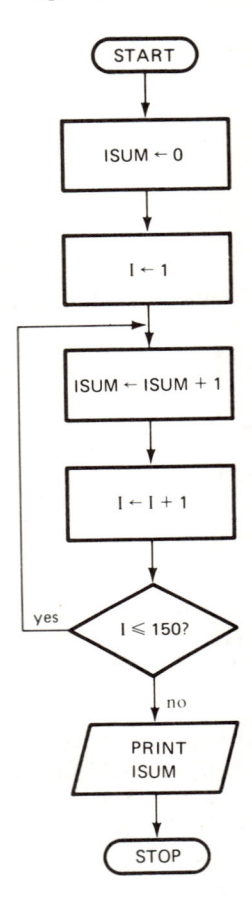

```
        ┌─────────┐
        │  START  │
        └────┬────┘
             │
        ┌────▼────┐
        │ ISUM ← 0│
        └────┬────┘
             │
        ┌────▼────┐
        │  I ← 1  │
        └────┬────┘
             │
   ┌─────────▼─────────┐
   │  ISUM ← ISUM + 1  │
   └─────────┬─────────┘
             │
        ┌────▼────┐
        │ I ← I+1 │
        └────┬────┘
             │
   yes    ┌──▼──┐
  ┌───────│I≤150?│
  │       └──┬──┘
  │          │ no
  │     ┌────▼────┐
  │     │  PRINT  │
  │     │  ISUM   │
  │     └────┬────┘
  │          │
  │     ┌────▼────┐
  │     │  STOP   │
  │     └─────────┘
```

Figure 6-2 Sum of the first 150 integers.

EXAMPLE 2. FIND THE LARGEST NUMBER

Array ALPHA contains the following values

1108	360	930
1700	635	315
520	1800	160

The FORTRAN program below finds the largest number and assigns it to the variable BETA. A flowchart is shown in Figure 6-3.

```
      C           LARGEST NUMBER PROGRAM
                  DIMENSION ALPHA(9)
                  ALPHA(1) = 1108.0
                  ALPHA(2) = 1700.0
```

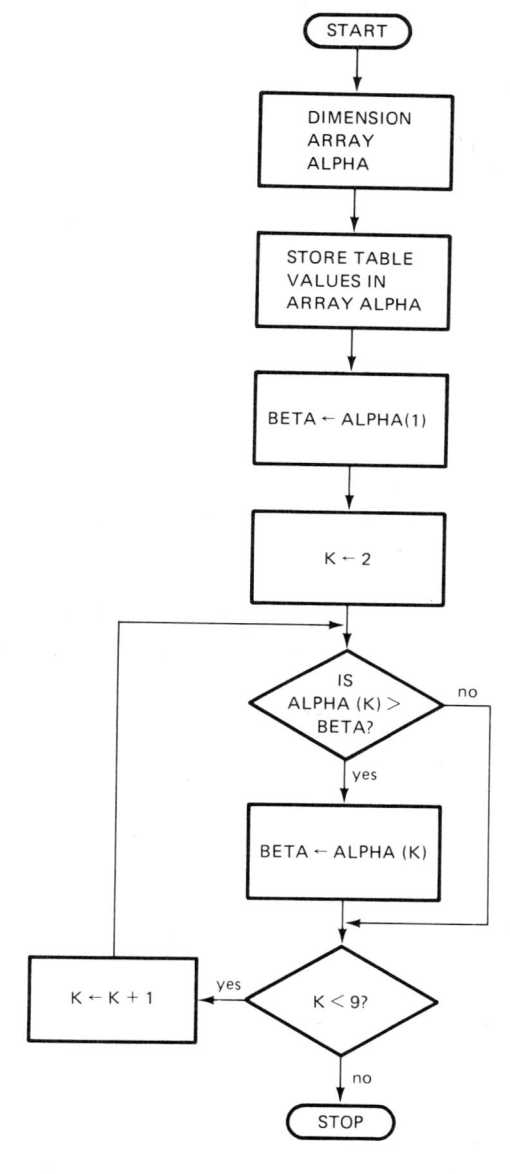

Figure 6-3 Find the largest number in array ALPHA.

```
            ALPHA(3) =  520.0
            ALPHA(4) =  360.0
            ALPHA(5) =  635.0
            ALPHA(6) = 1800.0
            ALPHA(7) =  930.0
            ALPHA(8) =  315.0
            ALPHA(9) =  160.0
            BETA = ALPHA(1)
            DO 10 K=2,9
            IF(ALPHA(K).GT.BETA)BETA=ALPHA(K)
         10 CONTINUE
            STOP
            END
```

Example 3. Numerical Integration

Numerical integration can be performed in a variety of ways. One way is to compute the area under a curve as the sum of areas of small rectangles. The area of each rectangle is the length of the base h times the height y_i. The base h represents the interval (a, b) divided by the number of rectangles that are to be summed, that is, $h = (b - a)/n$. One should make n sufficiently small to improve the accuracy of the answer. As this problem is defined, the area under the curve may be computed by obtaining the sum of $hy_0 + hy_1 + hy_2 + hy_3 + hy_4 + hy_5 + hy_6 + \cdots + hy_n$.

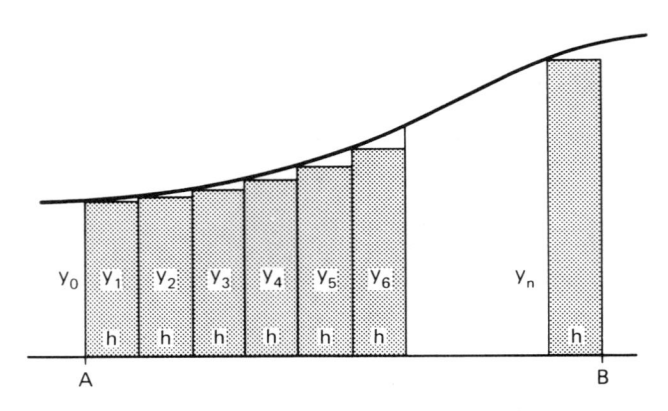

Figure 6-4.

The following program finds the area under the curve $f(x) = 3x^2 - 4x + 2$. The curve $f(x)$ will be integrated from point A to point B. These values are read into the computer and for this problem are equal to $A = 4$ and $B = 8$. The program will use an n of 1,000, which will give us a computed answer near the exact answer. A flowchart for this problem is shown in Figure 6-5.

```
      C         NUMERICAL INTEGRATION
                READ(2,10)A,B
           10   FORMAT(2F10.0)
```

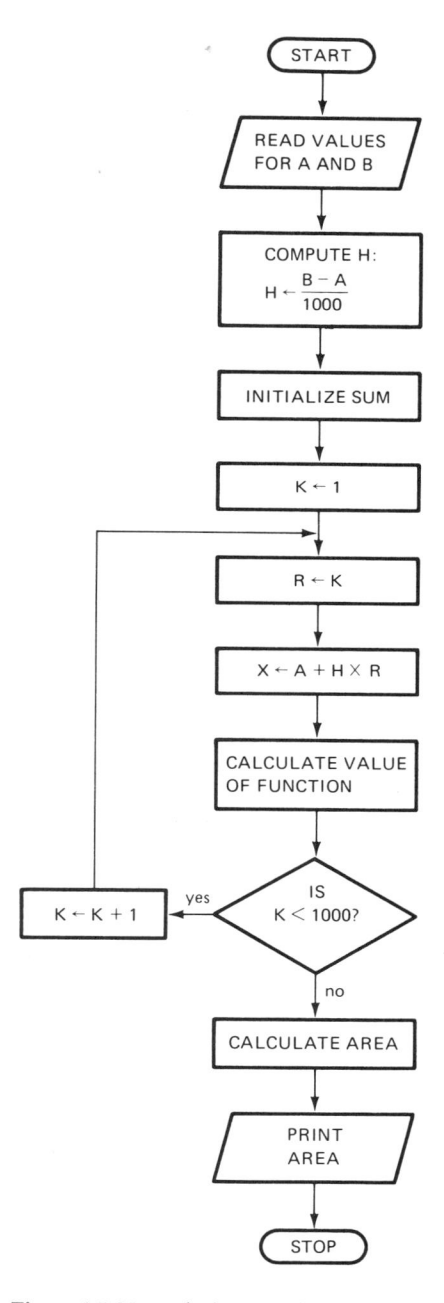

Figure 6-5 Numerical integration.

Chapter 6   Advanced FORTRAN   154

```
       C          CALCULATE H
                  H = (B - A) / 1000.0
       C          INITIALIZE SUM
                  SUM = 0.0
       C          CALCULATE VALUE OF FUNCTION
       C          AND SUM THE VALUES
                  DO 20 K = 1,1000
                  R = K
                  X = A + H * R
            20    SUM =SUM+3.0*X**2-4.0*X+2.0
       C          CALCULATE AREA
                  AREA = SUM * H
       C          PRINT ANSWER
                  WRITE(3,30)AREA
            30    FORMAT(1H1,E14.7)
                  STOP
                  END
```

EXAMPLE 4. SORTING

A flowchart of a simple way to sort or arrange a group of numbers in ascending order is shown in Figure 6-6. This procedure will take a given sequence of 20 numbers; say, 361, 22, 1, 31, 12, 81, 700, 6, 53, 99, 104, 123, 300, 461, 103, 411, 46, 7, 207, 650, and will arrange them in the order 1, 6, 7, 12, 22, 31, 46, 53, 81, 99, 103, 104, 123, 207, 300, 361, 411, 461, 650, 700. The procedure compares the first number with the second and interchanges them if the first number is larger than the second. The first number is then compared with the third number, and they are interchanged if out of order. The process is repeated until the first number has been compared with all numbers in the sequence. Then, starting with the second number, the same procedure is used, then the third number, and so on.

A FORTRAN program for the sorting procedure is shown below.

```
       C          SORTING
                  DIMENSION JJJ(20)
       C          READ TWENTY VALUES TO BE SORTED
                  READ(2,10)(JJJ(I), I=1,20)
            10    FORMAT(20I4)
                  K = 20
                  I = K - 1
                  DO 20 N=1,I
                  M = N + 1
                  DO 20 L=M,K
                  IF(JJJ(N) .LE. JJJ(L))GO TO 20
                  ITEMP = JJJ(N)
                  JJJ(N) = JJJ(L)
                  JJJ(L) = ITEMP
            20    CONTINUE
                  WRITE(3,10)(JJJ(I),I = 1,20)
                  STOP
                  END
```

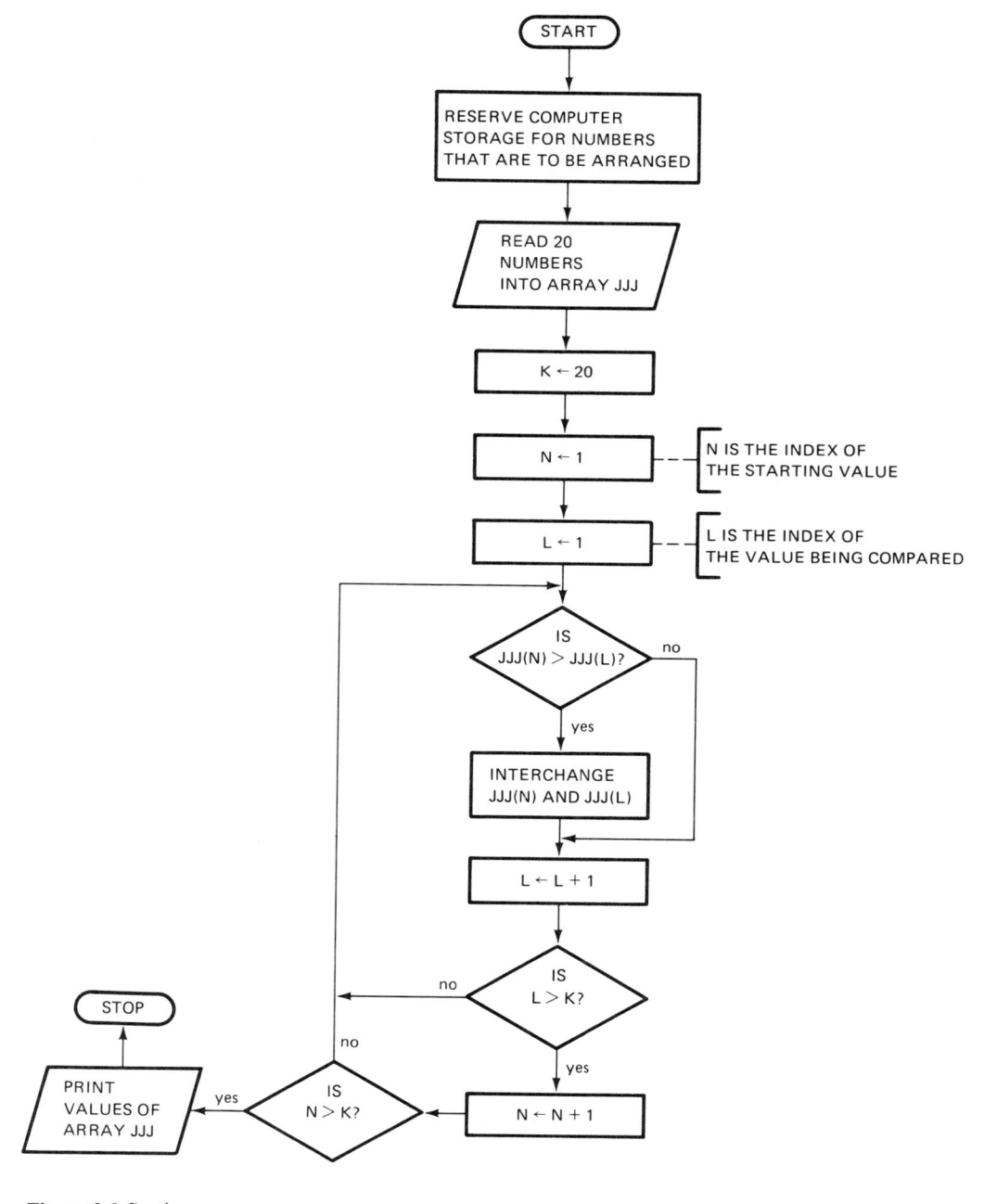

Figure 6-6 Sorting.

Chapter 6 Advanced FORTRAN

EXAMPLE 5. POLYNOMIAL EVALUATION

A polynomial of the form

$$P = a_1 x^n + a_2 x^{n-1} + \cdots + a_n x^1 + a_n + 1$$

may be solved for a given value of x by using a nesting procedure. For example, if

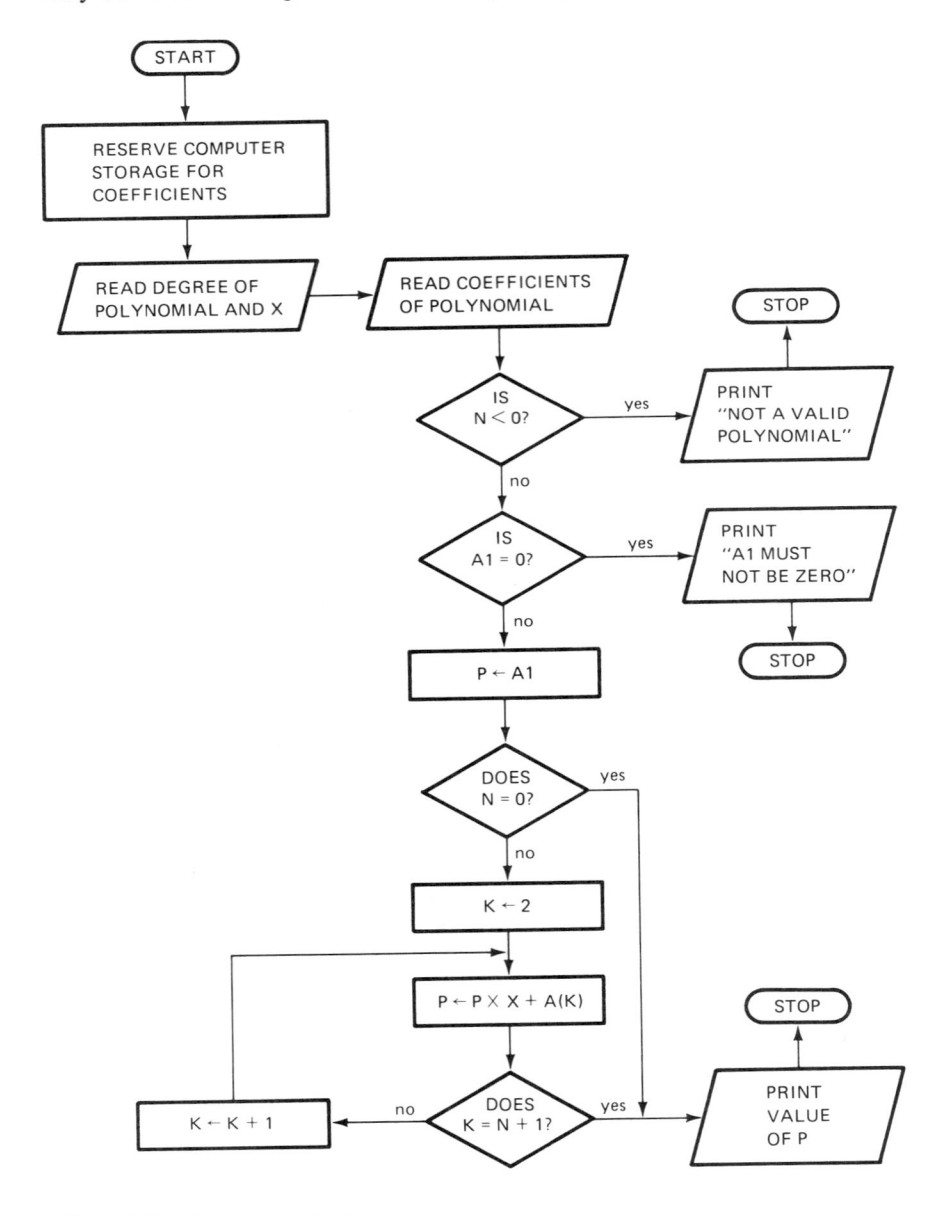

Figure 6-7 Polynomial evaluation.

Section 6.6   Sample Programs

$n = 5$, the nesting form would appear as

$$P = (x(x(x(x(x(a_1) + a_2) + a_3) + a_4) + a_5) + a_6)$$

The coefficient a_1 cannot be zero and if $n = 0$, the value of P is a_{n+1}. A flowchart of a program to evaluate a polynomial is shown in Figure 6-7 and a FORTRAN program is shown below.

```
C         POLYNOMIAL EVALUATION PROGRAM
C         N — DEGREE OF THE POLYNOMIAL
C         A — COEFFICIENTS OF POLYNOMIAL
          DIMENSION A(30)
C         READ DEGREE OF POLYNOMIAL AND X
          READ(2,10)N,X
      10  FORMAT(I5,F10.5)
C         READ COEFFICIENTS OF POLYNOMIAL
          READ(2,20)(A(I),I=1,N)
      20  FORMAT(F5.0)
          IF(N .GT. 0)GO TO 40
          WRITE(3,30)
      30  FORMAT(23H1NOT A VALID POLYNOMIAL)
          STOP
      40  IF(A(1) .NE. 0)GO TO 60
          WRITE(3,50)
      50  FORMAT(23H1A-ONE MUST NOT BE ZERO)
          STOP
      60  L = N + 1
          P = A(1)
          IF(N .EQ. 0)GO TO 80
          DO 70 I =2,1
      70  P = P * X + A(I)
C         PRINT VALUE OF POLYNOMIAL
      80  WRITE(3,90) P
      90  FORMAT(4H1P =,F14.5)
          STOP
          END
```

REVIEW EXERCISES

6.23 Given a one-dimensional array A, write a FORTRAN program segment that will calculate the sum of every fourth element, beginning with the third element, and place it in SUM. Array A contains 35 values. Assume that the elements are in computer memory and that the array has been previously dimensioned.

6.24 What elements of A were used in the above program segment? List the subscripts that identify the elements.

6.25 Write a FORTRAN program that will read the 10 values of array K into computer memory, calculate the sum of the values, and print the sum.

Chapter 6 Advanced FORTRAN 158

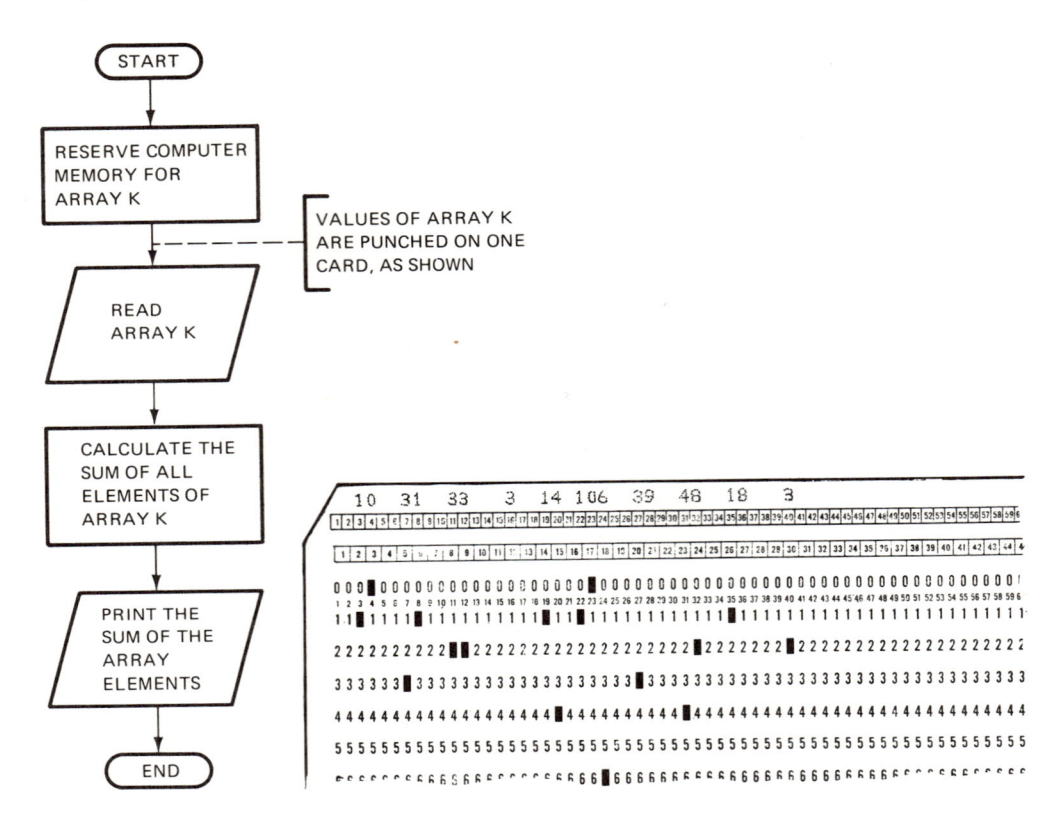

Exercise 6.25

6.26 Write a FORTRAN program to fill an array of 5 rows and 7 columns with the integers 1, 2, 3, ..., 35 by rows. Print the array.

6.27 Write a program to sum the numbers less than 200 that are divisible by 6. Use a DO statement in your program.

6.28 Draw a flowchart and write a FORTRAN program to read in a two-dimensional 10 by 10 array and determine the largest diagonal element. Then determine the largest nondiagonal elements in the row and in the column that intersect at the previously determined position. Set up the input as you desire. Print out the positions and values of all three of the maxima determined.

6.7 SPECIFICATION STATEMENTS

Most implementations of FORTRAN include the six specification statements—DIMENSION, COMMON, EXTERNAL, EQUIVALENCE, Type, and DATA. The DIMENSION statement was discussed earlier; the Type and DATA statements are covered in this section. The other three specification statements, which are of more concern to the professional programmer, are not discussed in this book. The reader interested in learning about these statements should consult one of the books listed in the bibliography.

Type Statements

In Chapter 2 we stated that integer variable names began with I, J, K, L, M, or N, and floating-point or real variable names started with other letters. Type statements are used to override variables named implicitly, that is, by the conventional IJKLMN naming rule. There are several FORTRAN Type statements; however, only three will be considered in this book.

The INTEGER Type statement has the form

    INTEGER AREA,X,OMEGA,K

It will cause the variables AREA, X, and OMEGA to be treated as integer variables in a program. Of course, the variable K was already implicitly defined as an integer variable, and it was not necessary to include it in the Type statement.

The statement

    REAL a,b,c,d, . . .

may be used in a program to establish a real mode for the variables listed in the statement; $a, b, c, d, \ldots$ can represent array or variable names.

The statement

    REAL MAGIC,NUMBER,C,L

will cause the variables MAGIC, NUMBER, and L to be treated as real variables in the program. It was not necessary to include C in the statement since C is already implicitly defined as a real variable.

Before an explicitly defined variable name can be used in an executable FORTRAN statement, it previously must have been defined by a Type statement.

All variables and arrays that are to be of the logical mode must be defined in the list of a LOGICAL Type statement. This statement has the form

    LOGICAL a,b,c,d, . . .

where $a, b, c, d, \ldots$ are variable or array names. A logical variable can take on only the values .TRUE. and .FALSE..

DATA Statement

Two of the common ways to make numeric assignments in a program are to use an arithmetic statement or to read the data value into memory. Both of these assignments are made while the program is being executed. Another way is to assign data values to a variable at compilation time. In this way, the data values become part of the source program.

Chapter 6   Advanced FORTRAN

This method uses the DATA statement, which has the general form

DATA $L_1/d_1,d_2,d_3,\ldots,d_n/,\ldots,L_n/d_1,d_2,d_3,\ldots,d_n/$

where each L_i represents a list of variables that are to receive data values, and the d's are the actual data values to be assigned to items in the list. The list is similar to the input/output list described earlier. The data values must be enclosed between slash marks.

Either of the statements

DATA A/6.3/,B/34.9/
DATA A,B/6.3,34.9/

would assign 6.3 to the variable A and 34.9 to the variable B.

The statement

DATA K,A(3),SPEED/71,10.0,107.2/

would accomplish the same assignment as the arithmetic statements

K = 71
A(3) = 10.0
SPEED = 107.2

or the data card in Figure 6-8 being read by the statements

READ(2,20)K,A(3),SPEED
20 FORMAT (I2,2X,F4.1,2X,F5.1).

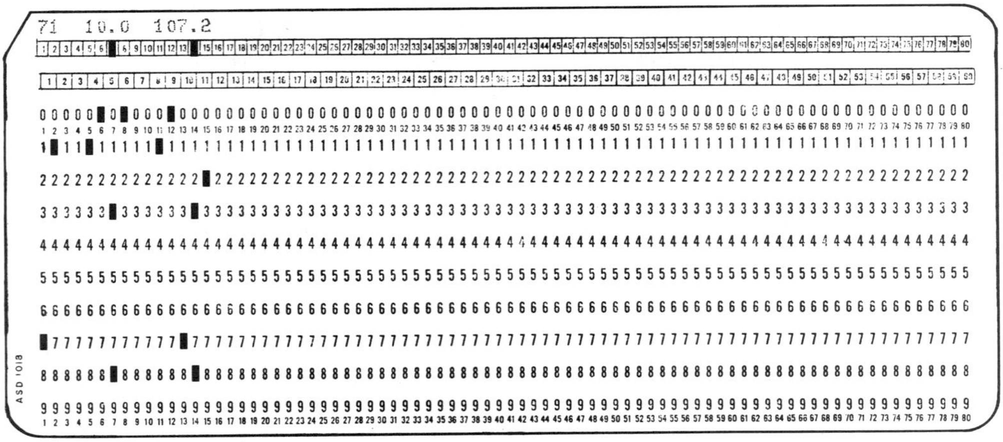

Figure 6-8.

Section 6.8 Subprograms

All elements in an array can, at the compiling stage, be set to zero by means of a DATA statement.

```
DIMENSION M(10,10)
DATA M /100 * 0/
```

Note that DATA statements are nonexecutable. Thus, a branch to the DATA statement, for example, cannot be made to reset arrays to zero. If, during program execution, certain arrays need to be set to zero, this must be achieved by way of a DO loop in the normal manner.

REVIEW EXERCISES

6.29 Write a Type statement to make the variables A, GAS, ORBIT, and PI of *integer* mode.

6.30 Write a Type statement to make the variables LAVA, NEON, MASS, and BORON of *real* mode.

6.31 The nine values of a 3 × 3 magic square are

8	1	6
3	5	7
4	9	2

Write a DATA statement that would assign these values to the nine elements of a two-dimensional array named M. The values of the magic square should be stored in the array in column order.

6.32 Write a DATA statement that could replace the following arithmetic statements.

```
I = 0
K = 7
ATOMIC = 36.4
```

6.8 SUBPROGRAMS

A routine is a series of instructions written to solve specific computations or program requirements. When these computations or requirements are used several times in the same program, it may simplify the programming task if they were written only once and then referenced in the program as many times as necessary. Each reference would accomplish the same task as though the instructions were written in that location of the program.

FORTRAN provides subprograms to avoid the necessity for multiple programming of similar routines. There are two classes of subprograms: subroutines and func-

Chapter 6   Advanced FORTRAN

tions. They are routines written once within the confines of the program and referenced as necessary from any point in the program.

In principles of operation, there are several degrees of similarity between subroutine and function subprograms. Each is a self-contained set of statements that will cause a specific computation to take place. The main difference between the functions and the subroutine is that functions always compute a single result, whereas a subroutine may compute more than one result.

Subroutines

A *subroutine* is a routine that performs some well-defined and often repeated operation. It is organized in such a way that it can be incorporated conveniently into a program. There are two types of subroutines: open and closed. An *open subroutine* is a set of statements inserted directly into the main stream of a program, simply becoming part of it. For example, if the open subroutine ROOT were to be used at four places in a program, the subroutine would be located at those four points in the program. If ROOT has consisted of 30 statements, the total number of statements required for this routine would be four times 30, or 120 statements. A *closed subroutine* is a set of statements that may be located physically outside the boundaries of the main program, but that are referenced at several places in the program.

Control must pass from the main program to the closed subroutine for the subroutine to perform its function. Such a coupling from the main program to the subroutine and back is sometimes called a *link*. If a main program referenced a closed subroutine, consisting of 30 statements, four times, the total number of statements required for the routine would consist of the 30 statements plus the statements necessary to send control and information to and from the closed subroutine four times.

Figure 6-9 illustrates the linkage between a main program and a closed subroutine. In this illustration, program control initially passes through MASS1, then goes to the subroutine, and after executing the statements in the subroutine, back to the main program at MASS2. Several other instructions in the main program would be executed before the second reference is made to the subroutine. Control would leave the main program at MASS3, go to the subroutine, and then back to MASS4. Several other main program instructions would be executed, and the process repeats at MASS5.

To create a subroutine, one needs only to enclose a set of statements between **SUBROUTINE** and **RETURN** statements and assign it a name. In other words, the general form of a subroutine is

```
SUBROUTINE    Name (argument, argument, ...)
    _____
    _____
    _____      } Subroutine Statements
    _____
    _____
RETURN
END
```

Section 6.8   Subprograms

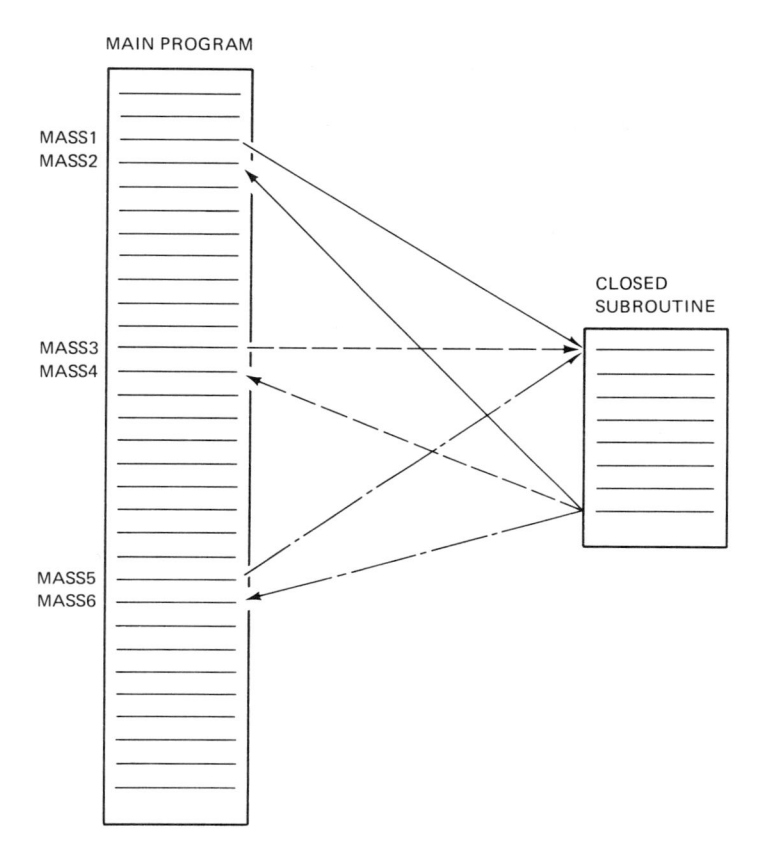

Figure 6-9 A closed subroutine being referenced from three locations in a main program.

where the SUBROUTINE statement is the first statement of the subroutine, *Name* is the name of the subroutine, and the *arguments*, if any, are nonsubscripted variable names or array names. The subroutine may use one or more of its arguments to return values to the main calling program. An argument used for this purpose must appear on the left side of an arithmetic statement or in the input list of an input statement within the subroutine. The arguments stated in the subroutine are *dummy* or formal *arguments* representing input and output variables.

The subroutine is terminated with a RETURN statement. This is the last statement in the subroutine that may be executed.

An example of a subroutine is shown below.

```
SUBROUTINE CALC(A, B, SUM, DIF)
SUM = A + B
DIF = A - B
RETURN
END
```

This subroutine finds the sum and difference of two real values. The name of the subroutine is CALC. The arguments are the real values to be used in the calculations, A and B, and the sum and difference, SUM and DIF. Notice that the first two arguments are used to send values to the subroutine and the other two arguments return data to the calling program. Within the subroutine, the sum and difference are calculated and assigned to the arguments. Then control returns to the calling program.

The RETURN statement is written as

> RETURN

and it signifies that program control is to be returned to the calling program. There may be more than one RETURN statement in a subprogram. For example, the subroutine illustrated below will exit at either statement 11, 21, or 31, depending upon the calculated value of X.

```
      SUBROUTINE CALX(A,B,D)
      X = A + B
      IF(X)10,20,30
   10 D = X - A
   11 RETURN
   20 D = X - B
   21 RETURN
   30 D = X + 30.0
   31 RETURN
      END
```

The proper manner for subroutine entry is via the subroutine CALL statement. The CALL statement has the form

> CALL *Name* (*argument, argument, . . .*)

Name is the symbolic name of the subroutine that is being called and the *arguments* are the *actual arguments* being supplied to the subroutine. The arguments to be used by the subroutine are enclosed within parentheses and may consist of any type of subscripted or unsubscripted variable, integer, or floating point constant, an arithmetic expression, or the name of a subprogram.

The CALL statement transfers control to the specified subroutine using the actual arguments in the subroutine calculations. When the calculations in the subroutine are finished, control is transferred to the statement following the CALL statement in the calling program. An example of a CALL statement is shown as follows:

```
   10 CALL SKILL(X,Y)
   11 ──────
```

The statement is calling a subroutine named SKILL, and there are two actual arguments. After the subroutine SKILL was executed, program control would be returned to statement number 11.

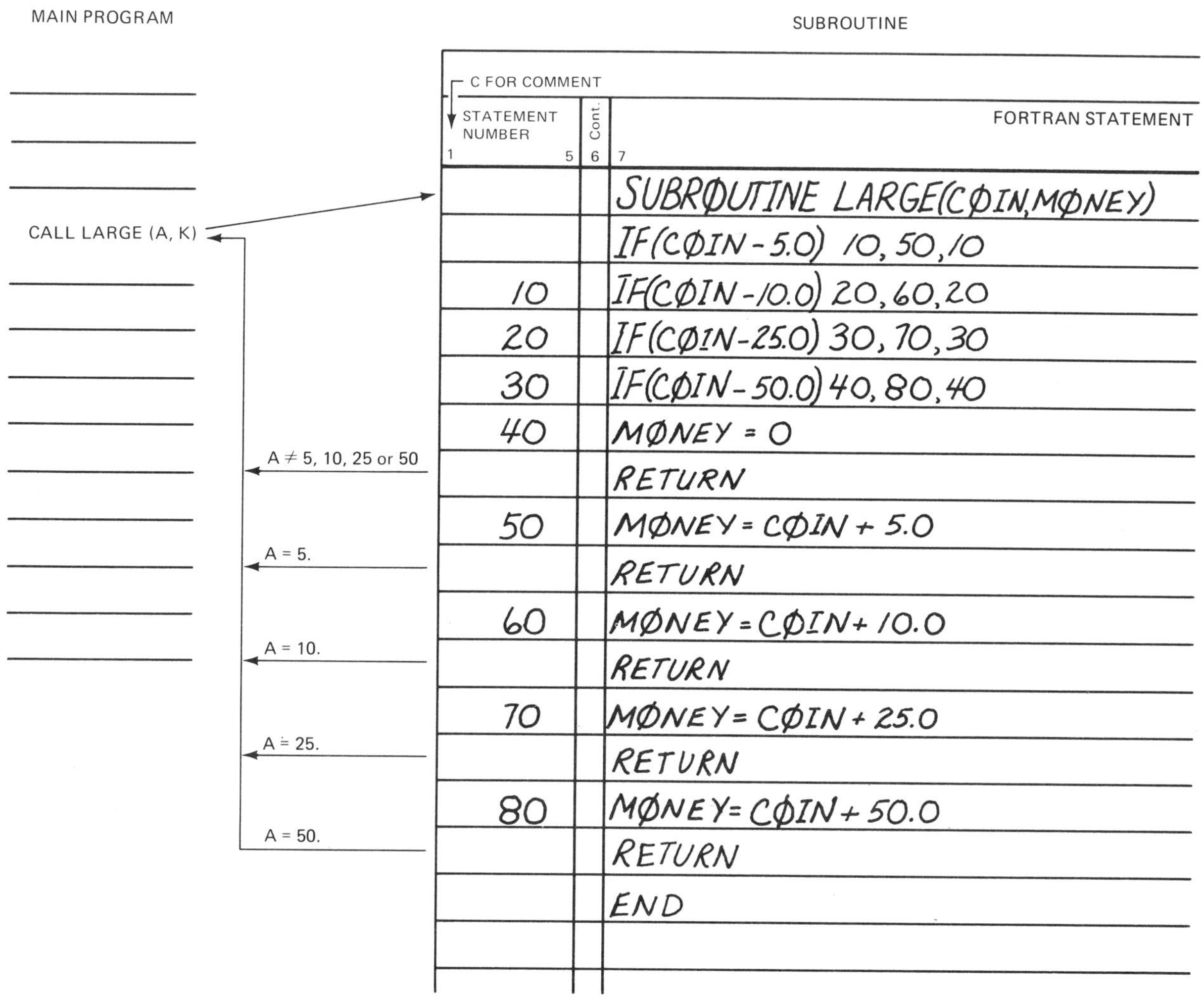

SUBROUTINE

STATEMENT NUMBER	Cont	FORTRAN STATEMENT
		SUBROUTINE LARGE(COIN,MONEY)
10		IF(COIN−5.0) 10,50,10
20		IF(COIN−10.0) 20,60,20
30		IF(COIN−25.0) 30,70,30
40		IF(COIN−50.0) 40,80,40
		MONEY = 0
		RETURN
50		MONEY = COIN + 5.0
		RETURN
60		MONEY = COIN + 10.0
		RETURN
70		MONEY = COIN + 25.0
		RETURN
80		MONEY = COIN + 50.0
		RETURN
		END

A ≠ 5, 10, 25 or 50
A = 5.
A = 10.
A = 25.
A = 50.

MAIN PROGRAM

CALL LARGE (A, K)

Figure 6-10 A main program reference to a subroutine.

Chapter 6   Advanced FORTRAN   166

An example of a main program and a subroutine is shown in Figure 6-10. In this example the subroutine LARGE is called on by the main program. The actual arguments (A and K) in the calling statement are used by the subroutine to compute a value. The dummy argument COIN is assigned the value of the actual argument A and the subroutine computes a value for the argument K by using the dummy argument MONEY. Control will be returned to the main program from one of the five subroutine exits. The choice of exit will depend upon the value of A. If A had a value of 5.0, the RETURN following statement 50 would be used; if A was equal to 10.0, the RETURN following statement 60 would be used, and so on. The example also illustrates that the arguments in a CALL statement must agree in number, type, and sequence with the corresponding arguments in the SUBROUTINE statement: that is, the arguments of the CALL statement, A and K, correspond with the dummy arguments, COIN and MONEY. If one of the arguments had been an array, the arguments also would have to agree in array size.

Functions

In mathematics, if a number—y, for example—depends upon another number—x, for example—in such a manner that when a value is assigned to x, a corresponding value of y is determined, then y is called a *function* of x. For example, in the equation

$$y = 3x^2 + 2x - 7$$

the value of y is determined for a given value of x. The assigned value of x is substituted in the above equation, and indicated operations are performed to find the corresponding value of y. This means that y is a function of x.

Often, when we wish to indicate that y is a function of x, we write

$$y = f(x)$$

This is read as *y equals a function of x*, and the parentheses does not imply f times x. When $f(x)$ is a given function, one may write, for example,

$$f(x) = 3x^2 + 4x - 2$$

If the number 3 was substituted for x, we would conveniently write $f(3)$. Thus, the above function would result as

$$f(3) = 3(3)^2 + 4(3) - 2 = 27 + 12 - 2 = 37$$

Likewise

$$f(2) = 3(2)^2 + 4(2) - 2 = 12 + 8 - 2 = 18$$
$$f(1) = 3(1)^2 + 4(1) - 2 = 3 + 4 - 2 = 5$$
$$f(0) = 3(0)^2 + 4(0) - 2 = 0 + 0 - 2 = -2$$
$$f(a) = 3(a)^2 + 4(a) - 2$$

Section 6.8 Subprograms

and
$$f(x + y) = 3(x + y)^2 + 4(x + y) - 2$$

The symbol $f(a)$ means that x is to be replaced by a in the defining expression of the function. Likewise, $f(x + y)$ means that $x + y$ is to be substituted for x in the equation.

In the expression
$$f(x) = x^2 + x + 4$$

$f(x)$ is a function and x is called an argument. Square Root (a) is a function called square root, whose argument is a. Tangent (x) is a function called tangent, whose argument is x. A function may have more than one argument. For example, Minimum (L, M) is a function that selects the smaller of a pair of arguments, that is, the smaller of two variables, L and M.

$$\text{Minimum } (2, 6) = 2$$
$$\text{Minimum } (2, 1) = 1$$

This function has two arguments.

A function in FORTRAN is very similar to a function in mathematics. A FORTRAN function is a relationship between a number of arguments, and its value depends upon the values assigned to the arguments of the function. A FORTRAN function will produce a single result using one or more arguments. Consider the function

$$f(x) = 5x^4 - 30x^2 - 6$$

The value of $f(x)$ will depend upon the value assigned to the argument of the function x. This function could be written in FORTRAN as

```
FUNC(X) = 5.0*X**4 - 30.0*X**2 - 6.0
```

and could be used in a FORTRAN statement as

```
TRICK = SILVER + FUNC(A)
```

The function FUNC(X) would compute a value by substituting an A for each X that appears in the expression. This value would be added to the variable SILVER to obtain a value for TRICK. The preceding statements are the same as writing the single statement

```
TRICK = SILVER + 5.0*A**4 - 30.0*A**2 - 6.0
```

There are three types of functions available in FORTRAN—library functions, arithmetic statement functions, and FUNCTION subprograms. Library functions were discussed in Chapter 2. Arithmetic statement functions and FUNCTION Subprograms are discussed in the following sections.

Arithmetic Statement Function

An arithmetic statement function is defined by a single arithmetic statement in the FORTRAN source program and applies only to the particular program or subprogram in which the definition appears. The arithmetic statement function has the general form

$$Name\ (argument_1, argument_2, \ldots, argument_n) = exp$$

where *Name* is the name of the function, *exp* is an arithmetic expression, and the *arguments* must be distinct, nonsubscripted variable names separated by commas. At least one argument must appear in the definition. The function *Name* may consist of up to five letters and digits, the first of which must be a letter. The type (real or integer) of a arithmetic statement function name is indicated in the same manner as variables. For example, the function

    CHESS (A,B,C) = A**2+B-C

uses the formal arguments A, B, and C in the expression $A^2 + B - C$. Upon execution of the statement function, the formal arguments are replaced by the actual arguments of the function reference. Thus, the actual arguments (B, E, and T) of the statement

    X = TEEKO + 37.0 + CHESS (B,E,T)

would replace the formal arguments of the arithmetic statement function CHESS. The preceding calculation of X is the same as would be accomplished by the statement

    X = TEEKO + 37.0 + B**2 + E - T

This example illustrates that the arguments of both the using statement and the arithmetic statement definition agree in order, number, and mode. Thus, the following arguments of a using statement

    A, K, ALPHA, STORM(2)

could correspond to the formal arguments

    B, LUCK, Q, SPEED

because they all agree in order, number, and mode. However, the actual arguments could not correspond to the following arrangement of formal arguments:

    MAX, VOLT, K

since they disagree in both number and mode.

The arithmetic expression *exp* on the right side of the *replaced by* symbol may contain references to previously defined arithmetic statement functions, library func-

Section 6.8   Subprograms

tions, or FUNCTION subprograms. For example, the arithmetic statement function.

$$RR(X,Y) = SQRT(X) + ABS(Y) + SQRT(304.0)$$

uses the SQRT and ABS library functions to calculate a value for the function RR.

The variable names used in the arithmetic statement function are dependent on the using program for their values. The following program illustrates this point.

```
C          ARITHMETIC FUNCTION ADD EXAMPLE
           ADD(X,Y,Z) = X + Y + Z + D
   5       READ(2,10) A,B,C,D
  10       FORMAT(4F10.3)
  15       SUM1 = 1.0 + ADD(A,B,C)
           WRITE(3,20) SUM1
  20       FORMAT(F10.0)
  25       READ(2,30) TI,TA,TØ
  30       FORMAT(3F10.0)
  35       SUM2 = 2.0 + ADD(TI,TA,TØ)
           WRITE(3,40) SUM2
  40       FORMAT(F10.2)
           STOP
           END
```

Statement 5 in the program reads into memory the values A, B, C, and D. Statement 15 calls on arithmetic statement function ADD to compute the sum of $A + B + C + D$. Note that only A, B, and C were specified as actual arguments. The function ADD uses the current value of D in the computation $A + B + C + D$ and again in the computation $TI + TA + TØ + D$ when statement 35 is executed.

All arithmetic statement functions of a given FORTRAN program must precede the first executable statement of the program.

As a last example of the arithmetic statement function, consider the problem of determining a root of the equation

$$4x^2 + 2x + 7 = 0$$

using the arithmetic statement function

$$ROOT(A,B,C) = (-B + SQRT(B**2 - 4.0*A*C))/(2.0*A)$$

The root may be found and stored in T by writing the statement

$$T = ROOT(4.0, 2.0, 7.0)$$

There are two serious restrictions placed upon the arithmetic statement function: 1) the definition is limited to *one* FORTRAN statement, and 2) the function can compute only *one* value. It will be seen in the next section that the FUNCTION subprogram provides additional capabilities and does not have one of the restrictions of the arithmetic statement function.

Chapter 6 Advanced FORTRAN

FUNCTION Subprograms

A FUNCTION subprogram is similar to the subroutine in that it may consist of many FORTRAN statements, and it is also similar to the arithmetic statement function in that it returns only one value to the calling program. The FUNCTION subprogram is used in situations where the particular function cannot be written in *one* arithmetic statement and only a single result is required. The function program may have several input arguments but only a single output value.

The general form of the FUNCTION subprogram is

FUNCTION *Name (argument$_1$, argument$_2$, ..., argument$_n$)*

where *Name* is the symbolic name of the function and the *arguments* must be non-subscripted variable names, or array names. There must be at least one argument in a FUNCTION subprogram. A FUNCTION subprogram begins with the FUNCTION declaration and returns control to the calling program by means of the RETURN statement. The name of the FUNCTION program must appear at least once between the FUNCTION and RETURN statements on the left side of an arithmetic statement or in an input list.

A FUNCTION subprogram is defined independently of the programs that call upon it. This means that variable names used within the FUNCTION subprogram assume values independent of the values assigned to them outside the FUNCTION subprogram. The FUNCTION subprogram *must* contain a RETURN statement that returns control to the calling program. The RETURN statement is the last executable statement in the subprogram; however, the last physical statement of a FUNCTION subprogram must be an END statement.

The arguments of the FUNCTION statement may be considered to be *formal arguments* of the subprogram. These arguments are replaced at the time of execution by the *actual arguments* included in the main program statement that is used to reference the subprogram. As was the case with subroutines, the actual arguments must agree in order, number, and mode to the formal arguments of the FUNCTION statement. Thus, the actual arguments of the following using statement

Y = A + B/C − L(A,Z,P,K)

agree in order, number, and mode to the formal arguments of the FUNCTION statement:

FUNCTION L(C,R,RED,M)

As an example of a FUNCTION subprogram, consider the subprogram in Figure 6-11, which computes the sum of the numbers from 1 to N. The variable N is used to represent the maximum number to be included in the sum. Thus, if N was 7, we would compute the sum of the numbers from 1 to 7.

1 + 2 + 3 + 4 + 5 + 6 + 7

Section 6.8   Subprograms

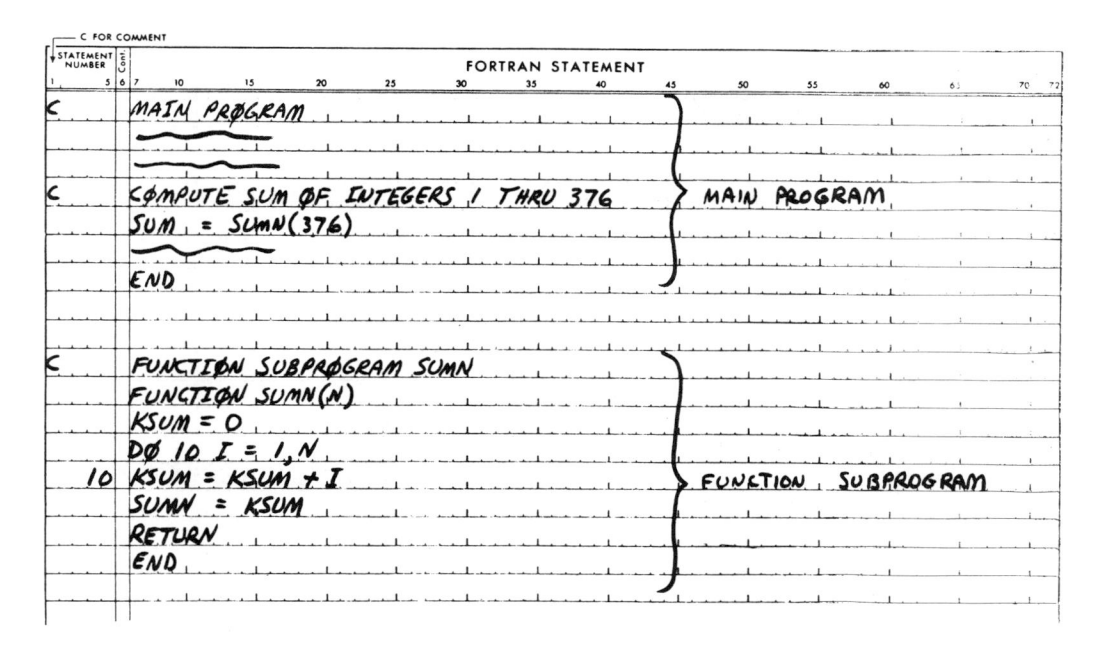

```
C  MAIN PROGRAM                    ⎫
                                    ⎬  MAIN PROGRAM
C  COMPUTE SUM OF INTEGERS 1 THRU 376
   SUM = SUMN(376)                  
   END                              ⎭


C  FUNCTION SUBPROGRAM SUMN        ⎫
   FUNCTION SUMN(N)                 
   KSUM = 0                         
   DO 10 I = 1,N                    ⎬  FUNCTION SUBPROGRAM
10 KSUM = KSUM + I                  
   SUMN = KSUM                      
   RETURN                           
   END                              ⎭
```

Figure 6-11 A main program/FUNCTION subprogram example.

If N was 134, we would compute the sum of the following numbers:

$$1 + 2 + 3 + 4 + 5 + \ldots + 131 + 132 + 133 + 134$$

The variable N is used as a formal argument in the subprogram.

The example in Figure 6-12 illustrates a FUNCTION subprogram with two RETURN statements. The subprogram name is COIN and it has three formal arguments, A, B and C. The subprogram will compute one of the following values:

$$COIN = D + E - F$$

or

$$COIN = D + E + D/F + E/F$$

depending upon the values of D and E of the main program. The subprogram will return control to the main program using the RETURN at statement 15 if D and E are not equal; otherwise, the RETURN at statement 25 is used, which means that D and E are equal values.

If a formal argument in the FUNCTION statement represents an array name, that array name must appear in a DIMENSION statement of the subprogram in which it occurs prior to any reference by an executable statement.

The last FUNCTION subprogram example is used to summarize the main requirements of a FUNCTION subprogram. The FUNCTION subprogram is referenced in the main program by using the subprogram name in an arithmetic statement. The

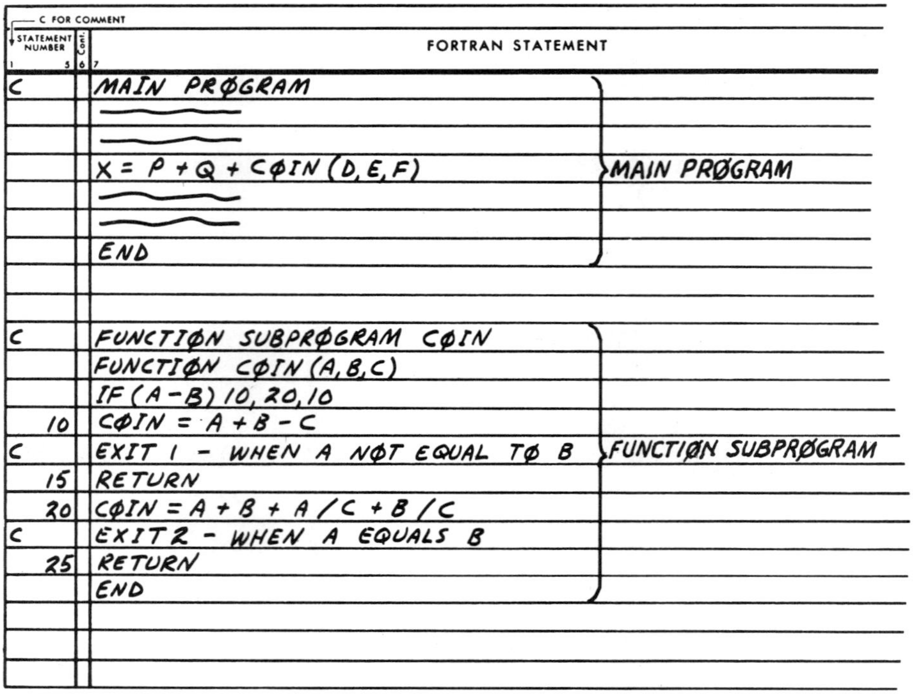

Chapter 6 Advanced FORTRAN

```
C       MAIN PROGRAM
                                                  ⎫
        X = P + Q + COIN(D,E,F)         MAIN PROGRAM
                                                  ⎭
        END


C       FUNCTION SUBPROGRAM COIN                  ⎫
        FUNCTION COIN(A,B,C)
        IF(A-B) 10,20,10
   10   COIN = A + B - C
C       EXIT 1 - WHEN A NOT EQUAL TO B    FUNCTION SUBPROGRAM
   15   RETURN
   20   COIN = A + B + A/C + B/C
C       EXIT 2 - WHEN A EQUALS B
   25   RETURN
        END                                       ⎭
```

Figure 6-12 A FUNCTION subprogram with two exits.

subprogram FORCE is referenced by the expression

$$\text{SOLVE} = A + B + \text{FORCE}(Y, H, G)$$

The function subprogram begins with a FUNCTION declaration and returns control to the main program by means of a RETURN statement. The subprogram FORCE is shown below.

```
C       FUNCTION SUBPROGRAM FORCE
        FUNCTION FORCE(X,R,B)
        BØ = X * 32.7
        FORCE = (BØ + B - 3.0 * R) / (4.0 * X)
        RETURN
        END
```

The subprogram FORCE appears in the subprogram on the left side of an arithmetic statement, the number, mode, and order of the arguments agree, the first statement of the subprogram is a FUNCTION statement, and the last executable statement in the subprogram is the RETURN statement. The last physical statement in the FUNCTION subprogram is the END statement.

Section 6.9   *Program Debugging Techniques*

The preceding use of a FUNCTION subprogram accomplishes the same calculation as would the statement

SOLVE = A + B + (Y * 32.7 + G - 3.0 * H) / (4.0 * Y)

REVIEW EXERCISES

6.33   Write a SUBROUTINE subprogram to compute the product of two matrices whose dimensions are specified in the call. Each element in the product is evaluated according to the formula

$$c_{ij} = \sum_{k=1}^{n} a_{ik} \cdot b_{kj}$$

6.34   The area of a triangle can be deduced from the formula

$$\text{AREA} = \frac{1}{4}\sqrt{(a+b+c)(-a+b+c)(a-b+c)(a+b-c)}$$

where *a*, *b*, and *c* are the lengths of the sides. Write an arithmetic statement function using this formula.

6.35   Write an arithmetic statement function to evaluate one root of a second degree equation, according to the fomula

$$x_1 = \frac{-b + \sqrt{a^2 - 4ac}}{2a}$$

It is assumed that $a \neq 0$.

6.36   Write a FUNCTION subprogram to evaluate cotangent *x* with the help of library functions for sine *x* and cosine *x*.

6.9 PROGRAM DEBUGGING TECHNIQUES

People accustomed to doing only tasks that do not require precision are in for a few surprises the first few times they try to code and run a computer program. Unfortunately, a computer is a totally obedient slave; it does *exactly* what you tell it to do—no more, no less. If you direct an IF statement to branch to a nonexistent location, the program will "blow up." If a subscript is negative, the program will "blow up." If you leave off a parentheses, the program will "blow up."

So many things can go wrong that, in practice, most people who write programs for computers find themselves spending a considerable amount of time debugging their programs. It sometimes is hard for one unfamiliar with programming to understand why a program does not work correctly the first time it is put on a computer. When a program is being prepared, it is possible to make mistakes at every step:

- The statement of the problem could be incorrect.
- The problem may be misunderstood by you.
- You could have analyzed the problem incorrectly.

- The problem could be incomplete.
- The flowchart may not incorporate all ideas of the problem.
- The flowchart could be incorrect.
- The flowchart may be interpreted incorrectly.
- You could make coding mistakes.
- The keypunch operator could produce mistakes.

Mistakes such as these will be minimized if good programming practices are used in the development of the program. Care must be taken when working in each area to minimize the chance for error. You must fully understand the original problem analysis. If you do not, the wrong problem may be coded. The flowchart must be carefully checked to see if it agrees with the program logic. Errors in problem analysis and flowcharts are of the rarest, but often the most serious, type. They are very easily overlooked. The coding should be checked, instruction by instruction, to see that it agrees with the flowchart. This is very tedious and time-consuming work, but many errors will be detected by this method.

Since programming mistakes can occur so frequently in the process of developing a computer program, it is important that you learn some of the techniques available to help you detect these mistakes. Many of the mistakes are obvious or easily detected; others are obscure and extremely hand to find. The use of a programming language such as FORTRAN tends to reduce programming mistakes, since many of the coding details are accomplished by the FORTRAN compiler.

Most of your mistakes may be classified as logical or clerical mistakes. A *logical mistake* is more likely to occur in the early stages of defining the problem, where problem understanding and determining a correct solution play an important part. Logical errors do not occur frequently, but they may be the most serious type when present. They tend to be overlooked and are often due to a misunderstanding of what the program is actually supposed to do.

Clerical mistakes are by far the most common type of mistakes found in computer programs. They usually result from *carelessness* and usually are relatively easy to find. Several clerical mistakes are listed below.

FORTRAN Statement	Mistake in Statement
Y = A + 3.76 + C	The variable C has not previously been assigned a value.
GO TO 200	Statement number 200 does not appear in the same program.
DO 30 A = 1, 10	Real variable used as an index.
Y = X + SQRT (A	Missing parentheses.
IF(X − 3.0), 10, 20, 30	Too many commas.
DIMINSION A(9,9)	Misspelling.
A = A12 + B36 + 21C	Incorrect variable name.
X − Y = 3.17 * Y * 2	Only one variable allowed on the left side of the *replaced by* symbol.

Section 6.9   *Program Debugging Techniques*   175

Another person who is familiar with the problem may be extremely helpful in early phases of program debugging. Since most errors occur from carelessness, the second person probably will not be blind to the same error. Talking over the analysis of a problem with another person is also an excellent way of detecting logical errors.

Knowing how to find mistakes in a program is as important as writing the program. A computer program is useless if it will not work or if it produces unpredictable results. One must expect to make mistakes and be able to find and correct them. Several steps that may help you to isolate mistakes in FORTRAN programs are presented in the next few sections.

Common Errors

It would be impossible to list every error that could be made in a FORTRAN program. Most of the errors would be of a specialized nature and would apply only to certain types of problems or computers. The following list covers some of the most common errors made in FORTRAN programs.

Logical errors

- Incorrect statement of problem.
- Misunderstanding of the problem.
- Choosing an incorrect solution to the problem.
- Not considering the entire problem.
- Incorrect flowchart of the problem.
- Incorrect interpretation of the flowchart.
- Transferring program control to an incorrect statement number.
- Interchanging the path of a flowchart decision box or FORTRAN IF statement.
- Not allowing for termination of a loop.

Clerical errors

- Misuse of FORTRAN operating symbols.
- Transferring program control to an incorrect statement number.
- DO range ending with a transfer of control statement.
- Omitting the decimal point in floating point constants.
- Not ending a FORTRAN program with an END statement.
- Omitting the comma between subscripts in a subscripted variable definition.
- Neglecting to DIMENSION an array.
- Omitting to initialize indexes.
- Use of an improper FORMAT statement for reading or printing data.
- Using an *OLD* program listing with a *NEW* program card deck.
- Omission of data cards.
- Data cards in incorrect order.

Chapter 6   Advanced FORTRAN

- Failure to DIMENSION the proper number of memory locations for an array.
- Omitting an operator symbol; for example, X * Y not XY.
- Using more than the allowed number of subscripts in a subscripted variable.
- Omitting the "C" in the COMMENT card.
- Nesting DO loops improperly.
- Not terminating the program.
- Two operating symbols appearing next to one another; for example, X * −Y instead of X * (−Y).
- Program is too large for the computer memory.
- Transfer into the range of a DO statement from outside its range.
- Interchange of individual cards of a source deck.
- Misuse of parentheses in an expression.
- Duplicate labels.
- Changing the indexes of a DO statement by an instruction within its range.
- Too many characters in a variable name.
- Variable name starting with a character other than a letter.
- Failure to discard old cards when inserting new correction cards in a source deck.
- Mode of the FORMAT field specification disagreeing with the associated variable in the input/output list.
- Not allowing for control of the printer paper when using the printer.
- Neglecting to enclose the arguments of a function in parentheses.
- Incorrect counting of a Hollerith FORMAT statement.
- Using a subscripted variable in a DO statement.
- Misspelling of key words; for example, SUBRUTINE instead of SUBROUTINE.
- Not including a RETURN statement in a subroutine or FUNCTION subprogram.
- Omitting commas and parentheses in FORTRAN statements.
- Placing commas in FORTRAN statements where they do not belong; for example, IF(X), 10,20,30.
- Referencing an undefined subprogram.

Most of these errors would be detected by the FORTRAN compiler, which is better at detecting clerical tasks than you are. This is why many students let the computer make the first debugging pass.

Visual Examination of the Coding Form

Before a program is keypunched into punched cards, it should be reviewed by its originator or, preferably, by another person familiar with what the program does. To have a program reviewed by the originator has the disadvantage that the originator may easily overlook a mistake by using the same reasoning he or she used when writing the program. Mistakes are more readily detected by another person because his or her point of view will be somewhat different than the originator's.

Section 6.9   *Program Debugging Techniques*   177

To minimize keypunching errors, the coding form should be examined for clarity. The letters of the alphabet should be written clearly in upper case.

Visual Examination of Source Program Cards

When cards are used as input medium, the statements from the FORTRAN coding sheet are punched on cards with a keypunch. As each character is punched in a card column, the character itself is printed near the top of the same column of the card. The cards can be used to verify the correctness of the punched cards and, occasionally, to reveal coding mistakes or keypunch operator mistakes. This method is not extremely useful if the program is large, but it often detects many mistakes in small programs. If the program is rather large, it is easier to use a printer listing of the punched cards rather than the cards themselves.

When it is determined that the punched source deck is a direct representation of the information on the FORTRAN coding form, the handwritten coding form should be thrown away. Old card decks also should be thrown away when new ones become available.

Visual Examination of the Program Listing

A visual examination of the source program deck is satisfactory for many small programs. However, for larger programs it is usually easier to examine a printer listing of the source cards. The printer listing should be compared to the coding form to determine if any mistakes occur. The listing should determine that all information was keypunched, that the order is correct, and that misleading handwritten characters were keypunched correctly. When it is determined that the printer listing is a representation of the handwritten coding form, the handwritten coding form should be destroyed.

FORTRAN Compiler Diagnostics

The time required to check out a program is in many cases far greater than the time needed to write the program. The removal of programming mistakes is an important and time-consuming task, which is commonly called *program debugging*.

The FORTRAN system eases the task of program debugging by 1) reducing the opportunity for clerical mistakes; 2) permitting the user to think in a language closer to what he or she is accustomed to rather than in a machine level computer language; 3) making address assignments, computer memory allocations, and input/output manipulations; and 4) providing an extensive selection of diagnostics.*

Diagnostic information is printed when the program is being compiled and will appear as part of the printer listing of the program. You should become familiar with the diagnostic messages produced by the computer that you use. They usually can be found in the systems FORTRAN REFERENCE MANUAL.

*A *diagnostic* is a comment that describes a program error.

Chapter 6   Advanced FORTRAN

Sample Calculations

To debug a program adequately, it is necessary to apply test data to the program. This data should be simple, and, if possible, hand calculations should be made to check the results. The hand calculations should employ the same general method of computation as is used by the program whenever feasible, so that intermediate results, as well as the final result, are available for examination.

Checking Large Programs in Segments

Large, complex programs are more easily checked out in smaller program segments. Each of the smaller segments should be free of errors before they are combined to form the total program. Once the first smaller segment has been debugged, another segment is attached, and both segments are debugged. Once these two segments are debugged, another segment is attached, and the three segments are debugged. This method of combining and debugging segments is used until the total program is debugged.

It is common practice for many users to let the computer find most of their key-punching and syntax errors. Although it is true that the compiler has an excellent capability of finding these errors and is much better and faster at finding them than you are, it is also expensive. This practice is commonly used in computing centers where the *turn around time** of their computer room is relatively fast or where low cost minicomputers are used. There are times, however, when one cannot afford this extra pass on the computer, and checking cards and printer listings for errors often is done prior to having the program compiled.

The Use of Remarks

Remarks may be printed at various points of program execution to provide supplementary information. The remark generating statement is generally placed at the conclusion of *key actions* of the program and should specify either that everything is all right or that something is wrong in the program. Typical remarks that may be printed are:

        VALUES DO NOT AGREE
        VALUE EXCEEDS LIMIT
        INPUT VALUE IN ERROR

Remark generating statements can be scattered freely throughout the program during the early stages of debugging a large FORTRAN program. After it is determined that the program is *error free*, the remark generating statements may be removed from the program. In FORTRAN, all that is required to produce a remark on the printer is a WRITE and FORMAT statement. Remarks are often of the informative

---

*The time required to process a job; time needed to compile and run a program and deliver the program results to the originator.

XYZ
PROGRAMMING
SCHOOL
"NOW ALL TOGETHER - SAY IT'S NOT THE PROGRAM'S FAULT"

type rather than being of a debugging nature. They are useful, however, to the person using the program and in many cases specify what the program actually does.

REVIEW EXERCISE

6.37 Willie Bigboy, the star halfback for the Midwest University football team, turned in the following **FORTRAN** program. Can you spot any mistakes in Willie's program? If you were Willie's teacher, what grade would you give the football star?

```
CCCCC    COMMENT - WILLIE'S PROGRAM
         DEMINSON A(10), B(30), C(15)
         FOOTBOLL = A(2,7)
         BASKETBALL = FOOTBOLL - √25
         HALFBK = SQUARE ROOT(R) * 20 *** 4
         IF(A(3) - 16) 10,30,10,20
   10    END
         A(4) = 10 ↑ 2
   20    STOP = 32.0 + 7
         GO TO A
         WRITE(6,30) A(7), FOOTBALL, 7
   30    FARMAT(I6,F36)
         A COMMENT - STOP COMPUTATION
   40    GO TO 10
   50    DO 20 R = 100,3
         STOP
```

6.10 A SUMMARY OF FORTRAN

The material on **FORTRAN** presented in this chapter and in Chapter 2 may be a little hard to follow. Therefore, it seems advisable at this point to summarize the more important features of the language.

FORTRAN, an acronym for **FOR**mula **TRAN**slation, is one of the most widely used programming languages for both scientific and business problems. Implementing **FORTRAN** requires, as do all other programming languages, a special translator

Section 6.10   *A Summary of FORTRAN*   181

program (called a *compiler*) written especially for each particular model of computer. The grammar, symbols, rules, and syntax used in FORTRAN are generally in common with easy-to-learn mathematical and English-language conventions, but the instructions must be explicit.

The computer user first analyzes the problem, designs an algorithm, and draws a flowchart. He or she then writes a FORTRAN program, generally on special coding forms. The program is first keypunched on cards and then executed and debugged on the computer, although on-line debugging* is often prohibited on many installations.

Variables and Constants

Variables are denoted by strings of letters and numbers in accordance with the following rules:

- The total number of characters in a FORTRAN variable may not exceed set limits, for example, 5, 6, or larger, depending upon which computer system you are using.
- Both capital letters and numbers may be used to form a variable name, but the first character must be a letter.
- The first letter of the name designating an integer variable must be I, J, K, L, M, or N (often called fixed-point variables).
- The first letter of the name designating a real (floating-point) variable may be any letter except those specifying integer, that is, A, B, . . . , or Z.

FORTRAN utilizes integer (fixed-point) and real (floating-point) numbers (constants).

- An integer constant is a positive or negative integer (-7 or 12).
- A real constant is one with a decimal point (for example, 36.0 or -100.72).

Mathematical Operations

The five basic operations provided by FORTRAN are

+	denotes	addition
−	denotes	subtraction
*	denotes	multiplication
/	denotes	division
**	denotes	raising to a power (exponentiation)

---

*On-line debugging means you are actually using the computer to help debug a program, contrasted with *off-line* debugging where you debug the program at some other location than on the computer system.

If there are no parentheses, the natural order of the operations within a FORTRAN statement is

- Raising to a power (**)
- Multiplication and division (* and /)
- Addition and subtraction (+ and −)

However, the natural order of the operations can be altered by inserting parentheses into FORTRAN statements.

An arithmetic expression is a properly formed sequence of variables, special symbols, constants, and functions operated on by arithmetic operators. For example, the mathematical expression $a + 26.3 - \sqrt{x}$ is expressed in FORTRAN as A + 26.3 − SQRT(X).

Expressions are evaluated using the following order of precedence:

First: operations within parentheses.
Second: exponentiation.
Third: multiplication and division.
Fourth: addition and subtraction.

The general form of the FORTRAN arithmetic statement is

$$V = e$$

where *e* represents the expression to be evaluated, the = (replaced by) symbol, and V is the variable that is set to the value of the expression. For example, the statement

$$X = 100.0 + SQRT(81.0)$$

would result in 109.0 being assigned to the variable X.

Program Control Statements

In general, FORTRAN commands are executed in normal sequence (the order in which they appear on the coding sheet or cards), but this order can be altered by the use of program control statements.

Unconditional transfers of program control are made possible by the GO TO statement. The statement

$$GO\ TO\ 200$$

will always transfer control to statement 200.

The Arithmetic IF statement transfers control on the condition of the happening of a certain event: IF (A − B)n_1, n_2, n_3. If the result of (A − B) is negative, control goes to statement n_1, if 0, to n_2, if positive, to n_3.

The general form of the Logical IF statement is

IF(E)L

where E is a logical expression and L is any executable statement except another Logical IF statement or a DO statement. For example, if you write the statement

IF(A .AND. B) GO TO 30

and both logical variables A and B are *true*, program control will be transferred to statement 30; otherwise program control continues with the statement following the Logical IF statement.

The following operators may be used in logical expressions:

Operator	Definition
.AND.	Logical *and* ($\vee$)
.OR.	Logical *or* ($\wedge$)
.NOT.	Logical not ($\bar{A}$)
.GT.	Greater than (>)
.LT.	Less than (<)
.EQ.	Equal to (=)
.NE.	Not equal to ($\neq$)
.GE.	Greater than or equal to ($\geq$)
.LE.	Less than or equal to ($\leq$)

These operators are always preceded and followed by a period.

IF statements allow the computer to make decisions as computation progresses; they also can be used to form loops of repeated calculations. This is accomplished by purposely transferring program control back to a previously executed program. Loops also can be set up by using the DO statement.

The DO statement makes it possible to repeat the same operation, changing only the variable. The general form of this statement is

DO *sn* i = m_1, m_2, m_3

where *sn* is a statement number, *i* is a nonsubscripted integer variable, and $m_1, m_2,$ and m_3 are each either unsigned integer constants or nonsubscripted integer variables. If m_3 is not stated, m_3 is understood to be 1. The DO statement directs the computer to execute repeatedly the statements that follow, up to and including the statement with the statement number *sn*. For the first iteration, the statements are executed with $i = m_1$. In each succeeding repetition, *i* is increased by the amount m_3. After the statements have been executed with *i* equal to the highest of the sequence of values that do not exceed m_2, program control passes to the statement following the statement *sn*. For example, the statement

DO 100 K = 1,5

Chapter 6   Advanced FORTRAN

informs the computer to execute all the commands up to and including statement 100, five times. The value of K is increased by 1 each time statement 100 is reached. The variable K usually appears within the loop as a working variable but this is not necessary.

Input-Output Statements

Data inputs can be introduced either *directly* by using an arithmetic statement such as

$$R = 326.0$$

or *indirectly* by using a pair of commands of the form

```
       READ(2,10)X,K
 10    FORMAT(F5.2,I3)
```

together with a set of data cards that are placed on the back of the source program deck as in Figure 6-13.

Another way to make numeric assignments in a program is to use the DATA statement. For example, the statement

```
DATA A,X,MASS/23.0,10.7,47/
```

would accomplish the same assignment as the arithmetic statements

```
A = 23.0
X = 10.7
MASS = 47
```

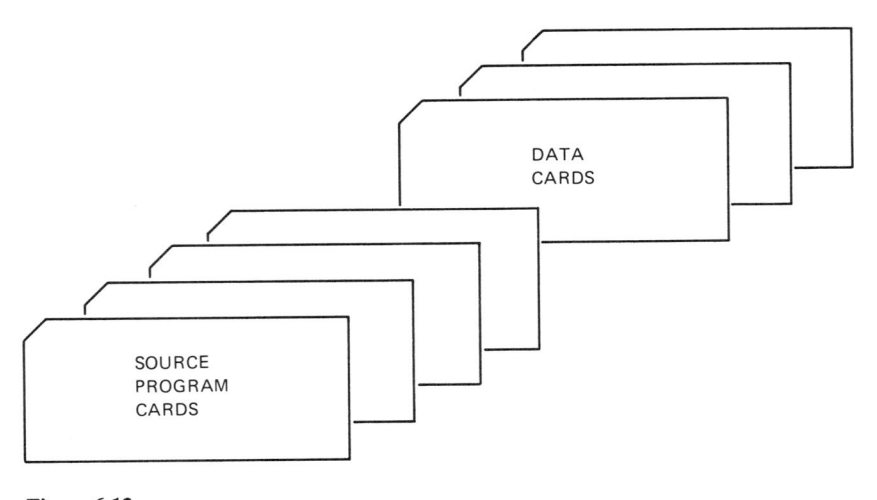

Figure 6-13.

Section 6.10   *A Summary of FORTRAN*

Assignments made by using the DATA statement are made at program compilation time rather than at program execution time.

WRITE statements are used to command the computer to print out its computed values. The statements

```
          WRITE(3,200)
200       FORMAT(26HCOMPUTERS ARE FOR EVERYONE)
```

for example, will cause the message

```
COMPUTERS ARE FOR EVERYONE
```

to be printed, whereas the pair

```
          WRITE(3,4000) ICE
4000      FORMAT(I7)
```

will print out the value of ICE in integer form.

The FORMAT statement, which must have a statement number, describes

- One punched card
- The specification of mode for each variable on the input-output list.
    1. I is used for Integer mode variables.
    2. F is used for Real variables punched in literal notation.
    3. E is used for Real variables punched in exponential notation.
    4. X is used to skip columns.
    5. H is used to describe Hollerith fields.
    6. The slash (/) is used to skip records (cards or printed lines).

Miscellaneous Statements

The STOP statement is used to halt the computation and return control back to the computer's operating system.

The END statement signals the FORTRAN compiler that it has reached the last statement in a program. The END *must* be the last statement in a FORTRAN program.

The CONTINUE statement does not cause any computer operation. The main purpose of a CONTINUE statement is to provide a convenient location for a statement number.

The INTEGER and REAL Type statements are used to override variables named implicitly, that is, by the conventional IJKLMN naming rule.

A statement such as

```
INTEGER A,X,Z
```

will cause the variables A, X, and Z to be treated as integer variables in a program. Likewise, the statement

Chapter 6   Advanced FORTRAN

REAL N,LOVE

will cause the variables N and LOVE to be treated as real variables in the program.

All variables and arrays that are to be of the logical mode must be defined in the list of LOGICAL Type statements. A logical variable can take on only the values .TRUE. and .FALSE..

Library Functions

Built-in library functions are of the utmost importance to computer users because they allow access to a set of useful elementary mathematical functions, such as square root, sines, cosines, logarithms, and exponentials. The following are examples.

Functions	Written As
$\sin x$	SIN(X)
$\cos x$	COS(X)
$\sqrt{x}$	SQRT(X)
$\|x\|$	ABS(X)
e^x	EXP(X)
$\ln x$	ALOG(X)
$\text{arctg } x$	ATAN(X)

Arrays and Subscripted Variables

Arrays and subscripted variables allow you to represent a number of variables with one name.

- Individual subscripted variables are called elements.
- The entire set of subscripted variables is called an array.
- Integer and Real elements cannot be mixed in an array.
- There are a number of rules for using subscripted variables.
    1. You must inform the computer which variables are subscripted.
    2. How many elements there are in each array.
    3. How many subscripts there are for each subscripted variable.
    4. Subscripts must be in integer mode or type.

Subscripted variables can represent any element of a one dimensional array (that is SPEED(K)) or any element of a two-dimensional array (that is SPEED(I, N)). The variable is still a FORTRAN variable of integer or real mode, depending upon its first letter. Every subscripted variable that appears in a program must also be listed in a DIMENSION statement. For example, the statement

Section 6.11   More FORTRAN

DIMENSION MASS(20,40)

causes the FORTRAN system to allocate computer storage for an array named MASS of 20 rows and 40 columns, or 800 elements. Several subscripted variables can be dimensioned in one DIMENSION statement. For example, the statement

DIMENSION TIC(60), TAC(40), TOE(30,50)

causes the FORTRAN system to set aside computer storage for a 60-element, one-dimensional array (TIC), a 40-element, one-dimensional array (TAC), and a 30 by 50 two-dimensional array (TOE).

6.11 MORE FORTRAN?

The material in Chapter 2 and in this chapter is not intended to represent a complete study of FORTRAN. It is rather a compilation of tidbits and scraps. If the sampling produced some interest, you are strongly advised to study any one of the numerous books devoted exclusively to an in-depth study of the FORTRAN language. Several excellent FORTRAN books are listed in the bibliography.

Chapter 7

Law enforcement agencies throughout the country use computers to help them fight crime. Computer systems hold records on such things as stolen cars, missing persons, wanted fugitives. (Courtesy *Sperry Rand Corp., Univac Division*)

Twelve Interesting FORTRAN Programs

The problems contained in this chapter again will serve as bridges between theory and practice. After having studied advanced FORTRAN programming features, it will be helpful to see them applied in the solution of several problems. Although most of the problems in this chapter are new, a few of them were discussed in Chapter 5.

Now we will see how we can improve on our programming techniques by utilizing advanced FORTRAN capabilities. Hence we also will be able to demonstrate that there is no single programming technique for the solution of a specific problem. Of course, some techniques are better than others and lend themselves more easily to a given problem. Usually, it is up to your imagination and abilities to utilize a specific set of FORTRAN statements for the solution of a given problem.

The sample problems in this chapter are intended to be read in the order presented, and each should increase the reader's understanding of problem solving. The problems are small and elementary, and, hopefully, the reader will have no trouble understanding them. A person just learning to write programs in FORTRAN should work with problems of this size until he or she feels confident that larger problems would not be too confusing. The FORTRAN programs are written in a straightforward manner and contain many comment statements, which should aid the reader in understanding the program.

7.1 MICHAEL'S DOG

The interest problem discussed in Chapter 5 can be rewritten incorporating the DO statement, which was presented in the last chapter. The following program illustrates how a DO loop greatly simplifies the coding task.

```
      C        MICHAEL'S DOG
               P = 200.0
               DO 10 N = 1,5
               P = P+ 0.12 * P
           10  CONTINUE
               WRITE(3,20)P
           20  FORMAT(4H P =,F14.3)
               STOP
               END
```

The program uses a CONTINUE statement to provide a reference point in the program to complete the loop.

7.2 THE MANHATTAN ISLAND PROBLEM

In Chapter 5 we discussed the Manhatten Island investment problem. Now we will solve this problem again, but this time by replacing the IF loop with a DO loop.

```
      C        THE MANHATTAN ISLAND PROBLEM
               PRI = 24.0
               RATE = .06
               DO 10 K = 1627,1976
           10  PRI = PRI + PRI * RATE
               WRITE(3,20)PRI
           20  FORMAT(30H PRESENT VALUE OF INVESTMENT =,F15.2)
               STOP
               END
```

The first statement is a comment statement. The next two statements assign the values 24 and .06 to the principal (PRI) and the interest rate (RATE), respectively. The DO statement will cause Statement 10 to be executed 350 times. After the loop is completed (that is, the number of iterations specified in the DO statement has been specified), the resulting principal (PRI) is printed.

7.3 FIREBALL WILLIAMS' AUTO RACES

This time Fireball Williams uses a DO statement in his program to compute the mean, the variance, and the standard deviation of last year's car races. The program also stores the 17 data input values in a one-dimensional array named X. The elements of

Section 7.5   Karl Gauss's Calculation

this array are X(1), X(2), X(3), ... X(17). Fireball's program is as follows:

```
C       FIREBALL WILLIAMS' AUTO RACES
C       COMPUTES THE MEAN, VARIANCE, AND SD. DEV.
        DIMENSION X(17)
        SUM = 0.0
        SUMSQ = 0.0
C       READ 17 VALUES OF X
        DO 20 N = 1,17
        READ(2,10)X(N)
   10   FORMAT(F5.0)
        SUMX = SUMX + X(N)
        SUMSQ = SUMSQ + X(N) * X(N)
   20   CONTINUE
C       COMPUTE THE MEAN
        XBAR = SUMX / 17.0
C       COMPUTE VARIANCE
        VAR = (SUMSQ-(SUMX**2/17.0))/(17.0 - 1.0)
C       COMPUTE STANDARD DEVIATION
        STDEV = SQRT(VAR)
C       PRINT STANDARD DEVIATION, VARIANCE, AND MEAN
        WRITE(3,30)STDEV,VAR,XBAR
   30   FORMAT(22H FIREBALL'S CAR SPEEDS,/,21H NUMBER OF RACES = 17,/,21H
       2STANDARD DEVIATION =,F16.4,/,11H VARIANCE =,F16.4,/,7H MEAN =,
       3F16.4)
        STOP
        END
```

7.4 CLASS ASSIGNMENT

Bob Wilson and Tom Fiddler attend the University. In one of their mathematics classes, the instructor gave them the following assignment: Write a FORTRAN program to calculate the sum of the squares of the first 200 positive integers. Bob's and Tom's programs are shown in Figure 7-1. Either program will cause the computer to sum the squares of the integers 1, 2, 3, ... , 200. In Bob's program, the IF statement recycles the computation until it equals 200. The DO loop in Tom's program accomplishes the same objective in a more compact manner. How would you have written this program?

7.5 KARL GAUSS'S CALCULATION

The following FORTRAN program computes the sum of the first 200 positive integers (1, 2, 3, ... , 200).

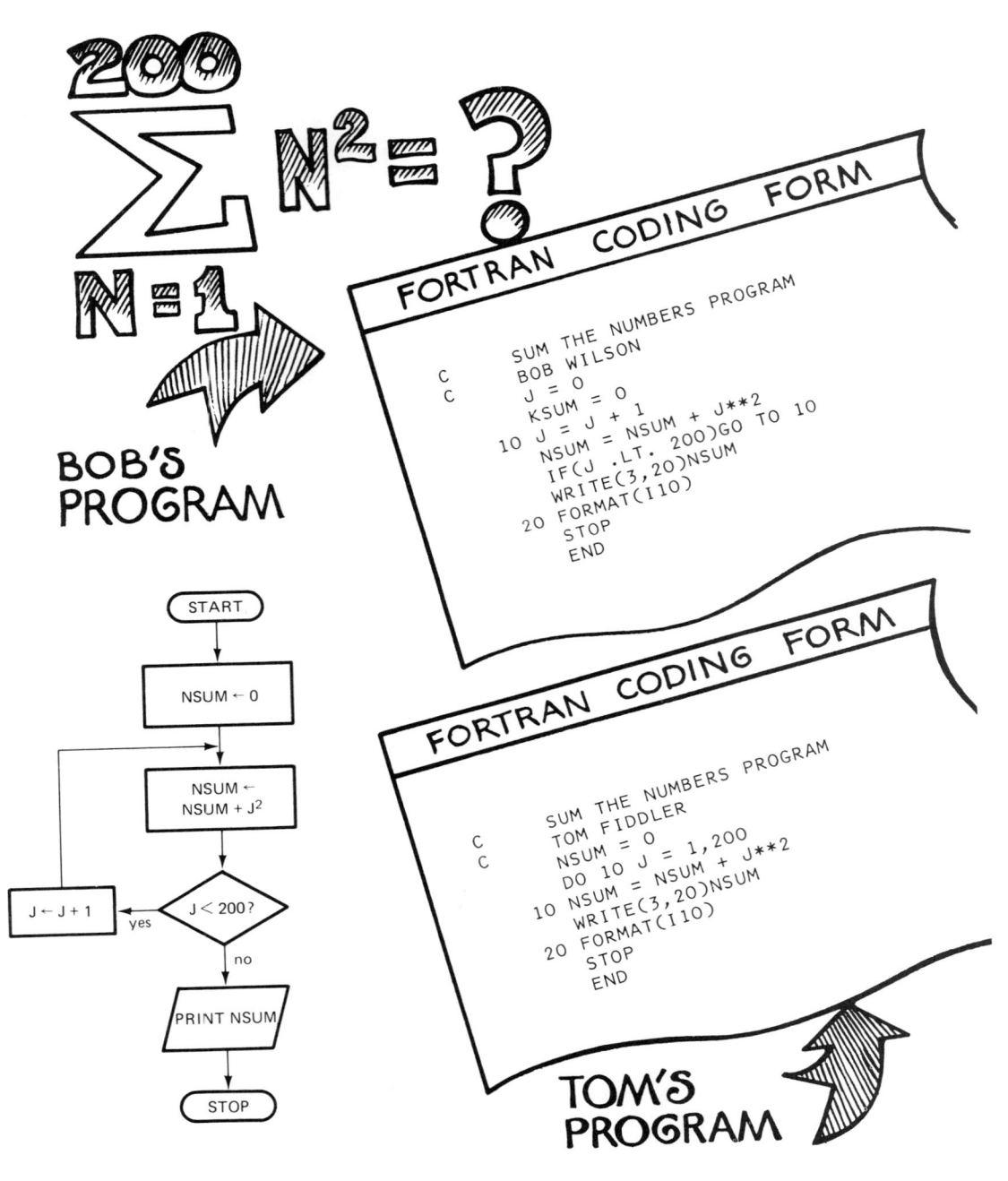

Figure 7-1 The sum of the squares of the first 200 positive integers can be calculated by using either of these two FORTRAN programs.

Section 7.5   Karl Gauss's Calculation

```
C        SUM OF THE FIRST 200 INTEGERS
         NUSUM = 0
         DO 10 K = 1,200
10       NUSUM = NUSUM + K
         WRITE(3,20) NUSUM
20       FORMAT(I5)
         STOP
         END
```

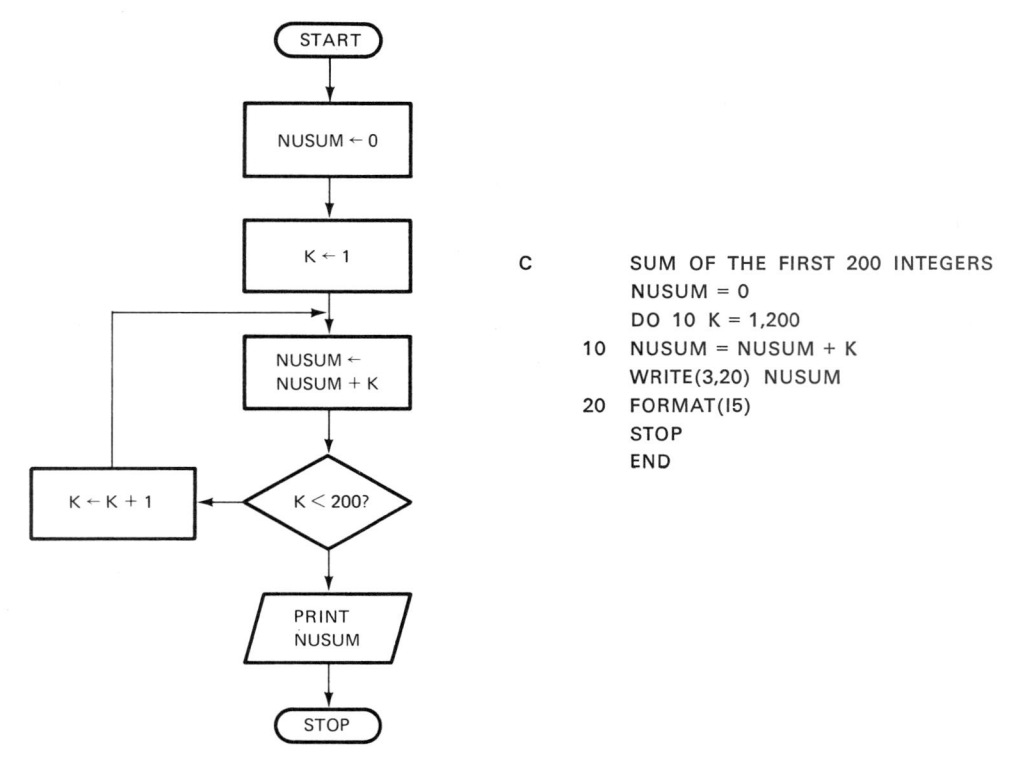

Figure 7-2.

Karl Friedrich Gauss, a German mathematician and astronomer, was able to solve this problem in just a few seconds. He paired off the numbers like this

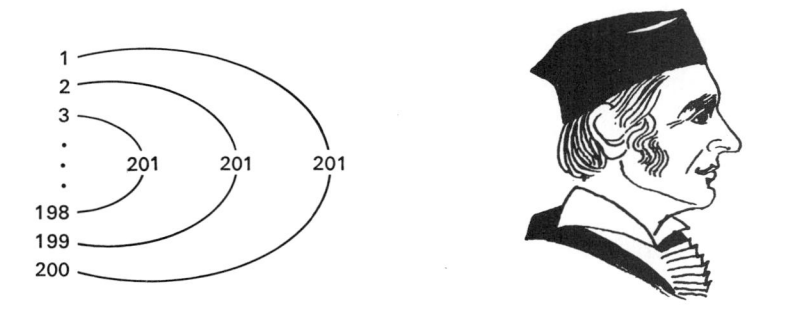

knowing that there would be 100 such pairs, each of whose sum was 201. Thus, the sum of the first 200 positive integers would be $100 \times 201 = 20100$!

Was Karl right? The following program computes the problem two ways—once the way previously shown and once the way Karl Gauss solved the problem.

Chapter 7   Twelve Interesting FORTRAN Programs   194

```
      C        SUM OF THE FIRST 200 INTEGERS
               NSUM = 0
               DO 10 K = 1,200
      10       NSUM = NSUM + K
      C        KARL GAUSS METHOD
               KGSUM = 100 * 201
               WRITE(3,20)NSUM,KGSUM
      20       FORMAT(22H SUM OF 200 INTEGERS =,I5,/,17H KARL GAUSS SUM =,I5)
               STOP
               END
```

If Karl Gauss was right, the variables NSUM and KGSUM should both equal 20100. Does Gauss's computational method work?

7.6 PERMUTATIONS

A *permutation* is an arrangement or a sequence of a set of objects. For example, there are six permutations of the letters A, B, and C. They are ABC, ACB, BAC, BCA, CAB, and CBA.

There are 24 permutations of the letters A, B, C, and D. They are as follows:

ABCD	BACD	CABD	DABC
ABDC	BADC	CADB	DACB
ACBD	BCAD	CBAD	DBAC
ACDB	BCDA	CBDA	DBCA
ADBC	BDAC	CDAB	DCAB
ADCB	BDCA	CDBA	DCBA

If there were 14 letters, there would be 87, 178, 291, 200 different ways of arranging the letters. How was this large number determined? One way is to use the fundamental counting principle. If we apply it to the case of 4 letters, each position of a letter can be represented by a box ☐☐☐☐. There are 4 ways of filling the first position, since any one of the letters can be placed there. Then there are 3 ways left to fill the second position, 2 ways to fill the third, and only 1 way left for the fourth: $\boxed{4\ 3\ 2\ 1}$. The number of arrangements for 4 letters is $4 \times 3 \times 2 \times 1 = 24$. For 14 letters, there are

$$14 \times 13 \times 12 \times 11 \times 10 \times 9 \times 8 \times 7 \times 6 \times 5 \times 4 \times 3 \times 2 \times 1$$
$$= 87, 178, 291, 200 \text{ different arrangements.}$$

A short way to write each of these products is to use a special mathematical symbol,

Section 7.6 Permutations

called a *factorial* symbol (!); $4 \times 3 \times 2 \times 1$ can be written as 4! (read as "four factorial").

$$14! = 14 \times 13 \times 12 \times 11 \times 10 \times 9 \times 8 \times 7 \times 6 \times 5 \times 4 \times 3 \times 2 \times 1$$

In general, the number of permutations of n objects is

$$n(n-1)(n-2) \ldots 3 \cdot 2 \cdot 1$$

or, written in factorial form, as

$$n! = n \ldots 4 \cdot 3 \cdot 2 \cdot 1$$

With this notation we can write the formula for the number of permutations of n objects:

$$_nP_n = n!$$

where the notation on the left means "the number of permutations of n objects taken n at a time." For example, the number of permutations of the letters COMPUTER is

$$_8P_8 = 8! = 8 \cdot 7 \cdot 6 \cdot 5 \cdot 4 \cdot 3 \cdot 2 \cdot 1 = 40,320$$

Now let us discuss a formula for the number of permutations of n objects taken r at a time. As an example, consider a certain club of 10 boys and 12 girls. They wish to elect officers in such a way that the president and treasurer are boys and the vice-president and secretary are girls. In how many ways can this be done? The number of different ways of selecting the president and treasurer is $_{10}P_2$. The number of ways of selecting the vice-president and secretary is $_{12}P_2$. The total number of ways of choosing officers is

$$_{10}P_2 \times {}_{12}P_2 = (10 \times 9) \times (12 \times 11) = 11,880$$

In general, the formula

$$_nP_r = \frac{n!}{(n-r)!}$$

gives the number of different ways of arranging r elements selected from a set of n elements; that is, the permutation of n things taken r at a time. The previous formula can be rewritten as:

$$_nP_r = n(n-1)(n-2)(n-3) \ldots (n-r+1)$$

which is a computational algorithm for $_nP_r$. The FORTRAN program shown in Figure 7-3 computes the number of permutations of n things taken r at a time using the latter

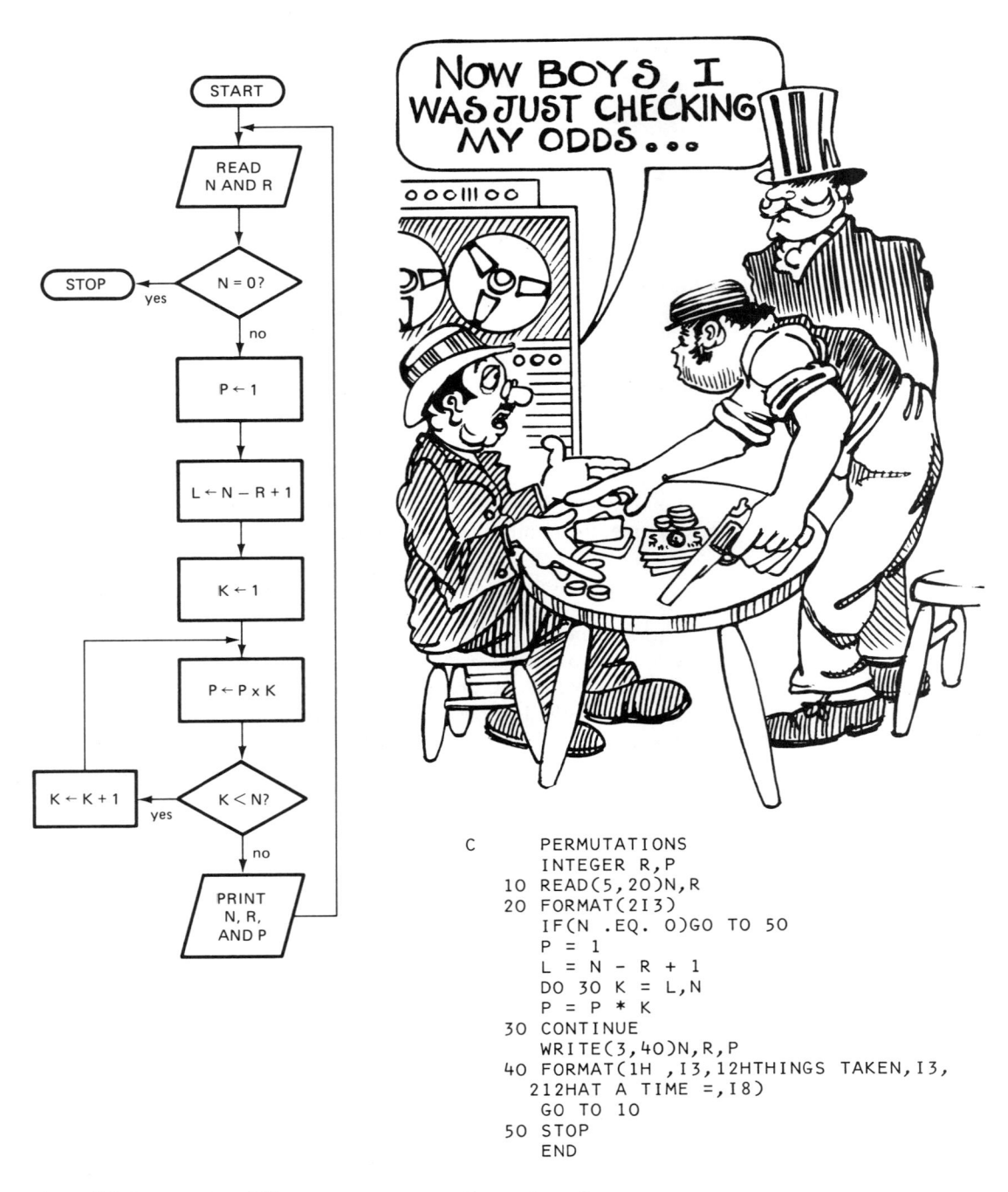

```
C       PERMUTATIONS
        INTEGER R,P
10      READ(5,20)N,R
20      FORMAT(2I3)
        IF(N .EQ. 0)GO TO 50
        P = 1
        L = N - R + 1
        DO 30 K = L,N
        P = P * K
30      CONTINUE
        WRITE(3,40)N,R,P
40      FORMAT(1H ,I3,12HTHINGS TAKEN,I3,
       2 12HAT A TIME =,I8)
        GO TO 10
50      STOP
        END
```

Figure 7-3 *Permutations.* This program computes the number of permutations of N things taken R at a time.

Section 7.7   Who Was Right?

formula. The program reads the following data cards

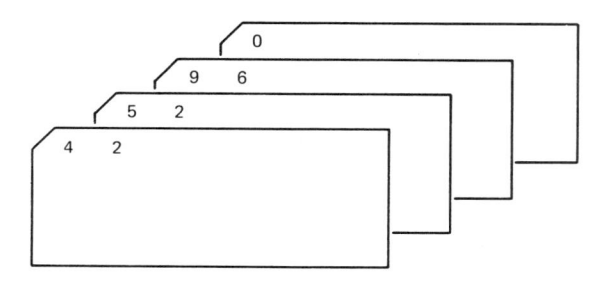

and produces the following printed output:

```
4 THINGS TAKEN 2 AT A TIME = 12
5 THINGS TAKEN 2 AT A TIME = 20
9 THINGS TAKEN 6 AT A TIME = 60,480
```

Note that the INTEGER Type statement was used to establish R and P in integer mode so that all computations could be performed in integer arithmetic.

7.7 WHO WAS RIGHT?

Marvin Smart said that the sum of the even positive integers less than or equal to 1,000 was 250,500. His barber, who spends his spare time studying number theory, said that the sum equals 249,500.

To settle the problem, each wrote a short FORTRAN program to prove his point. Marvin wrote the program at the top in Figure 7-4. His barber wrote the FORTRAN program at the bottom of Figure 7-4. Marvin's program printed the message

SUM OF EVEN INTEGERS = 250,500

Marvin's Program:

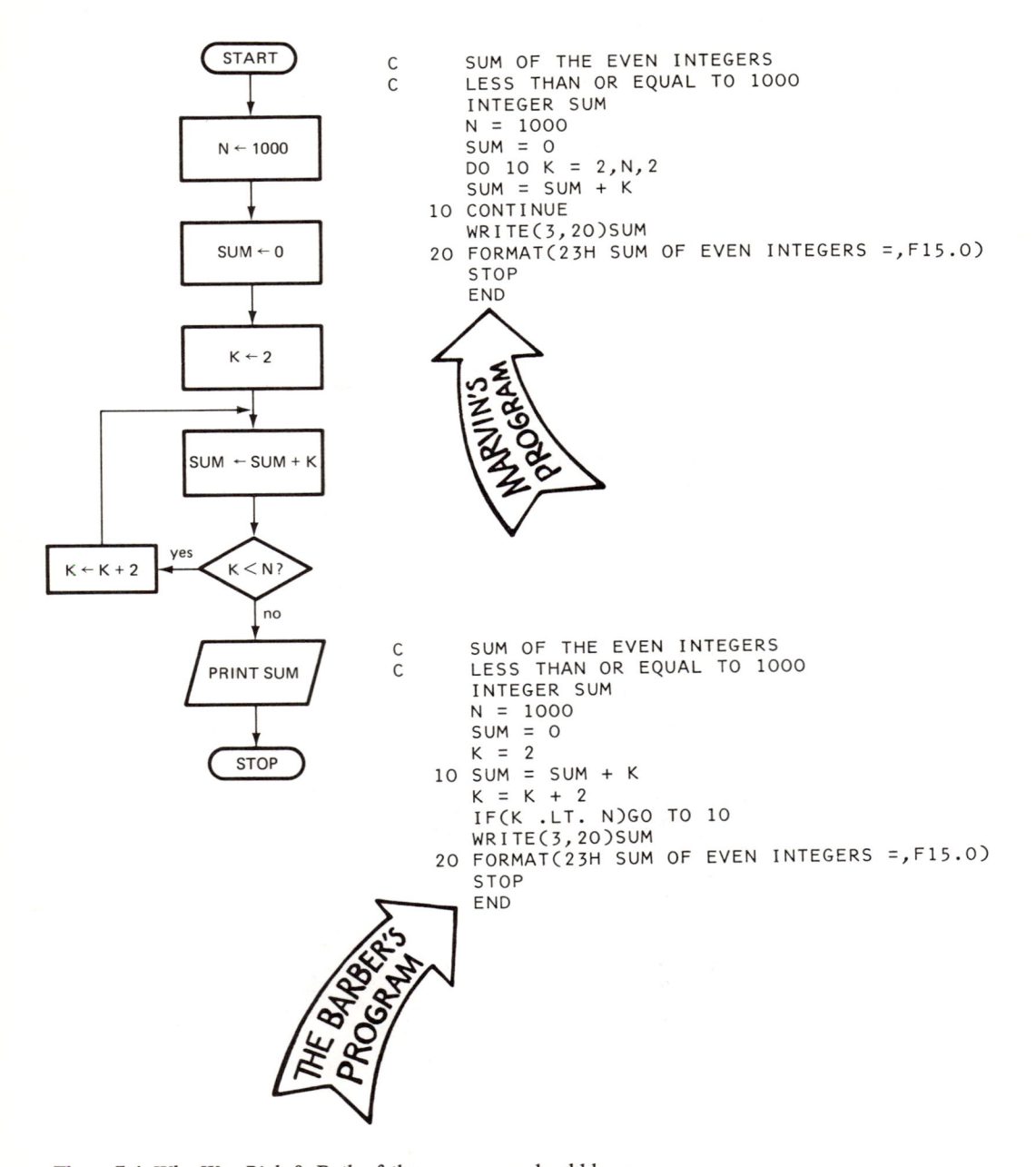

```
C     SUM OF THE EVEN INTEGERS
C     LESS THAN OR EQUAL TO 1000
      INTEGER SUM
      N = 1000
      SUM = 0
      DO 10 K = 2,N,2
      SUM = SUM + K
   10 CONTINUE
      WRITE(3,20)SUM
   20 FORMAT(23H SUM OF EVEN INTEGERS =,F15.0)
      STOP
      END
```

The Barber's Program:

```
C     SUM OF THE EVEN INTEGERS
C     LESS THAN OR EQUAL TO 1000
      INTEGER SUM
      N = 1000
      SUM = 0
      K = 2
   10 SUM = SUM + K
      K = K + 2
      IF(K .LT. N)GO TO 10
      WRITE(3,20)SUM
   20 FORMAT(23H SUM OF EVEN INTEGERS =,F15.0)
      STOP
      END
```

Figure 7-4 *Who Was Right?* Both of these programs should have determined the sum of the even positive integers less than or equal to 1000. However, one of the programs contains a mistake and gives an erroneous answer. Which one?

198

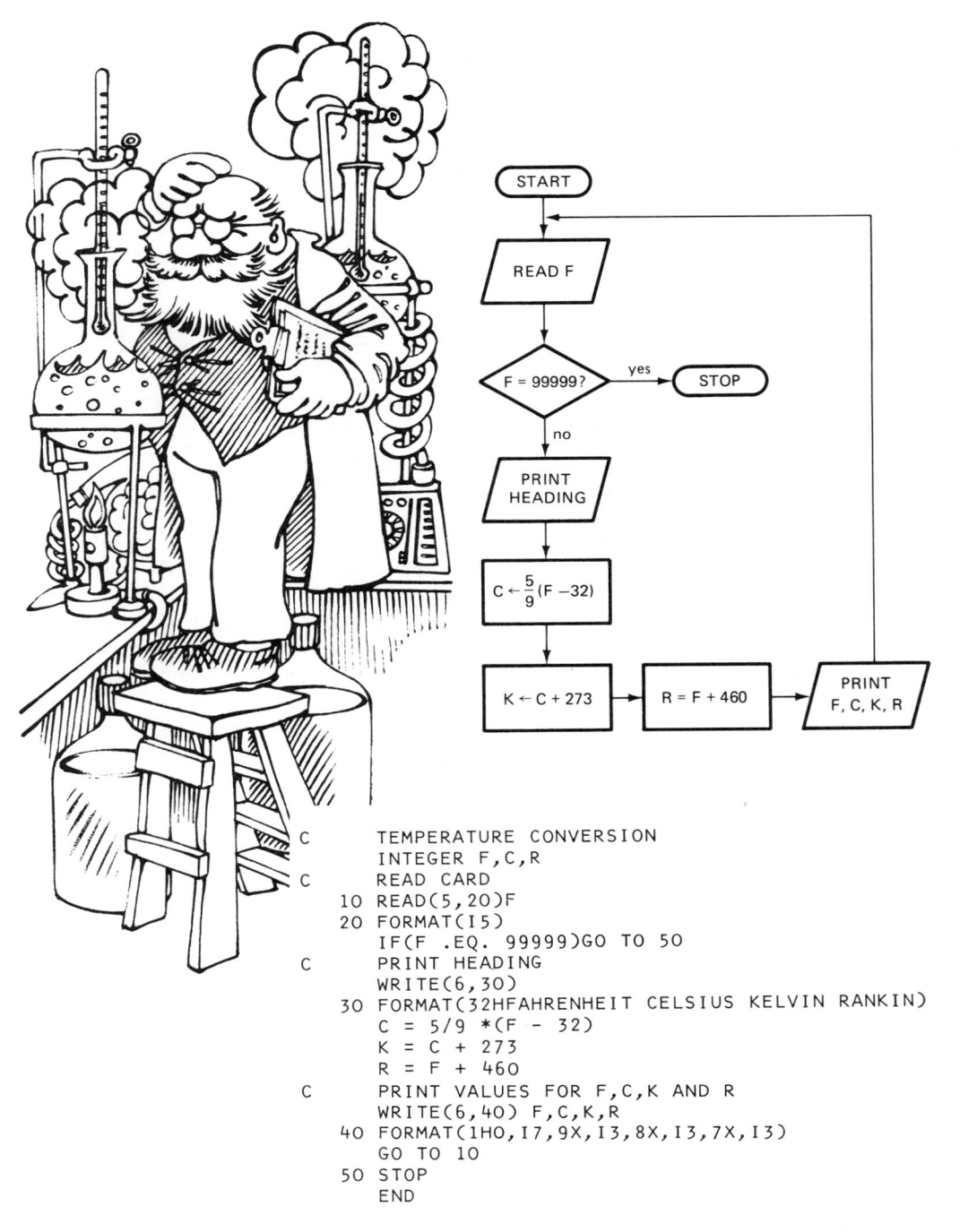

```
C        TEMPERATURE CONVERSION
         INTEGER F,C,R
C        READ CARD
   10    READ(5,20)F
   20    FORMAT(I5)
         IF(F .EQ. 99999)GO TO 50
C        PRINT HEADING
         WRITE(6,30)
   30    FORMAT(32HFAHRENHEIT CELSIUS KELVIN RANKIN)
         C = 5/9 *(F - 32)
         K = C + 273
         R = F + 460
C        PRINT VALUES FOR F,C,K AND R
         WRITE(6,40) F,C,K,R
   40    FORMAT(1H0,I7,9X,I3,8X,I3,7X,I3)
         GO TO 10
   50    STOP
         END
```

Figure 7-5 *The Absent-Minded Chemist*. This program helps Bob Sicard, the absent-minded chemist, convert Fahrenheit temperature readings to the equivalent values in Celsius, Kelvin, and Rankin temperature scales.

Chapter 7 Twelve Interesting FORTRAN Programs 200

His barber's program printed the message

SUM OF EVEN INTEGERS = 249,500

Examine both programs and see if you can determine which one has made a coding mistake (*hint:* Marvin had better not come back for a shave next week).

7.8 THE ABSENT-MINDED CHEMIST

Bob Sicard, the absent-minded chemist, can never remember how to convert from Fahrenheit temperatures to other forms of temperature such as Celsius, Kelvin, and Ranking. So, he wrote the program shown in Figure 7-5 to perform the conversions for him. The program converts Fahrenheit temperatures to Celsius by subtracting 32° from the Fahrenheit reading and multiplying the difference by 5/9. The product is the Celsius equivalent. It also converts Celsius temperatures to Kelvin by adding 273° to the Celsius reading, and converts Fahrenheit temperatures to Rankine by adding 460° to the Fahrenheit reading.

Bob's program accepts data cards as shown below (Figure 7-6). A Fahrenheit value is punched in columns 1–5. The last card in the deck has 99999 punched in the first five columns.

Bob's program uses the INTEGER Type statement to establish the variables for Fahrenheit (F), Celsius (C), and Rankin (R) in integer mode. The variable for Kelvin (K) is in integer mode because of the I, J, K, L, M, N naming convention. The pro-

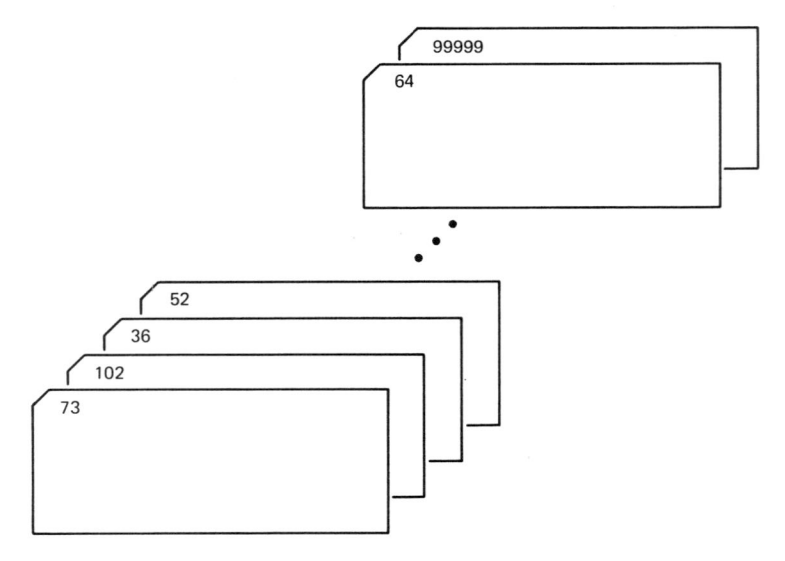

Figure 7-6.

Section 7.9   *Matrix Multiplication*

gram first reads a value of F, computes values for C, K, and R, and then prints a line containing the converted values. This procedure is repeated until the last card is read, wherein the program terminates execution.

7.9 MATRIX MULTIPLICATION

In 1858, Arthur Cayley introduced the theory of matrices. Within the last quarter century it has found many tasks to perform—in atomic physics, quantum mechanics, linear programming, circuit analysis, and many other areas.

A matrix is a rectangular or square array of numbers arranged in rows or columns. A 2×3 matrix would look like this:

$$\begin{bmatrix} 6 & 3 & 7 \\ 1 & 8 & 3 \end{bmatrix}$$

This matrix has two rows and three columns. A matrix with m rows and n columns is called an $m \times n$ matrix. If $m = n$, then we say we have a *square matrix*.

The addition or subtraction of two matrices of the same size is accomplished by adding or subtracting corresponding elements of each matrix. Likewise, to multiply matrix A by another matrix B, each element of the ith row of A is multiplied by the corresponding element of the jth column of B. The sum of the inner products so generated,

$$\sum A_{ij} B_{jk}$$

becomes the element C_{ik} of the product matrix C. The preceding rule can be expressed by the equation

$$C_{ik} = \sum_{j=1}^{n} A_{ij} B_{jk},$$

For example, consider the matrix equation

$$\begin{bmatrix} a_1 & b_1 & c_1 \\ a_2 & b_2 & c_2 \end{bmatrix} \times \begin{bmatrix} d_1 & e_1 \\ d_2 & e_2 \\ d_3 & e_3 \end{bmatrix} = \begin{bmatrix} a_1 d_1 + b_1 d_2 + c_1 d_3 & a_1 e_1 + b_1 e_2 + c_1 e_3 \\ a_2 d_1 + b_2 d_2 + c_2 d_3 & a_2 e_1 + b_2 e_2 + c_2 e_3 \end{bmatrix}.$$

Note the following:

1. Rows of the left matrix are multiplied into columns of the right.
2. The number of rows in the product equals the number of rows of the left matrix.
3. The number of columns in the product equals the number of columns of the right matrix.

Chapter 7   Twelve Interesting FORTRAN Programs

4. The number of rows in one matrix must equal the number of columns in the other matrix before multiplication can take place.

Numerical Example:

$$\text{Multiply} \begin{bmatrix} 3 & 1 & 2 \\ -1 & 2 & 3 \\ 2 & -5 & 7 \end{bmatrix} \times \begin{bmatrix} -2 & 1 & 1 \\ 3 & -1 & 2 \\ 0 & 1 & 0 \end{bmatrix}$$

$$= \begin{bmatrix} 3(-2) + & 1(3) + 2(0) & 3(1) + & 1(-1) + 2(1) & 3(1) + & 1(2) + 2(0) \\ -1(-2) + & 2(3) + 3(0) & -1(1) + & 2(-1) + 3(1) & -1(1) + & 2(2) + 3(0) \\ 2(-2) + & -5(3) + 7(0) & 2(1) + & -5(1) & + 7(1) & 2(1) + & -5(2) + 7(0) \end{bmatrix}$$

$$= \begin{bmatrix} -3 & 4 & 5 \\ 8 & 0 & 3 \\ -19 & 4 & -8 \end{bmatrix}$$

The following FORTRAN program multiplies the two matrices, A and B, where A has M rows and N columns, and B has N rows and K columns. The maximum size of M, N, and K is 10.

```
C         MATRIX MULTIPLICATION PROGRAM
          DIMENSION A(10,10),B(10,10),C(10,10)
C         READ NUMBER OF ROWS IN A AND COLUMNS IN B
          READ(2,5) ROWA,COLB
        5 FORMAL(2F3.0)
          IF(ROWA .EQ. COLB) GO TO 15
C         PRINT MESSAGE INDICATING INVALID CONDITION
          WRITE(3,10)
       10 FORMAT(52H1 ROWS OF MATRIX A AND COLUMNS OF MATRIX B NOT EQUAL)
          GO TO 40
C         INPUT VALUES FOR MATRICES A AND B
       15 READ(2,20) ((A(I,J),I=1,5),J=1,5),((B(I,J),I=1,5),J=1,5)
       20 FORMAT(25F2.0,/,25F2.0)
C         PRINT HEADING AND MATRICES A AND B
          WRITE(3,25)
       25 FORMAT(42H1MATRIX MULTIPLICATION,MATRIX A X MATRIX B)
          WRITE(3,30) ((A(I,J),J=1,5),I=1,5)
       30 FORMAT(1H0,5(//,5F8.0),/////)
          WRITE(3,30) ((B(I,J),J=1,5),I=1,5)
          DO 35 I = 1,5
          DO 35 K = 1,5
          C(I,K) = 0.0
          DO 35 J = 1,5
```

Section 7.9   Matrix Multiplication

```
       35   C(I,K) = C(I,K) + A(I,J) * B(J,K)
C           PRINT MATRIX C
            WRITE(3,30) ((C(I,J),J=1,5),I=1,5)
       40   STOP
            END
```

The program reads the following three data cards to determine what matrices to work with. The first data card indicates the number of rows in matrix A (5) and the number of columns in matrix B (5). The next two data cards contain the values for the A and B matrices.

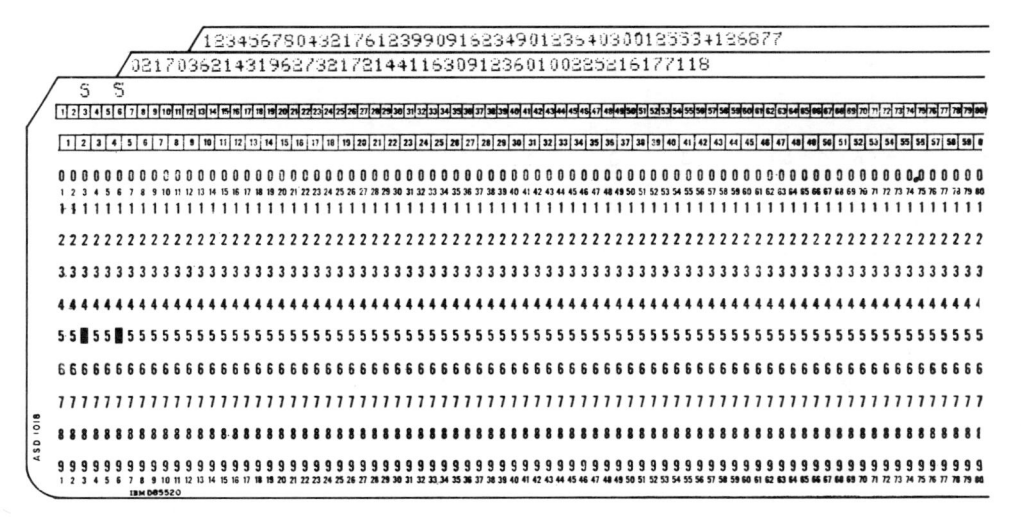

Figure 7-7.

A pictorial description of the data on the data cards is as follows:

$$A = \begin{bmatrix} 2 & 31 & 21 & 12 & 52 \\ 17 & 96 & 44 & 36 & 16 \\ 3 & 27 & 11 & 1 & 17 \\ 62 & 32 & 63 & 0 & 71 \\ 14 & 17 & 9 & 22 & 18 \end{bmatrix} \quad B = \begin{bmatrix} 12 & 32 & 9 & 23 & 55 \\ 34 & 17 & 16 & 64 & 34 \\ 56 & 61 & 23 & 3 & 12 \\ 78 & 23 & 49 & 0 & 68 \\ 4 & 99 & 1 & 12 & 77 \end{bmatrix}$$

The objective of the program is to calculate a product matrix and store the computed result in array C. The program also checks to see whether the number of rows of matrix A is equal to the number of columns of matrix B. If not, the multiplication

MATRIX MULTIPLICATIØN, MATRIX A X MATRIX B

2	31	21	12	52
17	96	44	36	16
3	27	11	1	17
62	32	63	0	71
14	19	9	22	18

12	32	9	23	55
34	17	16	64	34
56	61	23	3	12
78	23	49	0	68
4	99	1	12	77

3398	7296	1637	2717	6236
8804	7272	4481	6859	8407
1716	2932	778	2034	2592
5644	13400	2590	4515	10721
3106	3608	1733	1781	4406

Figure 7-8 Output of the Matrix Multiplication Program.

cannot take place, and a message ROWS OF MATRIX A AND COLUMNS OF MATRIX B NOT EQUAL is to be printed. After calculating the product matrix, the program causes all three matrices to be printed as shown in Figure 7-8. A flowchart for this problem is shown in Figure 7-9.

7.10 THE 15 PUZZLE

An algorithm for the 15 Puzzle was shown in Chapter 3. Shown here is a flowchart (see Figure 7-10) and the FORTRAN program on page 207.

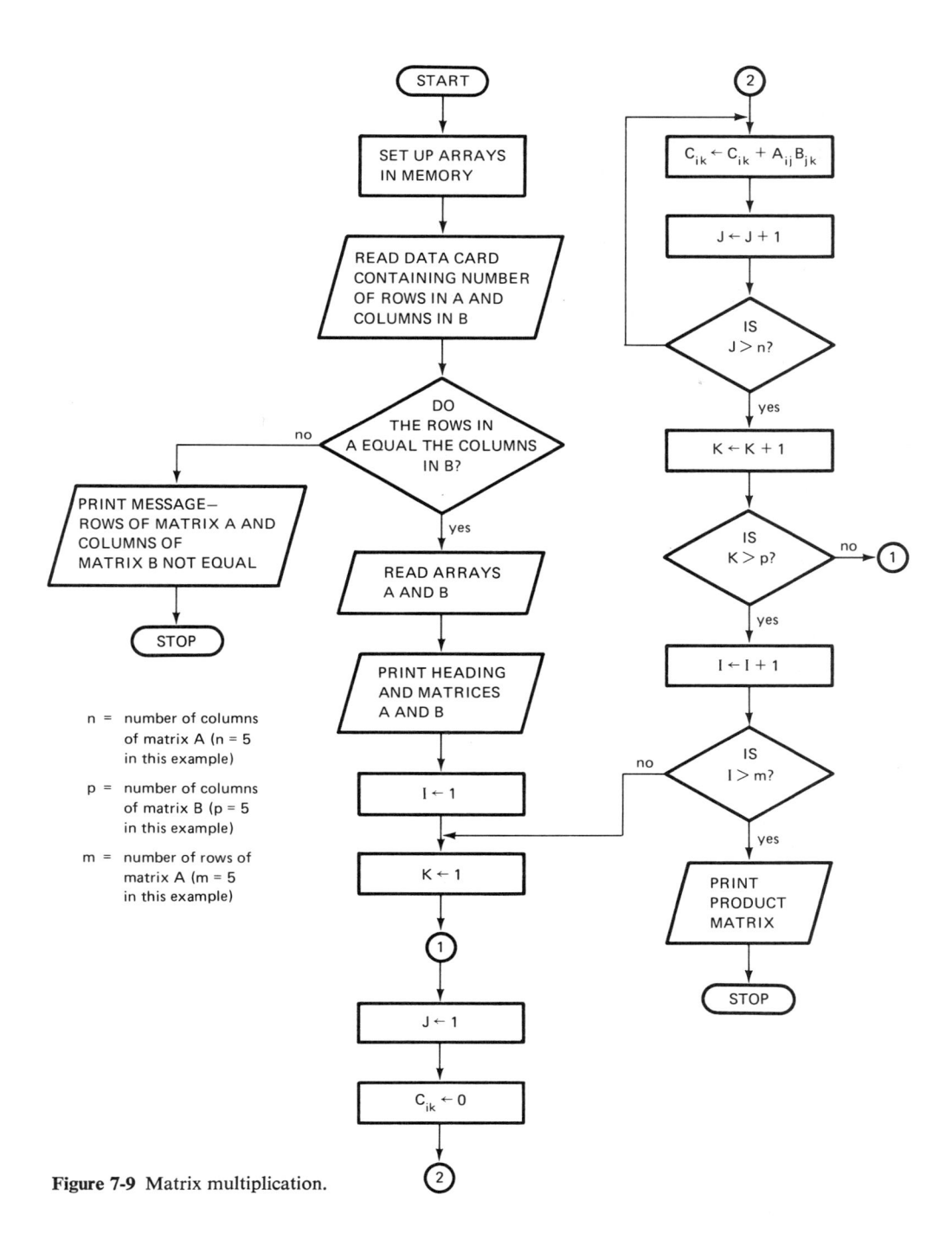

Figure 7-9 Matrix multiplication.

n = number of columns of matrix A (n = 5 in this example)

p = number of columns of matrix B (p = 5 in this example)

m = number of rows of matrix A (m = 5 in this example)

205

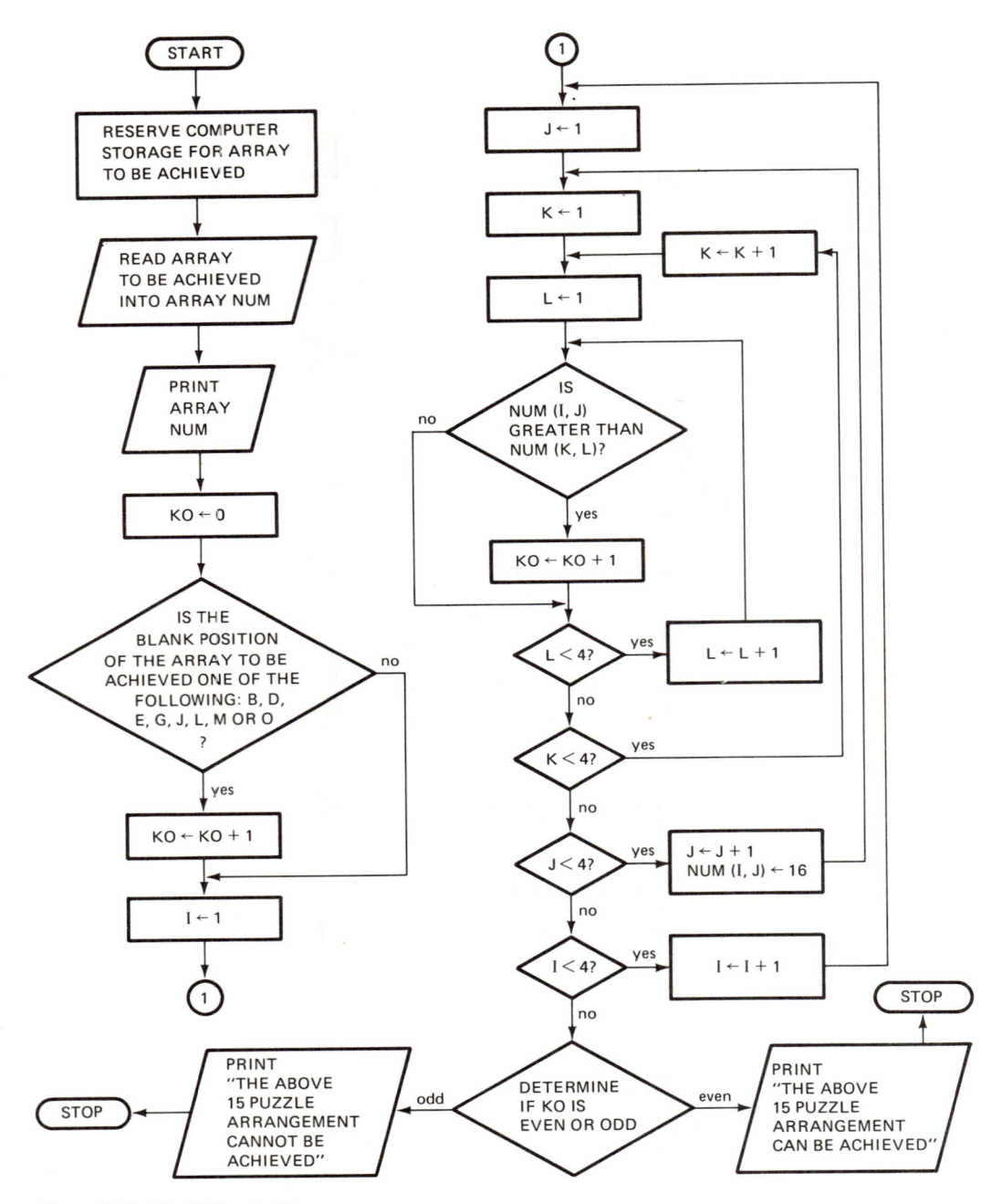

Figure 7-10 The 15 Puzzle Program.

Section 7.10   The 15 Puzzle   207

```
      C         15 PUZZLE
                DIMENSION NUM(4,4)
                READ(2,1)((NUM(I,J),I=1,4),J=1,4)
      1         FORMAT(16I2)
                WRITE(3,14)  ((NUM(I,J),J=1,4),I=1,4)
     14         FORMAT(1H1,/,4(10X,4I5,///),///)
                KO = 0
                IF(NUM(1,2) = 16) 2,9,2
      2         IF(NUM(1,4) = 16) 3,9,3
      3         IF(NUM(2,1) = 16) 4,9,4
      4         IF(NUM(2,3) = 16) 5,9,5
      5         IF(NUM(3,2) = 16) 6,9,6
      6         IF(NUM(3,4) = 16) 7,9,7
      7         IF(NUM(4,1) = 16) 8,9,8
      8         IF(NUM(4,3) = 16)10,9,10
      9         KO = KO + 1
     10         DO 13 I = 1,4
                DO 13 J = 1,4
                DO 12 K = 1,4
                DO 12 L = 1,4
                IF(NUM(I,J) - NUM(K,L))12,12,11
     11         KO = KO + 1
     12         CONTINUE
     13         NUM(I,J) = 16
                N = KO / 2
                IF(KO - 2 * N) 17,15,17
     15         WRITE(3,16)
     16         FORMAT(" THE ABOVE 15 PUZZLE ARRANGEMENT CAN BE ACHIEVED")
                GO TO 19
     17         WRITE(3,18)
     18         FORMAT(" THE ABOVE 15 PUZZLE ARRANGEMENT CANNOT BE ACHIEVED")
     19         STOP
                END
```

15	11	7	3
14	10	6	2
13	9	5	1
12	8	4	0

After determining whether a given number arrangement is possible, this program causes the number arrangement to be printed followed by one of the following messages:

        THE ABOVE 15 PUZZLE ARRANGEMENT CAN BE ACHIEVED
        THE ABOVE 15 PUZZLE ARRANGEMENT CANNOT BE ACHIEVED.

Chapter 7 Twelve Interesting FORTRAN Programs   208

7.11 MAGIC SQUARES

Magic squares were introduced in Chapter 3. Let us now develop a FORTRAN program that will produce odd-order magic squares of any size. As you may remember, a magic square is an array of numbers arranged in a square so that rows, columns, or main diagonals, when added up, yield the same total. This total sum is referred to as the *magic number* and is represented by the equation

$$\text{Magic number} = \frac{n(n^2 + 1)}{2},$$

where n is the size of the magic square; that is, $n = 3$ for a 3×3 square, $n = 7$ for a 7×7 square, and so forth.

Magic squares have little purpose other than amusement, but they do provide a challenging programming exercise.

Here is an example of a 3×3 magic square:

```
8 1 6
3 5 7
4 9 2
```

The sum or magic number of all rows, diagonals, and columns is 15, as determined by the equation

$$\frac{3(3^2 + 1)}{2} = 15.$$

An odd-order magic square can be computed by the following procedure. The example computes a 5×5 square. However, the procedure will work for all odd-order squares: 3×3, 5×5, 7×7, 9×9, 11×11, and so on.

1. Place the number 1 in the center box of the top row.
2. Move your pencil out of the box diagonally, through its upper right-hand corner. It will land outside the square. Move down this column and place the number 2 in the bottom row.
3. Move diagonally up to the right again, and put the number 3 in the next box you enter. Continue diagonally up to the right, and your pencil lands outside the square once more. Move left along this row, and put the number 4 in the left-hand column.
4. Go diagonally up to the right and enter the number 5. This completes a group of five numbers.
5. Go down one box to start the next group of five numbers. The 6 goes under the 5.
6. Move diagonally to the right, and place a number into each box you enter. When your pencil lands outside the square, move across to the opposite side of the row. After each group of five numbers, go down one box to start the next group of five.

Section 7.11 Magic Squares

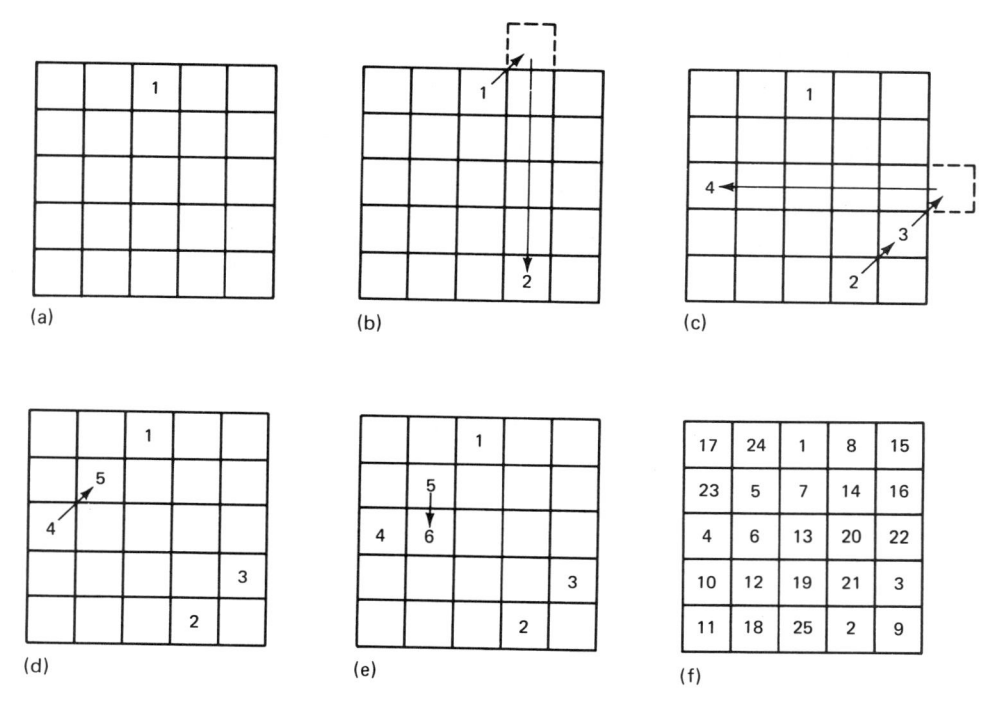

Figure 7-11.

When you finish the fifth group of five numbers, place the number 25 in the box in the center column of the bottom row.

The following **FORTRAN** program generated the 11 by 11 magic square shown in Figure 7-12. The size of the magic square is a data input to the program.

```
C          MAGIC SQUARES
C          THIS PROGRAM GENERATES A N BY N MAGIC SQUARE
           DIMENSION MAGIC (11,11)
C          READ SIZE OF SQUARE TO BE GENERATED
           READ(2,5) N
         5 FORMAT(I2)
           KTR = 1
           NUM = 1
           I = 1
           J = (N+1) / 2
C          PLACE A 1 IN THE CENTER CELL OF ROW 1
        10 MAGIC(I,J) = NUM
           NUM = NUM + 1
```

68	81	94	107	120	1	14	27	40	53	66
80	93	106	119	11	13	26	39	52	65	67
92	105	118	10	12	25	38	51	64	77	79
104	117	9	22	24	37	50	63	76	78	91
116	8	21	23	36	49	62	75	88	90	103
7	20	33	35	48	61	74	87	89	102	115
19	32	34	47	60	73	86	99	101	114	6
31	44	46	59	72	85	98	100	113	5	18
43	45	58	71	84	97	110	112	4	17	30
55	57	70	83	96	109	111	3	16	29	42
56	69	82	95	108	121	2	15	28	41	54

Figure 7-12 An 11 by 11 magic square.

```
      C        DETERMINE IF MAGIC SQUARE IS COMPLETE
               IF(NUM .LE. N*N)GO TO 40
      C        PRINT HEADING AND MAGIC SQUARE
               WRITE(3,20) N,N
            20 FORMAT(13H1MAGIC SQUARE,I4,2X,3H BY,I4)
               WRITE(3,30)  ((MAGIC(I,J),J=1,N),I = 1,N)
            30 FORMAT(1H0,/,11I5)
               STOP
```

Section 7.12 *Magic Square Checker*

```
C           DETERMINE IF KTR IS AN EVEN VALUE OF N
       40   IF(KTR .LT. N) GO TO 50
C           RESET KTR TO 1 AND SET ROW INDEX TO INDICATE NEXT ROW
            KTR = 1
            I = I + 1
            GO TO 10
C           INCREASE KTR BY 1 AND MOVE TO THE RIGHT AND UP
       50   KTR = KTR + 1
            I = I - 1
            J = J + 1
            IF(I .NE. 0) GO TO 60
C           MOVE WENT OUT OF TOP OF SQUARE — SET ROW INDEX TO N
            I = N
            GO TO 10
       60   IF(J .LE. N) GO TO 10
C           MOVE WENT OUT OF TOP OF SQUARE — SET COLUMN INDEX TO 1
       65   J = 1
            GO TO 10
            END
```

A flowchart of the logic used in the FORTRAN program is shown in Figure 7-13.

7.12 MAGIC SQUARE CHECKER

The following Magic Square Checking Program will read an array of numbers into Array MAGIC and determine if the number array is a magic square.

```
C           MAGIC SQUARE CHECKER
            DIMENSION MAGIC(9,9),IC(9),IR(9),ID(2)
            READ(2,3006)N,((MAGIC(I,J),I=1,9),J=1,9)
     3006   FORMAT(I3,2I3,/,24I3,/,24I3,/,10I3)
C           CALCULATE THE MAGIC NUMBER (SUM OF EACH COLUMN, ROW, AND DIAGONAL)
            MAGNU = (N * (N**2 + 1)) / 2
C           ADD ALL COLUMNS AND COMPARE AGAINST MAGIC NUMBER
            DO 3030 J = 1,N
            IC(J) = 0
            DO 3020 I = 1,N
     3020   IC(J) = IC(J) + MAGIC(I,J)
            IF(IC(J) - MAGNU) 3099,3030,3099
     3030   CONTINUE
            WRITE(3,3031)
     3031   FORMAT(35H ALL COLUMNS EQUAL THE MAGIC NUMBER)
C           ADD ALL ROWS AND COMPARE WITH MAGIC NUMBER
            DO 3050 I = 1,N
            IR(I) = 0
            DO 3040 J = 1,N
```

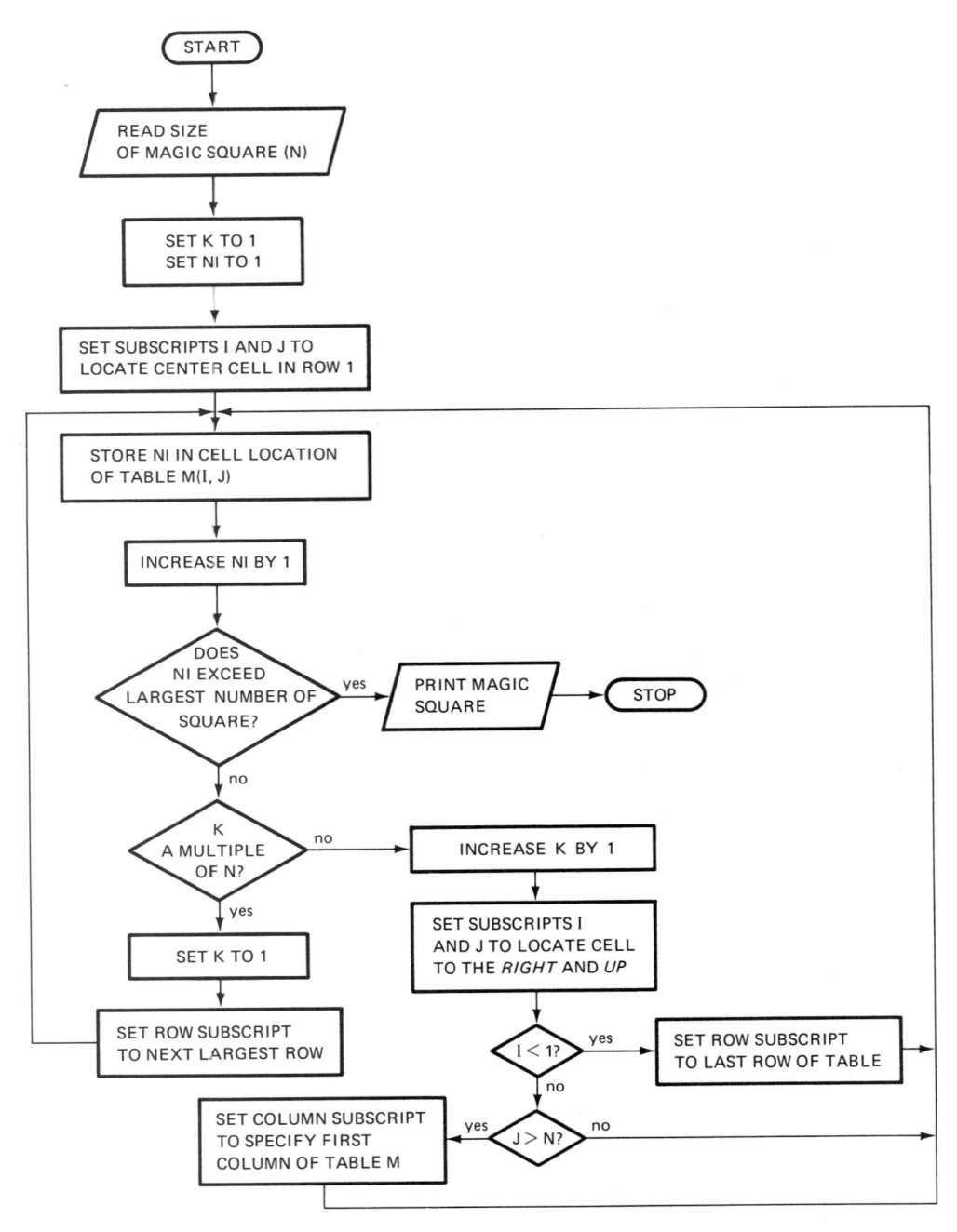

Figure 7-13 This flowchart shows the logic needed to generate an odd-order magic square of any size.

Section 7.12   Magic Square Checker

```
      3040  IR(I) = IR(I) + MAGIC(I,J)
            IF(IR(I) - MAGNU) 3099,3050,3099
      3050  CONTINUE
            WRITE(3,3051)
      3051  FORMAT(32H ALL ROWS EQUAL THE MAGIC NUMBER)
C     ADD BOTH DIAGONALS AND COMPARE WITH MAGIC NUMBER
            ID(1) = 0
            DO 3060 I = 1,N
            J = I
      3060  ID(1) = ID(1) + MAGIC(I,J)
            IF(ID(1) - MAGNU) 3099,3070,3099
      3070  CONTINUE
            WRITE(3,3071)
      3071  FORMAT(31H DIAGONAL 1 EQUALS MAGIC NUMBER)
C     ADD SECOND DIAGONAL
            ID(2) = 0
            DO 3080 I = 1,N
            J = N + 1 - I
      3080  ID(2) = ID(2) + MAGIC(I,J)
            IF(ID(2) - MAGNU) 3099,3090,3099
      3090  CONTINUE
            WRITE(3,3999)
      3999  FORMAT(31H DIAGONAL 2 EQUALS MAGIC NUMBER)
      3091  WRITE(3,3014)
      3014  FORMAT(23H THIS IS A MAGIC SQUARE,///)
            WRITE(3,3015) ((MAGIC(I,J),J=1,9),I=1,9)
      3015  FORMAT(1H0,/,(//9I5))
            GO TO 3100
      3099  WRITE(3,3007)
      3007  FORMAT(35H ARRYA DOES NOT FORM A MAGIC SQUARE)
            WRITE(3,3016) ((MAGIC(I,J),J=1,9),I=1,9)
      3016  FORMAT(1H0,/,(//9I5))
      3100  STOP
            END
```

The program first calculates the magic number, MAGNU, by using the following formula:

$$\text{MAGNU} = \frac{n(n^2 + 1)}{2}$$

where n is the size of the number square. The program compares the sum of each column row and main diagonal to the Magic Number (MAGNU). The following messages will be printed by the program if the sum of the specified values equals the Magic Number:

    ALL COLUMNS EQUAL THE MAGIC NUMBER
    ALL ROWS EQUAL THE MAGIC NUMBER
    DIAGONAL 1 EQUALS THE MAGIC NUMBER
    DIAGONAL 2 EQUALS THE MAGIC NUMBER

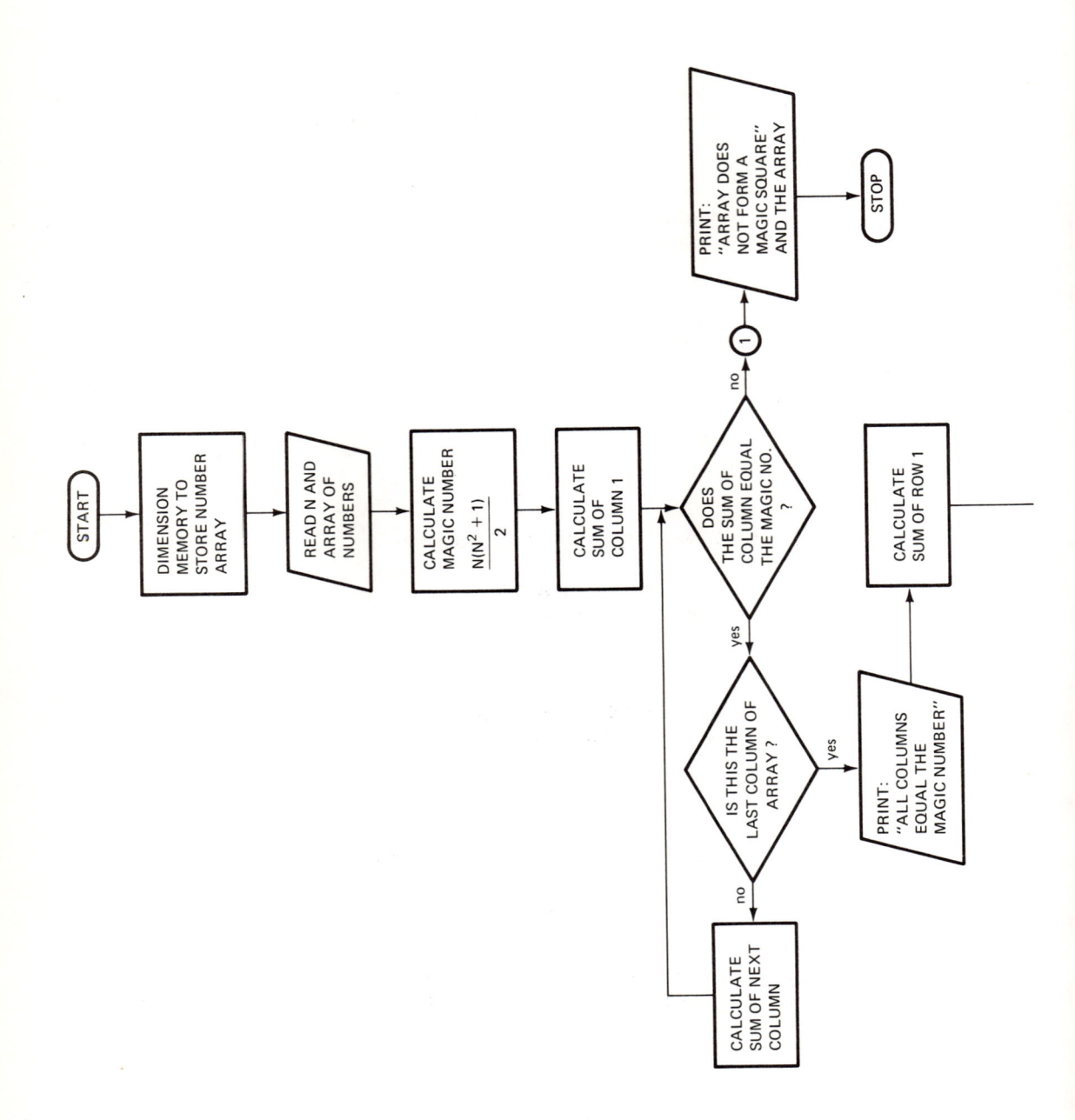

```
START → DIMENSION MEMORY TO STORE NUMBER ARRAY → READ N AND ARRAY OF NUMBERS → CALCULATE MAGIC NUMBER N(N² + 1)/2 → CALCULATE SUM OF COLUMN 1 → DOES THE SUM OF COLUMN EQUAL THE MAGIC NO.?
```

- no → (1) → PRINT: "ARRAY DOES NOT FORM A MAGIC SQUARE" AND THE ARRAY → STOP
- yes → IS THIS THE LAST COLUMN OF ARRAY?
  - no → CALCULATE SUM OF NEXT COLUMN → (loop back)
  - yes → PRINT: "ALL COLUMNS EQUAL THE MAGIC NUMBER" → CALCULATE SUM OF ROW 1

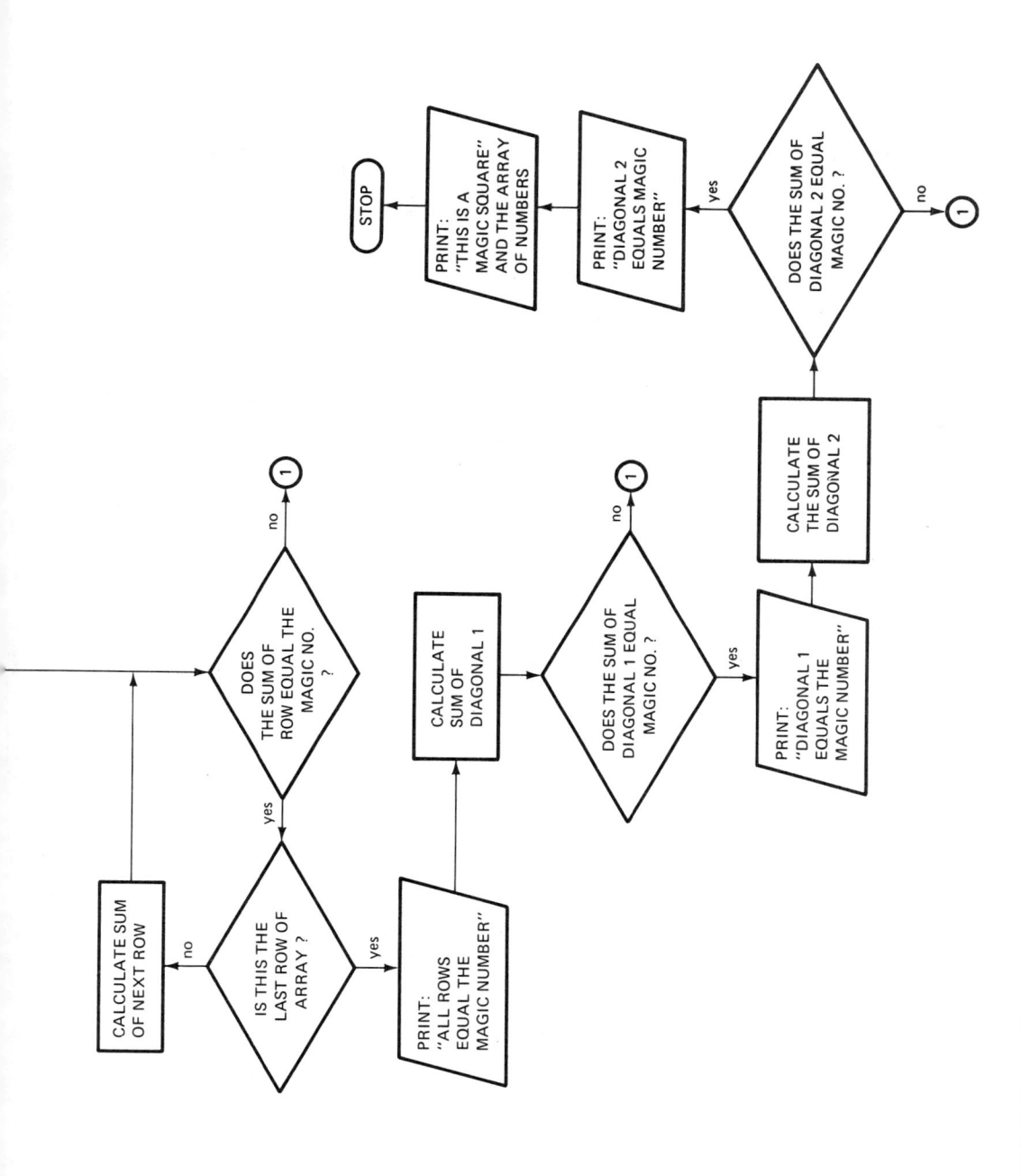

Figure 7-14 Magic Square Checking Program.

Chapter 7 Twelve Interesting FORTRAN Programs 216

If the above four messages are printed, the array of numbers is a magic square. The message

THIS IS A MAGIC SQUARE

along with the array of numbers also will be printed. The message

ARRAY DOES NOT FORM A MAGIC SQUARE

is printed if the number array is not a magic square. This would occur if the sum of any row, column, or main diagonal did not equal the magic number, MAGNU. Figure 7-14 illustrates a flowchart of the Magic Square Checking Program.

The program presented here is one of a large number that could be written to achieve the correct answer. A straightforward approach was used in determining a solution to the problem. Figure 7-15 illustrates the printer output that the program

```
ALL COLUMNS EQUAL THE MAGIC NUMBER
ALL ROWS EQUAL THE MAGIC NUMBER
DIAGONAL 1 EQUALS MAGIC NUMBER
DIAGONAL 2 EQUALS MAGIC NUMBER

THIS IS A MAGIC SQUARE
```

47	58	69	80	1	12	23	34	45
57	68	79	9	11	22	33	44	46
67	78	8	10	21	32	43	54	56
77	7	18	20	31	42	53	55	66
6	17	19	30	41	52	63	65	76
16	27	29	40	51	62	64	75	5
26	28	39	50	61	72	74	4	15
36	38	49	60	71	73	3	14	25
37	48	59	70	81	2	13	24	35

Figure 7-15 Output produced by the Magic Square Checking Program when the number array contained all the properties of a magic square.

Section 7.12   Magic Square Checker   217

ARRAY DØES NØT FØRM A MAGIC SQUARE

47	58	69	80	1	12	23	34	45
57	68	79	9	11	22	33	44	46
67	78	8	10	21	32	43	54	56
77	7	18	20	31	42	53	55	66
6	17	19	30	41	52	63	65	76
16	27	29	40	51	62	64	75	5
26	28	39	50	61	72	74	4	15
37	48	59	70	81	2	13	24	35
36	38	49	60	71	73	3	14	25

Figure 7-16 Output produced by the Magic Square Checking Program when the number array did not contain all the properties of a magic square.

generated when the number array contained all the properties of a magic square. Whenever the program detects a column, row, or diagonal sum that differs from the calculated magic number, a printout similar to the one shown in Figure 7-16 would be generated.

Chapter 8

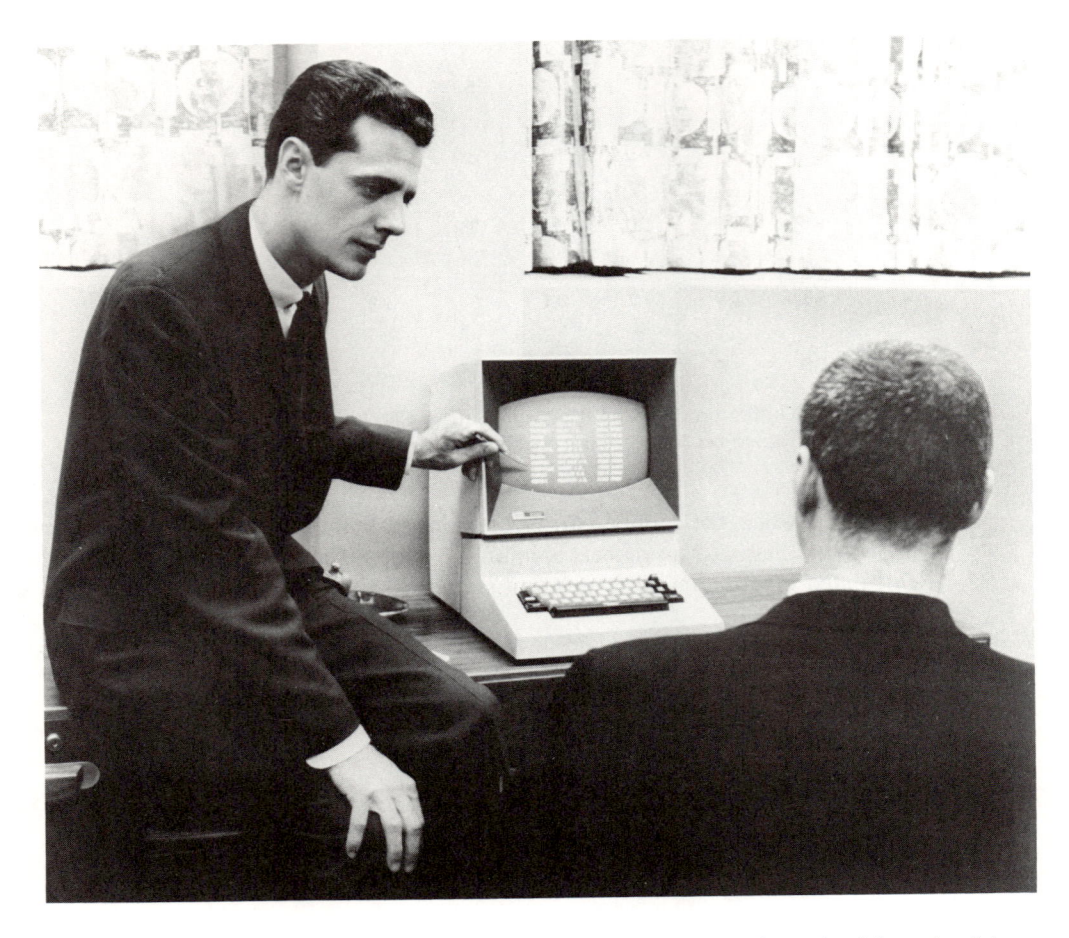

CRT display devices offer a simple and efficient way of entering information into a computer or receiving information from it. With one key stroke, for example, an important profit report can be called to the screen of the display device. Using a single display in his or her office, an executive can call up a variety of management reports. (Courtesy IBM Corp.)

Problems with Flowcharts

Chapters 8 and 9 present problems for reader solution. The problems in this chapter also include solutions in the form of flowcharts. They should be used by the reader as a guideline in coding FORTRAN programs. Some of these problems require a knowledge of first-year high school algebra, but most need no mathematical training.

The problems are presented in order of increasing difficulty. They have been selected from various fields: business, engineering, accounting, mathematics, social science, game playing, physics, number theory, and others.

The reader should remember that there often are many possible approaches to any problem. When solving problems by computers, you usually want to look for a technique that requires a minimum of computer processing time and storage.

8.1 INTEREST CALCULATION

Simple interest calculations involve arithmetic progessions. If P is the principal placed at an interest rate i for a period of n years, the amount A at the end of n years may be found by using the formula

$$A = P(1 + n \times i)$$

For example, if $P = 2000$, i is 7 percent, and n is 10, then

$$A = 2000(1 + (10 \times .07))$$
$$= 2000(1 + .7)$$
$$= 2000(1.7)$$
$$= \$3400$$

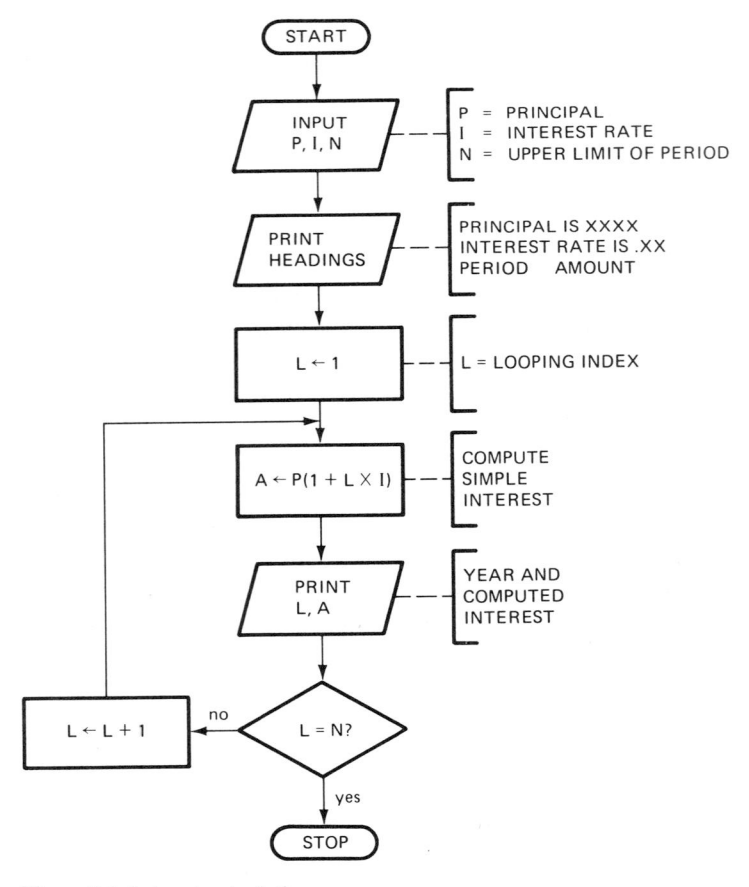

Figure 8-1 Interest calculation.

Section 8.3   *Checkerboard Interchange*   221

Figure 8-1 shows a method that will input values of principal, interest rate, and an upper limit to the period. The method calculates the amount at the end of each period from 1 to the limit, printing out values of the period and the amount. The output would appear similar to that shown below:

```
PRINCIPAL IS xxxx
INTEREST RATE IS .xx
PERIOD           AMOUNT
x                xxxx.xx
x                xxxx.xx
x                xxxx.xx
.                .
.                .
.                .
```

8.2 PRIME NUMBER POLYNOMIAL

Euclid proved that there is an infinite number of prime numbers. Mathematicians have looked in vain for a formula that would generate all the positive prime numbers. The formula $f(x) = x^2 - x + 41$ will generate primes for x in the range $1 \leq x \leq 40$.

$f(x)$	$x^2 - x + 41$
1	$1^2 - 1 + 41 = 41$
2	$2^2 - 2 + 41 = 43$
3	$3^2 - 3 + 41 = 47$
4	$4^2 - 4 + 41 = 53$
5	$5^2 - 5 + 41 = 61$
.	.
.	.
23	$23^2 - 23 + 41 = 547$
.	.
.	.
40	$40^2 - 40 + 41 = 1601$

A flowchart for generating primes using the formula $x^2 - x + 41$ is shown in Figure 8-2 on page 222.

8.3 CHECKERBOARD INTERCHANGE

Figure 8-3 illustrates a method to interchange the two main diagonals of an 8×8 checkerboard. In this example, the checkerboard is represented by a two-dimensional array named CHECK.

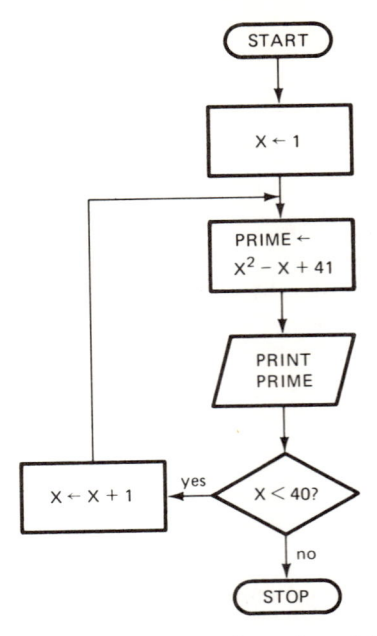

Figure 8-2 Prime number polynomial.

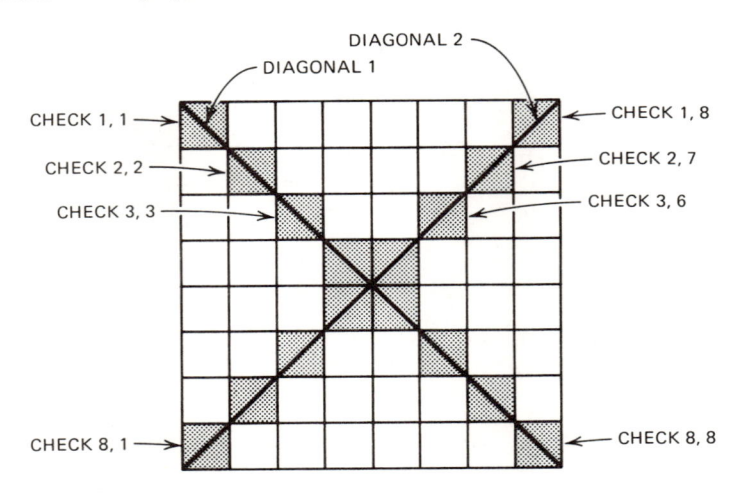

The interchange is accomplished by interchanging respective diagonal cells on the main diagonal lines. Thus,

$CHECK_{1,1}$ and $CHECK_{1,8}$ are interchanged
$CHECK_{2,2}$ and $CHECK_{2,7}$ are interchanged
$CHECK_{3,3}$ and $CHECK_{3,6}$ are interchanged
.
.
.
$CHECK_{8,8}$ and $CHECK_{8,1}$ are interchanged

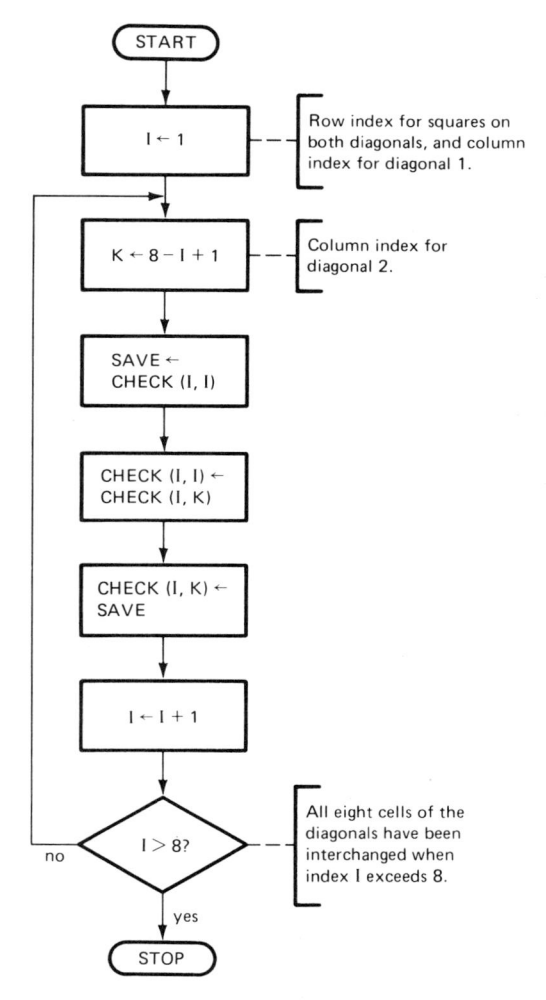

Figure 8-3 Checkerboard interchange.

The method employs a loop that uses the cell interchange portion of the problem eight times.

8.4 LAW OF COSINES

If two sides and the included angle are known, the third side of a triangle can be found by the Law of Cosines:

$$c^2 = a^2 + b^2 - 2ab \cos C$$

Figure 8-4 shows the flowchart of a method that will compute 100 values of c corresponding to 100 given values of a, b, and angle C.

```
                    ┌─────────┐
                    │  START  │
                    └────┬────┘
                         ▼
                    ┌─────────┐
                    │  I ← 1  │
                    └────┬────┘
                         ▼
                    ┌─────────┐
                    │  INPUT  │
                    │A, B, AND│
                    │ ANGLE C │
                    └────┬────┘
                         ▼
                    ┌──────────────┐
                    │      C ←     │
                    │ √A² + B² − 2AB cos C │
                    └──────┬───────┘
                           ▼
        ┌─────────┐  yes  ╱╲
        │ I ← I+1 │◄──────╱  ╲
        └────▲────┘      ╱ I<100? ╲
             │           ╲        ╱
             └────────────╲      ╱
                           ╲    ╱
                            ╲  ╱ no
                             ▼
                    ┌─────────┐
                    │  PRINT  │
                    │ A, B, C │
                    └────┬────┘
                         ▼
                    ┌─────────┐
                    │  STOP   │
                    └─────────┘
```

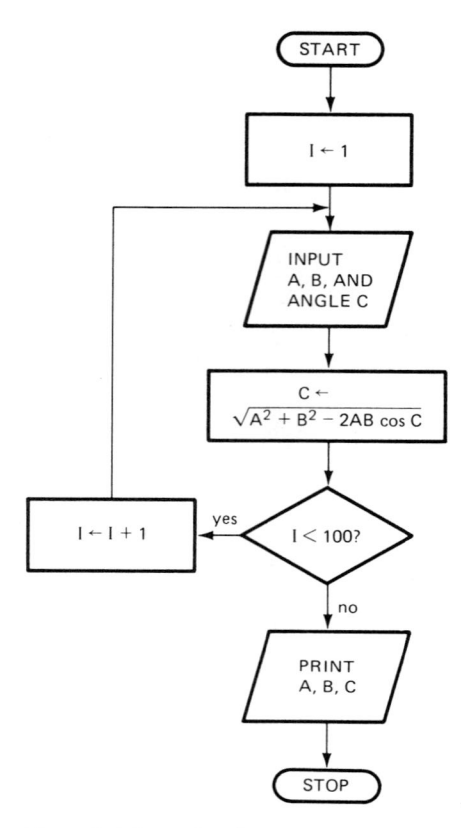

Figure 8-4 Law of cosines.

8.5 ACCOUNTING COMPUTATION

The Seven Flags Amusement Park wishes to use a computer to solve a simple accounting problem. A train worth $9000 is to be depreciated over 10 years by the use of a double declining-balance depreciation. Figure 8-5 shows a flowchart for the procedure to solve this problem. This procedure would produce a table such as the one that follows.

Year	Depreciation	Book Value
1	900.00	8100.00
2	810.00	7290.00
3	729.00	6561.00
4	656.10	5904.90
5	590.49	5314.41
6	531.44	4782.97
7	478.30	4304.67
8	430.47	3874.20
9	38/.42	3486.78
10	348.68	3138.10

Section 8.7 Real Estate Purchase

8.6 PRODUCT COST

Average cost per unit of production, a_c, is the ratio of the total cost to the number of units produced and is expressed

$$a_c = \frac{t_c}{n}$$

where t_c is the total cost and n is the number of units produced. Marginal cost is the cost of producing one more unit of the product.

The flowchart for this problem is shown in Figure 8-6. The procedure inputs as data the prices and total costs associated with 100 quantities, and calculates and outputs a table of average and marginal costs.

8.7 REAL ESTATE PURCHASE

Joan Wolcott has $7600 to spend and wants to purchase a lot having an area of at least 12,000 square feet. Given data for 300 lots, the procedure in Figure 8-7 will input Ms. Wolcott's requirements and determine whether they can be met by any of the given lots. Any lot or lots found to meet her requirements will be printed in the following format:

Chapter 8   Problems with Flowcharts   226

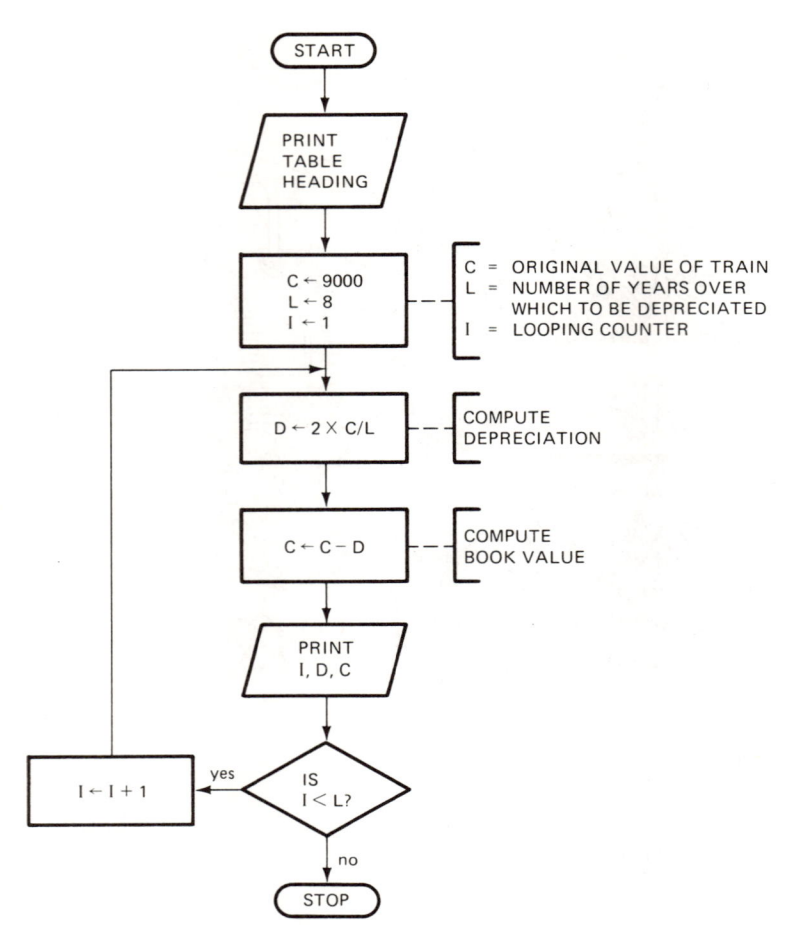

Figure 8-5 Accounting computation.

LOT ID	LENGTH	WIDTH	PRICE
67	110	120	$6400
107	120	131	$7200
153	100	120	$6000
158	100	180	$7400
261	110	200	$7600
.	.	.	.
.	.	.	.
.	.	.	.

8.8 CHECKER COUNTING

A standard checkerboard has 64 squares upon which *red checkers*, *black checkers*, *red kings*, or *black kings* may reside. The object is to determine how many of each checker type is on the checkerboard. The flowchart shown in Figure 8-8 uses an array

Section 8.8   *Checker Counting*

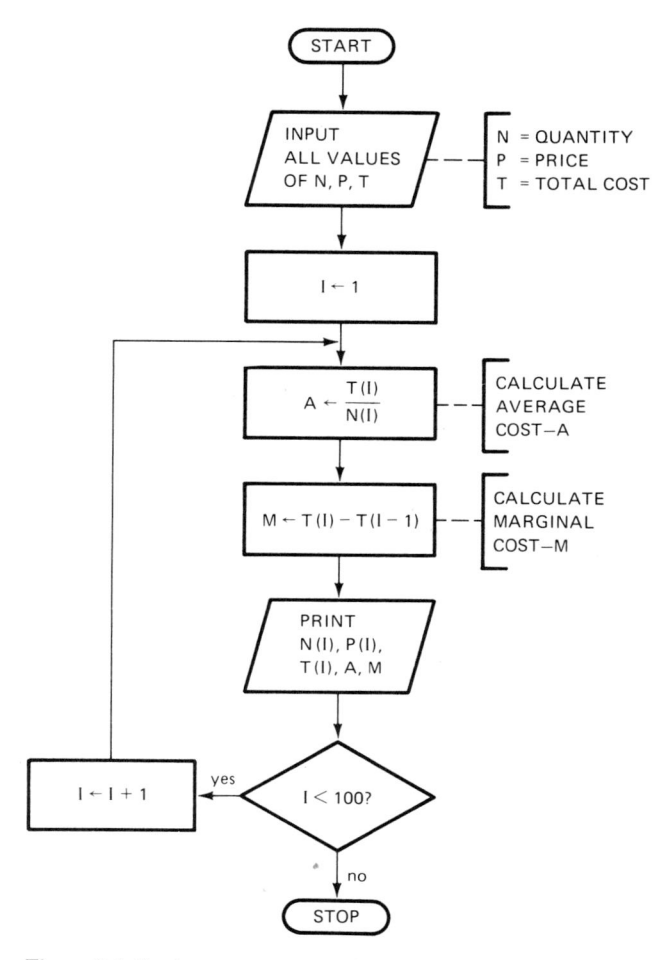

```
                    ┌─────────┐
                    │  START  │
                    └────┬────┘
                         │
                 ╱───────────────╲
                ╱   INPUT          ╲       ┌ N = QUANTITY
                ╲   ALL VALUES     ╱ ──── ─┤ P = PRICE
                 ╲  OF N, P, T    ╱        └ T = TOTAL COST
                  ───────┬───────
                         │
                  ┌─────────────┐
                  │   I ← 1     │
                  └──────┬──────┘
                         │
          ┌──────────────▼──────┐
          │                     │         ┌ CALCULATE
          │   A ← T(I)/N(I)     │ ──── ───┤ AVERAGE
          │                     │         └ COST—A
          └──────────┬──────────┘
                     │
          ┌──────────▼──────────┐         ┌ CALCULATE
          │ M ← T(I) − T(I−1)   │ ──── ───┤ MARGINAL
          └──────────┬──────────┘         └ COST—M
                     │
              ╱──────────────╲
             ╱    PRINT         ╲
             ╲   N(I), P(I),    ╱
              ╲  T(I), A, M    ╱
               ─────┬─────────
                    │
   ┌──────────┐ yes ◇
   │ I ← I+1  │◄────│ I < 100? │
   └────▲─────┘     ◇
        │            │ no
        │       ┌────▼────┐
        │       │  STOP   │
        │       └─────────┘
```

Figure 8-6 Product cost computation.

called CHECK to represent the checkerboard and the subscripts I and J to locate a position within the array. Each of the array elements could represent one of the following:

Red Checker   —10—RC
Black Checker—20—BC
Red King   —30—RK
Black King   —40—BK

The value following the checker type is used by the procedure to identify the type of checker, and the variable names following the values are used by the procedure to store the count of each checker type. The method generates a count for each checker

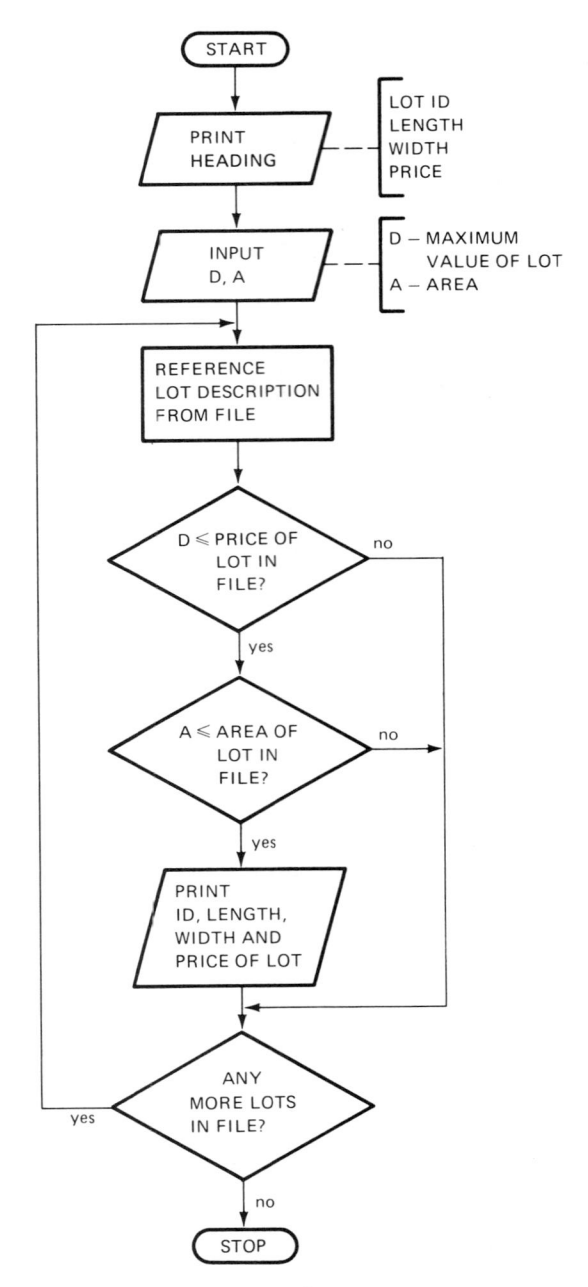

Figure 8-7 Real estate purchase.

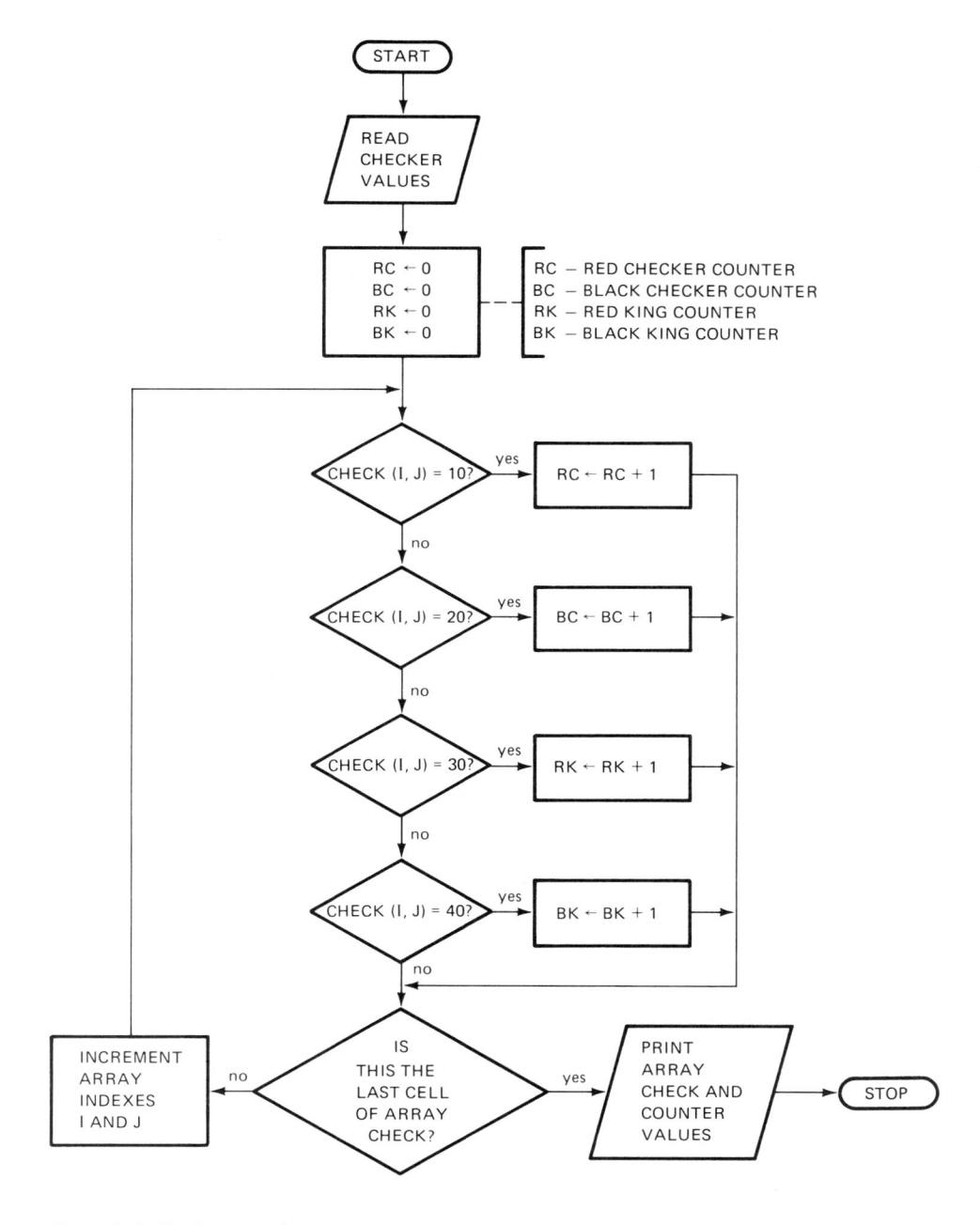

Figure 8-8 Checker counting procedure.

type by examining each element of the array and incrementing the respective counts each time a checker is detected.

8.9 CHI-SQUARE

Very often in statistical studies, one is called upon to make *statistical decisions* about populations on the basis of sample information. However, the results obtained in samples do not always agree exactly with theoretical results expected according to rules of probability. For example, although theoretical considerations lead us to expect 50 heads and 50 tails when we toss a fair coin 100 times, it is rare that these results are obtained exactly.

Suppose that in a particular sample a set of possible events $E_1, E_2, E_3, \ldots, E_k$ are observed to occur with frequencies $f_1, f_2, f_3, \ldots, f_k$, called *observed frequencies*, and that according to probability rules they are expected to occur with frequencies $e_1, e_2, e_3, \ldots, e_k$, called *expected frequencies*. We often wish to know whether observed frequencies differ significantly from expected frequencies. A measure of the discrepancy existing between observed and expected frequencies is supplied by the statistic x^2 (read *chi-square*) given by

$$x^2 = \frac{(f_1 - e_1)^2}{e_1} + \frac{(f_2 - e_2)^2}{e_2} + \frac{(f_3 - e_3)^2}{e_3} + \cdots + \frac{(f_k - e_k)^2}{e_k}$$

The following table illustrates the distribution of the digits 0 through 9 in a random number table of 250 digits.

Digit	0	1	2	3	4	5	6	7	8	9
Observed Frequency	17	31	29	18	14	20	35	30	20	36
Expected Frequency	25	25	25	25	25	25	25	25	25	25

Figure 8-9 shows the flowchart for a procedure that examines this distribution and computes x^2.

8.10 COMPOUND INTEREST

The compound interest formula is

$$a = p\left(1 + \frac{i}{100}\right)^n$$

where p is the principal (the amount originally invested or deposited), i is the yearly rate of interest, n is the number of years, and a is the amount (principal + interest). The flowchart shown in Figure 8-10 is of a method for computing the values of an initial deposit of $3000 invested at 12 percent interest for 10 to 30 years. This procedure illustrates a simple loop, which is repeated 20 times.

Section 8.11   Customer Billing

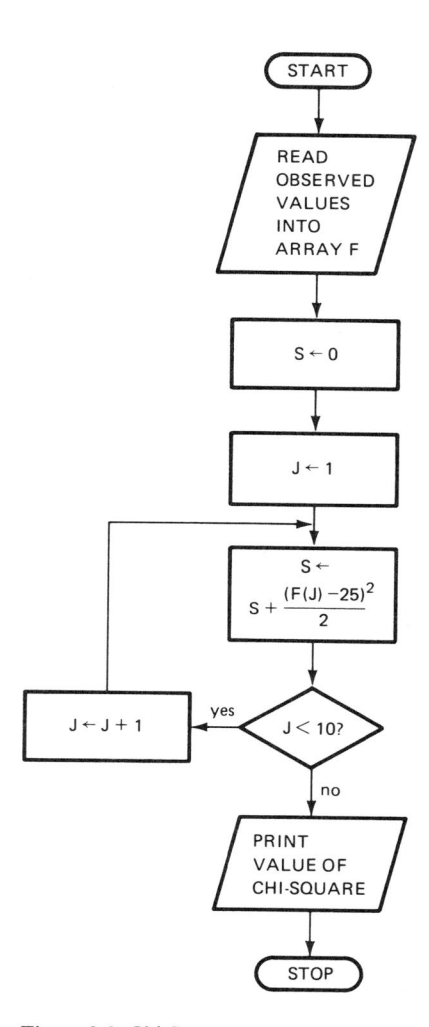

```
                    ┌───────┐
                    │ START │
                    └───┬───┘
                        ▼
                ╱─────────────╲
               ╱  READ         ╲
              ╱   OBSERVED      ╲
              ╲   VALUES        ╱
               ╲  INTO         ╱
                ╲  ARRAY F    ╱
                 ╲───────────╱
                        │
                        ▼
                  ┌──────────┐
                  │  S ← 0   │
                  └────┬─────┘
                       ▼
                  ┌──────────┐
                  │  J ← 1   │
                  └────┬─────┘
                       ▼
                  ┌──────────────┐
                  │  S ←         │
                  │       (F(J)−25)² │
                  │  S + ─────────── │
                  │           2      │
                  └────┬─────────┘
                       ▼
   ┌───────────┐  yes  ╱╲
   │ J ← J + 1 │◀──────╱  ╲
   └─────▲─────┘      ╱J<10?╲
         │            ╲      ╱
         │             ╲    ╱
         │              ╲  ╱
         │               ╲╱
         │               │ no
         │               ▼
         │         ╱──────────╲
         │        ╱  PRINT      ╲
         │       ╱   VALUE OF    ╲
         │       ╲   CHI-SQUARE  ╱
         │        ╲─────────────╱
         │               │
         │               ▼
         │           ┌──────┐
         │           │ STOP │
         │           └──────┘
```

Figure 8-9 Chi-Square.

8.11 CUSTOMER BILLING

The flowchart in Figure 8-11 shows how a furniture store handles the billing of overdue accounts. A late payment penalty is charged to accounts 30 days overdue. The amount of the penalty is based on the unpaid balance in the account. If the balance is over $300, the penalty is 5 percent; otherwise a 2 percent charge is levied. The amount of the penalty must be added to the next bill sent to the customer. If the account is 60 days or more overdue, a message (PAST DUE) is printed on the statement. The procedure also causes a statement to be printed for all accounts that are overdue 30

Chapter 8   Problems with Flowcharts   232

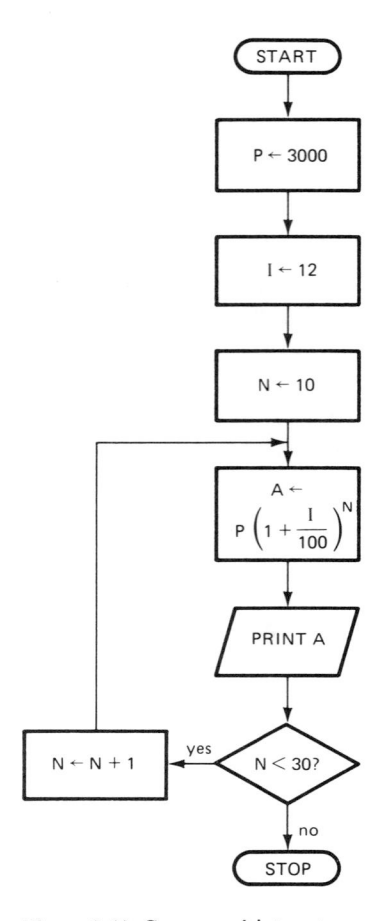

```
                    START
                      │
                      ▼
                  ┌───────┐
                  │P ← 3000│
                  └───────┘
                      │
                      ▼
                  ┌───────┐
                  │ I ← 12│
                  └───────┘
                      │
                      ▼
                  ┌───────┐
                  │N ← 10 │
                  └───────┘
                      │
         ┌────────────▼
         │       ┌─────────────┐
         │       │     A ←     │
         │       │P(1 + I/100)^N│
         │       └─────────────┘
         │            │
         │            ▼
         │        ╱────────╲
         │        │ PRINT A │
         │        ╲────────╱
         │            │
         │    yes     ▼
    ┌─────────┐   ◇───────◇
    │N ← N + 1│◀──│ N < 30?│
    └─────────┘   ◇───────◇
                      │ no
                      ▼
                    STOP
```

Figure 8-10 Compound interest.

days or less. The store's credit manager handles, on an individual basis, those accounts that remain unpaid after a certain time.

8.12 CHANGE MAKER

Since computer users have an affinity for change (changing their flowcharts, changing their minds, changing their jobs, and so on), the procedure shown in Figure 8-12 should be appealing to them. Such a change maker procedure has its uses in payroll programs where actual money must be divided into pay envelopes. An input value of 5367 ($53.67), for example, would generate: 1 fifty-dollar bill, 3 one-dollar bills, 1 fifty-cent coin, 1 dime, 1 nickle, and 2 pennies. The United States currency system includes paper bills in denominations of $1, 2, 5, 10, 20, 50, 100, 500, 1000, 5000, and 10,000 and coins of 1, 5, 10, 25, 50, and 100¢ (silver dollar). The amount to be converted to change is reduced to the number of each of these denominations needed by a succes-

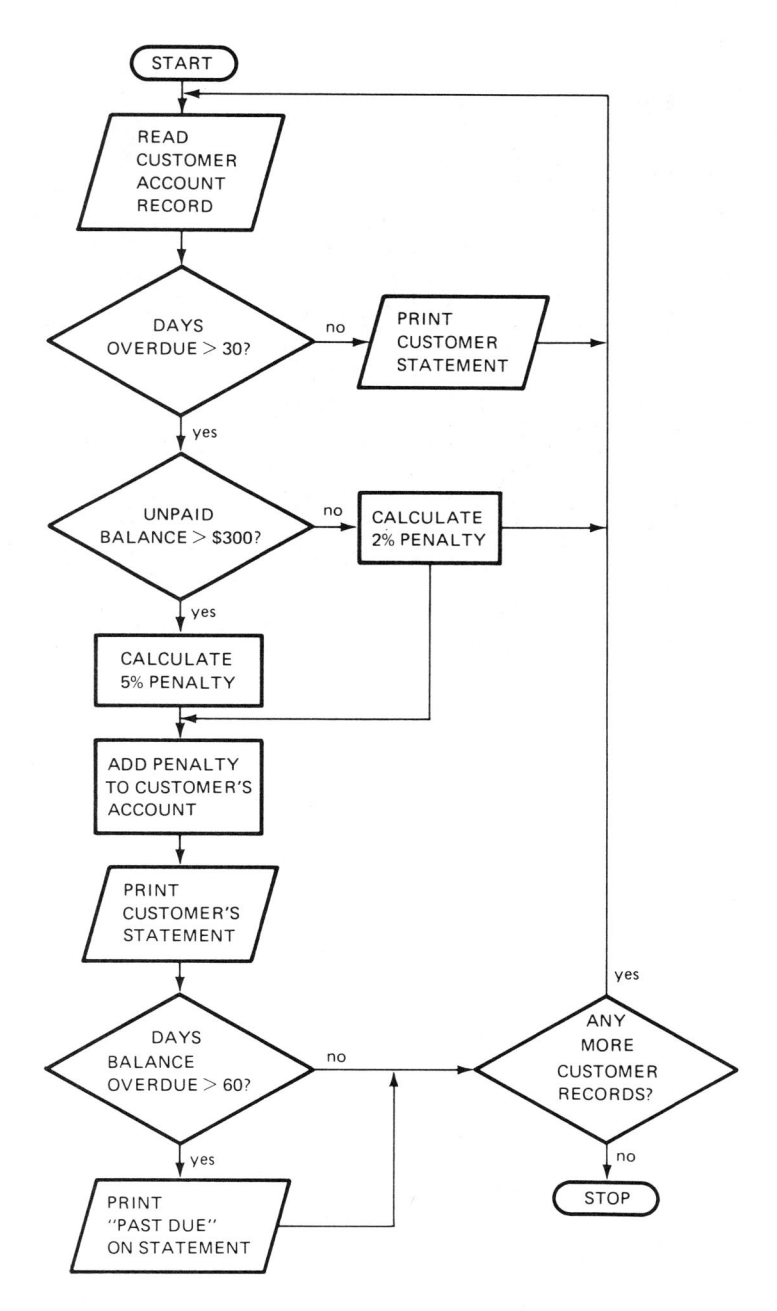

Figure 8-11 Customer billing.

Chapter 8   Problems with Flowcharts   234

sive series of tests and divisions starting with the largest denominator. The $2 bill and 100 (silver dollar) coin are not included due to their infrequent use in change making. The coin conversion table used in this procedure is as follows:

Coin Conversion Table

N	X(N)	A(N)	T(N)
1	1000000	Ten Thousand Dollar Bill	0
2	500000	Five Thousand Dollar Bill	0
3	100000	One Thousand Dollar Bill	0
4	50000	Five Hundred Dollar Bill	0
5	10000	One Hundred Dollar Bill	0
6	5000	Fifty Dollar Bill	0
7	2000	Twenty Dollar Bill	0
8	1000	Ten Dollar Bill	0
9	500	Five Dollar Bill	0
10	100	One Dollar Bill	0
11	50	Fifty Cent Coin	0
12	25	Quarter	0
13	10	Dime	0
14	5	Nickle	0
15	1	Penny	0

Section 8.13   *Trigonometric Functions*   235

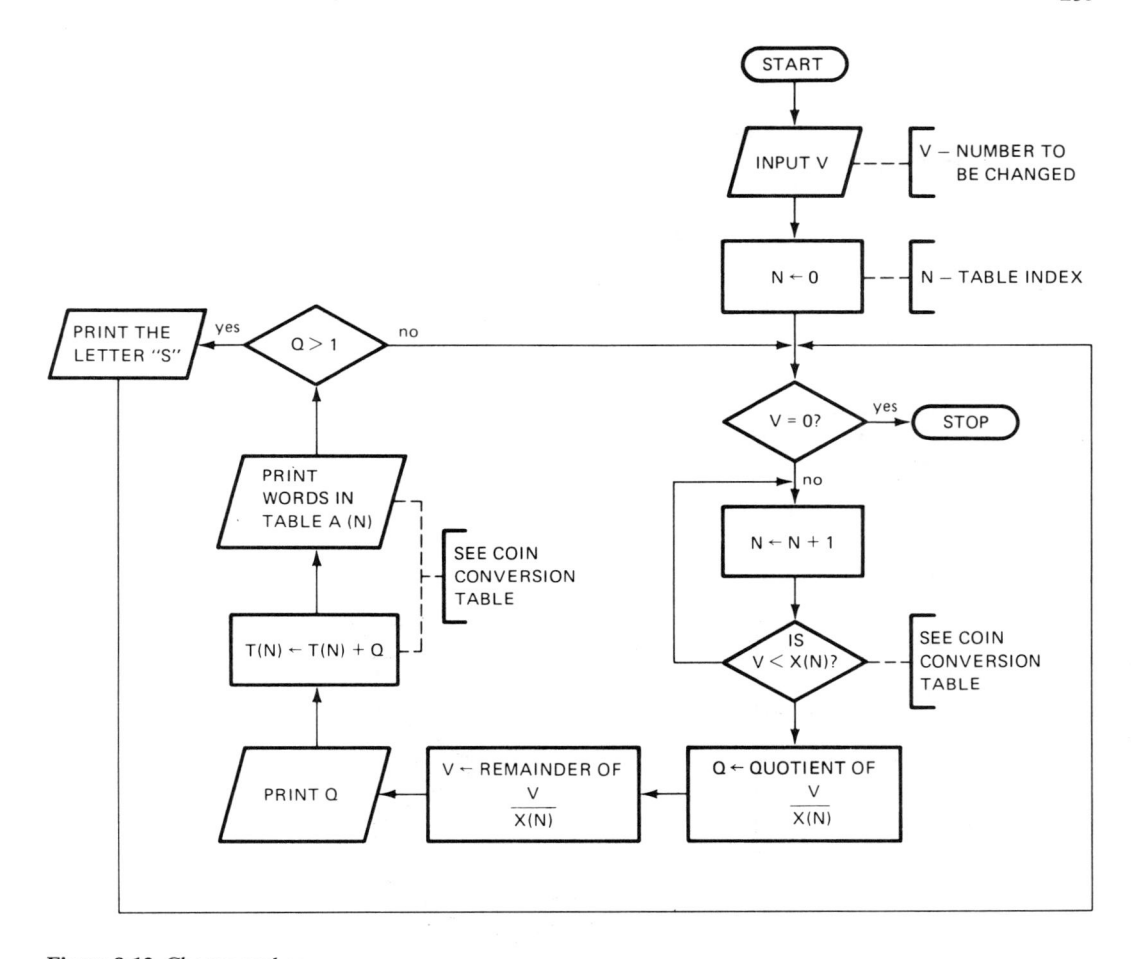

Figure 8-12 Change maker.

8.13 TRIGONOMETRIC FUNCTIONS

Figure 8-13 shows the flowchart for computing and printing a table of trigonometric functions. The procedure uses the following relationships and approximations for the sine, cosine, tangent, and cotangent:

$$\sin x = x - \frac{x^3}{3!} + \frac{x^5}{5!} - \frac{x^7}{7!} + \frac{x^9}{9!} - \frac{x^{11}}{11!} + \cdots,$$

$$\cos x = 1 - \frac{x^2}{2!} + \frac{x^4}{4!} - \frac{x^6}{6!} + \frac{x^8}{8!} - \frac{x^{10}}{10!} + \cdots,$$

$$\tan x = \frac{\sin x}{\cos x},$$

$$\cot x = \frac{\cos x}{\sin x}.$$

Chapter 8　Problems with Flowcharts　　236

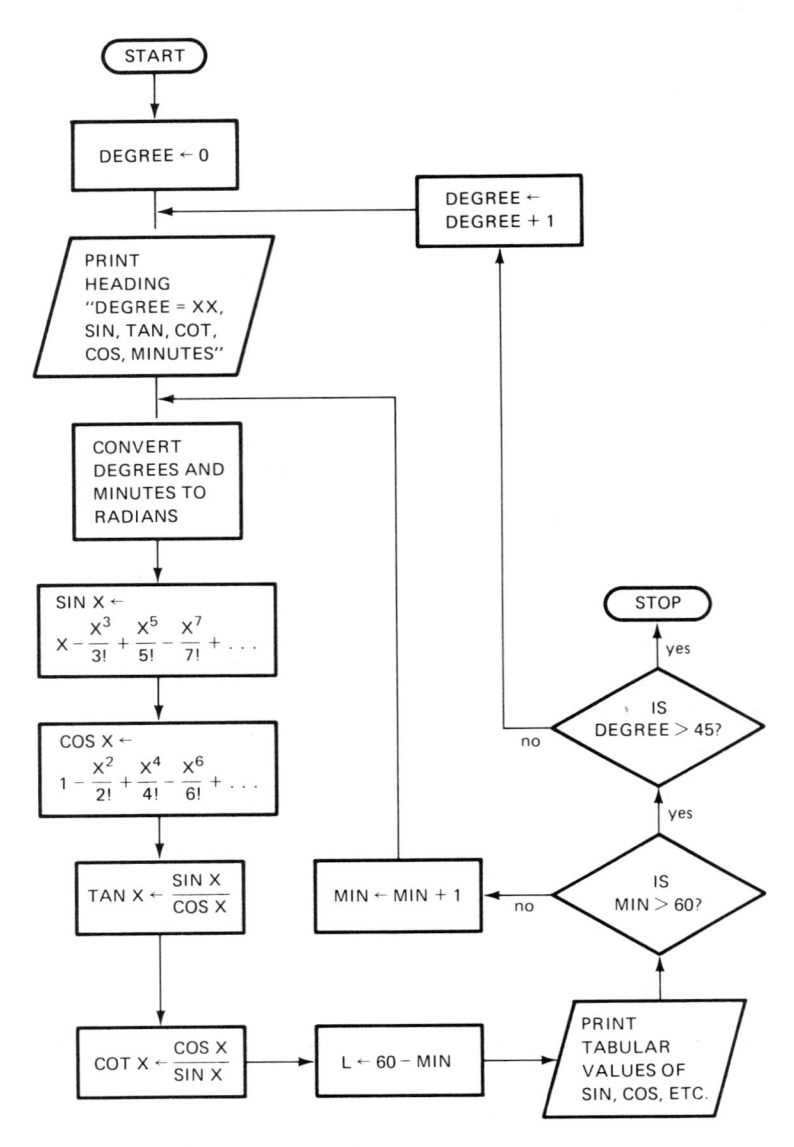

Figure 8-13　Trigonometric functions.

8.14 EMPLOYEE PAYROLL

This example shows the method of computation for the weekly wage of an employee. The method computes the weekly wage and prints the computed value along with the employees identification number. Input to the program is a data record containing

Section 8.14   Employee Payroll

the employee's ID number, hours worked, standard weekly pay rate, and overtime rate. After determining the number of hours that the employee worked, the program determines the wage, using either the standard rate or the overtime rate. If the number of hours exceeds 40, the procedure uses the overtime rate for all hours over 40 and the standard rate for the first 40 hours. If the number of hours was 40 or less, the program multiplies the number of hours by the standard rate. A flowchart of this problem is shown in Figure 8-14.

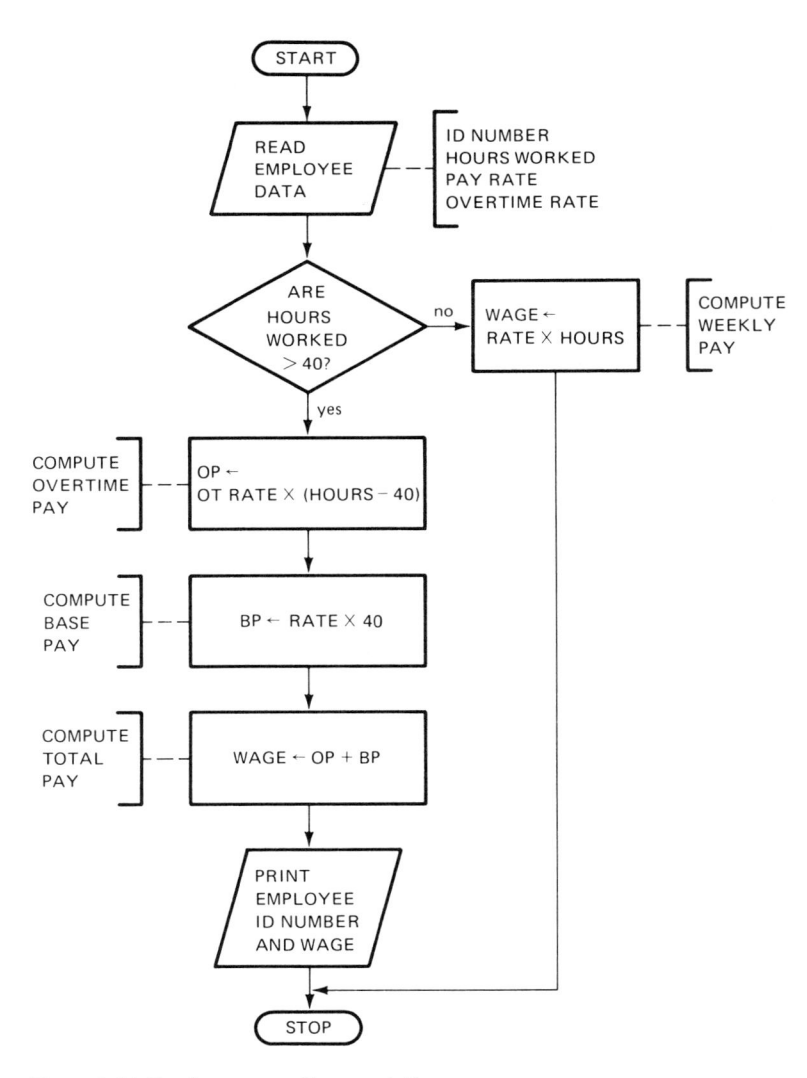

Figure 8-14 Employee payroll computation.

8.15 COMPANY PAYROLL

It is possible to perform the same computation described in the previous problem for 450 employees of the Southern Construction Company. The flowchart in Figure 8-15

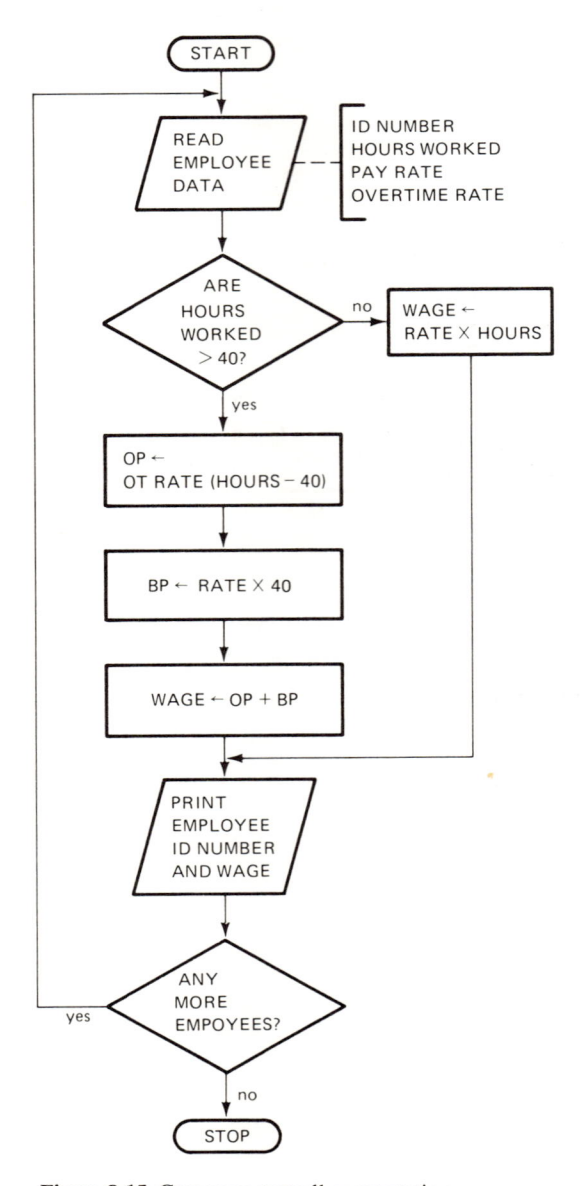

```
                START
                  │
                  ▼
            ┌───────────┐      ┌ ID NUMBER
            │   READ    │      │ HOURS WORKED
            │ EMPLOYEE  │──── ─┤ PAY RATE
            │   DATA    │      │ OVERTIME RATE
            └───────────┘      └
                  │
                  ▼
              ╱ ARE  ╲
             ╱ HOURS  ╲   no    ┌─────────────┐
            ╱ WORKED   ╲──────▶│   WAGE ←    │
             ╲  > 40?  ╱        │ RATE × HOURS│
              ╲       ╱         └─────────────┘
                │ yes                  │
                ▼                      │
        ┌───────────────────┐          │
        │      OP ←         │          │
        │ OT RATE (HOURS−40)│          │
        └───────────────────┘          │
                │                      │
                ▼                      │
        ┌───────────────────┐          │
        │   BP ← RATE × 40  │          │
        └───────────────────┘          │
                │                      │
                ▼                      │
        ┌───────────────────┐          │
        │   WAGE ← OP + BP  │          │
        └───────────────────┘          │
                │                      │
                ◀──────────────────────┘
                ▼
            ┌───────────┐
            │   PRINT   │
            │ EMPLOYEE  │
            │ ID NUMBER │
            │ AND WAGE  │
            └───────────┘
                  │
                  ▼
               ╱ ANY ╲
              ╱ MORE  ╲  yes
              ╲EMPOYEES?╱─────▶ (back to READ)
               ╲     ╱
                 │ no
                 ▼
               STOP
```

Figure 8-15 Company payroll computation.

Section 8.17   Roman Numeralizer   239

illustrates how the Employee Payroll Computation flowchart can be altered to effect this computation.

8.16 THE 50 PUZZLE

The 6 by 6 array in Figure 8-16 contains 36 numbered squares.

28	3	8	32	18	13
7	30	1	20	17	4
36	17	27	9	13	12
19	2	25	14	5	21
10	19	29	8	23	16
16	11	36	13	31	28

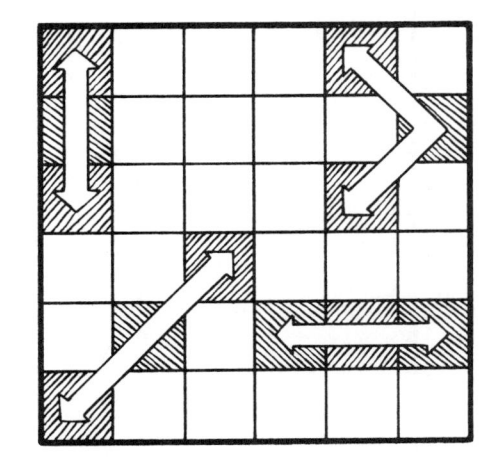

Figure 8-16.

The object of the puzzle is to connect any 3 consecutive squares, either in a vertical line, a horizontal line, or on diagonal lines, that add up to exactly 50. Typical connections that would be allowed are shown below. The flowchart in Figure 8-17 may be used to write a program to solve the 50 puzzle.

8.17 ROMAN NUMERALIZER

Conversion of numbers from binary to decimal is a rather common function to computer users. The decimal numbers are expressed by a combination of Arabic numerals 0 through 9. This, however, is not the only way to express numbers. In fact, long before the Arabic decimal system of number notation became popular, the Romans had their own number system, called Roman numerals. Conversion of binary numbers to Roman numerals does not lend itself to a mathematical conversion due to lack of a symmetrical relationship between the "digits" of the Roman numeral system. A reduction conversion method is used instead, as shown in Figure 8-18. The Romans had no concept of fractions, and so all their numerals were integers. At the time their system was initiated, 1000 was as large as could be conceived and was given the letter M (magna = large). Other decimal equivalents are shown in the following table.

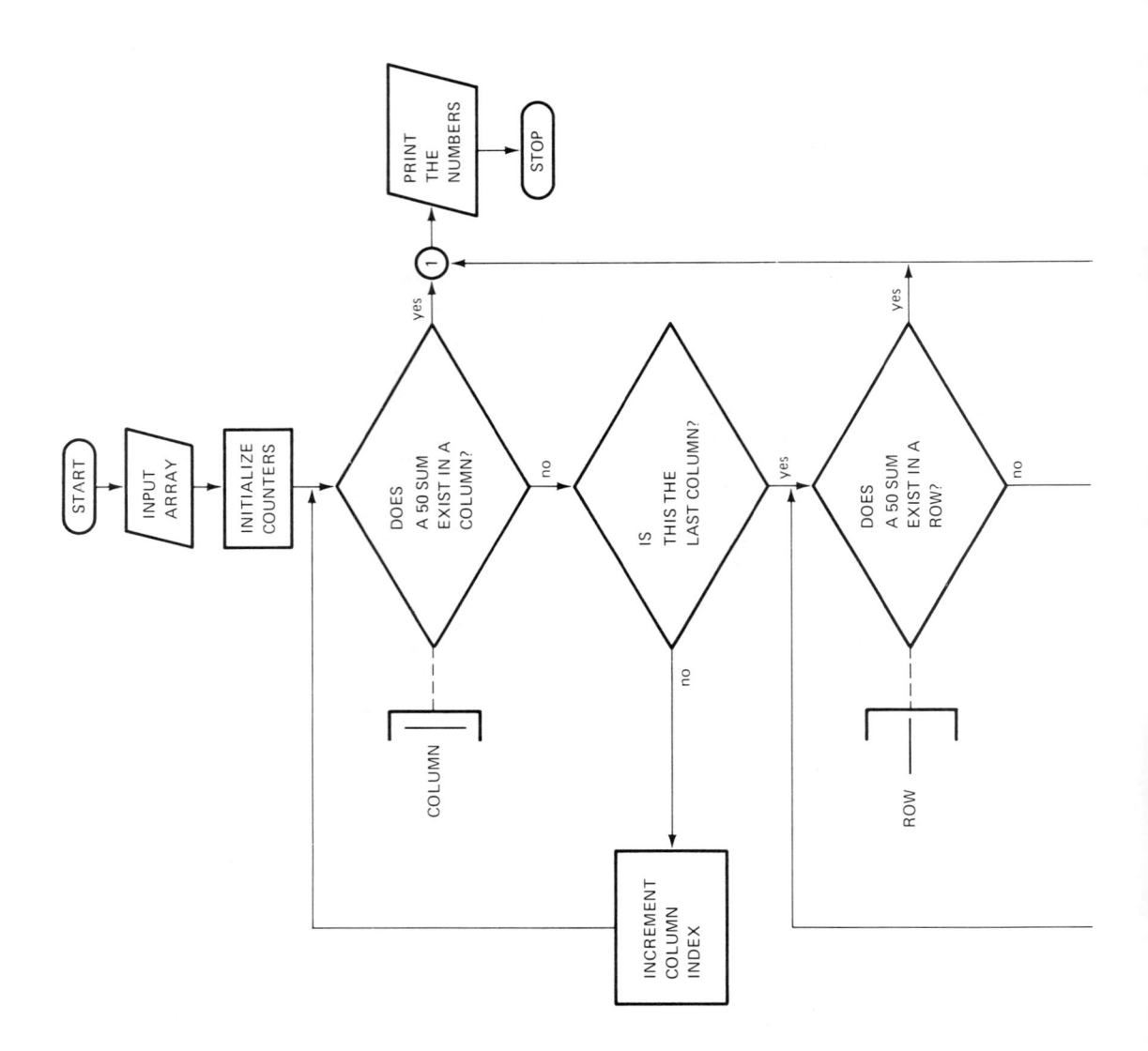

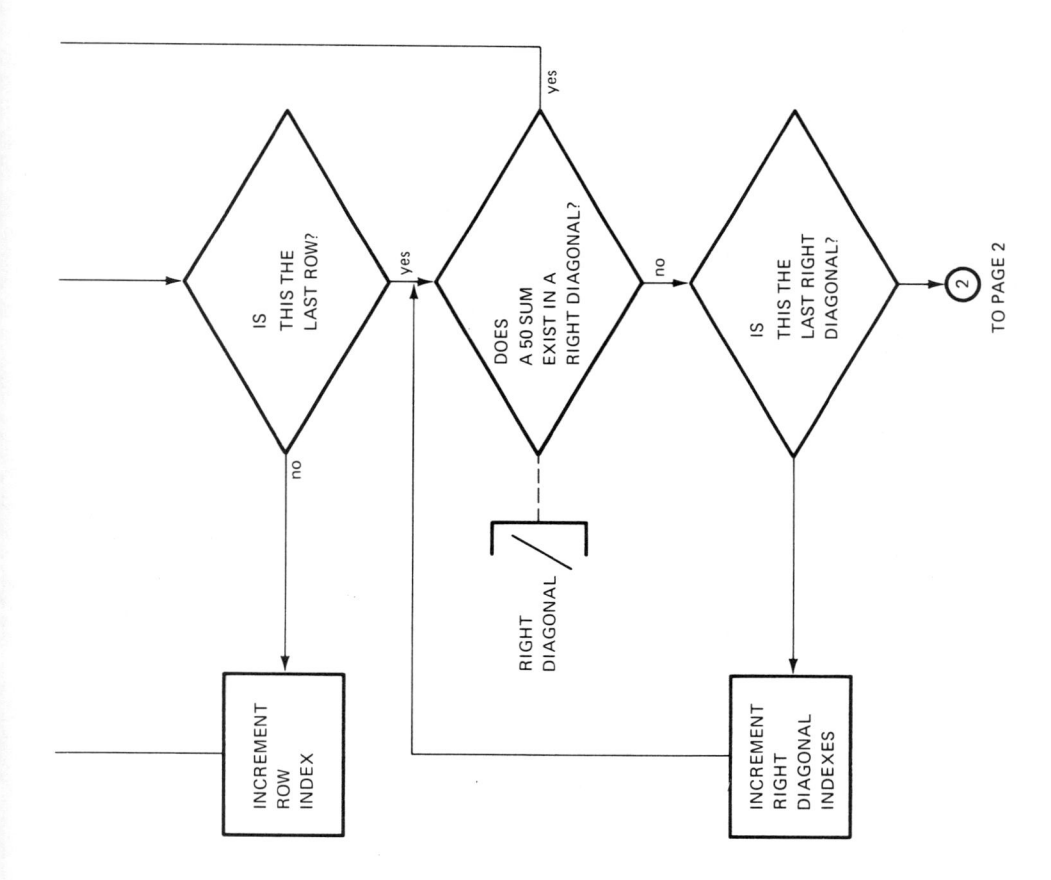

Figure 8-17 The 50 Puzzle, *Page 1*.

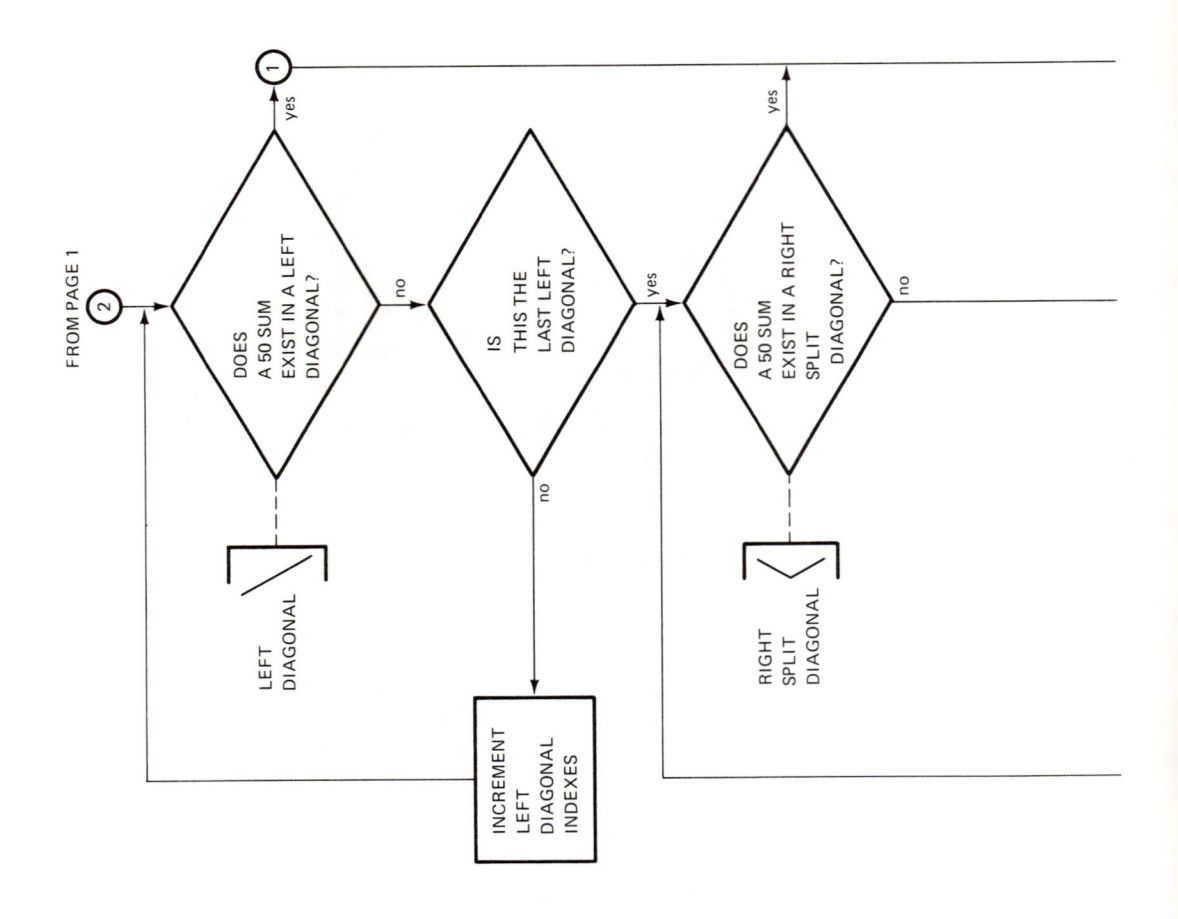

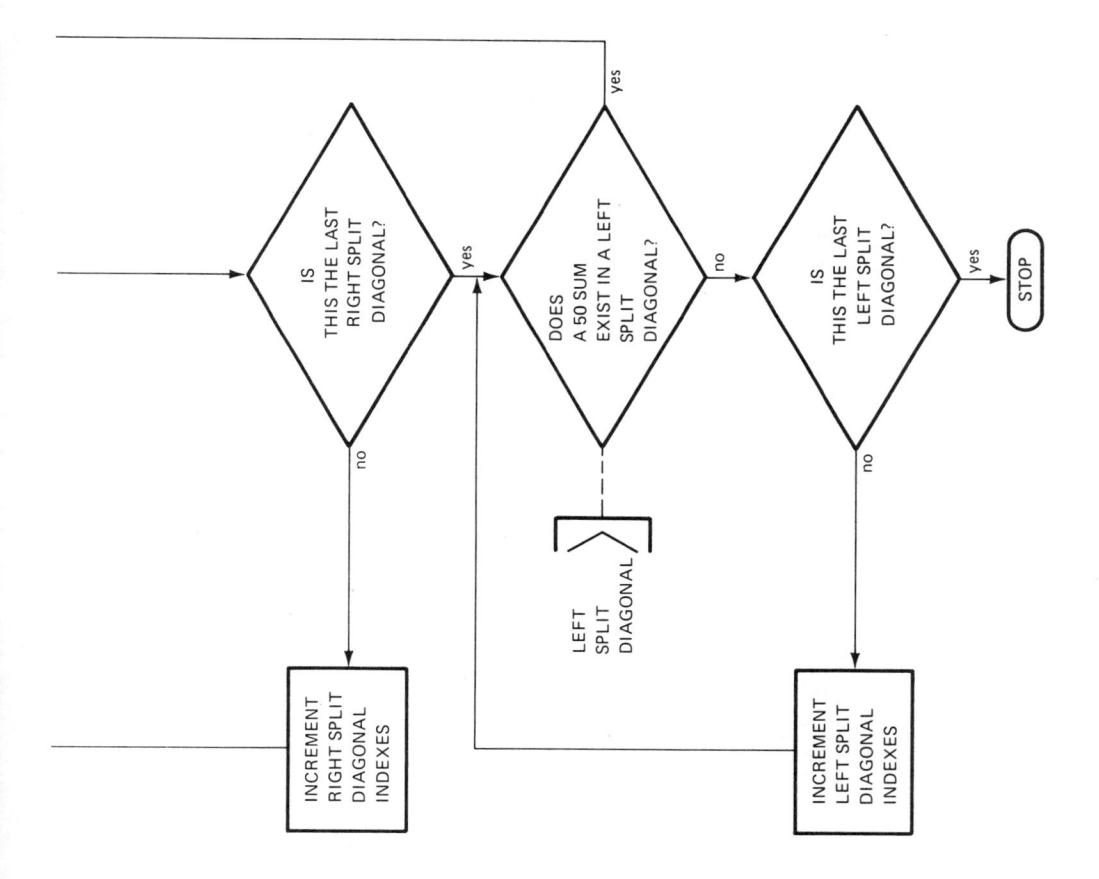

Figure 8-17 The 50 Puzzle, *Page 2*.

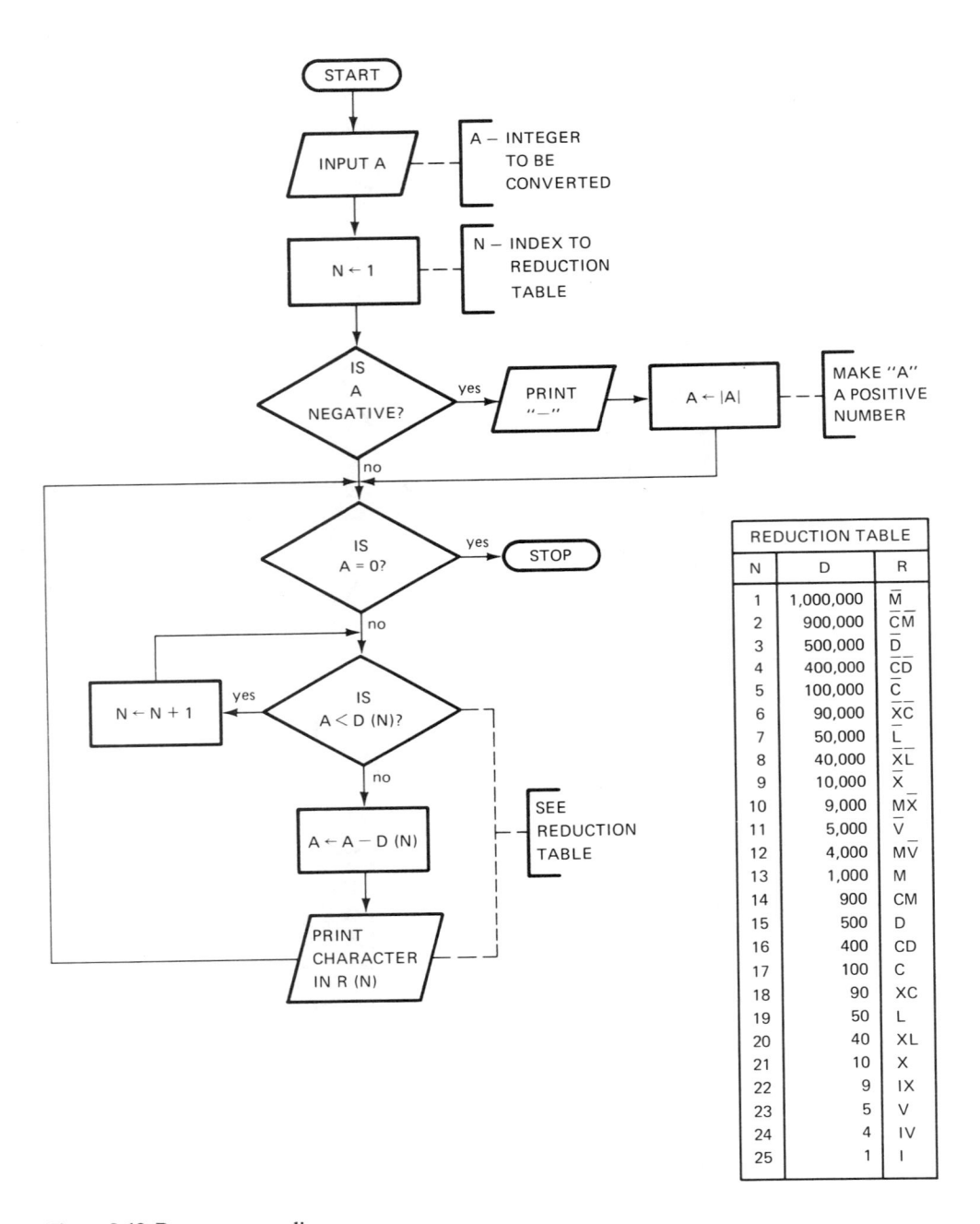

Figure 8-18 Roman numeralizer.

REDUCTION TABLE		
N	D	R
1	1,000,000	M̄
2	900,000	C̄M̄
3	500,000	D̄
4	400,000	C̄D̄
5	100,000	C̄
6	90,000	X̄C̄
7	50,000	L̄
8	40,000	X̄L̄
9	10,000	X̄
10	9,000	MX̄
11	5,000	V̄
12	4,000	MV̄
13	1,000	M
14	900	CM
15	500	D
16	400	CD
17	100	C
18	90	XC
19	50	L
20	40	XL
21	10	X
22	9	IX
23	5	V
24	4	IV
25	1	I

Section 8.18   *Payroll Deduction*

Roman/Decimal Equivalents

I = 1	$\overline{V}$ = 5,000
V = 5	$\overline{X}$ = 10,000
X = 10	$\overline{L}$ = 50,000
L = 50	$\overline{C}$ = 100,000
C = 100	$\overline{D}$ = 500,000
D = 500	$\overline{M}$ = 1,000,000
M = 1,000	

A later modification to the Roman numeral system extended the range a thousandfold by defining any "digit" with a bar over it as being 1000 times the normal value.

$$\text{Thus, } M = 1000 \text{ and } \overline{M} = 1{,}000{,}000$$

In this way, numbers as high as 1,000,000 can be expressed, and by use of multiple $\overline{M}$'s, even larger numbers are converted, for example

$$1975 = \text{MCMLXXV}$$
$$3398353 = \overline{\text{MMMCCCXCV}}\text{MMMCCCLIII}$$

8.18 PAYROLL DEDUCTION

Figure 8-19 illustrates a flowchart for a procedure to compute the Social Security deduction and accumulated gross pay of the employees of Liberty Insurance Company.

Employee's Name	Employee's ID Number	Gross Pay for Current Week	Accumulated Gross Pay
Todd Shirah	10643	100	14600
Michael Sicard	11218	163	17700
Mitch Wolcott	21600	250	19740
Steven Spencer	19846	210	8560
Tom Smith	21107	110	14800
Bill Wilson	22406	206	8400
Ron Taylor	19327	253	9960

The program should input the employee's ID number, gross pay for the current week, and accumulated gross pay for the current year. The program should output the employee's ID number, updated gross pay, Social Security deduction for the current week, and net pay for the current week. The Social Security deduction used in this example is 7 percent of the gross pay up to an accumulated gross pay of 10,000.

Chapter 8   Problems with Flowcharts   246

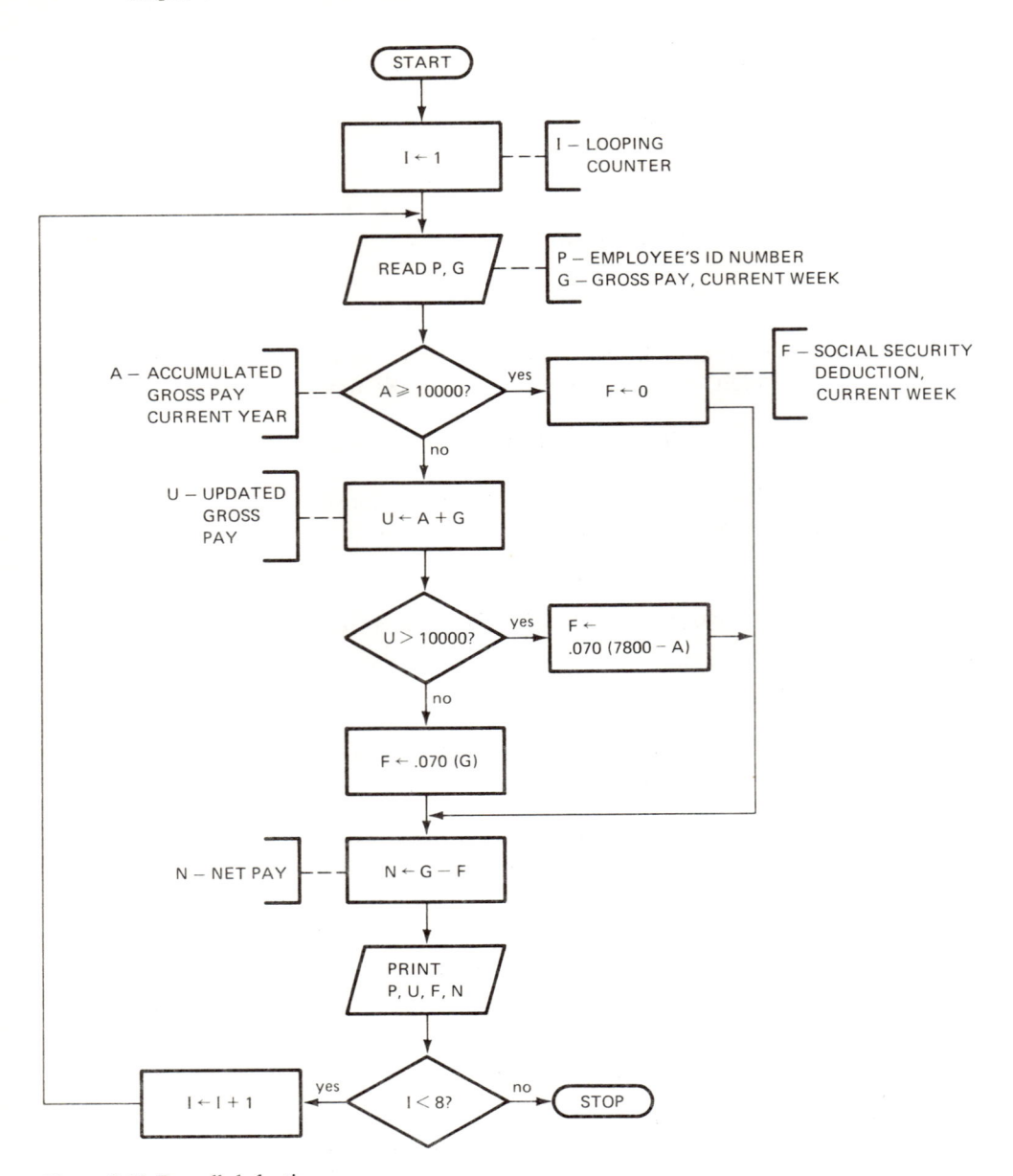

```
                        START
                          │
                          ▼
                      ┌───────┐
                      │ I ← 1 │────── I – LOOPING COUNTER
                      └───────┘
                          │
           ┌──────────────▼
           │          ┌─────────┐
           │          │ READ P,G│────── P – EMPLOYEE'S ID NUMBER
           │          └─────────┘        G – GROSS PAY, CURRENT WEEK
           │              │
           │              ▼
  A – ACCUMULATED     ◇ A ≥ 10000? ──yes──┐ F ← 0 ├──── F – SOCIAL SECURITY
  GROSS PAY           ◇                    └───────┘     DEDUCTION,
  CURRENT YEAR            │no                            CURRENT WEEK
           │              ▼
  U – UPDATED         ┌─────────┐
  GROSS PAY  ─ ─ ─ ─ │ U ← A+G │
                      └─────────┘
                          │
                          ▼
                      ◇ U > 10000? ──yes──┐ F ←        │
                          │                │ .070(7800-A)│──┐
                          │no              └─────────────┘  │
                          ▼                                 │
                      ┌──────────────┐                      │
                      │ F ← .070 (G) │                      │
                      └──────────────┘                      │
                          │◄─────────────────────────────────┘
                          ▼
  N – NET PAY  ─ ─ ─  ┌─────────┐
                      │ N ← G-F │
                      └─────────┘
                          │
                          ▼
                      ┌─────────┐
                      │ PRINT   │
                      │P,U,F,N  │
                      └─────────┘
                          │
           ┌──────────────▼
           │ yes                 no
    ┌─────────┐  ◇ I < 8? ────────► STOP
    │ I ← I+1 │◄────
    └─────────┘
```

Figure 8-19 Payroll deduction.

8.19 SLOT MACHINE SIMULATOR

A flowchart (Figure 8-20) is provided for readers who wish to "gamble" with their computers. The computer's typewriter (or CRT keyboard/display device) is used as the "slot machine"—a typewriter (or CRT keyboard) input is the "handle," and instead

Section 8.19   *Slot Machine Simulator*

of figures showing behind the "windows," the typewriter (or CRT display) outputs three words representing the figures. There are six "figures," and the payoffs vary approximately the same as the slot machines at Las Vegas.

Payoff Table

Special Combinations			Payoff
CHERRY	—	—	2
CHERRY	CHERRY	—	5
LEMON	LEMON	LEMON	8
LIME	LIME	—	5
LIME	LIME	LIME	10
ORANGE	ORANGE	—	5
ORANGE	ORANGE	ORANGE	10
BAR	BAR	BAR	18
STAR	STAR	STAR	100

The coin size of the simulator is 25 cents. The "figures" are chosen in random order. The money won or lost by the operator is typed after each "pull."

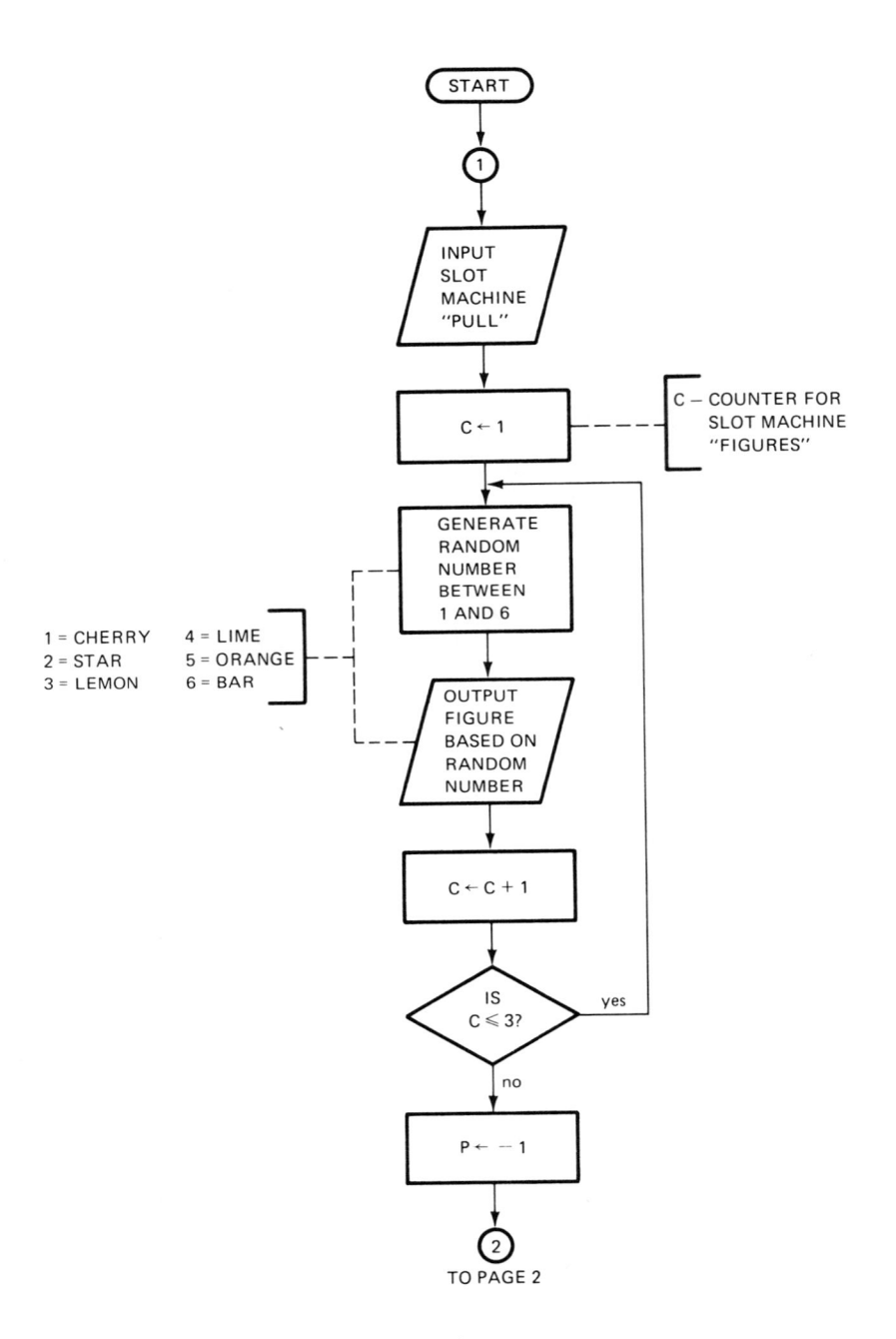

Figure 8-20 Slot machine simulator, *Page 1*.

Section 8.20   *Decimal-to-English Conversion*   249

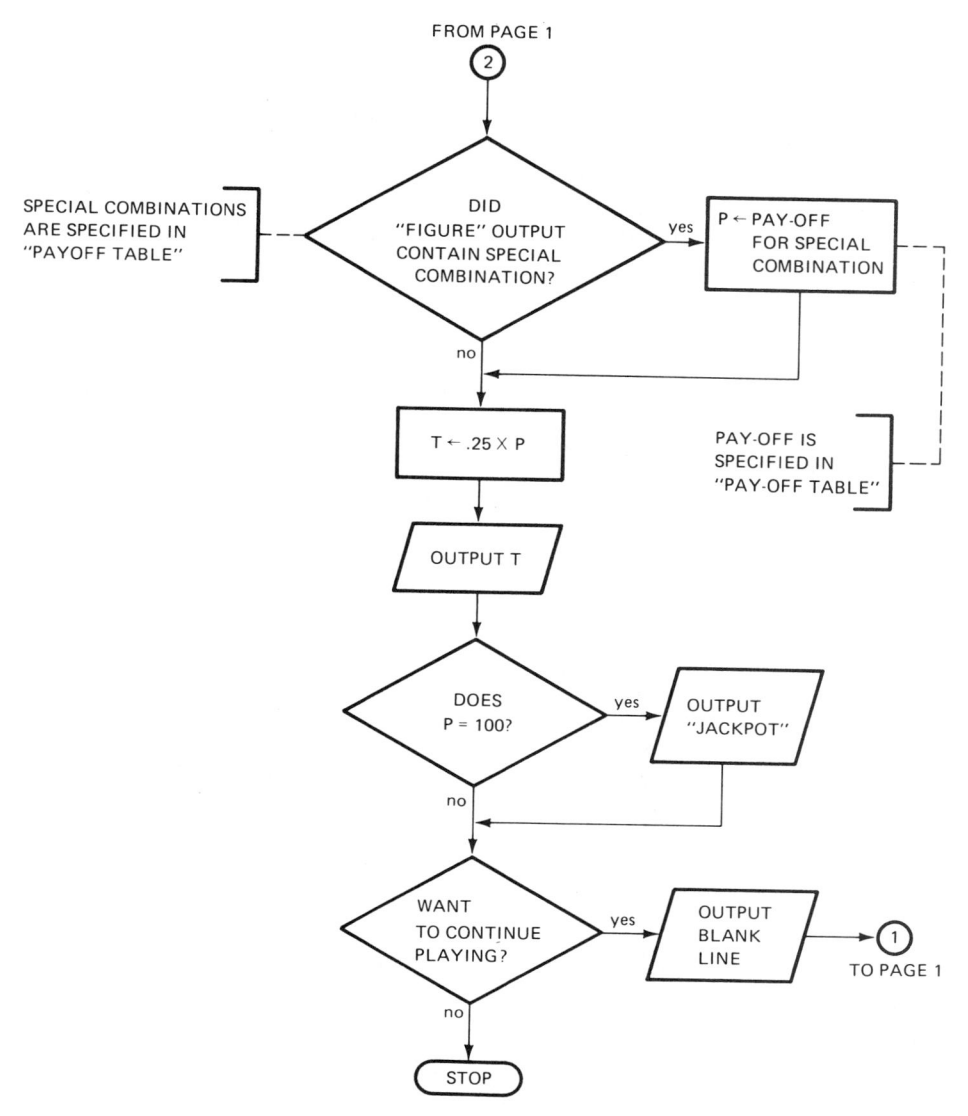

Figure 8-20 Slot machine simulator, *Page 2.*

8.20 DECIMAL-TO-ENGLISH CONVERSION

Numbers are usually represented by a sequence of Arabic digits. However, there are applications where an English word representation of a number is required, such as on a check. This procedure will convert decimal numbers to English.

Since the English language has proven illogical in spelling, definitions, and so on,

Chapter 8   Problems with Flowcharts

it is only fitting that no simple relationship occurs between a decimal number and its English language equivalent. It is interesting to note, however, that the conversion process between 1 to 999 repeats itself every time a decimal number has a comma. Example: 123, 456, 789, 212 could be broken at the commas into 4 numbers—123 ...456...789...212. Each group is followed by the appropriate word, such as thousand or million, to complete the conversion. Therefore, 123, 456, 789, 212 after conversion is one hundred and twenty-three billion, four hundred and fifty-six million, seven hundred and eighty-nine thousand, two hundred and twelve.

Figure 8-21 shows the flowchart of a procedure that will convert a given decimal number into its English language equivalent.

8.21 PRIME NUMBERS

A *prime* is a positive whole number that cannot be written as the product of two smaller factors (other than 1). The numbers 3 and 7 are primes, but 6 and 10 are not since $6 = 2 \cdot 3$ and $10 = 2 \cdot 5$. The first primes are:

1, 2, 3, 5, 7, 11, 13, 17, 19, 23, 29, 31, 37, 41, 43, 47, 53, ...

A glance reveals that this sequence does not follow any simple law. In fact, the structure of the sequence of primes is extremely complex. No formula exists that produces all possible primes.

One way of finding primes is by the *Sieve of Eratosthenes*. First, write all the numbers 1, 2, 3, 4, 5, ... as far as you care to go. Then strike out all those you know are not primes; those that are left constitute the table of primes. Since all even numbers can be divided by 2, the only *even prime*, all other even numbers can be canceled immediately. Next, every number divisible by 3 (except 3 itself) is crossed out, then every number divisible by 5, and so on. In other words, leave in each number that is not crossed out, divide all the others by it, and cross out all its multiples. The following diagram shows the process for the primes up to 50.

1	2	3	4̸	5	6̸	7	8̸	9̸	1̸0̸
11	1̸2̸	13	1̸4̸	1̸5̸	1̸6̸	17	1̸8̸	19	2̸0̸
2̸1̸	2̸2̸	23	2̸4̸	2̸5̸	2̸6̸	2̸7̸	2̸8̸	29	3̸0̸
31	3̸2̸	3̸3̸	3̸4̸	3̸5̸	3̸6̸	37	3̸8̸	3̸9̸	4̸0̸
41	4̸2̸	43	4̸4̸	4̸5̸	4̸6̸	47	4̸8̸	4̸9̸	5̸0̸

First, the numbers divisible by 2 are crossed out, then those divisible by 3, then by 5 and 7. We need not test with the numbers from 11 on, because $11 > \sqrt{50}$; hence, if 11 divides any of the remaining numbers, the quotient is one of the already determined primes less than 11.

Figure 8-22 shows the flowchart for a procedure that will find all prime numbers less than 1000 by means of the Sieve of Eratosthenes.

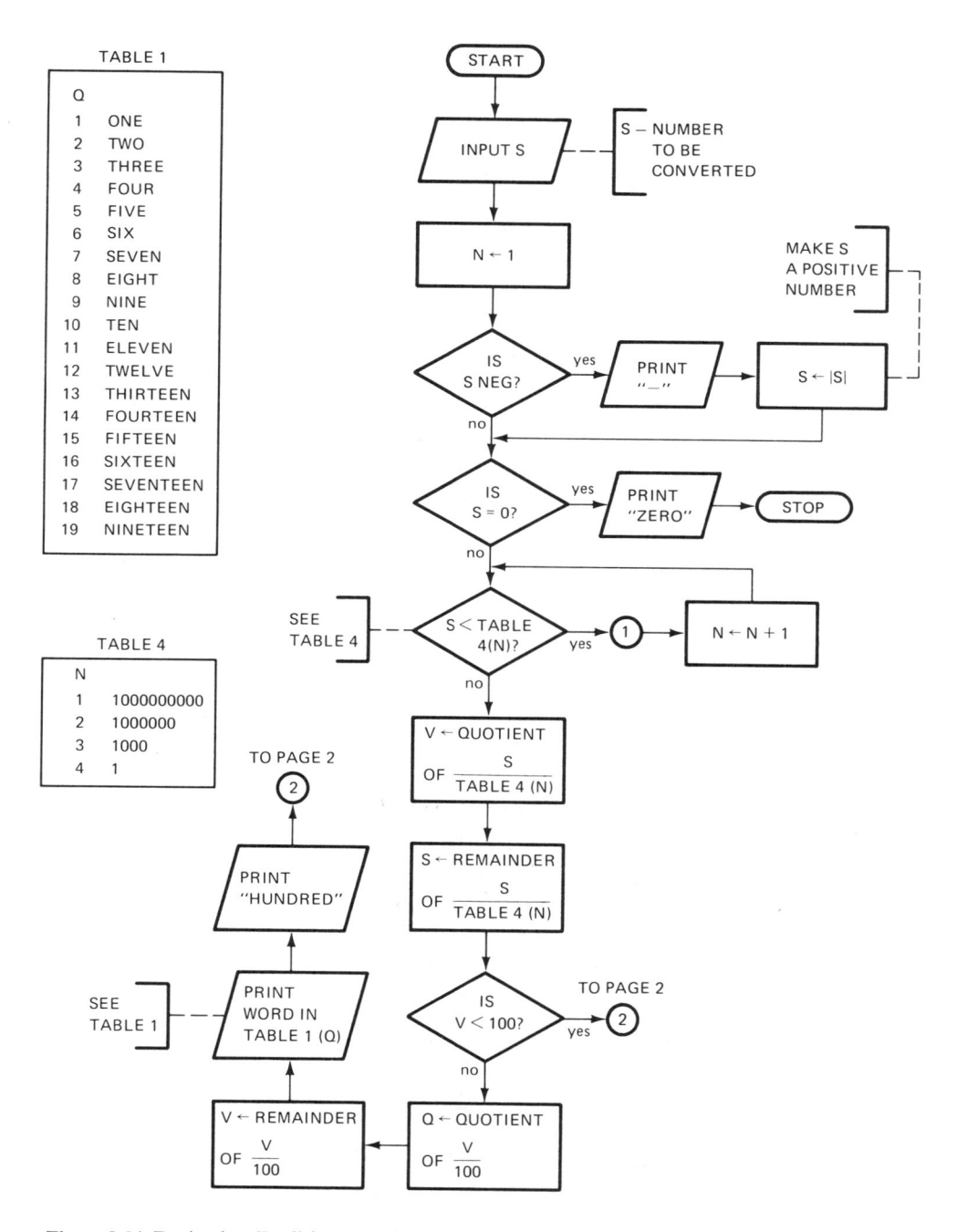

TABLE 1	
Q	
1	ONE
2	TWO
3	THREE
4	FOUR
5	FIVE
6	SIX
7	SEVEN
8	EIGHT
9	NINE
10	TEN
11	ELEVEN
12	TWELVE
13	THIRTEEN
14	FOURTEEN
15	FIFTEEN
16	SIXTEEN
17	SEVENTEEN
18	EIGHTEEN
19	NINETEEN

TABLE 4	
N	
1	1000000000
2	1000000
3	1000
4	1

Figure 8-21 Decimal-to-English conversion, *Page 1*.

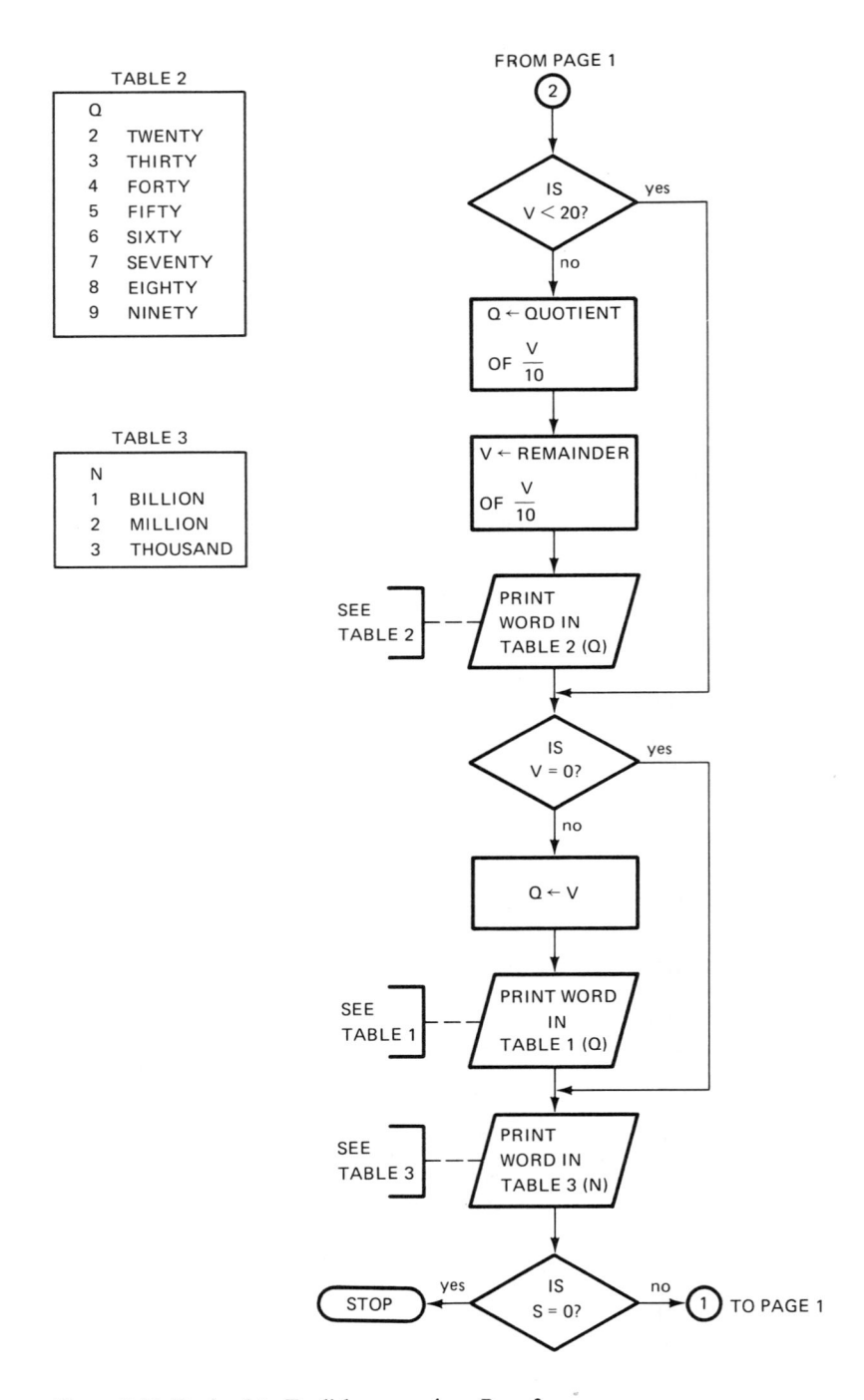

TABLE 2	
Q	
2	TWENTY
3	THIRTY
4	FORTY
5	FIFTY
6	SIXTY
7	SEVENTY
8	EIGHTY
9	NINETY

TABLE 3	
N	
1	BILLION
2	MILLION
3	THOUSAND

Figure 8-21 Decimal-to-English conversion, *Page 2*.

Section 8.21   Prime Numbers

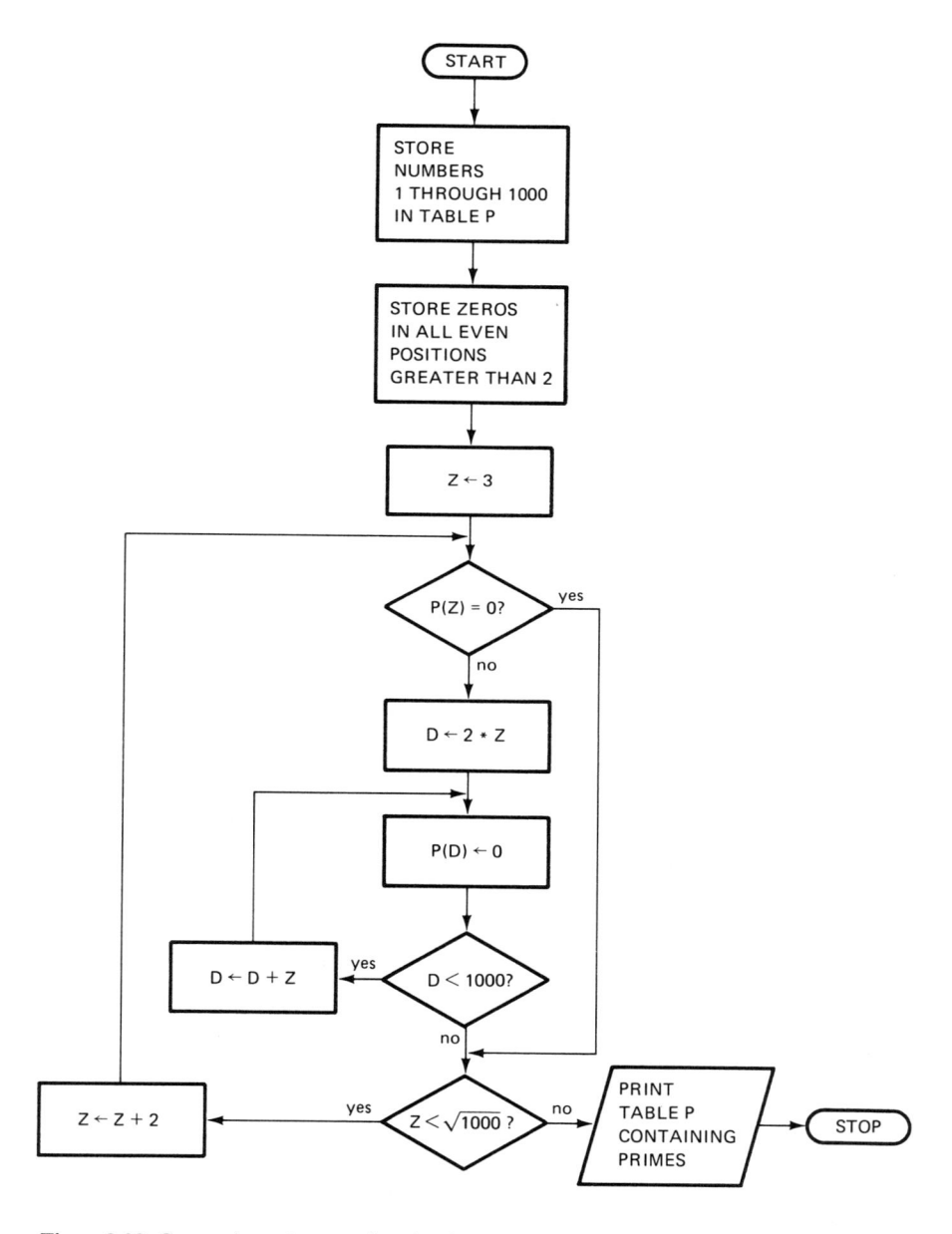

Figure 8-22 Generating prime numbers by the Sieve of Eratosthenes.

Since we know that 2 is the only even prime, a better way to generate primes would be to examine only the odd numbers, starting with the number 3, and divide each succeeding odd number up to some final desired value by all the primes we have found. The flowchart for this procedure is shown in Figure 8-23.

Chapter 8   Problems with Flowcharts   254

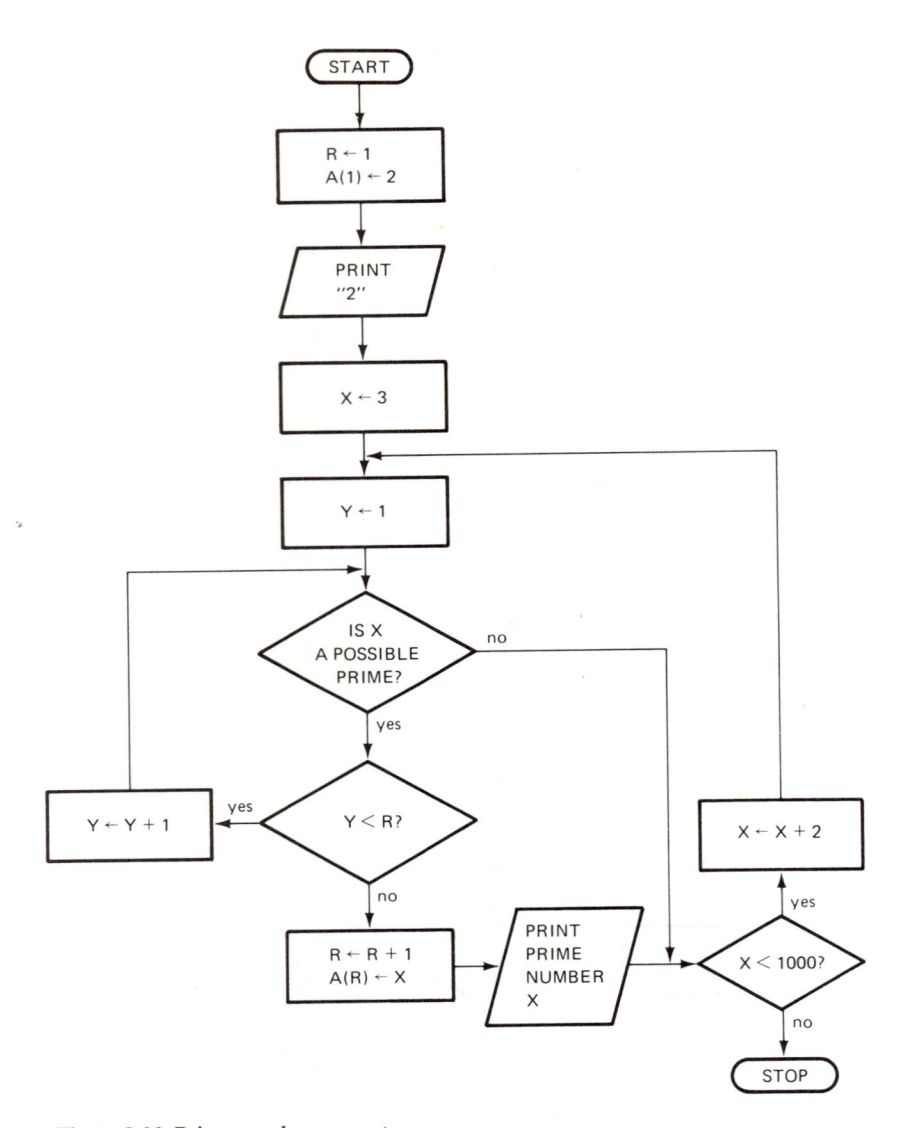

Figure 8-23 Prime number generator.

8.22 BILLIARD SIMULATION

The following shows how a computer procedure can simulate a real situation. We will see how to simulate the path of an eight ball on a billiard table.

The ball is projected at 45° from the lower left-hand corner of the table, which is 12 units wide and 16 units long. We assume that the ball travels back and forth across

Section 8.22 Billiard Simulation

the table, always rebounding at 45° from each edge. This procedure determines the position of the ball on the table at the end of a specified time, assuming that the ball travels at a constant speed on the table.

With vertical and horizontal directions represented by the x and y coordinates, the position of the ball at any particular time is specified by the values of x and y. The values of x and y at the end of, say, 22 time intervals are $x = 2$, $y = 10$. Let us follow the path of the ball in terms of x and y, starting at 0. At the end of the first time interval, $x = 1$ and $y = 1$. At the end of the second interval, $x = 2$ and $y = 2$. Thus, in each interval we add 1 to x and 1 to y.

At the end of 12 intervals, $x = 12$ and $y = 12$: the ball strikes the edge of the table and rebounds. The ball now begins to travel back across the table in a direction that makes x smaller (y continues to increase as before). Later (when $y = 16$), the ball strikes and rebounds from the top of the table. Thereafter, the ball's direction is such that both x and y decrease with the passage of time.

We must develop our procedure to detect when x becomes equal to the width of the table and then to modify the procedure to subtract 1 from the value of x, rather than adding as before. When y becomes equal to the length of the table, the procedure must then make the same modification for y. A flowchart for accomplishing this billiard table calculation is shown in Figure 8-24.

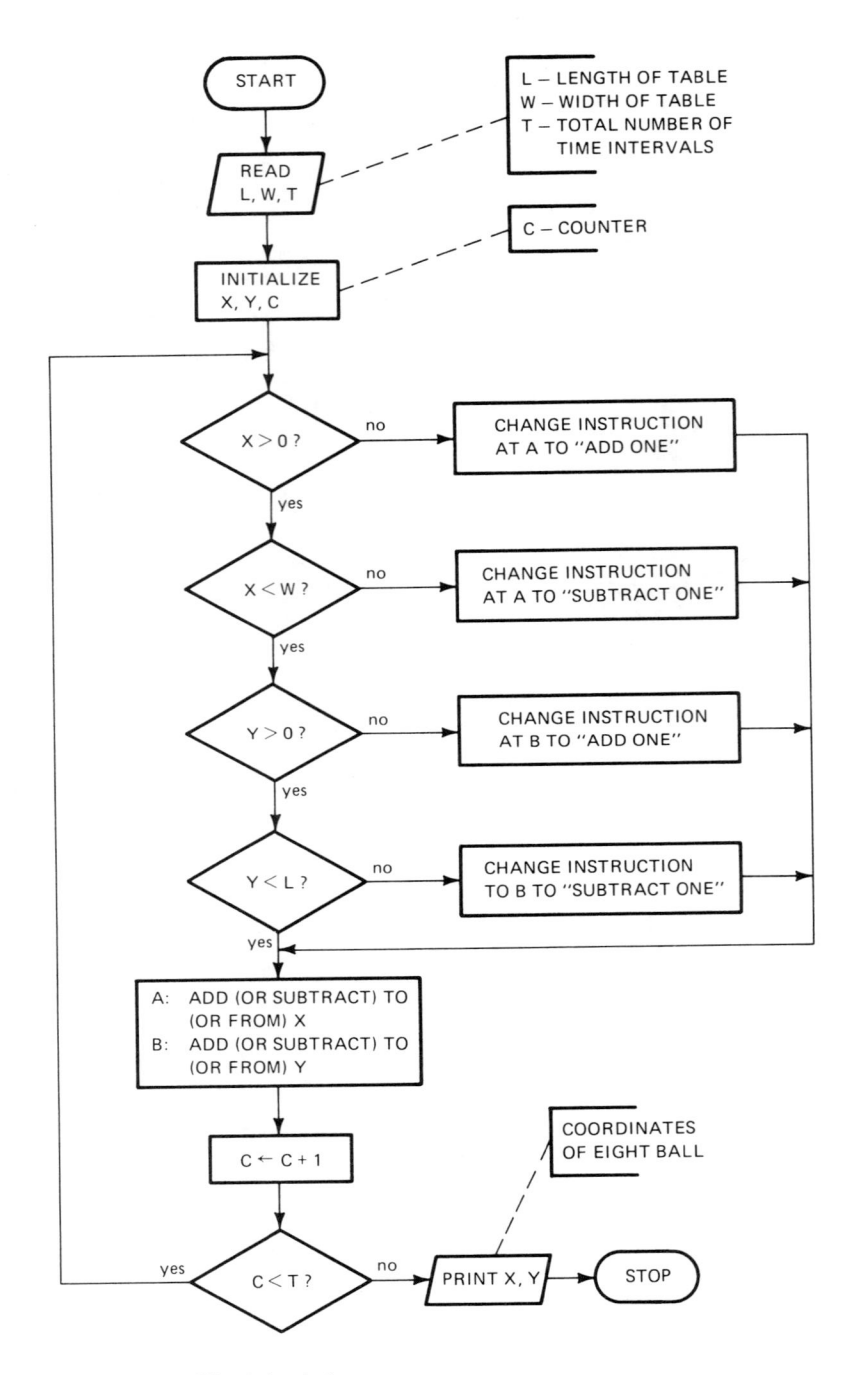

Figure 8-24 Billiard simulation.

Section 8.23   Mouse in a Maze

We first read in the table length (16 units), the width (12 units), and the total time (22 intervals), and we set x, y, and the interval counter to 0. We set two instructions A and B (shown toward the bottom of the flowchart) to *add* 1. These are the instructions that can be modified to *subtract* as the values of x and/or y require.

Looking at the flowchart, let us see what happens when $x = 5$ and $y = 5$. A test of x at the first test point shows that x is greater than 0. We therefore bypass the instruction modification and go to the second test point, which shows that x is less than the width. Therefore, we again bypass to a similar pair of tests for y, which disclose that y is also greater than 0 and that it is less than the length. Thus, the two instructions A and B add 1 to x and y, respectively.

Next let us examine the situation where $x = 12$ and $y = 12$; the first point of rebound from a table edge. Now, the first test point shows that x is again greater than 0, so we again take the bypass to the second test point. Here, since x is now equal to the width, we do not bypass the instruction modification, and thus change the instruction at A so that it *subtracts* from x. Testing the y value, we find that no instruction modification is necessary, and that y is incremented by one.

Continuing to follow the ball's upward journey, we reach the top edge where the ball's rebound causes x and y to enter a phase in which both coordinates decreases Thus, step by step, we make the flowchart picture the eight ball's journey.

This procedure can be varied in many ways to match different conditions. For example, it may be varied to follow a ball shot from the lower right corner, or to take into account the effect of *English* on the ball's path and recoil pattern, or the energy sapping effects of friction. Since these physical factors are represented by numerical quantities in the procedure, we can make a computer "model," or simulate, as many possible physical conditions as we please.

8.23 MOUSE IN A MAZE

Figure 8-25a shows a maze with places of entry and exit for a mouse. After the mouse enters the maze, the entry is closed. The maze, consisting of a pattern of horizontal and vertical paths, can be represented as an array containing 5 rows and 5 columns (Figure 8-25b). The entry is located at Row 4, Column 1, and the exit at Row 2, Column 5.

The object of the problem is to follow the mouse through the maze from entry to exit. A move, which is defined as a transfer from one position to some other position at a distance of one row or one column, is determined by a random number 1 to 4, each of which specifies the direction of the move, as follows:

1—right
2—left
3—up
4—down

Chapter 8   Problems with Flowcharts   258

(a)

(b)

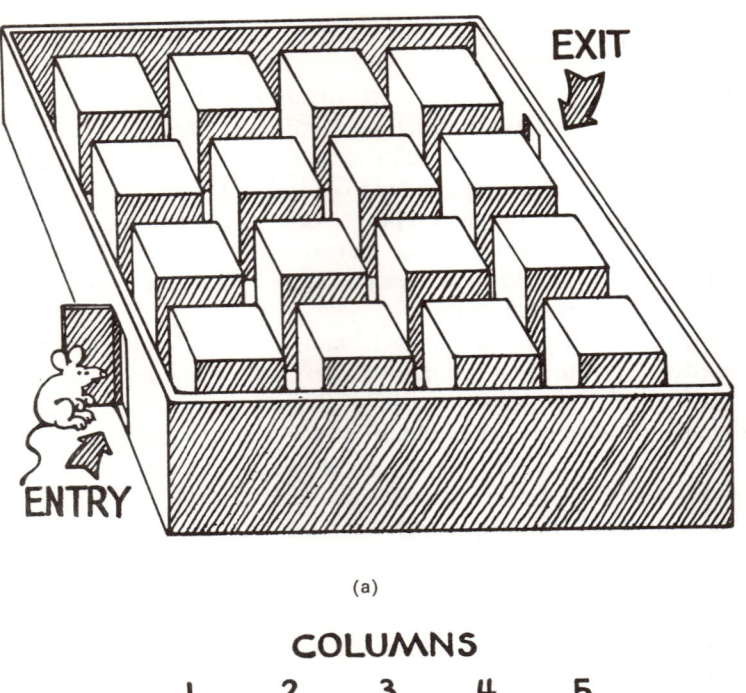

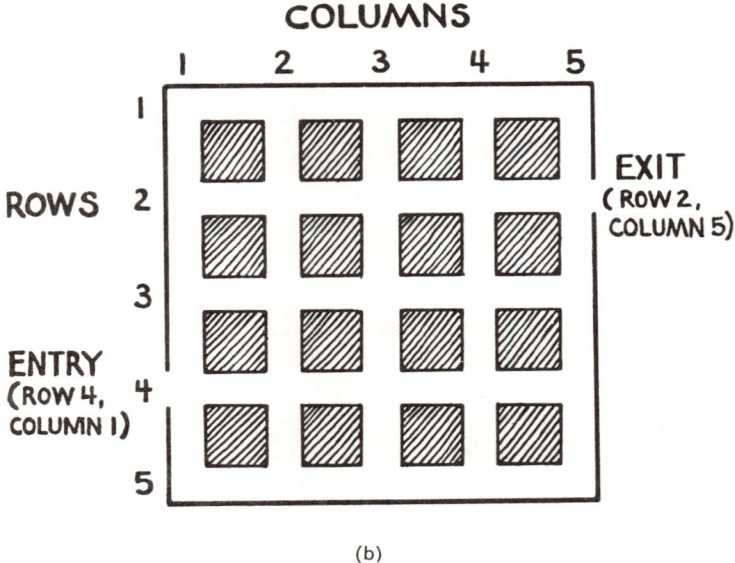

Figure 8-25.

A move is disregarded whenever the random number selected directs the mouse outside the boundaries of the maze. For example, the random number 2 would be disregarded if generated as the first move of the mouse, because a move can be made only up, down, or to the right at the entry position.

Section 8.23   Mouse in a Maze

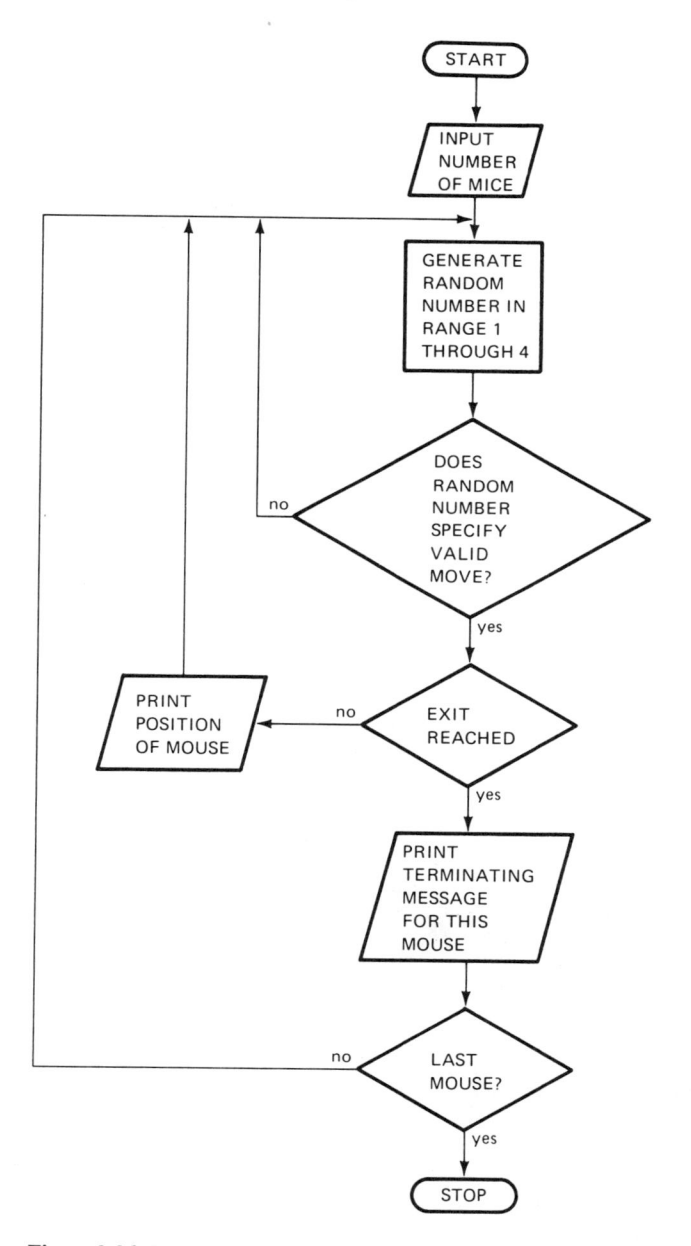

Figure 8-26 Mouse in a maze.

A flowchart for a procedure that generates routes of an unspecified number of mice through the maze is shown in Figure 8-26. The number of different mice that may tour the maze is an input to the procedure.

Chapter 9

Computers aboard this carrier-based, twin jet aircraft help the U.S. Navy to protect ships from submarine attack and the continental United States from intercontinental ballistic missiles launched from enemy submarines. (Courtesy Sperry Rand Corp., Univac Division)

Problems for Computer Solution

The 58 problems in this chapter can be solved through FORTRAN programming. Taken from many disciplines and covering a wide range of difficulty, the problems, should stimulate creative work and demonstrate the reader's understanding of algorithm development, flowcharting, and some FORTRAN programming. Some of the problems are little more than elementary exercises; others may require many hours in the development of a suitable solution.

An attempt has been made to arrange the problems in order of difficulty; however, since the difficulty of any problem depends upon the background and aptitude of the person attempting to solve it, the arrangement should be considered with reservations. You should not assume that difficulty with a particular problem will imply greater difficulty with succeeding problems.

One word of advice: First, be sure you fully understand the problem. Next, develop an algorithm and draw a flowchart. Only then are you ready to write a FORTRAN program to solve the problem.

Happy problem solving!

9.1 3 BY 3 MAGIC SQUARE

The following diagram illustrates a form that may be used to generate one of the 8 possible number arrangements of a 3 by 3 Magic Square.

a + b	a − (b + c)	a + c
a − (b − c)	a	a + (b − c)
a − c	a + (b + c)	a − b

Draw the flowchart and write a **FORTRAN** program that uses this method to generate a magic square.

9.2 CHRISTMAS TREE

Construct **FORTRAN** statements that will produce on the printer the Christmas tree design.

```
            *
          * * *
        * * * * *
      * * * * * * *
    * * * * * * * * *
            *
            *
```

9.3 POWERS OF TWO

Draw a flowchart and write a program to print out a table of powers of 2 that are less than 1000.

```
              2
              4
              8
             16
             32
              .
              .
              .
```

262

9.4 INVESTMENT CALCULATION

You have just invested $100 in the Shifty Real Estate Company. The board of directors guarantees that you double your investment every two years. Draw a flowchart and write a FORTRAN program that will compute your investment each year. The procedure should print a list similar to the following:

2	YEARS	$	200.00
4	YEARS	$	400.00
6	YEARS	$	800.00
8	YEARS	$	1,600.00
10	YEARS	$	3,200.00
12	YEARS	$	6,400.00
14	YEARS	$	12,800.00
16	YEARS	$	25,600.00
18	YEARS	$	51,200.00
20	YEARS	$	102,400.00
22	YEARS	$	204,800.00
24	YEARS	$	409,600.00
26	YEARS	$	819,200.00
28	YEARS	$1,638,400.00
30	YEARS	$3,276,800.00

9.5 SATELLITE SPEED

The time that it takes a satellite at a certain altitude to circle the earth is a function of its speed. The formula for an altitude of 100 miles is

$$t = \frac{1540}{s}$$

where t is the time in minutes and s is the speed of the satellite in thousands of miles per hour.

Draw a flowchart and write a FORTRAN program that will compute and print t for s equal to 18, 19, 20, ..., 23, 24.

9.6 FOOTBALL FRANCHISE

The International Football League is starting to be in direct competition with the National Football League. You purchase a franchise in the newly formed association, and you are told that your profit (in $1000 units) can be projected for the next 8 years by the formula

$$p = t^3 - 5t^2 + 10t - 51$$

(p represents your profit, t the time in years)

At $t = 0$, the time of the purchase of the franchise, $p = -51$. Your cost of the franchise, therefore, is $51,000, a negative profit indicating a loss.

Draw a flowchart and write a FORTRAN program to determine your total profit (or loss) for the cumulative 8 years.

9.7 PAYROLL

Draw a flowchart and write a program that computes a weekly payroll for a firm employing 12 people.

1. Compute regular wages on a 40-hour basis.
2. Overtime is determined at time and a half.
3. Include standard deductions of 15 percent federal income tax, 6 percent state income tax, and 7 3/4 percent FICA (Social Security).
4. Your output should include the employee number and should have the following format:

Emp No.	Hours	Rate	Gross Pay	Fed Tax	ST Tax	Fica	Net Pay
1	50	$5.20					
2	40	4.60					
3	35	6.60					
4	40	3.50					
5	42	4.00					
6	48	3.00					
7	40	7.80					
8	34	4.25					
9	40	3.50					
10	40	5.60					
11	42	2.80					
12	50	3.10					

9.8 LAW OF SINES

The Law of Sines states that for any triangle ABC,

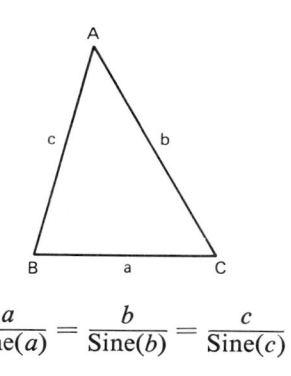

$$\frac{a}{\text{Sine}(a)} = \frac{b}{\text{Sine}(b)} = \frac{c}{\text{Sine}(c)}$$

Given the measures of the sides a and b and measure of angle C, draw a flowchart

Chapter 9   Problems for Computer Solution

and write a program that will determine the measure of angle *B*, and using the Law of Cosines, determine the measure of *c* and angle *C*. The Law of Cosines states that for any triangle *ABC*, $c^2 = a^2 + b^2 - 2ab\text{Cosine}(C)$.

9.9 MULTIPLICATION TABLE

Draw a flowchart and write a program to compute and output a 12×12 multiplication table; that is, one times one through twelve, two times one through twelve, up to twelve times one through twelve.

9.10 BIRDS

If 5 pairs of birds each raise 3 eggs to adulthood, then die, leaving the remaining 15 birds to mate and also raise 3 eggs per pair to adulthood, then die, and so on. . .

Draw a flowchart and write a program to determine how many birds there will be at the end of 5 years.

9.11 FOURTH POWERS

The following table shows the fourth powers of the numbers 1 to 10. Draw a flowchart and write a program that will compute and print a similar table containing the fourth powers of the first 50 integers.

Number	Fourth Power
1	1
2	16
3	81
4	256
5	625
6	1296
7	2401
8	4096
9	6561
10	10,000

9.12 AVERAGE DISTANCE

The Wilson family went on vacation last week. They drove 440 kilometers on Monday, 0 kilometers on Tuesday, 100 kilometers on Wednesday, 320 kilometers on Thursday, and 40 kilometers on Friday. Write a FORTRAN program to determine the average distance traveled per day.

Section 9.13   Volume of a Dam

9.13 VOLUME OF A DAM

An engineer who builds earthfill dams wants a procedure to calculate the volume of earth required for a given dam. All dams are shaped as shown below; they vary only in dimension. Draw a flowchart and write a program to calculate the volume in cubic yards.

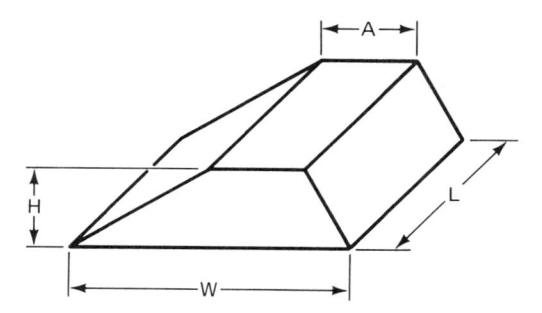

Figure 9-1.

Chapter 9   Problems for Computer Solution   268

9.14 STUDENT AVERAGES

Draw a flowchart and write a program to compute the averages for a class of up to 50 students. The input data should consist of 5 scores and a name for each student. A negative value for the first score can be used to end the input. The program output should show the name, average, and 5 scores of each student.

9.15 EMPLOYMENT

Mr. Smith is offered employment by the Rapid Toy Company, with the opportunity of taking two different methods of payment. He can receive a monthly wage of $500 and a $5 raise each month, or he can receive a monthly wage of $500 with a yearly raise of $80.

Draw a flowchart and write a FORTRAN program that will determine the monthly wages for the next 10 years in each case. The program should determine the cumulative wages after each month, and from the information determine which is the better method of payment.

9.16 LARGEST NUMBER

Draw a flowchart and write a program that will find the largest of 30 numbers. Assume that the following 30 numbers are located in Array A.

34	6	22	12	1	20
21	47	28	4	9	12
8	13	30	49	10	16
9	32	17	27	4	3
6	2	16	7	31	14

The program must determine and print out the largest number in the array.

9.17 BOUNCING BALL

A ball is dropped from a height of 10 feet. It bounces back each time to a height two-thirds the height of the last bounce. Draw a flowchart and write a program to determine how far the ball will have traveled when it hits the ground on the 40th bounce.

9.18 POLYGON

Draw a flowchart and write a FORTRAN program to compute and print the area A and length of perimeter P of a polygon with n sides of circumscribed about a circle of radius r. Input values for r and n and output the values of A and P. For example, if $n = 5$, you have the shown figure:

Section 9.19   *Cricket Thermometer*   269

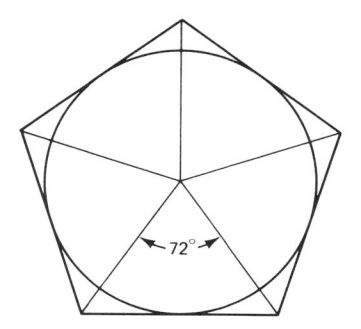

Figure 9-2.

9.19 CRICKET THERMOMETER

The number of chirps that a cricket makes in a minute is a function of the temperature. As a result, it is possible to tell how warm it is by using a cricket as a thermometer!

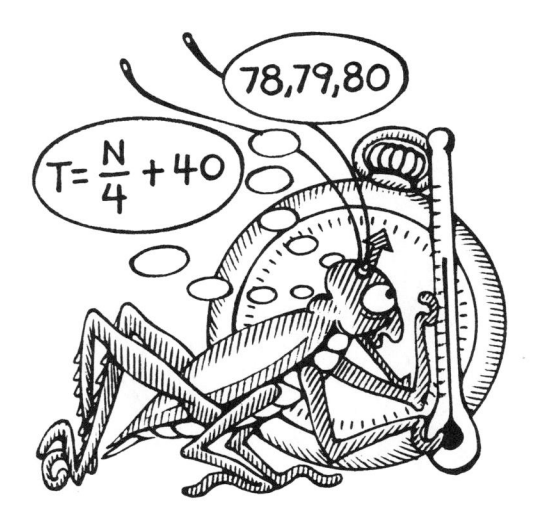

A formula for the function is

$$t = \frac{n}{4} + 40$$

where *t* represents the temperature in degrees Fahrenheit and *n* represents the number of cricket chirps in one minute.

Draw a flowchart and write a program that will determine and output values for *t* for *n* equal to 40, 50, 60, 70, . . . , 140, 150.

Chapter 9   Problems for Computer Solution   270

9.20 AVERAGE TEMPERATURE

The average temperatures for a 12-month period in Anyplace, U.S.A., are as follows:

SPRING	March	38	SUMMER	June	79
	April	47		July	84
	May	69		August	92
FALL	September	82	WINTER	December	46
	October	64		January	38
	November	55		February	31

Draw a flowchart and write a FORTRAN program that will compute the average spring, summer, fall, and winter temperatures in Anyplace. After the values have been computed, the program is to output the following messages and the values that complete them.

AVERAGE SPRING TEMPERATURE IS x
AVERAGE SUMMER TEMPERATURE IS x

AVERAGE FALL TEMPERATURE IS x
AVERAGE WINTER TEMPERATURE IS x

9.21 NUMBER SEARCH

Draw a flowchart and write a FORTRAN program to input 50 numbers into an array, find the values of the largest and smallest numbers in the array, and print out these two numbers, along with the 10 numbers in the array.

9.22 DRAG AND LIFT FORCE

The drag and lift forces on a rocket can be approximated by the equations

$$\text{Drag} = C_D \, d \, A V^2$$
$$\text{Lift} = C_L \, d \, A V^2$$

where C_D and C_L are the experimentally determined drag coefficient and lift coefficient, respectively; d is the density of air; A is the cross-sectional area of the missile; and V is its velocity.

Draw a flowchart and write a program that will input the required data and compute and print out the values of the drag and lift forces.

9.23 MAGIC SQUARE CHECKER

Draw a flowchart and write a program to determine if the following number arrangement is a Magic Square. You may wish to reference the program shown in Section 7.12.

15	16	22	3	9
8	14	20	21	2
1	7	13	19	25
24	5	6	12	18
17	23	4	10	11

9.24 STUDENT ENROLLMENT SURVEY

A survey is being made of the number of students in Quincey College. The research committee has set up a list of the number of sections of each grade, and this was punched onto successive cards with -777 used to separate the grades and -999 used to indicate the end of the list. Draw a flowchart for a subroutine that adds up the number of students within each grade (freshmen, sophmores, juniors, seniors) and prints the total, in a mainline program that accumulates the number of students in the college grade by grade, and finally prints out the total number in Quincey College.

9.25 STATISTICAL CALCULATION

The following table give the normal low and high temperatures in Atlanta and Houston for each month of the year.

	Atlanta Low	Atlanta High	Houston Low	Houston High
January	45	55	46	54
February	46	56	48	56
March	49	60	50	61
April	52	63	52	62
May	53	65	59	69
June	55	71	61	73
July	58	82	62	93
August	61	93	63	99
September	59	91	63	99
October	53	81	59	87
November	46	73	54	73
December	47	59	51	69

Draw a flowchart and write a FORTRAN program that will input the given temperatures and calculate the average yearly high and low temperatures for Atlanta and Houston.

9.26 ROW INTERCHANGE

Draw a flowchart and write a FORTRAN program that will interchange rows 4 and 6 of the following number arrangement.

37	48	59	70	81	2	13	24	35
36	38	49	60	71	73	3	14	25
26	28	39	50	61	72	74	4	15
16	27	29	40	51	62	64	75	5
6	17	19	30	41	52	63	65	76
77	7	18	20	31	42	53	55	66
67	78	8	10	21	32	43	54	56
57	68	79	9	11	22	33	44	46
47	58	69	80	1	12	23	34	45

9.27 MEAN, MEDIAN, AND MODE

The arithmetic *mean* is the sum of all values divided by the number of values. The *median* is the "middle value." Half of the values are larger than the median and half of the values are smaller. The *mode* is that value occuring most frequently. As an example, consider finding the mean, median, and mode of the following 10 test results.

90, 75, 60, 75, 80, 85, 83, 75, 70, 77

To compute the mean score, add up the 10 scores and divide by 10:

$$\frac{90 + 75 + 60 + 75 + 80 + 85 + 83 + 75 + 70 + 77}{10} = \frac{770}{10} = 77$$

The mean score is 77.

To compute the median score, arrange the scores in ascending order.

60
70
75
75
75
77
80
83
85
90

There are 10 scores with 75 as the fifth score and 77 as the sixth score. The median score is 76 since there are 5 scores below 76 and 5 scores above 76.

To compute the mode, scan the list to determine the most frequent score—75 is the mode.

For the given test scores, the mean is 77, the median is 76, and the mode is 75.

Draw a flowchart and write a program that will determine the mean, median, and mode of the following set of values: 153, 158, 161, 157, 150, 153, 149, 153, 155, 162.

9.28 CUBE ROOT

The cube root of a number may be found by using the recursive relationship

$$x_n = \frac{1}{3}\left(2x_0 + \frac{n}{x_0^2}\right),$$

where n is the number and x_0 is the first guess. Then

$$x_n \text{ will replace } x_o \text{ until } |x_n - x_o| < E$$

Draw the flowchart of a procedure to compute the cube root of n, using a first guess of x_o. The procedure should input values for n, x_o, and E. After calculating $\sqrt[3]{n}$, the procedure should output n and the cube root of n.

9.29 GUESSING GAME

Draw a flowchart and write a FORTRAN program to play the following game. Enter your guesses for 5 consecutive throws of a die. Have the program simulate the throwing of a die. If none of your guesses matches the corresponding throw, you pay $5; with one match, you win $1; 2 matches, $3; 3 matches, $10; 4 matches, $100; and 5 matches, $1,000. The program should keep track of winnings and losses, and print its tosses each time.

9.30 WHAT IS THE NUMBER?

The computer tries to guess a number you have in mind. First, it guesses a number and you tell it if the number is too high, too low, or correct. On the basis of the information you give, the computer guesses again. This continues until the computer guesses right.

Draw a flowchart and write a program that will play this guessing game.

9.31 BATTING AVERAGE

Players on a cricket team have batting figures for a season set out in a table as shown here:

Section 9.33   Temperature Simulation

Player's Number	Runs	Number of Innings	Times Not Out	Average
1	536	17	0	
2	642	14	2	
3	559	14	3	
.	.	.	.	.
.	.	.	.	.
.	.	.	.	.
16	43	3	3	

Input the figures shown, calculate the batting averages, and print the complete table in descending order of averages.

9.32 MOST POPULAR PLAYER

A western university conducted a student survey to determine the most popular football player. The numbers 1, 2, 3, and 4 were used to determine the student votes.

　　1—vote for J. Superspeed, the halfback
　　2—vote for S. Bigboy, the tackle
　　3—vote for P. Smarts, the quarterback
　　4—vote for B. Hands, the end

Fifty-two people participated in the survey and cast the following votes: 4, 1, 1, 2, 4, 1, 2, 3, 4, 4, 4, 1, 3, 3, 2, 4, 1, 2, 1, 4, 3, 3, 4, 1, 2, 4, 3, 2, 4, 4, 3, 1, 2, 4, 4, 3, 1, 1, 3, 4, 4, 4, 2, 1, 2, 4, 2, 4, 2, 1, 3, 4. Find out which football player was voted the most popular.

9.33 TEMPERATURE SIMULATION

A family is trying to determine the most economical nighttime setting for the thermostat in their house. The utility company estimates the cost, in cents, for each night at

$$\frac{(m-t)^2}{10} + \frac{(72-t)^2}{100}$$

where m is the mean nighttime temperature and t is the thermostat setting, both measured in degrees Fahrenheit. The mean nighttime temperature m varies uniformly between 20°F and 70°F during the year.

　　Write a FORTRAN program that will simulate the values of m for one year and calculate the utility cost for a given value of t. Use the program with various values of t to find the most economical setting.

9.34 LOT PURCHASE

Joan Wilson has $7600 to spend and wants to purchase a lot having an area of at least 12,000 square feet. Make up data for 30 lots, write a program to input Ms. Wilson's requirements, and determine whether they can be met by any of the given lots.

The program should print out the identification, size, and price of all lots that meet Ms. Wilson's lot requirements.

9.35 GAS MILEAGE

Write a FORTRAN program to compute the average for and variance of the gas mileage of a delivery truck that traveled 200 miles, 180 miles, 155 miles, 230 miles, 143 miles, 190 miles, respectively. The gallons of gas used for each trip are 13.2, 10.8, 9.6, 12.5, 9.5, and 11.6. The formula for computing the variance is

$$\text{Variance} = \frac{(\text{average} - X_i)^2}{N - 1}$$

$$i = 1 \text{ to } N$$

where N = number of trips and X_i = miles traveled for trip i.

Section 9.39   Interest Table   277

9.36 SALES CHART

Write a FORTRAN program to compute and print out the following sales chart. Each dealer gets a 10 percent commission on sales.

Sales Chart

	Mon	Tues	Wed	Thurs	Fri	Total	Comm
DEALER 17	103.76	108.75	0.00	98.76	282.65	_____	____
DEALER 38	0.00	123.65	115.75	85.67	238.50	_____	____
DEALER 47	88.75	0.00	146.60	138.85	227.65	_____	____
DEALER 62	110.50	95.35	158.17	0.00	295.64	_____	____
TOTALS	_____	_____	_____	_____	_____	_____	____

9.37 SALARY CONVERSION TABLE

Ms. Watson of the ABC Employment Agency has asked you to supply her with a salary conversion table. Since the agency states all salaries on an annual basis, you will be required to show the annual salary and its equivalent in monthly and weekly terms. Your FORTRAN program should print a table converting salary ranges from $3800 to $7500 annually in increments of $50.

9.38 RADIUS OF CURVATURE

The radius of curvature of a highway is determined by using the formula

$$R = 0.258 V^2$$

where R is the radius of a circular curve.

V is the velocity in mph.

0.258 is a constant factor that takes into consideration gravity, tire friction, and a maximum super elevation slope of 0.10.

Write a FORTRAN program that would output R for 20 different values of V.

9.39 INTEREST TABLE

Set up a table of amounts that $100 will be at the end of 10, 15, 20, and 25 years at the following percentages—5, 5 1/2, 6, 6 1/2, 7 1/2 per year compounded monthly. Print the years across the top and the rates in the first column of each row.

Chapter 9   Problems for Computer Solution   278

9.40 HOUSE MORTGAGE

The Brown family is buying a house with a mortgage from the Security Savings Bank. The original loan was for $45,000 at 8 percent interest per year. The Browns make a monthly payment of $375, which includes the interest and payment toward the loan. The interest is computed each month on the "unpair balance" of the loan. The first month, the interest is

$$i = (45,000) \times (.08) \times \frac{1}{12} = 300.$$

Therefore, the amount of the monthly payment toward the loan is $375 - $300 = $75. The unpaid balance becomes $45,000 - $75 = $44,925. The interest for the second month is calculated on this new balance. Write a FORTRAN program that will print a payment table for the first 72 months.

9.41 MERCHANDISE COST

The string Instrument Manufacturing Company determines the cost of the guitars it has sold by using the following formula:

$$CGS = BMI + P - EMI - PRA$$

Section 9.42   College Admission Record   279

where BMI is the Beginning Merchandise Inventory ($).

P is the Purchases ($).

EMI is the Ending Merchandise Inventory ($).

PRA is the Purchase Returns and Allowances ($).

Write a **FORTRAN** program to determine the cost of guitars sold for each fiscal period, given the following data.

January—June	July—December
BMI—$4000	BMI—$6200
P —$2100	P —$2860
EMI—$3260	EMI—$3590
PRA—$ 190	PRA—$ 460

9.42 COLLEGE ADMISSION RECORD

All students entering Southern Technical University must submit a high school mathematics average to the admissions office. A table is constructed that assigns a one-digit code for the averages.

Average	Code
0– 49	0
50– 59	1
60– 69	2
70– 79	3
80– 89	4
90–100	5

Each student's record is contained on an accounting card. Columns 78 and 80 contain the student's average, recorded to the nearest percent. For example, 91 percent is recorded as 091 in columns 78, 79, and 80. Write a FORTRAN program that will accumulate the numbers of students with code 0, code 1, code 2, and so on. So that the program can sense the last card, enter into columns 78 to 80 the number 999. This artificial mark can be placed after the data and used to stop the counting.

9.43 SALES JOURNAL

Prepare a sales journal. Provide columns for the following data: date (month, day, year), account name, account number, invoice number, invoice date, terms, and amount. Total the amount column, using the following card input format:

Card Columns	Data
1– 6	Account Number
7–26	Account Name
27–41	Account Address
42–46	Invoice Number
47–48	Invoice Date—Month
49–50	Invoice Date—Day
51–52	Invoice Date—Year
53–59	Terms
60–66	Amount
67–80	Blank

You are to determine the output format. All information requested must be printed.

9.44 ACCOUNTS RECEIVABLE

A few companies with many accounts receivable find it to their advantage to age their accounts receivable on the basis of the invoice date. Using the same data as in problem 9.43, prepare a report indicating the age of each of the outstanding accounts receivable and the total amount that should be allowed for doubtful accounts (using 10 percent of the total dollar value of all accounts over 90 days old). Your output report should

Section 9.47   Big Words

provide sufficient identifying data on each account so that collection procedures may be initiated.

9.45 COLLEGE EXAM SCORES

The following scores were recorded on a mathematics college entrance exam: 83, 74, 69, 100, 92, 95, 89, 75, 92, 82, 85, 97, 74, 91, 78, 83, 61, 100, 93, 54, 87, 82, 79, 68, 72, 75, 86, 92, 53, 100, 99, 67, 97, 79, 82, 81, 85, 98, 99. Write a FORTRAN program to determine and print the median of the scores. Also print the scores in descending order.

9.46 ONE PILE PICKUP

This game is a slight variation of Nim and uses only one pile of articles. Each player is required to pick up at least one but less than k articles. The *loser* of the game is the person picking up the last article.

Consider the following game, where two players start with 9 checkers. Each player must not pick up more than two checkers at any one time; therefore, $k = 3$.

Starting Pile of Checkers	000000000
Player 1 takes 2 checkers leaving 7	0000000
Player 2 takes 1 checker leaving 6	000000
Player 1 takes 1 checker leaving 5	00000
Player 2 takes 1 checker leaving 4	0000
Player 1 takes 1 checker leaving 3	000
Player 2 takes 1 checker leaving 2	00
Player 1 wins the game by taking 1 checker and leaving 1 checker for Player 2 to take.	0

In general, the first player able to leave $nk + 1$ checkers can win by leaving $n(k - 1) + 1$ checkers at the next play.

Player 1 in the illustrated game used this strategy when he took two checkers on the first move ($nk + 1 = 2 \cdot 3 + 1 = 7$ checkers), and again when he left five checkers after his second move ($n(k - 1) + 1 = 2(3 - 1) + 1 = 5$), three checkers after his third move ($1(3 - 1) + 1 = 3$ checkers), and 1 checker after his last move ($0(3 - 1) + 1 = 1$ checker).

Draw a flowchart and write a FORTRAN program to play this game.

9.47 BIG WORDS

Some people like to throw big words around without really saying anything when they want to sound important. The following table of 27 words can be used to produce impressive-sounding three-word phrases.

Chapter 9   Problems for Computer Solution   282

Item Number	List A	List B	List C
1	integrated	policy	flexibility
2	total	third-generation	hardware
3	parallel	management	capability
4	balanced	organizational	contigency
5	systematized	monitored	mobility
6	functional	reciprocal	programming
7	optional	logistical	concept
8	responsive	digital	time-phase
9	synchronized	transitional	projection

To produce a phrase, choose any three-digit number—the first digit selects a word from List A, the second digit a word from List B, and the third digit a word from List C. Some examples are:

477—balanced logistical concept

359—parallel monitored projection

182—integrated digital hardware

Draw a flowchart and write a FORTRAN program that will select a three-word phrase based on a three-digit number that is input to the program.

9.48 DATE FINDER

The following rules are used to Pick-a-Date.

1. Pick a date.
2. Add 1/4 of the last two digits of the year to the last two digits of the year.
3. Add the month number shown in the following list:

January	Add 1	Leap Year 0
February	Add 4	Leap Year 3
March	Add 4	
April	Add 0	
May	Add 2	
June	Add 5	
July	Add 0	
August	Add 3	
September	Add 6	
October	Add 1	
November	Add 4	
December	Add 6	

4. Add the day.

5. Add the year number shown in the following:

1900–2000	Add 0
1800–1900	Add 2
9/14/1752–1800	Add 4
1700–9/2/1752	Add 1
1600–1700	Add 2

6. Divide by 7.
7. The day is found in the following by using the remainder.

Sunday	1		Wednesday	4
Monday	2		Thursday	5
Tuesday	3		Friday	6
		Saturday	0	

EXAMPLE:

What day did September 3, 1848, fall on?

1. The date is September 3, 1848.
2. $1/4(48) = 12$ $48 + 12 = 60$
3. $60 + 6 = 66$
4. $66 + 3 = 69$
5. $69 + 2 = 71$
6. $71 \div 7 =$ Quotient $= 10$ Remainder $= 1$
7. Remainder 1 specifies the day Sunday.

Write a FORTRAN program that will specify the day for any given date. The following dates can be used to check out your procedure logic: January 4, 1756 = Sunday; February 12, 1803 = Saturday; April 30, 1875 = Friday; June 8, 1920 = Tuesday; August 24, 1961 = Thursday; October 4, 1975 = Saturday; November 17, 1985 = Sunday; and December 25, 1999 = Saturday.

9.49 LUCKY NUMBERS

Stanislav Ulam and a group of investigators at Los Alamos Scientific Laboratory created a new sequence of numbers by using computers. Ulam called these numbers, which are strikingly similar to primes, *lucky* numbers.

The lucky numbers were determined by a process that begins with all the natural numbers (up to a specified limit) written in order. In each step, select the next highest surviving number after 1, call it *n*, and counting from the beginning, strike out every *n*th number. The first step, with all the numbers surviving, eliminates all even numbers. The next step, when *n* is 3, eliminates every third surviving number. In the next three steps, *n* is 7, 9, and 13. The process is continued until it fails to remove any more numbers from the table. The first 13 lucky numbers are 1, 3, 7, 9, 13, 15, 21, 25, 31, 33, 37, 43, 49.

Chapter 9   Problems for Computer Solution   284

Draw a flowchart and write a FORTRAN program that will generate all the lucky numbers between 1 and 48,600. Your program should determine that there are 4571 lucky numbers.

9.50 WHEEL OF FORTUNE

The Wheel of Fortune is a giant wheel with a diameter of about 5 feet. The rim of the wheel is divided into 50 sections. In 48 of these sections is paper money in denominations of $1, $2, $5, $10, and $20. The remaining two sections contain a joker and a flag. The Wheel of Fortune layout, which consists of 7 corresponding numbers and symbols, is used by the players for placing bets. The wheel is spun and players bet that it will come to rest with the pointer at a specified money denomination.

- A player will win even money if he or she bet on $1 and the pointer stopped at the $1 bill.
- A player will win $2 if he or she bet on $2 and the pointer stopped at the $2 bill.
- If the wheel stops at the $5 bill, the player will collect $5 if he or she bet on that value.
- If the wheel stops at the $10 bill, the player will win $10 if he or she has bet on that denomination.
- If the wheel stops at the $20 bill, the player will win $20 if he or she was betting on that value.

- The joker and flag pay off at 40 to 1 odds, and a player betting on this value would collect $40 if the wheel stopped on either one.

On most wheels there are twenty-two $1 bills, fourteen $2 bills, seven $5 bills, three $10 bills, two $20 bills, one Joker, and one flag, located on the outer rim.

Draw a flowchart and write a FORTRAN program to simulate play on the Wheel of Fortune.

9.51 PERFECT NUMBERS

The number 6 has a curious property. By adding the divisors of 6 (other than 6 itself), a sum equal to the number itself is found:

$$3 + 2 + 1 = 6$$

This is also true of the number 28.

$$14 + 7 + 4 + 2 + 1 = 28$$

These numbers are called *perfect*. A formula for generating perfect numbers is

$$2^{n-1}(2^n - 1)$$

in which the factor $2^n - 1$ must be a prime number. For many years, only 12 perfect numbers were known, namely those computed by setting n equal to 2, 3, 5, 7, 13, 17, 19, 31, 61, 89, 107, and 127 in the previous formula.

n	$2^{n-1}(2^n - 1)$
2	6
3	28
5	496
7	8128
13	33,550,336
17	8,589,869,056
.	.
.	.
.	.

In recent years, computers have been used to generate very large perfect numbers. Draw a flowchart and write a FORTRAN program to compute perfect numbers.

9.52 SYMMETRY GAME

Here is a game that has a winning strategy based on symmetry. An object is placed on each corner of a regular polygon—say a nonagon, for example. Two players take turns removing either one object or two objects that are next to each other. The player who picks up the last object wins.

Chapter 9   Problems for Computer Solution   286

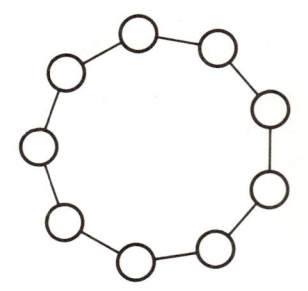

The game is not fair because the player who goes second can always win. Suppose the first player picks up two objects, leaving the board as shown in the left part of Figure 9-3. The second player should then take the penny exactly opposite, so that the board looks like the diagram in the right part of Figure 9-3. What should the second player do from this point on to be sure of winning the game? If the first player picks up only one penny at the start, what should the second player's original move be?

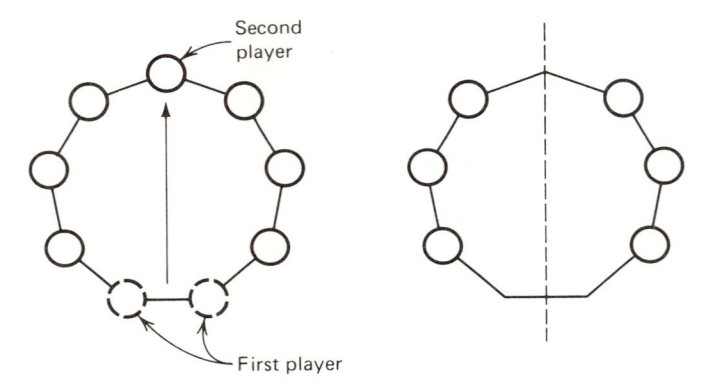

Figure 9-3.

After answering these questions, draw a flowchart and write a FORTRAN program to play this game.

9.53 THE SWIMMING POOL

A rectangular swimming pool has dimensions 120 feet by 50 feet. A person standing at corner A wishes to go to corner C in the least possible time. She has the option of running the entire distance around (170 feet), swimming diagonally across (130 feet), or combining some running with some swimming. She determines that the fastest route is the combination. Her running rate is 3 ft./sec. and her swimming rate is 2 ft./sec.

Section 9.54   *Calculate the Sum*   287

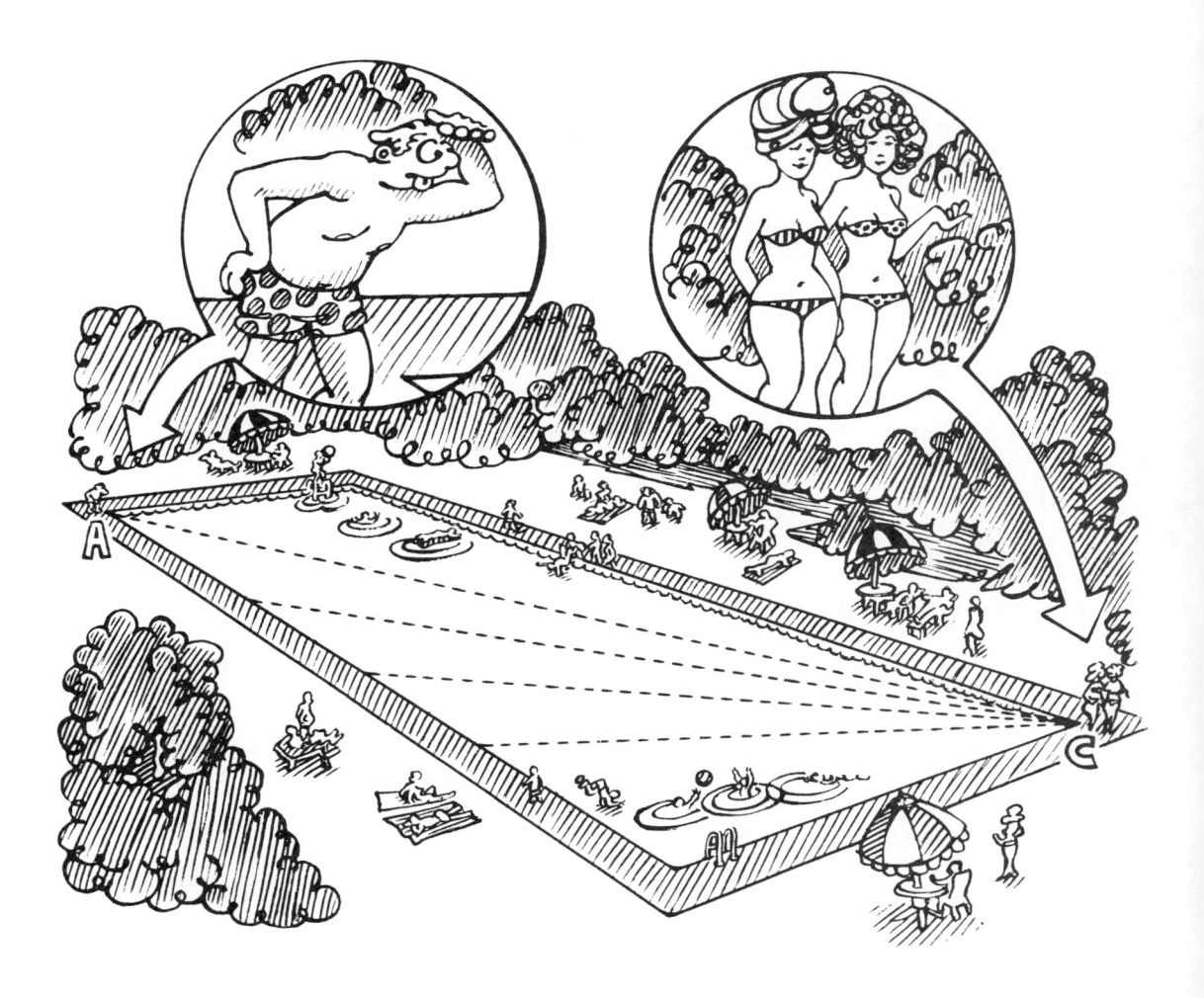

Draw a flowchart and write a FORTRAN program that determines the running distance and the swimming distance which determine the least required time to go from corner A to corner C. The procedure should output the running distance, the swimming distance, and the minimum time.

9.54 CALCULATE THE SUM

You are given a two-dimensional array. Each box in the array has an integer inside, and you are to find the sum of all the numbers in the shaded area (see Figure 9-4). Draw a flowchart and write a FORTRAN program using two nested loops to find the sum of the items.

Chapter 9   Problems for Computer Solution   288

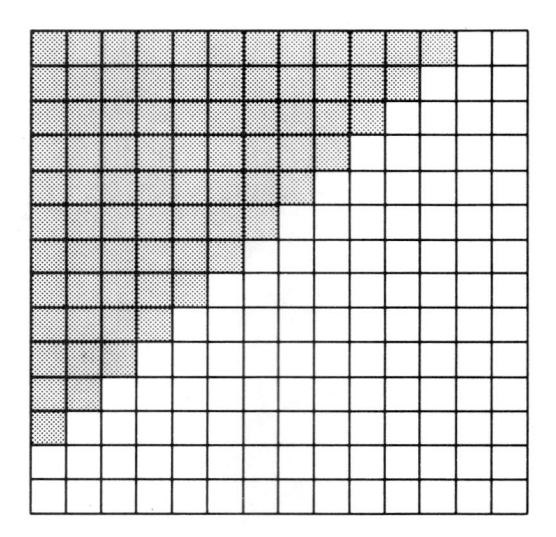

Figure 9-4.

9.55 TABLE OF TRIGONOMETRIC FUNCTIONS

Draw a flowchart and write a FORTRAN program that calculates and outputs a table of trigonometric functions in the following format:

DEG	SIN	TAN	COT	COS	DEG
0	0.00000	0.00000	INF	1.00000	90
1	0.01745	0.01746	57.28996	0.99985	89
2	0.03490	0.03492	28.63625	0.00039	88
.	.	.	.	.	.
.	.	.	.	.	.
.	.	.	.	.	.
45	0.70711	1.00000	1.00000	0.70711	45

9.56 MAZE

Modify the maze problem (Section 8.23) so that entry and exit points are as those shown in Figure 9-5. All other maze specifications are as stated in Section 8.23.

Draw a flowchart and write a FORTRAN program that would generate routes through the new maze.

9.57 KING'S TOUR OF THE CHESSBOARD

The king's power of movement on the chessboard is very limited. He can move only one square at a time. He can go into any of the squares—front, back, or side—adja-

Figure 9-5.

Figure 9-6.

cent to the square on which he stands, as shown in Figure 9-6. To complete a king's tour, the king must move successively to every cell on the board. The following figure illustrates such a tour. An interesting thing about this tour is that the numbers indicating the path form a magic square.

61	62	63	64	1	2	3	4
60	11	58	57	8	7	54	5
12	59	10	9	56	55	6	53
13	14	15	16	49	50	51	52
20	19	18	17	48	47	46	45
21	38	23	24	41	42	27	44
37	22	39	40	25	26	43	28
36	35	34	33	32	31	30	29

Draw a flowchart and write a FORTRAN program that will produce the king's tour of the chessboard.

9.58 FLIGHT PATH COMPUTATION

Many of the airlines flying the North Atlantic use computers to find minimum-time jet flight paths, taking into account the strong winds that usually occur at jet cruising altitudes and the restrictions on possible routes imposed by air traffic control requirements. Savings on the order of 15 minutes on the nominal seven-hour flight are

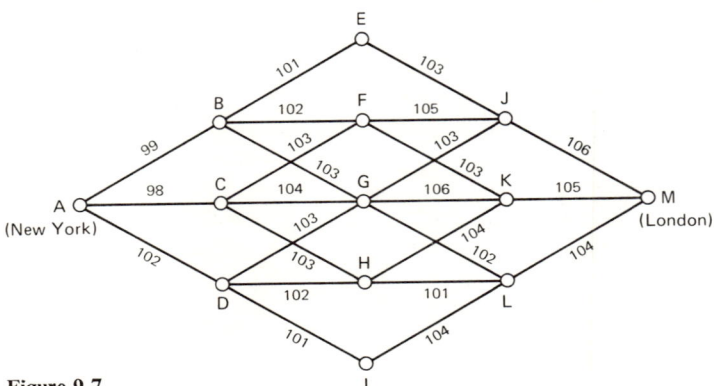

Figure 9-7.

Section 9.58   Flight Path Computation

obtained in this way. A grid of checkpoints is selected, and all routes must consist of generally east-west, straight-line segments between checkpoints. A simplified version of such a grid is shown in Figure 9-7. Imagine that checkpoint A is New York and M is London. Checkpoints B through L are points in the ocean (located by giving their longitude and latitude). Using wind data from weather ships on the North Atlantic and characteristics of the particular jet airplane the airline uses, the flight planner computes the time to fly each segment (results for east-to-west flights differ, of course, from west-to-east flights). In practice, there are many more checkpoints than are shown in the figure so that a computer solution is essential.

Draw a flowchart and write a FORTRAN program to find and print the minimum-time route.

Appendices

Appendix A
Keypunching A Source Deck

Many times students are required to keypunch their own source program decks when doing class problems. If you are unfamiliar with keypunching operations, this can be very frustrating. This appendix is for students who are required to do their own keypunching but who have had no experience in doing so.

Shown in Figure A-1 is the IBM 029 keypunch, a common device for punching programs and data cards. It may be used to punch numerical, alphabetic, and special character information. To begin punching, place blank cards in the hopper of the machine and sit at a typewriterlike keyboard. The card hopper holds approximately 500 cards. The cards are inserted face forward with the 12 edge up. At the touch of the REL (release) button, cards are fed down to the *card bed* and move across it from right to left. As the card moves, it passes under the punching and reading stations. Punching is done by hitting the keys of the keyboard. As each key is depressed, the proper code is punched and printed in the column under the punching station. Then the card moves to the left, advancing one column at a time. When the card reaches the left end

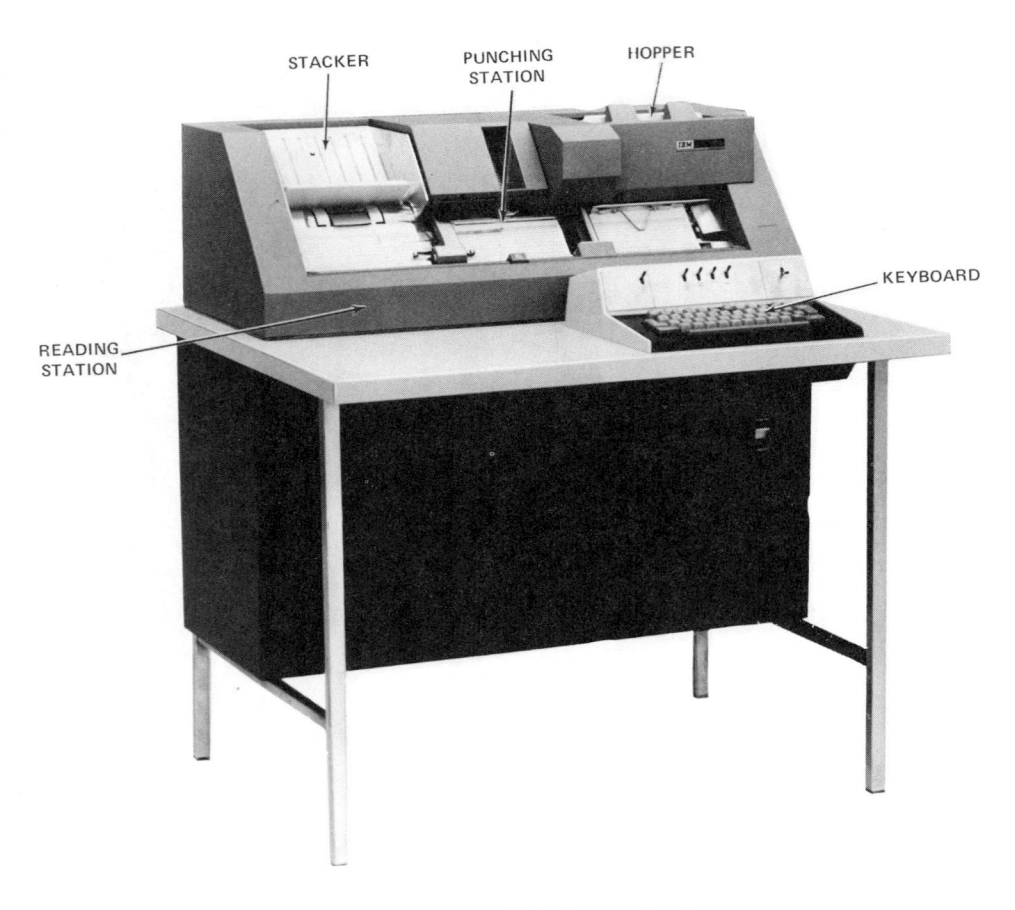

Figure A-1 The IBM 029 keypunch. (*Courtesy* IBM Corporation.)

Appendix A Keypunching a Source Deck 297

of the card bed, it is placed in the stacker; at the same time, a new card is taken from the hopper and placed at the right-hand end of the card bed. After keypunching is complete, the newly punched card is automatically placed in the stacker on the left of the machine.

Keypunches are available with more than one type of keyboard. One keyboard is used for recording numeric data only. Figure A-2 illustrates the combination keyboard used for punching alphabetic, numeric, and special character information in a card.

Figure A-2 Keyboard and switches of the IBM 029 keypunch. (*Courtesy* IBM Corporation.)

Appendix A   Keypunching a Source Deck

Observe the shaded keys in Figure A-2. They are used for punching both letters and numbers. For example, the K key will punch both K and the number 5. The letter is punched by merely depressing the indicated key; the number is punched by depressing the NUMERIC key along with the indicated key. Using the keypunch keyboard is similar to typing on a typewriter, and you can become proficient with only a small amount of training and practice.

The keypunch includes several features that aid in punching cards. Basically, the features consist of a skip key, a duplicate key, a program card, and a special key for inserting zeros in the unused columns of a numeric field.

A *skip key* is provided to move quickly from one punching field to another. It is similar to a tabulator bar on a typewriter. The key is used in conjunction with a program card. The *program card* automatically provides for skipping, duplicating, and shifting. Each of these operations is designated by a specific code punched in a program card, which automatically controls the punching operation column by column. A separate program card must be prepared for each job. For example, one program card must be prepared for punching information in cards for payroll, another for punching information for student registration.

A program card is shown below.

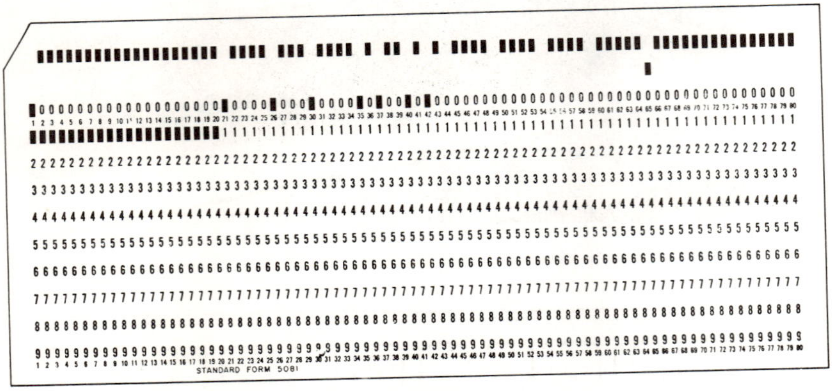

Figure A-3.

This card is prepared for each different punching application and can be used repeatedly. Proper punching in this program card controls the automatic operations for the corresponding columns of the cards being punched. Each punch in the program card governs a specific function:

Punches	Function
0	Automatic Duplication—a punch in the 0 position in the first column of a field automatically starts duplication, which is then continued by the 12s punched in the remaining columns of the field.

Appendix A   Keypunching a Source Deck

1	Alphabetic Punching—a punch in the 1 position shifts the keypunch keyboard to the alphabetic position so that alphabetic characters will be punched in the field.
11	Automatic Skip—a 11 punch in the first column of any field automatically starts a skip, which is then continued by the 12s punched in the remaining columns of the field.
12	Field Definition—a 12 punch must be recorded in every column except the first of every field to be automatically skipped, duplicated, or manually punched.
blank (no punch)	A blank column on the program card indicates the beginning of a field in which numeric data are to be punched on the keypunch by the operator.

The IBM 029 keypunch allows for following two separate programs punched in one program card. You can switch from one program to the other by merely depressing either the PROG ONE or PROG TWO keys (see Figure A-2). One program is punched at the top of the program card, and the other is punched near the middle of the card (rows 4, 5, 6, and 7 instead of rows 12, 11, 0, and 1).

Cards can be duplicated on the keypunch. Pressing a duplicate key (DUP) on the keyboard causes a sensing device to read the punches in the card at the reading station and punches this information into the card at the punching station (see Figure A-1 for locations of the reading and punching stations). After a card has been duplicated, accuracy can be determined by a "sight check" of the cards. This is accomplished by placing the duplicated card in front of the original card and holding them both up to the light to insure that daylight appears in all punched columns.

With program control, zeros punched to the left of the first significant digit in a numeric field determined by 12s in the program card are automatically suppressed in normal printing (00036 is printed 36). The IBM 029 keypunch is equipped with a special key (the LEFT ZERO key), which, when depressed, will automatically determine the number of zeros needed and will cause the extra zeros to be punched. The LEFT ZERO key works in conjunction with a program card placed in the machine.

The keyboard of the IBM 029 keypunch locks when certain errors occur during operation. For example, the keyboard locks if a strictly alphabetic key such as A is pressed when in numeric shift; or if the FEED key is pressed when a card is already registered at the punching station; or if a blank column is duplicated in a field programmed for numeric punching. The keyboard can be unlocked by pressing the ERROR RESET key.

If a card is wrinkled or has a nick in it, it may have to be duplicated before it can be read by a card reader. To do this, turn off AUTO FEED and AUTO SKIP DUP (see switches in Figure A-2), and clear the machine of cards. After straightening the card as best you can, proceed as follows:

- Insert the damaged card through the plastic guides at the reading station.
- Place a blank card through the guides at the punching station.

Appendix A   Keypunching a Source Deck

- Press the REG key to register the cards at the reading and punching station.
- Press the DUP key until all of the data in the damaged card is punched into the new card. Then press the REL key to release both cards.
- Clear the cards from the machine.

The same type of duplicating procedure used for damaged cards can also be used for making minor corrections to a source card. Suppose, for example, that you punched a card as follows:

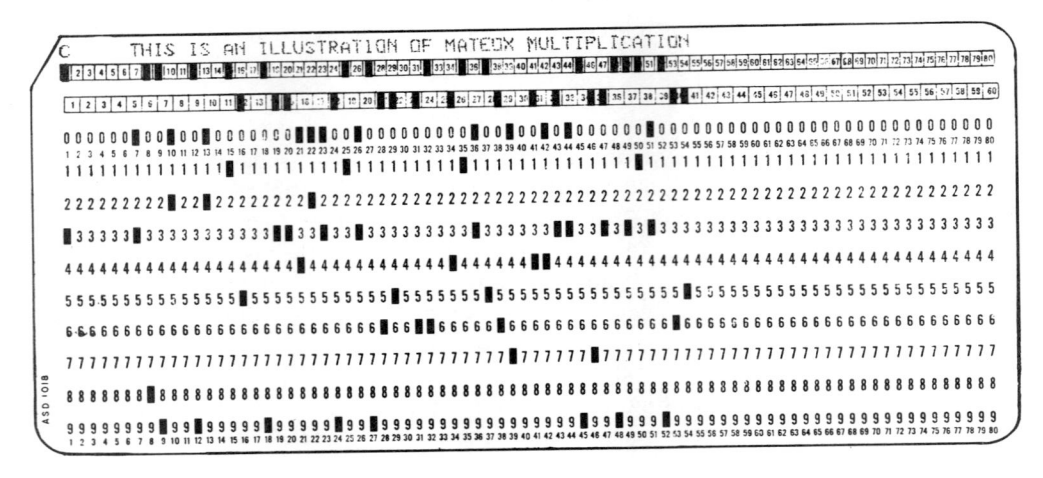

[Punched card showing: THIS IS AN ILLUSTRATION OF MATEOX MULTIPLICATION]

Figure A-4.

Since only **MATEOX** is incorrect—it should be **MATRIX**—it would be wasted effort to keypunch the entire card. Instead, insert the error card in the reading station and a blank card at the punching station. Register the cards and press the DUP key until the first error column is reached—in this case, column 34. After keypunching RI (in columns 34 and 35), press the DUP key again until all source data from the first card is duplicated into the second card. Then, clear the cards from the machine.

There are many more keypunching procedures that could be explained. With little practice, however, the information here should enable you to do your own keypunching. If something unexpected occurs, such as a card jam, it is best to get help from your instructor or an experienced keypunch operator.

Appendix B
Program Flowcharting Symbols

Represents

PROCESS—used to represent calculations, processing, or any function not described by a more specific symbol.

INPUT/OUTPUT—used to represent the making available of information for processing (input) or the recording of processed information (output).

DECISION—used to represent a decision, question, or comparison.

TERMINAL—used to represent the start or end of a procedure or subroutine.

ANNOTATION—used to contain descriptive comments or clarifying notes about a procedure.

PREDEFINED PROCESS—used to represent a subroutine.

CONNECTOR—used to represent a junction in a line of flow, to connect broken paths in the line of flow, and to connect several pages of the same flowchart.

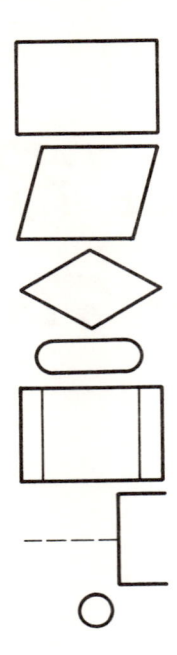

Other Symbols Frequently Used on Flowcharts

Symbol	Function
>	Greater than
≥	Greater than or equal to
<	Less than
≤	Less than or equal to
=	Equal or assignment
≠	Not equal
(	Left parenthesis
)	Right parenthesis
+	Plus sign
−	Minus sign
×, or ·, or ∗	Multiplication
÷ or /	Division
?	Question mark
$	Currency (dollar sign)
←	Assignment
Y	Yes
N	No

Appendix C
Glossary

absolute value. The quantitative value of a number, exclusive of its sign.

acronym. An identifying word or expression from initials or segments of a name, term, or phrase; for example, BASIC from Beginners All-Purpose Symbolic Instruction Code or FORTRAN from FORmula TRANslation.

algorithm. A list of instructions specifying a sequence of operations that will give the answer to any problem of a given type.

alphanumeric. Consisting of alphabetical and numerical characters combined.

analysis. The investigation of a problem by a consistent method.

annotation. An added descriptive comment or explanatory note.

ANSI. American National Standards Institute. An organization that acts as a national clearinghouse and coordinator for voluntary standards in the United States. ANSI standards exist for *flowcharting* (X3.5-1970), *FORTRAN* (X3.9-1966), and other programming languages, techniques, and procedures.

application. The problem for which a computer solution is designed.

arithmetic statement. A type of FORTRAN statement that specifies a numerical computation.

array. An ordered arrangement of items.

auxiliary operation. An operation performed on equipment not under direct control of the computer. See *off-line*.

BASIC. A programming language similar to FORTRAN.

batch processing. A system in which similar input items are grouped together for processing in the same computer run.

branch. A technique used to transfer control from one sequence of a program to another.

card. A storage medium in which data is represented by means of holes punched in vertical columns in a paper card.

central processing unit. The components of a computer system that contains the arithmetic and logic unit, storage unit, and control circuits. Commonly called the CPU.

code. A set of symbols and rules for representing information.

coding. The writing of computer instructions in a programming language for acceptance by a computer.

column. The verticle numbers of one line of an array, a print column, or punches in one line of a card.

compare. To examine the representation of a quantity to determine its relationship to zero or to examine two quantities usually for the purposes of determining identity or relative magnitude.

compiler. A program used to translate a source language program, such as FORTRAN programs, into machine language programs suitable for execution on a particular computer.

computer program. See *Program*.

computer science. The field of knowledge embracing all aspects of the design and use of computers.

Appendix C   Glossary   305

computer system. A digital computer, its related peripheral equipment, and associated software.

computing. The act of using computing equipment for processing data.

conditional transfer. A variation of control based on some condition.

constant. A quantity that does not change, for example, 26 or 48.3. In FORTRAN an integer constant does not have a decimal point, for example, 73 or 200, and a real constant must contain a decimal point, for example, 48.0, 32.6, or 103.0E2.

continuation card. A card used to continue a previous FORTRAN statement.

control statement. An operation that terminates the sequential execution of instructions by transferring control to a statement elsewhere in a program.

counter. A variable used to determine the number of times an operation is performed.

data. A representation of facts or concepts in a formalized manner suitable for communication, interpretation, or processing by people or by automatic means.

data processing. The generic term for operations performed with automatic equipment, which may or may not include a computer.

debugging. The process of eliminating errors (commonly called bugs) from a flowchart or computer program.

decision. The process of comparing values or conditions.

decrement. Decreasing the value of a quantity.

diagnostics. Messages to the computer user automatically printed by the computer, which pinpoint improper program statements.

digit. One of the symbols of a number system used to designate a quantity.

digital computer. A machine designed to execute a sequence of mathematical or logical operations automatically, that is, without human intervention.

display. A visual representation of data.

documentation. The process of organizing information about a problem into a useful file. Usually includes problem statement, associated algorithms, flowcharts, punched cards, program listings, and program operating instructions.

element. An item of data within an array.

execute. To perform the operations specified by a computer program.

exponentiation. Representation of a number in terms of a power of a base.

file. An organized collection of related data.

fixed-point quantity. See *Integer Quantity*.

floating-point quantity. See *Real Quantity*.

flow. A general term to indicate a sequence of events.

flowchart. A pictorial description of a computer solution to a problem, used as a guideline for the preparation of a computer program.

flowcharting symbol. A symbol used to represent operations or flow on a flowchart.

flowcharting template. A plastic guide containing cutouts of the flowcharting symbols that are used in drawing a flowchart.

Appendix C   Glossary

flowline. A means of connecting two flowchart symbols on a flowchart.

format. The general makeup of items, including arrangement and location of all information; in FORTRAN, a statement (FORMAT) associated with every READ and WRITE statement.

FORTRAN (FORmula TRANslation). A programming language in which the commands resemble algebraic equations.

function. A specific purpose or a characteristic action.

hardware. The physical equipment of a computer system; contrasted with *Software*.

information. Data that have been organized into a meaningful sequence.

initialize. To preset a variable or counter to proper starting values before commencing a calculation.

input. To enter information into the computer.

input/output. A general term for the equipment, data, or media used in the entering or recording function, commonly abbreviated I/O.

instruction. A command to be executed by the computer.

integer quantity. Any value that does not include a decimal point (also called fixed-point). In FORTRAN, an integer variable begins with one of the letters I,J,K,L,M, or N.

keypunch. A typewriterlike machine to punch holes in cards for use in computer processing operations.

library function. A special subprogram that is permanently included with the FORTRAN language for use when needed.

loop. A sequence of operations usually repeated a controlled number of times within a program.

LSI. Large scale integration.

matrix. A rectangular array of elements.

memory. The storage area of a computer.

microcomputer. A small, low cost computer built from LSI circuitry.

minicomputer. A small, low cost digital computer.

mixed mode expression. A FORTRAN expression involving both integer and real variables.

nesting. A method of grouping items completely within another group of items.

normal directional flow. On a flowchart, the direction of flow from left to right or top to bottom.

off-line. Peripheral devices that operate independently of the computer; devices not under the control of the computer.

one-dimensional array. An array consisting of a single row or column of elements.

on-line. Peripheral devices operating under the direct control of the computer.

operating system. Software that controls the execution of computer programs and may provide scheduling, input-output control, compilation, data management, debugging, storage assignment, accounting, and other similar functions.

operation. The process of executing a defined action.

operator. A symbol specifying that a defined action is to take place; for example, in FORTRAN notation, + is the symbol for addition, * for multiplication.

Appendix C Glossary   307

output. To transfer information from the computer to some useable form, such as a hard copy printout or CRT display.

peripheral device. The input-output machines that may be placed under the control of a computer. Examples are card readers, CRT display units, line printers, typewriters, magnetic disk units, magnetic tape units, digital plotters, paper tape readers, and others.

power. A symbolic representation of the number of times a number is multiplied by itself. The process is called *exponentiation*. In FORTRAN, the operation symbol is **.

predefined process. An identifiable predetermined process or operation.

print. To transfer information, usually from the computer's internal storage to a paper printing device.

printer. A device that prints results from a computer on paper.

problem definition. The formulation of the logic used to define a problem. A description of a task to be performed.

processing. A term including any operation or combination of operations on data, where an operation is the execution of a defined action.

program. An ordered list of statements that directs the computer to perform certain operations in a specified sequence to solve a problem.

programming. The technique for translating the steps in the solution of a problem into a form the computer understands.

programming language. A language used to prepare computer programs, such as FORTRAN, BASIC, COBOL, APL, PL/1, RPG.

punched card. A card that is punched with a combination of holes to represent letters, digits, or special characters.

read. To sense data from an input medium.

real quantity. Any value that includes a decimal point (also called floating-point). In FORTRAN, real variables begin with any letter other than I, J, K, L, M, or N.

record. A set of data pertaining to a particular item.

relation operator. A symbol that specifies a comparative relationship between two items of data; for example, less than (<), equal to (=), greater than (>).

routine. A set of instructions for carrying out a specific processing operation.

row. The horizontal members of one line of an array.

run. To perform the operations specified by a computer program.

sequence. An arrangement of items according to a specific set of rules.

software. Programs and associated material for use on a computer. Includes computer programs, flowcharts, punched cards, program listings, and so on; contrasted with *Hardware*.

sort. To arrange data into some predefined order.

source deck. A card deck comprising a computer program, in symbolic language, and data cards.

source language. The original form in which a program is prepared prior to processing by the computer, for example, FORTRAN or BASIC.

Appendix C   Glossary   308

source program. A source program written in a symbolic programming language, for example, FORTRAN program. A compiler is used to translate the FORTRAN source program into one that can be executed on a computer.

special character. A graphic character that is neither a letter or a digit—for example, + or ?.

standard. An accepted and approved criterion for drawing flowcharts, writing computer programs, and so on.

standardize. To establish standards or to cause conformity with established standards.

statement. A FORTRAN order of instruction to the computer to perform some sequence of operations.

statement number. A reference number associated with a FORTRAN statement.

storage. The part of the computer that retains information.

subroutine. A group of statements to perform a particular operation that may be used repeatedly in a program.

subscript. An expression that represents the position of an element in an array.

subscripted variable. A symbol whose numeric value can change. It is denoted by an array name followed by a subscript, for example, CHESS (2,4) or A(7).

symbolic language. Any programming language in which the commands resemble scientific equations, business arithmetic, or easy-to-remember abbreviations of words.

system. A collection of people, machines, and methods required to accomplish a specific objective.

template. See *flowcharting template*.

terminal. A point in a computer system or communication network at which information (programs or data) can either enter or leave.

two-dimensional array. An array having both 2 or more columns and 2 or more rows.

variable. A symbol whose numeric value can change.

write. To obtain data from storage.

Bibliography

There are many good books available on computers, problem solving, flowcharting and FORTRAN programming. Here are a few suggestions for further reading:

ADAMS, J. M., and D. H. HADEN, *Computers: Appreciation, Applications, Implications*. New York: John Wiley & Sons, 1973.

BAER, R. M., *The Digital Villain*. Reading, Mass.: Addison-Wesley Publishing Company, 1972.

BARRODABLE, I., F. ROBERTS, and B. EHLE, *Elementary Computer Applications*. New York: John Wiley & Sons, 1971.

BECKER, J., *The First Book of Information Science*. Washington, D.C.: Atomic Energy Commission, 1973.

BOHL, M., *Flowcharting Techniques*. Chicago: Science Research Associates, 1971.

CALTER, P., *Problem Solving with Computers*. New York: McGraw-Hill Book Company, 1973.

CAMPBELL, G. M., and W. E. SINGLETARY, *FORTRAN IV with Watfiv*. New York: Petrocelli/Charter, 1975.

DAWSON, C. B., and T. C. WOOL, *From Bits to IF's*. New York: Harper & Row, 1971.

DINTER, H., *Introduction to Computing*. New York: Macmillan Publishing Company, 1973.

DORF, R. C., *Introduction to Computers and Computer Science*. Boyd & Fraser Publishing Company, 1972.

DORN, W. S., G. G. BITTER, and D. L. HECTOR, *Computer Applications for Calculus*. Boston: Prindle, Weber & Schmidt, 1972.

GROSS, J. L., and W. S. BRAINERD, *Fundamental Programming Concepts*. New York: Harper & Row, 1972.

GRUENBERGER, F., *Computing: An Introduction*. New York: Harcourt, Brace & World, 1969.

GRUENBERGER, F., and G. JAFFRAY, *Problems for Computer Solution*. New York: John Wiley & Sons, 1965.

HAWKES, N., *The Computer Revolution*. New York: E. P. Dutton, 1972.

JACKSON, P. C., *Introduction to Artificial Intelligence*. New York: Petrocelli Books, 1974.

JAMISON, R. V., *Introduction to Computer Science Mathematics*. New York: McGraw-Hill Book Company, 1973.

KATZAN, H., *Information Technology: The Human Use of Computers*. New York: Petrocelli Books, 1974.

KOCHENBERGER, G. A., B. A. MCCARL, T. L. ISENHOUR, and P. C. JURS, *Introduction to Computer Programming in Business*. Boston: Nolbrook Press, 1974.

KOCHENBURGER, R. J., and C. J. TURCIO, *Computers in Modern Society*. Santa Barbara, Calif.: Hamilton Publishing Company, 1974.

LOGSDON, T., *An Introduction to Computer Science and Technology*. Palisade, N.J.: Franklin Publishing Company, 1974.

MAURER, H. A., and M. R. WILLIAMS, *A Collection of Programming Problems and Techniques*. Englewood Cliffs, N.J.: Prentice-Hall, 1972.

MCCRACKEN, D. D., *FORTRAN with Engineering Applications*. New York: John Wiley & Sons, 1967.

MOURSUND, D. G., *How Computers Do It*. Belmont, Calif.: Wadsworth Publishing Company, 1969.

NICKERSON, R. C., *Fundamentals of FORTRAN Programming*. Cambridge, Mass.: Winthrop Publisher, Inc., 1975.

ROTHMAN, S., and C. MOSMANN, *Computers and Society*. Chicago: Science Research Associates, 1972.

SAGE, E. R., *Fun and Games With the Computer*. Newburyport, Mass.: Entelek Inc., 1975.

SAXON, J. A., *Basic Data Processing Mathematics*. Englewood Cliffs, N.J.: Prentice-Hall, 1972.

SPENCER, D. D., *Computers and Programming Guide for Engineers*. New York: Howard W. Sams & Co., 1973.

———, *Computer Dictionary*, Ormond Beach, Fla.: Camelot Publishing Company, 1977.

———, *Computers In Action* (2nd ed.) Rochelle Park, N.J.: Hayden Book Company, 1978.

———, *Computers In Society*. Rochelle Park, N.J.: Hayden Book Company, 1974.

———, *Computer Science Mathematics*, Columbus, Ohio: Charles E. Merrill, 1976.

———, *Data Processing*. Columbus, Ohio: Charles E. Merrill, 1978.

———, *Fun with Computers and BASIC*. Ormond Beach, Fla.: Camelot Publishing Company, 1976.

———, *Game Playing With Computers* (2nd ed.). Rochelle Park, N.J.: Hayden Book Company, 1975.

———, *Introduction to Information Processing* (2nd ed.). Columbus, Ohio: Charles E. Merrill, 1977.

———, *Problems for Computer Solution*. Ormond Beach, Fla.: Camelot Publishing Company, 1977.

———, *What Computers Can Do*, Ormond Beach, Fla.: Camelot Publishing Company, 1977.

STUART, F., *FORTRAN Programming*. New York: John Wiley & Sons, 1969.

TEAGUE, R., *Computing Problems for FORTRAN Solution*. San Francisco, Calif.: Canfield Press, 1972.

VINTURELLA, J. B., *Introduction to FORTRAN*. New York: Petrocelli/Charter, 1975.

Index

A

Acronym, 17
Addition, 24, 28
Algorithm development, 58-70
Algorithms, 11, 57-70, 74
.AND. operator, 34
Annotation symbol, 100-101
ANSI (American National Standards Institute), 18, 75
Arguments, 163
Arithmetic:
   expression, 28-30
   IF statement, 49-51, 183
   operators, 28, 181
   statement, 30-31
Arithmetic expression, 28-30
Arithmetic IF statement, 49-51, 183
Arithmetic operators, 28, 181
Arithmetic statement, 30-31
Arithmetic statement function, 168-69
Arrays, 140-46, 186-87
   one-dimensional, 140
   two-dimensional, 140-41

B

BACKSPACE statement, 37
Bibliography, 309

C

CALL statement, 164-66
Carriage control, 44
Cayley, Arthur, 201
Character set, 24
Coding form, 19-20, 176
Column, array, 140
Comma, field separator, 45-46
Comment card, 19
Comments:
   in a program, 19
   in a flowchart, 100-101
COMMON statement, 158
Compiler, FORTRAN, 138, 177
Composite symbol, 24

Computed GO TO statement, 49
Computers, importance of, 4-5
Connector symbol, 99-100
Constant, 25, 34, 181
   fixed point, 25
   floating point, 25
   integer, 25
   logical, 34
   real, 25
Continuation, 19
CONTINUE statement, 138-39, 185
Control statements, 48-52, 182-84

D

DATA statement, 159-61
Debugging, program, 15, 173-80
Decision statements,
   GO TO, 49, 138, 182
   IF, 49-51, 138
Decision symbol, 84-88
Diamond symbol, 84-88
DIMENSION statement, 142, 158, 171, 186-87
Division, 24, 28
DO loop, 136-38
DO statement, 136-38, 183-84

E

E field, 41-42
END statement, 52, 185
ENDFILE statement, 37
.EQ. operator, 34
EQUIVALENCE statement, 158
Exponentiation, 24-25, 28-29
Expression:
   arithmetic, 28-30
   logical, 34-35
   relational, 34-35
EXTERNAL statements, 158

F

F fields, 40-42

Index

Fibonacci numbers:
  algorithm, 65-66
  program, 109-10, 113-14
Field descriptors (*see* FORMAT field descriptors)
Fifteen puzzle:
  algorithm, 66
  program, 204-7
Fixed-point constants (*see* Integer constants)
Floating-point constants (*see* Real constants)
Flowcharts 11-13, 73-102
  construction, 80-82
  guidelines, 78
  symbols, 74-78, 81-88
  template, 79-80
Flowcharting guidelines, 78
Flowcharting symbols, 74-78, 302
Flowcharting template, 79-80
Flowline, 78
FORMAT field descriptors, 39-46
  E field, 41-42
  F field, 40-42
  H field, 43-44
  I field, 39-40
  X specification, 42-43
FORMAT field separators, 45-46
  comma, 45-46
  slash, 45-46
FORMAT statement, 37-46
FORTRAN:
  acronym, 17
  coding form, 19-20, 176
  constant, 25, 34, 181
  expression, 28-30, 34-35
  functions, 166-73
  operators, 28, 34-35, 181, 183
  programs, 106-33, 149-57, 189-217
  statements, 17-55, 136-49, 158-73
  subroutine, 162-66
  summary, 180-87
  variables, 25-27, 142, 181, 186-87
FORTRAN programs:
  absent-minded chemist, 200
  area of triangle, 53
  average of 15 numbers, 54
  California chemical laboratory, 125

FORTRAN programs *(cont.)*:
  class assignments, 191
  electric bill calculation, 54
  fifteen puzzle, 204
  find the largest number, 150
  Fireball Williams' auto races, 119, 190
  force calculation, 52-53
  gas station robbery, 132
  how much current, 128
  jolly green giant, 114
  Karl Gauss's calculation, 191
  magic square checker, 211
  magic square generator, 208
  Manhattan Island, 109, 190
  Mary goes to the circus, 109
  matrix multiplication, 201
  Michael's dog, 108, 190
  N-th Fibonacci numbers, 114
  numerical integration, 152
  painting the gazebo, 106
  permutations, 194
  polynomial evaluation, 156
  Rodney's new calculator, 117
  roots of an equation, 114
  sorting, 154
  square root, 123
  sum of 100 integers, 54
  sum of the first 150 integers, 149
  who was right, 197
FORTRAN reference manual, 177
Functional parts of a computer, 6-7
Functions, 166-73
  arithmetic statement function, 168-69
  FUNCTION subprograms, 170-73

G

.GE. operator, 34
Glossary, 303
GO TO statements, 49, 138, 182
  computed, 49
  unconditional, 49
.GT. operator, 34

H

H fields, 43-44

Index 317

Hardware, 7
Hierarchy of operations, 29-30, 36, 182
Hollerith field, 43-44

I

I fields, 39-40
Identification field, 19-20
IF statements 49-51, 138
   arithmetic, 49-51
   logical, 51
Increment of loop, 137
Index of loop, 136
Input/Output (I/O), 37-46, 147-48, 184-85
   devices, 7, 37
   FORMAT, 37-46
   list, 37
   READ, 37-38, 147-48, 184-85
   WRITE, 38, 147-48, 184-85
Input/Output devices, 7, 37
Input/Output list, 37
Input/Output statements, 37-48, 147-48, 184, 185
Integer constants, 25-26
INTEGER statement, 159, 185
Integer variables, 26-27

K

Keypunching programs, 19, 296-300
Königsberg bridge algorithm, 68-70

L

Last statement of program, 52
.LE. operator, 34
Library functions, 33, 186
Link, 162
Logical, 33-37
   constant, 34
   expression, 34
   IF statement, 51. 183
   operators, 34, 183
   statement, 36
   variable, 34

Logical constants, 34
Logical end of a program, 52
Logical expressions, 34-35
Logical IF statement, 51, 183
Logical operators, 34, 183
LOGICAL statement, 36, 159, 186
Logical statements, 36
Logical variable, 34
Looping, 89-97
   controlled loops, 92-94
   nested loops, 95-97
.LT. operator, 34

M

Magic Squares, 144
   algorithm, 58
   checking program, 211-17, 271
   program, 208-11
Main program, 162-66
Manhattan Island problem, 109, 111
Mantissa, 25-26
Mathematical symbols, 78
Matrix multiplication, 201-5
Mixed mode arithmetic, 29-30
Mode, 29-30
Multiplication, 24, 28

N

Names of variables, 26-27
.NE. operator, 34
Nested loops, 95-97, 137
.NOT. operator, 34
Number game algorithm, 65
Numbers, statement, 19

O

One-dimensional array, 140
Operations:
   arithmetic, 28, 181
   logical, 34, 183
   relational, 34-35

Index

Operators:
   addition, 28, 181
   division, 28, 181
   exponentiation, 24-25, 28-29
   multiplication, 28, 181
   order of, 29-30, 36, 182
   relational, 34, 35
   subtraction, 28, 181
   symbols for, 28, 181
.OR. operator, 34
Output, 37-38, 147-48, 184-85
Oval symbol, 81

P

Parallelogram symbol, 81-82
Parentheses, 28-29
Permutations, 194-96
Physical end of a program, 52
Predefined process symbol, 102
PRINT statement, 37
Printer carriage control characters, 44
Problem analysis, 58
Problem definition, 8, 11
Problem solving steps, 8-15
Problems for reader solution:
   accounting computation, 224
   accounts receivable, 280
   average distance, 266
   average temperature, 270
   batting average, 274
   big words, 281
   billiard simulation, 254
   birds, 266
   bouncing ball, 268
   calculate the sum, 287
   change maker, 232
   checker counting, 266
   checkerboard interchange, 221
   chi-square, 230
   Christmas tree, 262
   college admission record, 279
   college exam scores, 281
   company interest, 230
   company payroll, 238
   cricket thermometer, 269
   cube root, 274

Problems for reader solution *(cont.)*:
   customer billing, 231
   date finder, 282
   decimal-to-English conversion, 249
   drag and lift force, 271
   employee payroll, 236
   employment, 268
   fifty puzzle, 239
   flight path computation, 290
   football franchise, 264
   fourth powers, 266
   gas mileage, 276
   guessing game, 274
   house mortage, 278
   interest calculation, 220
   interest table, 277
   investment calculation, 263
   king's tour of the chessboard, 288
   largest number, 268
   law of cosines, 223
   law of sines, 265
   lot purchase, 276
   lucky numbers, 283
   magic square checker, 271
   maze, 288
   mean, median, and mode, 273
   merchandise cost, 278
   most popular player, 275
   mouse in a maze, 257
   multiplication table, 266
   number search, 271
   one pile pickup, 281
   payroll, 265
   payroll deduction, 245
   perfect numbers, 285
   polygon, 268
   powers of two, 262
   prime number polynomial, 221
   prime numbers, 250
   product cost, 225
   radius of curvature, 277
   real estate purchase, 225
   roman numeralizer, 239
   row interchange, 273
   salary conversion table, 277
   sales chart, 277
   sales journal, 280
   satellite speed, 264

Index 319

Problems for reader solution *(cont.)*:
   slot machine simulator, 246
   statistical calculation, 272
   student averages, 268
   student enrollment survey, 271
   symmetry game, 285
   table of trigonometric functions, 288
   temperature simulation, 275
   three by three magic square, 262
   trigonometric functions, 235
   volume of a dam, 267
   what is the number?, 274
   wheel of fortune, 284
Program, 7-8
Program card, 296
Program debugging 15, 173-80
Program mistakes, 13, 15, 174-76
Programs (*see* FORTRAN programs)
Programming language, 13
PUNCH statement, 37
Punched card, 21

R

READ statement, 37-38
Real:
   constant, 25-26
   varible, 26-27
Real constants, 25-26
REAL statement, 159, 185
Real variables, 26-27
Rectangle symbol, 81
Relational expressions, 34-35
Relational operators, 34-35
Replaced by symbol, 30-31
RETURN statement, 162-64, 170-72
REWIND statement, 37
Right justified, 39
Roots of an equation program, 112, 114
Row in array, 140

S

Sequence number, 19-20
Slash (/):
   arithmetic operator, 24

Slash (/) *(cont.)*:
   in FORMAT statement, 45-46
Software, 7
Source deck, 19
Source program, 19
Specification statements, 158-61
Square root, 123-25
Statement, FORTRAN, 17-55, 136-49, 158-73
Statement field, 19
Statement numbers, 19
Statements, FORTRAN:
   CALL, 164-66
   computed GO TO, 49
   CONTINUE, 138-39, 185
   DATA, 159-61
   DIMENSION, 142, 158, 171, 186-87
   DO, 136-38, 183-84
   END, 52, 185
   ENDFILE, 37
   EQUIVALENCE, 158
   EXTERNAL, 158
   FORMAT, 37-46
   GO TO, 49, 138, 182
   IF, 49-51, 138
   INTEGER, 159, 185
   LOGICAL, 36, 159, 186
   PRINT, 37
   PUNCH, 37
   READ, 37-38
   REAL, 159, 185
   RETURN, 162-64, 170-72
   REWIND, 37
   STOP, 51-52, 138, 185
   SUBROUTINE, 162-66
   WRITE, 38
STOP statement, 51-52, 138, 185
Subprograms, 161-66
   functions, 166
   subroutines, 162-66
SUBROUTINE statement, 162-66
Subroutine symbol, 102
Subroutines, 162-66
   open subroutine, 162
   closed subroutine, 162
Subscript, 140
Subscripted variable, 142, 186-87
Subtraction, 24, 28

Index

Symbol, flowcharting:
   annotation, 76-78, 100-101
   connector, 76, 99-100
   decision, 76-77, 84-88
   input-output, 76, 82
   pre-defined process, 76, 102
   process, 76-77, 82
   terminal, 76, 81
Symbol, FORTRAN, 24-25

T

Template, flowcharting, 79-80
Terminal start and stop symbol, 81
Transfer of control, 49-51, 138, 182
   CALL, 164-66
   computed GO TO, 49
   DO, 136-38, 183-84
   GO TO, 49
   IF, 49-51, 138
   RETURN, 162-64, 170-72
   unconditional, 49
Truncation, 30
Turn around time, 178
Two-dimensional arrays, 140-41
Type statements, 159
   INTEGER, 159

Type statements *(cont.)*:
   LOGICAL, 36, 159
   REAL, 159

U

Unconditional transfer statement, 49

V

Variables, 26, 181
   integer, 26
   names of, 25-27
   real, 26
   subscripted, 142, 186-87

W

WRITE statement, 38

X

X fields, 42-43